Mind Design II

Mind
Design II

Philosophy
Psychology
Artificial Intelligence

Revised and enlarged edition

edited by
John Haugeland

A Bradford Book
The MIT Press
Cambridge, Massachusetts
London, England

Second printing, 1997
© 1997 Massachusetts Institute of Technology

Book design and typesetting by John Haugeland. Body text set in Adobe Garamond 11.5 on 13; titles set in Zapf Humanist 601 BT. Printed and bound in the United States of America.

Library of Congress Cataloging-in-Publication Data

Mind design II / edited by John Haugeland. — 2nd ed., rev. and enlarged.
    p.   cm.
"A Bradford book."
Includes bibliographical references.
    ISBN 0-262-08259-4 (hc : alk. paper). — ISBN 0-262-58153-1 (pb : alk. paper)
    1. Artificial intelligence. 2. Cognitive psychology.
I. Haugeland, John, 1945–
Q335.5.M492 1997
006.3—dc21   96-45188
                                     CIP

for Barbara and John III

Contents

Mind Design II

What Is Mind Design?

John Haugeland
1996

MIND DESIGN is the endeavor to understand *mind* (thinking, intellect) in terms of its *design* (how it is built, how it works). It amounts, therefore, to a kind of cognitive psychology. But it is oriented more toward structure and mechanism than toward correlation or law, more toward the "how" than the "what", than is traditional empirical psychology. An "experiment" in mind design is more often an effort to *build* something and make it work, than to observe or analyze what already exists. Thus, the field of artificial intelligence (AI), the attempt to construct intelligent artifacts, systems with minds of their own, lies at the heart of mind design. Of course, natural intelligence, especially human intelligence, remains the final object of investigation, the phenomenon eventually to be understood. What is distinctive is not the goal but rather the means to it. Mind design is *psychology by reverse engineering*.

Though the idea of intelligent artifacts is as old as Greek mythology, and a familiar staple of fantasy fiction, it has been taken seriously as science for scarcely two generations. And the reason is not far to seek: pending several conceptual and technical breakthroughs, no one had a clue how to proceed. Even as the pioneers were striking boldly into the unknown, much of what they were really up to remained unclear, both to themselves and to others; and some still does. Accordingly, mind design has always been an area of *philosophical* interest, an area in which the conceptual foundations—the very questions to ask, and what would count as an answer—have remained unusually fluid and controversial.

The essays collected here span the history of the field since its inception (though with emphasis on more recent developments). The authors are about evenly divided between philosophers and scientists. Yet, all of the essays are "philosophical", in that they address fundamental issues and basic concepts; at the same time, nearly all are also "scientific" in that they are technically sophisticated and concerned with the achievements and challenges of concrete empirical research.

Several major trends and schools of thought are represented, often explicitly disputing with one another. In their juxtaposition, therefore, not only the lay of the land, its principal peaks and valleys, but also its current movement, its still active fault lines, can come into view.

By way of introduction, I shall try in what follows to articulate a handful of the fundamental ideas that have made all this possible.

1 Perspectives and things

None of the present authors believes that intelligence depends on anything immaterial or supernatural, such as a vital spirit or an immortal soul. Thus, they are all *materialists* in at least the minimal sense of supposing that matter, suitably selected and arranged, suffices for intelligence. The question is: How?

It can seem incredible to suggest that mind is "nothing but" matter in motion. Are we to imagine all those little atoms thinking deep thoughts as they careen past one another in the thermal chaos? Or, if not one by one, then maybe collectively, by the zillions? The answer to this puzzle is to realize that things can be viewed from different *perspectives* (or described in different terms)—and, when we look differently, what we are able to see is also different. For instance, what is a coarse weave of frayed strands when viewed under a microscope is a shiny silk scarf seen in a store window. What is a marvellous old clockwork in the eyes of an antique restorer is a few cents' worth of brass, seen as scrap metal. Likewise, so the idea goes, what is mere atoms in the void from one point of view can be an intelligent system from another.

Of course, you can't look at anything in just any way you please—at least, not and be right about it. A scrap dealer couldn't see a wooden stool as a few cents' worth of brass, since it isn't brass; the antiquarian couldn't see a brass monkey as a clockwork, since it doesn't work like a clock. Awkwardly, however, these two points taken together seem to create a dilemma. According to the first, what something is—coarse or fine, clockwork or scrap metal—depends on how you look at it. But, according to the second, how you can *rightly* look at something (or describe it) depends on what it is. Which comes first, one wants to ask, seeing or being?

Clearly, there's something wrong with that question. What something is and how it can rightly be regarded are not essentially distinct; neither comes before the other, because they are the same. The advantage of emphasizing perspective, nevertheless, is that it highlights the following question: What *constrains* how something can rightly be regarded or described (and thus determines what it is)? This is important, because the answer will be different for different kinds of perspective or description—as our examples already illustrate. Sometimes, what something is is determined by its shape or form (at the relevant level of detail); sometimes it is determined by what it's made of; and sometimes by how it works or even just what it does. Which—if any— of these could determine whether something is (rightly regarded or described as) *intelligent*?

1.1 The Turing test

In 1950, the pioneering computer scientist A. M. Turing suggested that intelligence is a matter of behavior or behavioral capacity: whether a system has a mind, or how intelligent it is, is determined by what it can and cannot do. Most materialist philosophers and cognitive scientists now accept this general idea (though John Searle is an exception). Turing also proposed a pragmatic criterion or test of what a system can do that would be sufficient to show that it is intelligent. (He did not claim that a system would not be intelligent if it could not pass his test; only that it would be if it could.) This test, now called the *Turing test*, is controversial in various ways, but remains widely respected in spirit.

Turing cast his test in terms of simulation or imitation: a non-human system will be deemed intelligent if it acts so like an ordinary person *in certain respects* that other ordinary people can't tell (from these actions alone) that it isn't one. But the imitation idea itself isn't the important part of Turing's proposal. What's important is rather the specific sort of behavior that Turing chose for his test: he specified *verbal* behavior. A system is surely intelligent, he said, if it can carry on an ordinary conversation like an ordinary person (via electronic means, to avoid any influence due to appearance, tone of voice, and so on).

This is a daring and radical simplification. There are many ways in which intelligence is manifested. Why single out *talking* for special emphasis? Remember: Turing didn't suggest that talking in this way is required to demonstrate intelligence, only that it's sufficient. So there's no worry about the test being too hard; the only question is whether it might be too lenient. We know, for instance, that there are systems that can regulate temperatures, generate intricate rhythms, or even fly airplanes without being, in any serious sense, intelligent. Why couldn't the ability to carry on ordinary conversations be like that?

Turing's answer is elegant and deep: talking is unique among intelligent abilities because it gathers within itself, at one remove, all others. One cannot generate rhythms or fly airplanes "about" talking, but one certainly can *talk about* rhythms and flying—not to mention poetry, sports, science, cooking, love, politics, and so on—*and,* if one doesn't know what one is talking about, it will soon become painfully obvious. Talking is not merely one intelligent ability among others, but also, and essentially, the ability to *express* intelligently a great many (maybe all) other intelligent abilities. And, without *having* those abilities in fact, at least to some degree, one cannot talk intelligently about them. That's why Turing's test is so compelling and powerful.

On the other hand, even if not too easy, there is nevertheless a sense in which the test does obscure certain real difficulties. By concentrating on conversational ability, which can be exhibited entirely in writing (say, via computer terminals), the Turing test completely ignores any issues of real-world perception and action. Yet these turn out to be extraordinarily difficult to achieve artificially at any plausible level of sophistication. And, what may be worse, ignoring real-time environmental interaction distorts a system designer's assumptions about how intelligent systems are related to the world more generally. For instance, if a system has to deal or cope with things around it, but is not continually tracking them externally, then it will need somehow to "keep track of" or *represent* them internally. Thus, neglect of perception and action can lead to an overemphasis on representation and internal modeling.

1.2 Intentionality

"Intentionality", said Franz Brentano (1874/1973), "is the mark of the mental." By this he meant that everything mental has intentionality, and nothing else does (except in a derivative or second-hand way), and, finally, that this fact is the *definition of the mental.* 'Intentional' is used here in a medieval sense that harks back to the original Latin meaning of "stretching toward" something; it is not limited to things like plans and purposes, but applies to all kinds of mental acts. More specifically, intentionality is the character of one thing being "of" or "about" something else, for instance by representing it, describing it, referring to it, aiming at it, and so on. Thus, intending in the narrower modern sense (planning) is also intentional in Brentano's broader and older sense, but much else is as well, such as believing, wanting, remembering, imagining, fearing, and the like.

Intentionality is peculiar and perplexing. It looks on the face of it to be a relation between two things. My belief that Cairo is hot is intentional because it is *about* Cairo (and/or its being hot). That which an intentional act or state is about (Cairo or its being hot, say) is called its *intentional object*. (It is this intentional object that the intentional state "stretches toward".) Likewise, my desire for a certain shirt, my imagining a party on a certain date, my fear of dogs in general, would be "about"—that is, have as their intentional objects—that shirt, a party on that date, and dogs in general. Indeed, *having* an object in this way is another way of explaining intentionality; and such "having" seems to be a relation, namely between the state and its object.

But, if it's a relation, it's a relation like no other. Being-inside-of is a typical relation. Now notice this: if it is a fact about one thing that it is inside of another, then not only that first thing, but also the second has to *exist*; *X* cannot be inside of *Y*, or indeed be related to *Y* in any other way, if *Y* does not exist. This is true of relations quite generally; but it is *not* true of intentionality. I can perfectly well imagine a party on a certain date, and also have beliefs, desires, and fears about it, even though there is (was, will be) no such party. Of course, those beliefs would be false, and those hopes and fears unfulfilled; but they would be intentional—be about, or "have", those objects—all the same.

It is this puzzling ability to have something as an object, whether or not that something actually exists, that caught Brentano's attention. Brentano was no materialist: he thought that mental phenomena were one kind of entity, and material or physical phenomena were a completely different kind. And he could not see how *any* merely material or physical thing could be *in fact* related to another, if the latter didn't exist; yet *every* mental state (belief, desire, and so on) has this possibility. So intentionality is the definitive mark of the mental.

Daniel C. Dennett accepts Brentano's definition of the mental, but proposes a materialist way to view intentionality. Dennett, like Turing, thinks intelligence is a matter of how a system behaves; but, unlike Turing, he also has a worked-out account of what it is about (some) behavior that makes it intelligent—or, in Brentano's terms, makes it the behavior of a system with intentional (that is, *mental*) states. The idea has two parts: (i) behavior should be understood not in isolation but in *context* and as part of a consistent *pattern* of behavior (this is often called "holism"); and (ii) for some systems, a consistent pattern of behavior in context can be construed as *rational* (such construing is often called "interpretation").[1]

Rationality here means: acting so as best to satisfy your goals overall, given what you know and can tell about your situation. Subject to this constraint, we can surmise what a system wants and believes by watching what it does—but, of course, not in isolation. From all you can tell in isolation, a single bit of behavior might be manifesting any number of different beliefs and/or desires, or none at all. Only when you see a *consistent pattern of rational behavior*, manifesting the *same* cognitive states and capacities repeatedly, in various combinations, are you justified in saying that *those* are the states and capacities that this system has—or even that it has *any* cognitive states or capacities at all. "Rationality", Dennett says (1971/78, p. 19), "is the mother of intention."

This is a prime example of the above point about *perspective*. The constraint on whether something can rightly be regarded as having intentional states is, according to Dennett, not its shape or what it is made of, but rather what it does—more specifically, a consistently rational pattern in what it does. We infer that a rabbit can tell a fox from another rabbit, always wanting to get away from the one but not the other, from having observed it behave accordingly time and again, under various conditions. Thus, on a given occasion, we impute to the rabbit *intentional* states (beliefs and desires) *about* a particular fox, on the basis not only of its current behavior but also of the pattern in its behavior over time. The consistent pattern lends both specificity and credibility to the respective individual attributions.

Dennett calls this perspective the *intentional stance* and the entities so regarded *intentional systems*. If the stance is to have any conviction in any particular case, the pattern on which it depends had better be broad and reliable; but it needn't be perfect. Compare a crystal: the pattern in the atomic lattice had better be broad and reliable, if the sample is to be a crystal at all; but it needn't be perfect. Indeed, the very idea of a *flaw* in a crystal is made intelligible by the regularity of the pattern around it; only insofar as *most* of the lattice is regular, can particular parts be deemed flawed in determinate ways. Likewise for the intentional stance: only because the rabbit behaves rationally almost always, could we ever say on a particular occasion that it happened to be *wrong*—had *mistaken* another rabbit (or a bush, or a shadow) for a fox, say. False beliefs and unfulfilled hopes are intelligible as isolated lapses in an overall consistent pattern, like flaws in a crystal. This is how a specific intentional state can rightly be attributed, even though its supposed intentional object doesn't exist—and thus is Dennett's answer to Brentano's puzzle.

1.3 Original intentionality

Many material things that aren't intentional systems are nevertheless "about" other things—including, sometimes, things that don't exist. Written sentences and stories, for instance, are in some sense material; yet they are often about fictional characters and events. Even pictures and maps can represent nonexistent scenes and places. Of course, Brentano knew this, and so does Dennett. But they can say that this sort of intentionality is only *derivative*. Here's the idea: sentence inscriptions—ink marks on a page, say—are only "about" anything because we (or other intelligent users) *mean* them that way. Their intentionality is second-hand, borrowed or derived from the intentionality that those users already have.

So, a sentence like "Santa lives at the North Pole", or a picture of him or a map of his travels, can be "about" Santa (who, alas, doesn't exist), but *only because* we can *think* that he lives there, and *imagine* what he looks like and where he goes. It's really *our* intentionality that these artifacts have, second-hand, because we use them to *express* it. Our intentionality itself, on the other hand, cannot be likewise derivative: it must be *original*. ('Original', here, just means *not* derivative, not borrowed from somewhere else. If there is any intentionality at all, at least some of it must be original; it can't all be derivative.)

The problem for mind design is that artificial intelligence systems, like sentences and pictures, are also artifacts. So it can seem that their intentionality too must always be derivative—borrowed from their designers or users, presumably—and never original. Yet, if the project of designing and building a system with a mind of its own is ever really to succeed, then it must be possible for an artificial system to have genuine *original* intentionality, just as we do. Is that possible?

Think again about people and sentences, with their original and derivative intentionality, respectively. What's the reason for that difference? Is it really that sentences are artifacts, whereas people are not, or might it be something else? Here's another candidate. Sentences don't *do* anything with what they mean: they never pursue goals, draw conclusions, make plans, answer questions, let alone *care* whether they are right or wrong about the world—they just sit there, utterly inert and heedless. A person, by contrast, relies on what he or she believes and wants in order to make sensible choices and act efficiently; and this entails, in turn, an ongoing concern about whether those beliefs are really true, those goals really beneficial, and so on. In other words, real beliefs and desires are integrally involved in a rational, active existence, intelligently engaged with its environment. Maybe this active, rational engagement is more pertinent to whether the intentionality is original or not than is any question of natural or artificial origin.

Clearly, this is what Dennett's approach implies. An intentional system, by his lights, is just one that exhibits an appropriate pattern of consistently rational *behavior*—that is, active engagement with the world. If an artificial system can be produced that behaves on its own in a rational manner, consistently enough and in a suitable variety of circumstances (remember, it doesn't have to be flawless), then it has *original* intentionality—it has a mind of its own, just as we do.

On the other hand, Dennett's account is completely silent about how, or even whether, such a system could actually be designed and built. Intentionality, according to Dennett, depends entirely and exclusively on a certain sort of pattern in a system's behavior; internal structure and mechanism (if any) are quite beside the point. For scientific mind design, however, the question of how it actually works (and so, how it could be built) is absolutely central—and that brings us to computers.

2 Computers

Computers are important to scientific mind design in two fundamentally different ways. The first is what inspired Turing long ago, and a number of other scientists much more recently. But the second is what really launched AI and gave it its first serious hope of success. In order to understand these respective roles, and how they differ, it will first be necessary to grasp the notion of 'computer' at an essential level.

2.1 Formal systems

A formal system is like a game in which tokens are manipulated according to definite rules, in order to see what configurations can be obtained. In fact, many familiar games—among them chess, checkers, tic-tac-toe, and go—simply *are* formal systems. But there are also many games that are not formal systems, and many formal systems that are not games. Among the former are games like marbles, tiddly-winks, billiards, and baseball; and among the latter are a number of systems studied by logicians, computer scientists, and linguists.

This is not the place to attempt a full definition of formal systems; but three essential features can capture the basic idea: (i) they are (as indicated above) token-manipulation systems; (ii) they are digital; and

(iii) they are medium independent. It will be worth a moment to spell out what each of these means.

TOKEN-MANIPULATION SYSTEMS. To say that a formal system is a token-manipulation system is to say that you can define it *completely* by specifying three things:

(1) a set of types of formal tokens or pieces;

(2) one or more allowable starting positions—that is, initial formal arrangements of tokens of these types; and

(3) a set of formal rules specifying how such formal arrangements may or must be changed into others.

This definition is meant to imply that token-manipulation systems are entirely *self-contained*. In particular, the formality of the rules is two-fold: (i) they specify *only* the allowable next formal arrangements of tokens, and (ii) they specify these in terms *only* of the current formal arrangement—nothing else is *formally* relevant at all.

So take chess, for example. There are twelve types of piece, six of each color. There is only one allowable starting position, namely one in which thirty-two pieces of those twelve types are placed in a certain way on an eight-by-eight array of squares. The rules specifying how the positions change are simply the rules specifying how the pieces move, disappear (get captured), or change type (get promoted). (In chess, new pieces are never added to the position; but that's a further kind of move in other formal games—such as go.) Finally, notice that chess is entirely self-contained: nothing is ever relevant to what moves would be legal other than the current chess position itself.[2]

And every student of formal logic is familiar with at least one logical system as a token-manipulation game. Here's one obvious way it can go (there are many others): the kinds of logical symbol are the types, and the marks that you actually make on paper are the tokens of those types; the allowable starting positions are sets of well-formed formulae (taken as premises); and the formal rules are the inference rules specifying steps—that is, further formulae that you write down and add to the current position—in formally valid inferences. The fact that this is called *formal* logic is, of course, no accident.

DIGITAL SYSTEMS. Digitalness is a characteristic of certain techniques (methods, devices) for *making* things, and then (later) *identifying* what was made. A familiar example of such a technique is writing something down and later reading it. The thing written or made is supposed to be of a specified type (from some set of possible types), and identifying it later is telling what type that was. So maybe you're supposed to write down specified letters of the alphabet; and then my job is to tell, on the basis of what you produce, which letters you were supposed to write. Then the question is: how well can I do that? How good are the later identifications at recovering the prior specifications?

Such a technique is *digital* if it is positive and reliable. It is *positive* if the reidentification can be *absolutely perfect*. A positive technique is *reliable* if it not only can be perfect, but almost always is. This bears some thought. We're accustomed to the idea that nothing—at least, nothing mundane and real-worldly—is ever quite *perfect*. Perfection is an ideal, never fully attainable in practice. Yet the definition of 'digital' requires that perfection be not only possible, but reliably achievable.

Everything turns on what counts as success. Compare two tasks, each involving a penny and an eight-inch checkerboard. The first asks you to place the penny *exactly* 0.43747 inches in from the nearest edge of the board, and 0.18761 inches from the left; the second asks you to put it *somewhere* in the fourth rank (row) and the second file (column from the left). Of course, achieving the first would also achieve the second. But the first task is strictly impossible—that is, it can never actually be achieved, but at best approximated. The second task, on the other hand, can in fact be carried out *absolutely perfectly*—it's not even hard. And the reason is easy to see: any number of slightly different actual positions would equally well count as *complete* success—because the penny only has to be *somewhere* within the specified square.

Chess is digital: if one player produces a chess position (or move), then the other player can reliably identify it *perfectly*. Chess positions and moves are like the second task with the penny: slight differences in the physical locations of the figurines aren't differences at all from the chess point of view—that is, in the positions of the chess pieces. Checkers, go, and tic-tac-toe are like chess in this way, but baseball and billiards are not. In the latter, unlike the former, arbitrarily small differences in the exact position, velocity, smoothness, elasticity, or whatever, of some physical object can make a significant difference to the game. Digital systems, though concrete and material, are insulated from such physical vicissitudes.

MEDIUM INDEPENDENCE. A concrete system is medium independent if what it is does not depend on what physical "medium" it is made of or implemented in. Of course, it has to be implemented in *something*;

and, moreover, that something has to support whatever structure or form is necessary for the kind of system in question. But, apart from this generic prerequisite, nothing specific about the medium matters (except, perhaps, for extraneous reasons of convenience). In this sense, only the *form* of a formal system is significant, not its matter.

Chess, for instance, is medium independent. Chess pieces can be made of wood, plastic, ivory, onyx, or whatever you want, just as long as they are sufficiently stable (they don't melt or crawl around) and are movable by the players. You can play chess with patterns of light on a video screen, with symbols drawn in the sand, or even—if you're rich and eccentric enough—with fleets of helicopters operated by radio control. But you can't play chess with live frogs (they won't sit still), shapes traced in the water (they won't last), or mountain tops (nobody can move them). Essentially similar points can be made about logical symbolism and all other formal systems.

By contrast, what you can light a fire, feed a family, or wire a circuit with is not medium independent, because whether something is flammable, edible, or electrically conductive depends not just on its form but also on what it's made of. Nor are billiards or baseball independent of their media: what the balls (and bats and playing surfaces) are made of is quite important and carefully regulated. Billiard balls can indeed be made either of ivory or of (certain special) plastics, but hardly of wood or onyx. And you couldn't play billiards or baseball with helicopters or shapes in the sand to save your life. The reason is that, unlike chess and other formal systems, in these games the details of the physical interactions of the balls and other equipment make an important difference: how they bounce, how much friction there is, how much energy it takes to make them go a certain distance, and so on.

2.2 Automatic formal systems

An *automatic* formal system is a formal system that "moves" by itself. More precisely, it is a physical device or machine such that:

(1) some configurations of its parts or states can be regarded as the tokens and positions of some formal system; and

(2) in its normal operation, it automatically manipulates these tokens in accord with the rules of that system.

So it's like a set of chess pieces that hop around the board, abiding by the rules, all by themselves, or like a magical pencil that writes out formally correct logical derivations, without the guidance of any logician.

Of course, this is exactly what computers are, seen from a formal perspective. But, if we are to appreciate properly their importance for mind design, several fundamental facts and features will need further elaboration—among them the notions of implementation and universality, algorithmic and heuristic procedures, and digital simulation.

IMPLEMENTATION AND UNIVERSALITY. Perhaps the most basic idea of computer science is that you can use one automatic formal system to *implement* another. This is what *programming* is. Instead of building some special computer out of hardware, you build it out of software; that is, you write a program for a "general purpose" computer (which you already have) that will make it act exactly as if it were the special computer that you need. One computer so implements another when:

(1) some configurations of tokens and positions of the former can be regarded as the tokens and positions of the latter; and

(2) as the former follows its own rules, it automatically manipulates those tokens of the latter in accord with the latter's rules.

In general, those configurations that are being regarded as tokens and positions of the special computer are themselves only a fraction of the tokens and positions of the general computer. The remainder (which may be the majority) are the program. The general computer follows its own rules with regard to *all* of its tokens; but the program tokens are so arranged that the net effect is to manipulate the configurations implementing the tokens of the special computer in exactly the way required by its rules.

This is complicated to describe, never mind actually to achieve; and the question arises how often such implementation is possible in principle. The answer is as surprising as it is consequential. In 1937, A. M. Turing—the same Turing we met earlier in our discussion of intelligence—showed, in effect, that it is *always* possible. Put somewhat more carefully, he showed that there are some computing machines—which he called *universal* machines—that can implement *any* well-defined automatic formal system whatsoever, provided only that they have enough storage capacity and time. Not only that, he showed also that universal machines can be amazingly simple; and he gave a complete design specification for one.

Every ordinary (programmable) computer is a universal machine in Turing's sense. In other words, the computer on your desk, given the right program and enough memory, could be made equivalent to any computer that is possible at all, in every respect except speed. Anything any computer can do, yours can too, in principle. Indeed, the machine on your desk can be (and usually is) lots of computers at once. From one point of view, it is a "hardware" computer modifying, according to strict formal rules, complex patterns of tiny voltage tokens often called "bits". Viewed another way, it is simultaneously a completely different system that shuffles machine-language words called "op-codes", "data" and "addresses". And, depending on what you're up to, it may also *be* a word processor, a spell checker, a macro interpreter, and/or whatever.

ALGORITHMS AND HEURISTICS. Often a specific computer is designed and built (or programed) for a particular purpose: there will be some complicated rearrangement of tokens that it would be valuable to bring about automatically. Typically, a designer works with facilities that can carry out simple rearrangements easily, and the job is to find a combination of them (usually a sequence of steps) that will collectively achieve the desired result. Now there are two basic kinds of case, depending mainly on the character of the assigned task.

In many cases, the designer is able to implement a procedure that is guaranteed always to work—that is, to effect the desired rearrangement, regardless of the input, in a finite amount of time. Suppose, for instance, that the input is always a list of English words, and the desired rearrangement is to put them in alphabetical order. There are known procedures that are guaranteed to alphabetize any given list in finite time. Such procedures, ones that are sure to succeed in finite time, are called *algorithms*. Many important computational problems can be solved algorithmically.

But many others cannot, for theoretical or practical reasons. The task, for instance, might be to find the optimal move in any given chess position. Technically, chess is finite; so, theoretically, it would be possible to check every possible outcome of every possible move, and thus choose flawlessly, on the basis of complete information. But, in fact, even if the entire planet Earth were one huge computer built with the best current technology, it could not solve this problem even once in the life of the Solar System. So chess by brute force is impractical. But that, obviously, does not mean that machines can't come up with good chess moves. How do they do that?

They rely on general estimates and rules of thumb: procedures that, while not guaranteed to give the right answer every time, are fairly reliable most of the time. Such procedures are called *heuristics*. In the case of chess, sensible heuristics involve looking ahead a few moves in various directions and then evaluating factors like number and kind of pieces, mobility, control of the center, pawn coordination, and so on. These are not infallible measures of the strength of chess positions; but, in combination, they can be pretty good. This is how chess-playing computers work—and likewise many other machines that deal with problems for which there are no known algorithmic solutions.

The possibility of heuristic procedures on computers is sometimes confusing. In one sense, every digital computation (that does not consult a randomizer) is algorithmic; so how can any of them be heuristic? The answer is again a matter of perspective. Whether any given procedure is algorithmic or heuristic depends on how you describe the task. One and the same procedure can be an algorithm, when described as counting up the number and kinds of pieces, but a mere heuristic rule of thumb, when described as estimating the strength of a position.

This is the resolution of another common confusion as well. It is often said that computers never make mistakes (unless there is a bug in some program or a hardware malfunction). Yet anybody who has ever played chess against a small chess computer knows that it makes plenty of mistakes. But this is just that same issue about how you describe the task. Even that cheap toy is executing the algorithms that implement its heuristics flawlessly every time; seen that way, it never makes a mistake. It's just that those heuristics aren't very sophisticated; so, seen as a chess player, the same system makes lots of mistakes.

DIGITAL SIMULATION. One important practical application of computers isn't really token manipulation at all, except as a means to an end. You see this in your own computer all the time. Word processors and spreadsheets literally work with digital tokens: letters and numerals. But image processors do not: pictures are *not* digital. Rather, as everybody knows, they are "digitized". That is, they are divided up into fine enough dots and gradations that the increments are barely perceptible, and the result looks smooth and continuous. Nevertheless, the computer can store and modify them because—*redescribed*—those pixels are all just digital numerals.

The same thing can be done with dynamic systems: systems whose states interact and change in regular ways over time. If the relevant variables and relationships are known, then time can be divided into small intervals too, and the progress of the system computed, step by tiny step. This is called *digital simulation*. The most famous real-world example of it is the massive effort to predict the weather by simulating the Earth's atmosphere. But engineers and scientists—including, as we shall see, many cognitive scientists—rely on digital simulation of non-digital systems all the time.

2.3 Computers and intelligence

Turing (1950 [chapter 2 in this volume], 442 [38]) predicted—falsely, as we now know, but not foolishly—that by the year 2000 there would be computers that could pass his test for intelligence. This was before any serious work, theoretical or practical, had begun on artificial intelligence at all. On what, then, did he base his prediction? He doesn't really say (apart from an estimate—quite low—of how much storage computers would then have). But I think we can see what moved him.

In Turing's test, the only relevant inputs and outputs are *words*—all of which are (among other things) formal tokens. So the capacity of human beings that is to be matched is effectively a formal input/output function. But Turing himself had shown, thirteen years earlier, that *any* formal input/output function from a certain very broad category could be implemented in a routine universal machine, provided only that it had enough memory and time (or speed)—and those, he thought, would be available by century's end.

Now, this isn't really a proof, even setting aside the assumptions about size and speed, because Turing did not (and could not) show that the human verbal input/output function fell into that broad category of functions to which his theorem applied. But he had excellent reason to believe that any function computable by any *digital* mechanism would fall into that category; and he was convinced that there is nothing immaterial or supernatural in human beings. The only alternative remaining would seem to be *non*digital mechanisms; and those he believed could be digitally simulated.

Notice that there is *nothing* in this argument about how the mind might actually work—nothing about actual *mind design*. There's just an assumption that there must be *some* (nonmagical) way that it works, and that, whatever that way is, a computer can either implement it or simulate it. In the subsequent history of artificial intelligence, on the other hand, a number of very concrete proposals have been made about the actual design of human (and/or other) minds. Almost all of these fall into one or the other of two broad groups: those that take seriously the idea that the mind itself is essentially a digital computer (of a particular sort), and those that reject that idea.

3 GOFAI

The first approach is what I call "good old-fashioned AI", or *GOFAI*. (It is also sometimes called "classical" or "symbol-manipulation" or even "language-of-thought" AI.) Research in the GOFAI tradition dominated the field from the mid-fifties through at least the mid-eighties, and for a very good reason: it was (and still is) a well-articulated view of the mechanisms of intelligence that is both intuitively plausible and eminently realizable. According to this view, the mind just *is* a computer with certain special characteristics—namely, one with internal states and processes that can be regarded as explicit *thinking* or *reasoning*. In order to understand the immense plausibility and power of this GOFAI idea, we will need to see how a computer could properly be regarded in this way.

3.1 Interpreted formal systems

The idea of a formal system emerged first in mathematics, and was inspired by arithmetic and algebra. When people solve arithmetic or algebraic problems, they manipulate tokens according to definite rules, sort of like a game. But there is a profound difference between these tokens and, say, the pieces on a chess board: they *mean* something. Numerals, for instance, represent numbers (either of specified items or in the abstract), while arithmetic signs represent operations on or relationships among those numbers. (Tokens that mean something in this way are often called *symbols*.) Chess pieces, checkers, and go stones, by contrast, represent nothing: they are not symbols at all, but *merely* formal game tokens.

The rules according to which the tokens in a mathematical system may be manipulated and what those tokens mean are closely related. A simple example will bring this out. Suppose someone is playing a formal game with the first fifteen letters of the alphabet. The rules of this game are very restrictive: every starting position consists of a string of letters ending in 'A' (though not every such string is legal); and, for each starting position, there is one and only one legal move—which is to append a *particular* string of letters after the 'A' (and then the game is over). The question is: What (if anything) is going on here?

Suppose it occurs to you that the letters might be just an oddball notation for the familiar digits and signs of ordinary arithmetic. There are, however, over a trillion possible ways to translate fifteen letters into fifteen digits and signs. How could you decide which—*if any*—is

Eight sample games (before translation):			
Starting position	*Legal move*	*Starting position*	*Legal move*
OEO A	N	MMCN A	JJ
NIBM A	G	OODF A	OO
HCHCH A	KON	IDL A	M
KEKDOF A	F	NBN A	O

First translation scheme:			Sample games, by first translation:	
A ⇒ 1	F ⇒ 6	K ⇒ +	= 5 = 1	÷
B ⇒ 2	G ⇒ 7	L ⇒ −	÷ 92 × 1	7
C ⇒ 3	H ⇒ 8	M ⇒ ×	83838 1	+ = ÷
D ⇒ 4	I ⇒ 9	N ⇒ ÷	+5+4=6 1	6
E ⇒ 5	J ⇒ 0	O ⇒ =		

Sample games, by first translation (continued):

× × 3 ÷ 1	00
= = 46 1	= =
94 − 1	×
÷ 2 ÷ 1	=

Second translation scheme:			Sample games, by second translation:	
A ⇒ =	F ⇒ 0	K ⇒ 5	9 ÷ 9 =	8
B ⇒ +	G ⇒ 1	L ⇒ 6	83 + 7 =	1
C ⇒ −	H ⇒ 2	M ⇒ 7	2 − 2 − 2 =	598
D ⇒ ×	I ⇒ 3	N ⇒ 8	5 ÷ 5 × 90 =	0
E ⇒ ÷	J ⇒ 4	O ⇒ 9		

77 − 8 =	44
99 × 0 =	99
3 × 6 =	2
8 + 8 =	9

Third translation scheme:			Sample games, by third translation:	
A ⇒ =	F ⇒ 0	K ⇒ 5	1 + 1 =	2
B ⇒ ÷	G ⇒ 9	L ⇒ 4	27 ÷ 3 =	9
C ⇒ ×	H ⇒ 8	M ⇒ 3	8 × 8 × 8 =	512
D ⇒ −	I ⇒ 7	N ⇒ 2	5 + 5 − 10 =	0
E ⇒ +	J ⇒ 6	O ⇒ 1		

33 × 2 =	66
11 − 0 =	11
7 − 4 =	3
2 ÷ 2 =	1

Table 1.1: Letter game and three different translation schemes.

the "right" way? The problem is illustrated in table 1.1. The first row gives eight sample games, each legal according to the rules. The next three rows each give a possible translation scheme, and show how the eight samples would come out according to that scheme.

The differences are conspicuous. The sample games as rendered by the first scheme, though consisting of digits and arithmetic signs, look no more like real arithmetic than the letters did—they're "arithmetic salad" at best. The second scheme, at first glance, looks better: at least the strings have the shape of equations. But, on closer examination, construed as equations, they would all be *false*—*wildly* false. In fact, though the signs are plausibly placed, the digits are just as randomly "tossed" as the first case. The third scheme, by contrast, yields strings that not only look like equations, they *are* equations—they're all *true*. And this makes that third scheme seem much more acceptable. Why?

Consider a related problem: translating some ancient documents in a hitherto unknown script. Clearly, if some crank translator proposed a scheme according to which the texts came out gibberish (like the first one in the table) we would be unimpressed. Almost as obviously, we would be unimpressed if they came out *looking like* sentences, but *loony* ones: not just false, but scattered, silly falsehoods, unrelated to one another or to anything else. On the other hand, if some careful, systematic scheme finds in them detailed, sensible accounts of battles, technologies, facts of nature, or whatever, that we know about from other sources, then we will be convinced.[3] But again: why?

Translation is a species of interpretation (see p. 5 above). Instead of saying what some system thinks or is up to, a translator says what some strings of tokens (symbols) mean. To keep the two species distinct, we can call the former *intentional* interpretation, since it attributes intentional states, and the latter (translation) *semantic* interpretation, since it attributes meanings (= semantics).

Like all interpretation, translation is holistic: it is impossible to interpret a brief string completely out of context. For instance, the legal game 'HDJ A N' happens to come out looking just as true on the second as on the third scheme in our arithmetic example ('$2 \times 4 = 8$' and '$8 - 6 = 2$', respectively). But, in the case of the second scheme, this is obviously just an isolated coincidence, whereas, in the case of the third, it is part of a consistent pattern. Finding meaning in a body of symbols, like finding rationality in a body of behavior, is finding a certain kind of consistent, reliable *pattern*.

Well, what *kind* of pattern? Intentional interpretation seeks to construe a system or creature so that what it thinks and does turns out to be consistently reasonable and sensible, given its situation. Semantic interpretation seeks to construe a body of symbols so that what they mean ("say") turns out to be consistently reasonable and sensible, given the situation. This is *why* the third schemes in both the arithmetic and ancient-script examples are the acceptable ones: they're the ones that "make sense" of the texts, and *that's* the kind of pattern that translation seeks. I don't think we will ever have a precise, explicit definition of any phrase like "consistently reasonable and sensible, given the situation". But surely it captures much of what we mean (and Turing meant) by *intelligence*, whether in action or in expression.

3.2 Intelligence by explicit reasoning

Needless to say, interpretation and automation can be combined. A simple calculator, for instance, is essentially an automated version of the letter-game example, with the third interpretation. And the system that Turing envisioned—a computer with inputs and outputs that could be understood as coherent conversation in English—would be an interpreted automatic formal system. But it's *not* GOFAI.

So far, we have considered systems the inputs and outputs of which can be interpreted. But we have paid no attention to what goes on *inside* of those systems—*how* they get from an input to an appropriate output. In the case of a simple calculator, there's not much to it. But imagine a system that tackles harder problems—like "word problems" in an algebra or physics text, for instance. Here the challenge is not doing the calculations, but figuring out what calculations to do. There are many possible things to try, only one or a few of which will work.

A skilled problem solver, of course, will not try things at random, but will rely on experience and rules of thumb for guidance about what to try next, and about how things are going so far (whether it would be best to continue, to back-track, to start over, or even to give up). We can imagine someone muttering: "If only I could get that, then I could nail this down; but, in order to get that, I would need such and such. Now, let me see ... well, what if ..." (and so on). Such canny, methodical exploration—neither algorithmic nor random—is a familiar sort of articulate *reasoning* or *thinking* a problem out.

But each of those steps (conjectures, partial results, subgoals, blind alleys, and so on) is—from a formal point of view—just another token string. As such, they could easily be intermediate states in an interpreted automatic formal system that took a statement of the problem as input and gave a statement of the solution as output. Should these intermediate strings themselves then be *interpreted as* steps in thinking or reasoning the problem through? If two conditions are met, then the case becomes quite compelling. First, the system had better be able to handle with comparable facility an open-ended and varied range of problems, not just a few (the solutions to which might have been "pre-canned"). And, it had better be arriving at its solutions actually via these steps. (It would be a kind of fraud if it were really solving the problem in some other way, and then tacking on the "steps" for show afterwards.)

GOFAI is predicated on the idea that systems can be built to solve problems by reasoning or thinking them through in this way, and, moreover, that this is how people solve problems. Of course, we aren't always consciously aware of such reasoning, especially for the countless routine problems—like those involved in talking, doing chores, and generally getting along—that we "solve" all the time. But the fact that we are not aware of it doesn't mean that it's not going on, subconsciously or somehow "behind the scenes".

The earliest GOFAI efforts emphasized problem-solving methods, especially the design of efficient heuristics and search procedures, for various specific classes of problems. (The article by Newell and Simon reviews this approach.) These early systems, however, tended to be quite "narrow-minded" and embarrassingly vulnerable to unexpected variations and oddities in the problems and information they were given. Though they could generate quite clever solutions to complicated problems that were carefully posed, they conspicuously lacked "common sense"—they were hopelessly *ignorant*—so they were prone to amusing blunders that no ordinary person would ever make.

Later designs have therefore emphasized broad, common-sense knowledge. Of course, problem-solving heuristics and search techniques are still essential; but, as research problems, these were overshadowed by the difficulties of large-scale "knowledge representation". The biggest problem turned out to be organization. Common-sense knowledge is vast; and, it seems, almost any odd bit of it can be just what is needed to avoid some dumb mistake at any particular moment. So all of it has to be at the system's "cognitive fingertips" all the time. Since repeated exhaustive search of the entire knowledge base would be quite impractical, some shortcuts had to be devised that would work most of the time. This is what efficient organizing or structuring of the knowledge is supposed to provide.

Knowledge-representation research, in contrast to heuristic problem solving, has tended to concentrate on natural language ability, since this is where the difficulties it addresses are most obvious. The principal challenge of ordinary conversation, from a designer's point of view, is that it is so often ambiguous and incomplete—mainly because speakers take so much for granted. That means that the system must be able to fill in all sorts of "trivial" gaps, in order to follow what's being said. But this is still GOFAI, because the filling in is being done rationally. Behind the scenes, the system is explicitly "figuring out" what the speaker must have meant, on the basis of what it knows about the world and the context. (The articles by Minsky and Dreyfus survey some of this work, and Dreyfus and Searle also criticize it.)

Despite its initial plausibility and promise, however, GOFAI has been in some ways disappointing. Expanding and organizing a system's store of explicit knowledge seems at best partially to solve the problem of common sense. This is why the Turing test will not soon be passed. Further, it is surprisingly difficult to design systems that can adjust their own knowledge in the light of experience. The problem is not that they can't modify themselves, but that it's hard to figure out just which modifications to make, while keeping everything else coherent. Finally, GOFAI systems tend to be rather poor at noticing unexpected similarities or adapting to unexpected peculiarities. Indeed, they are poor at recognizing patterns more generally—such as perceived faces, sounds, or kinds of objects—let alone *learning* to recognize them.

None of this means, of course, that the program is bankrupt. Rome was not built in a day. There is a great deal of active research, and new developments occur all the time. It *has* meant, however, that *some* cognitive scientists have begun to explore various alternative approaches.

4 New-fangled AI

By far the most prominent of these new-fangled ideas—we could call them collectively *NFAI* (*en*-fai)—falls under the general rubric of *connectionism*. This is a diverse and still rapidly evolving bundle of systems and proposals that seem, on the face of it, to address some of GOFAI's most glaring weaknesses. On the other hand, connectionist systems are not so good—at least not yet—at matching GOFAI's most obvious strengths. (This suggests, of course, a possibility of joining forces; but, at this point, it's too soon to tell whether any such thing could work, never mind how it might be done.) And, in the meantime, there are other NFAI ideas afloat, that are neither GOFAI nor connectionist. The field as a whole is in more ferment now than it has been since the earliest days, in the fifties.

4.1 Connectionist networks

Connectionist systems are networks of lots of simple active units that have lots of connections among them, by which they can interact. There is no central processor or controller, and also no separate memory or storage mechanism. The only activity in the system is these little units changing state, in response to signals coming in along those connections, and then sending out signals of their own. There are two ways in which such a network can achieve a kind of memory. First, in the short term, information can be retained in the system over time insofar as the units tend to change state only slowly (and, perhaps, regularly). Second, and in the longer term, there is a kind of memory in the connections themselves. For, each connection always connects the same two units (they don't move around); and, more significant, each connection has a property, called its "weight" or "strength", which is preserved over time.

Obviously, connectionist networks are inspired to some extent by brains and neural networks. The active units are like individual neurons, and the connections among them are like the axons and dendrites along which electro-chemical "pulses" are sent from neuron to neuron. But, while this analogy is important, it should not be overstressed. What makes connectionist systems interesting as an approach to AI is not the fact that their structure mimics biology at a certain level of description, but rather what they can do. After all, there are countless other levels of description at which connectionist nets are utterly *un*biological; and, if some GOFAI account turns out to be right about human intelligence, then there will be *some* level of description at which it too accurately models the brain. Connectionist and allied research may someday show that neural networks are the level at which the brain implements psychological structures; but this certainly cannot be assumed at the outset.

In order to appreciate what is distinctive about network models, it is important to keep in mind how simple and relatively isolated the active units are. The "state" of such a unit is typically just a single quantitative magnitude—specifiable with a single number—called its *activation level.* This activation level changes in response to signals arriving from other units, but only in a very crude way. In the first place, it pays no attention to which signals came from which other units, or how any of those signals might be related to others: it simply adds them indiscriminately together and responds only to the total. Moreover, that response, the change in activation, is a simple function of that total; and the signal it then sends to other units is just a simple function of that resulting activation.

Now there is one small complication, which is the root of everything interesting about these models. The signal that a unit receives from another is not the same as the signal that the other unit sent: it is multiplied—increased or decreased—by the weight or strength of the connection between them. And there are always many more connections in a network than there are units, simply because each unit is connected to many others. That means that the *overall* state of the network—that is, the *pattern* of activations of all its units—can change in very subtle and sophisticated ways, as a function of its initial state. The overall pattern of connection weights is what determines these complicated changes, and thus the basic character of the network.

Accordingly, connectionist networks are essentially *pattern processors*. And, it turns out, they can be quite good at certain psychologically important kinds of pattern processing. In particular, they are adept at finding various sorts of similarities among patterns, at recognizing repeated (or almost repeated) patterns, at filling in the missing parts of incomplete patterns, and at transforming patterns into others with which they have been associated. People are good at these kinds of pattern processing too; but GOFAI systems tend not to be, except in special cases. Needless to say, this is what gets cognitive scientists excited about connectionist models.

Two more points. First, when I say that networks are good at such pattern processing, I mean not only that they can do it well, but also that they can do it quickly. This is a consequence of the fact that, although each unit is very simple, there are a great many of them working at once—in *parallel*, so to speak—so the cumulative effect in each time increment can be quite substantial. Second, techniques have been discovered by means of which networks can be *trained* through exposure to examples. That is, the connection weights required for some desired pattern-processing ability can be induced ("taught") by giving the network a number of sample instances, and allowing it slowly to adjust itself. (It should be added, however, that the training techniques so far discovered are not psychologically realistic: people learn from examples too, but, for various reasons, we know it can't be in quite these ways.)

I mentioned a moment ago that GOFAI systems are not so good at pattern processing, except in special cases. In comparing approaches to mind design, however, it is crucial to recognize that some of these "special cases" are extremely important. In particular, GOFAI systems are remarkably *good* at processing (recognizing, transforming, producing) *syntactical* (grammatical) patterns of the sort that are characteristic of logical formulae, ordinary sentences, and many inferences. What's more, connectionist networks are *not* (so far?) particularly good at processing *these* patterns. Yet language is surely a central manifestation of (human) intelligence. No approach to mind design that cannot accommodate language ability can possibly be adequate.

Connectionist researchers use computers in their work just as much as GOFAI researchers do; but they use them differently. Pattern-processing networks are not themselves automatic formal systems: they do not manipulate formal tokens, and they are not essentially digital. To be sure, the individual units and connections are sharply distinct from one another; and, for convenience, their activations and weights are sometimes limited to a handful of discrete values. But these are more akin to the "digitization" of images in computer image processing than to the essential digitalness of chess pieces, logical symbols, and words. Thus, connectionist mind design relies on computers more in the way the weather service does, to simulate digitally systems that are not in themselves digital.

It has been shown, however, that some connectionist networks can, in effect, *implement* symbol manipulation systems. Although these implementations tend not to be very efficient, they are nevertheless interesting. For one thing, they may show how symbol manipulation could be implemented in the brain. For another, they might yield ways to build and understand genuine *hybrid* systems—that is, systems with the advantages of both approaches. Such possibilities aside, however, symbolic implementation would seem at best Phyrric victory: the network would be relegated to the role of "hardware", while the psychological relevance, the actual *mind design*, would still be GOFAI.

GOFAI is inspired by the idea that intelligence as such is made possible by explicit thinking or reasoning—that is, by the rational manipulation of internal symbol structures (interpreted formal tokens). Thus, GOFAI intentionality is grounded in the possibility of translation—*semantic* interpretation. Connectionist NFAI, by contrast, is inspired initially by the structure of the brain, but, more deeply, by the importance and ubiquity of non-formal pattern processing. Since there are no formal tokens (unless implemented at a higher level), there can be no semantically interpreted symbols. Thus, to regard these systems as having intentional states would be to adopt Dennett's intentional stance—that is, *intentional* interpretation.

In this volume, connectionist models are introduced and promoted in the articles by Rumelhart, by Smolensky, and by Churchland. The approach is criticized in the articles by Rosenberg and by Fodor and Pylyshyn. The articles by Ramsey, Stich and Garon and by Clark don't so much take sides as explore further what might be involved in the very idea of connectionism, in ways that might make a difference to those who do take sides.

4.2 Embodied and embedded AI

GOFAI is a fairly coherent research tradition, based on a single basic idea: thinking as internal symbol manipulation. 'NFAI', by contrast, is more a grab-bag term: it means, roughly, scientific mind design that is not GOFAI. Connectionism falls under this umbrella, but several other possibilities do as well, of which I will mention just one.

Connectionist and GOFAI systems, for all their differences, tend to have one feature in common: they accept an input from somewhere, they work on it for a while, and then they deliver an output. All the "action" is *within* the system, rather than being an integral part of a larger *interaction* with an active body and an active environment. The alternative, to put it radically (and perhaps a bit contentiously), would be to have the intelligent system *be* the larger interactive *whole*, including the body and environment as essential components. Now, of course, this whole couldn't be intelligent if it weren't for a special "subsystem" such as might be implemented in a computer or a brain; but, equally, perhaps, that subsystem couldn't be intelligent either except as part of a whole comprising the other components as well.

Why would anyone think this? It goes without saying that, in general, intelligent systems ought to be able to *act* intelligently "in" the world. That's what intelligence is for, ultimately. Yet, achieving even basic competence in real robots turns out to be surprisingly hard. A simple example can illustrate the point and also the change in perspective that motivates some recent research. Consider a system that must be able, among other things, to approach and unlock a door. How will it get the key in the lock? One approach would equip the robot with:

(1) precise sensors to identify and locate the lock, and monitor the angles of the joints in its own arm and hand;

(2) enough modelling power to convert joint information into a representation of the location and orientation of the key (in the coordinate system of the lock), compute the exact key motion required, and then convert that back into joint motions; and

(3) motors accurate enough to effect the computed motions, and thereby to slide the key in, smooth and straight, the first time.

Remarkably, such a system is utterly impractical, perhaps literally impossible, even with state-of-the-art technology. Yet insects, with far less compute power on board, routinely perform much harder tasks.

How would insectile "intelligence" approach the key-lock problem? First, the system would have a crude detector to notice and aim at locks, more or less. But, it would generate no central representation of the lock's position, for other subsystems to use in computing arm movements. Rather, the arm itself would have its own ad hoc, but more local, detectors that enable it likewise to home in on a lock, more or less (and also, perhaps, to adjust its aim from one try to the next). And, in the meantime, the arm and its grip on the key would both be quite flexible, and the lock would have a kind of funnel around its opening, so any stab that's at all close would be guided physically right into the lock. Now *that's* engineering—elegant, cheap, reliable.

But is it *intelligence*? Well surely not much; but that may not be the right question to ask. Instead, we should wonder whether some similar essential involvement of the body (physical flexibility and special purpose subsystems, for instance) and the world (conveniences like the funnel) might be integral to capacities that are more plausibly intelligent. If so, it could greatly decrease the load on central knowledge, problem solving, and even pattern processing, thereby circumventing (perhaps) some of the bottlenecks that frustrate current designs.

To get a feel for the possibilities, move for a moment to the other end of the spectrum. Human intelligence is surely manifested in the ability to design and make things—using, as the case may be, boards and nails. Now, for such a design to work, it must be possible to drive nails into pieces of wood in a way that will hold them together. But neither a designer nor a carpenter ever needs to think about that—it need never even *occur* to them. (They take it for granted, as a fish does water.) The suitability of these materials and techniques is embedded in the structure of their culture: the logging industry, the manufacture of wire, the existence of lumber yards—and, of course, countless bodily skills and habits passed down from generation to generation.

Think how much "knowledge" is contained in the traditional shape and heft of a hammer, as well as in the muscles and reflexes acquired in learning to use it—though, again, no one need *ever* have thought of it. Multiply that by our food and hygiene practices, our manner of dress, the layout of buildings, cities, and farms. To be sure, some of this was explicitly figured out, at least once upon a time; but a lot of it wasn't— it just evolved that way (because it worked). Yet a great deal, perhaps even the bulk, of the basic expertise that makes human intelligence what it is, is maintained and brought to bear in these "physical" structures. It is neither stored nor used inside the head of *anyone*—it's in their bodies and, even more, out there in the world.

Scientific research into the kinds of systems that might achieve intelligence in this way—embodied and embedded mind design—is still in an early phase. Two rather different theoretical and empirical strategies are presented here in the articles by Brooks and van Gelder.

5 What's missing from mind design?

A common complaint about artificial intelligence, of whatever stripe, is that it pays scant attention to feelings, emotions, ego, imagination, moods, consciousness—the whole "phenomenology" of an inner life. No matter how smart the machines become, so the worry goes, there's still "nobody home". I think there is considerable merit in these misgivings, though, of course, more in some forms than in others. Here, however, I would like briefly to discuss only one form of the worry, one that strikes me as more basic than the others, and also more intimately connected with cognition narrowly conceived.

No current approach to artificial intelligence takes *understanding* seriously—where understanding itself is understood as distinct from knowledge (in whole or in part) and prerequisite thereto. It seems to me that, taken in this sense, *only people* ever understand anything—no animals and no artifacts (yet). It follows that, in a strict and proper sense, no animal or machine genuinely believes or desires anything either—How could it believe something it doesn't understand?—though, obviously, in some other, weaker sense, animals (at least) have plenty of beliefs and desires. This conviction, I should add, is not based on any in-principle barrier; it's just an empirical observation about what happens to be the case at the moment, so far as we can tell.

So, what is it for a system to understand something? Imagine a system that makes or marks a battery of related distinctions in the course of coping with some range of objects. These distinctions can show up in the form of differing skillful responses, different symbol structures, or whatever. Let's say that, for each such distinction, the system has a *proto-concept*. Now I suggest that a system *understands* the objects to which it applies its proto-concepts insofar as:

(1) it takes responsibility for applying the proto-concepts correctly;

(2) it takes responsibility for the empirical adequacy of the proto-concepts themselves; and

(3) it takes a firm stand on what can and cannot happen in the world, when grasped in terms of these proto-concepts.

When these conditions are met, moreover, the proto-concepts are not merely *proto*-concepts, but *concepts* in the full and proper sense.

The three conditions are not unrelated. For, it is precisely in the face of something *impossible* seeming to have happened, that the question of *correct* application becomes urgent. We can imagine the system responding in some way that we would express by saying: "This *can't* be right!" and then trying to figure out what went wrong. The responsibility for the concepts themselves emerges when, too often, it can't find any mistake. In that event, the conceptual structure itself must be revised, either by modifying the discriminative abilities that embody the concepts, or by modifying the stand it takes on what is and isn't possible, or both. Afterward, it will have (more or less) new concepts.

A system that appropriates and takes charge of its own conceptual resources in this way is not merely going through the motions of intelligence, whether evolved, learned, or programmed-in, but rather grasps the point of them for itself. It does not merely make discriminations or produce outputs that, when best interpreted by us, come out true. Rather, such a system appreciates for itself the difference between truth and falsity, appreciates that, in these, it must accede to the world, that the world determines which is which—and it *cares*. That, I think, is *understanding*.[4]

Notes

1. Both parts of this idea have their roots in W. V. O. Quine's pioneering (1950, 1960) investigations of meaning. (Meaning is the linguistic or symbolic counterpart of intentionality.)

2. Chess players will know that the rules for castling, stalemate, and capturing *en passent* depend also on *previous* events; so, to make chess strictly formal, these conditions would have to be encoded in further tokens (markers, say) that count as part of the current position.

3. A similar point can be made about code-cracking (which is basically translating texts that are contrived to make that especially difficult). A cryptographer knows she has succeeded when and only when the decoded messages come out consistently sensible, relevant, and true.

4. These ideas are explored fruther in the last four chapters of Haugeland (1997).

Computing Machinery and Intelligence

A. M. Turing
1950

1 The imitation game

I propose to consider the question "Can machines think?" This should begin with definitions of the meaning of the terms 'machine' and 'think'. The definitions might be framed so as to reflect so far as possible the normal use of the words, but this attitude is dangerous. If the meaning of the words 'machine' and 'think' are to be found by examining how they are commonly used it is difficult to escape the conclusion that the meaning and the answer to the question, "Can machines think?" is to be sought in a statistical survey such as a Gallup poll. But this is absurd. Instead of attempting such a definition I shall replace the question by another, which is closely related to it and is expressed in relatively unambiguous words.

The new form of the problem can be described in terms of a game which we call the "imitation game". It is played with three people, a man (A), a woman (B), and an interrogator (C) who may be of either sex. The interrogator stays in a room apart from the other two. The object of the game for the interrogator is to determine which of the other two is the man and which is the woman. He knows them by labels X and Y, and at the end of the game he says either "X is A and Y is B" or "X is B and Y is A". The interrogator is allowed to put questions to A and B thus:

C: Will X please tell me the length of his or her hair?

Now suppose X is actually A, then A must answer. It is A's object in the game to try to cause C to make the wrong identification. His answer might therefore be

A: My hair is shingled, and the longest strands are about nine inches long.

In order that tones of voice may not help the interrogator the answers should be written, or better still, typewritten. The ideal arrangement is to have a teleprinter communicating between the two rooms. Alternatively the question and answers can be repeated by an intermediary. The object of the game for the third player (B) is to help the interrogator. The best strategy for her is probably to give truthful answers. She can add such things as "I am the woman, don't listen to him!" to her answers, but it will avail nothing as the man can make similar remarks.

We now ask the question, "What will happen when a machine takes the part of A in this game?" Will the interrogator decide wrongly as often when the game is played like this as he does when the game is played between a man and a woman? These questions replace our original, "Can machines think?"

2 Critique of the new problem

As well as asking, "What is the answer to this new form of the question?" one may ask, "Is this new question a worthy one to investigate?" This latter question we investigate without further ado, thereby cutting short an infinite regress.

The new problem has the advantage of drawing a fairly sharp line between the physical and the intellectual capacities of a man. No engineer or chemist claims to be able to produce a material which is indistinguishable from the human skin. It is possible that at some time this might be done, but even supposing this invention available we should feel there was little point in trying to make a "thinking machine" more human by dressing it up in such artificial flesh. The form in which we have set the problem reflects this fact in the condition which prevents the interrogator from seeing or touching the other competitors, or hearing their voices. Some other advantages of the proposed criterion may be shown up by specimen questions and answers. Thus:

Q: Please write me a sonnet on the subject of the Forth Bridge.

A: Count me out on this one. I never could write poetry.

Q: Add 34957 to 70764.

A: (Pause about 30 seconds and then give as answer) 105621.

Q: Do you play chess?

A: Yes.

Q: I have K at my K1, and no other pieces. You have only K at K6
and R at R1. It is your move. What do you play?

A: (After a pause of 15 seconds) R–R8 mate.

The question and answer method seems to be suitable for introducing almost any one of the fields of human endeavor that we wish to
include. We do not wish to penalize the machine for its inability to
shine in beauty competitions, nor to penalize a man for losing in a race
against an airplane. The conditions of our game make these disabilities
irrelevant. The "witnesses" can brag, if they consider it advisable, as
much as they please about their charms, strength or heroism, but the
interrogator cannot demand practical demonstrations.

The game may perhaps be criticized on the ground that the odds
are weighted too heavily against the machine. If the man were to try
and pretend to be the machine he would clearly make a very poor
showing. He would be given away at once by slowness and inaccuracy
in arithmetic. May not machines carry out something which ought to
be described as thinking but which is very different from what a man
does? This objection is a very strong one, but at least we can say that if,
nevertheless, a machine can be constructed to play the imitation game
satisfactorily, we need not be troubled by this objection.

It might be urged that when playing the "imitation game" the best
strategy for the machine may possibly be something other than imitation of the behavior of a man. This may be, but I think it is unlikely
that there is any great effect of this kind. In any case there is no intention to investigate here the theory of the game, and it will be assumed
that the best strategy is to try to provide answers that would naturally
be given by a man.

3 The machines concerned in the game

The question which we put in section 1 will not be quite definite until
we have specified what we mean by the word 'machine'. It is natural
that we should wish to permit every kind of engineering technique to
be used in our machines. We also wish to allow the possibility that an
engineer or team of engineers may construct a machine which works,
but whose manner of operation cannot be satisfactorily described by
its constructors because they have applied a method which is largely
experimental. Finally, we wish to exclude from the machines men born
in the usual manner. It is difficult to frame the definitions so as to satisfy these three conditions. One might for instance insist that the team

of engineers should be all of one sex, but this would not really be satisfactory, for it is probably possible to rear a complete individual from a single cell of the skin (say) of a man. To do so would be a feat of biological technique deserving of the very highest praise, but we would not be inclined to regard it as a case of "constructing a thinking machine". This prompts us to abandon the requirement that every kind of technique should be permitted. We are the more ready to do so in view of the fact that the present interest in "thinking machines" has been aroused by a particular kind of machine, usually called an "electronic computer" or "digital computer". Following this suggestion we only permit digital computers to take part in our game.

This restriction appears at first sight to be a very drastic one. I shall attempt to show that it is not so in reality. To do this necessitates a short account of the nature and properties of these computers.

It may also be said that this identification of machines with digital computers, like our criterion for "thinking", will only be unsatisfactory if (contrary to my belief), it turns out that digital computers are unable to give a good showing in the game.

There are already a number of digital computers in working order, and it may be asked, "Why not try the experiment straight away? It would be easy to satisfy the conditions of the game. A number of interrogators could be used, and statistics compiled to show how often the right identification was given." The short answer is that we are not asking whether all digital computers would do well in the game nor whether the computers at present available would do well, but whether there are imaginable computers which would do well. But this is only the short answer. We shall see this question in a different light later.

4 Digital computers

The idea behind digital computers may be explained by saying that these machines are intended to carry out any operations which could be done by a human computer. The human computer is supposed to be following fixed rules; he has no authority to deviate from them in any detail. We may suppose that these rules are supplied in a book, which is altered whenever he is put on to a new job. He has also an unlimited supply of paper on which he does his calculations. He may also do his multiplications and additions on a "desk machine", but this is not important.

If we use the above explanation as a definition, we shall be in danger of circularity of argument. We avoid this by giving an outline of the means by which the desired effect is achieved. A digital computer can usually be regarded as consisting of three parts:

(i) Store.

(ii) Executive unit.

(iii) Control.

The store is a store of information, and corresponds to the human computer's paper, whether this is the paper on which he does his calculations or that on which his book of rules is printed. Insofar as the human computer does calculations in his head, a part of the store will correspond to his memory.

The executive unit is the part which carries out the various individual operations involved in a calculation. What these individual operations are will vary from machine to machine. Usually fairly lengthy operations, such as "Multiply 3540675445 by 7076345687", can be done, but in some machines only very simple ones, such as "Write down 0", are possible.

We have mentioned that the "book of rules" supplied to the computer is replaced in the machine by a part of the store. It is then called the "table of instructions". It is the duty of the control to see that these instructions are obeyed correctly and in the right order. The control is so constructed that this necessarily happens.

The information in the store is usually broken up into packets of moderately small size. In one machine, for instance, a packet might consist of ten decimal digits. Numbers are assigned to the parts of the store in which the various packets of information are stored, in some systematic manner. A typical instruction might say:

Add the number stored in position 6809 to that in 4302 and put the result back into the latter storage position.

Needless to say it would not occur in the machine expressed in English. It would more likely be coded in a form such as 6809430217. Here 17 says which of various possible operations is to be performed on the two numbers—in this case the operation that is described above, namely, "Add the number …". It will be noticed that the instruction takes up 10 digits and so forms one packet of information, very conveniently. The control will normally take the instructions to be obeyed in the order of the positions in which they are stored, but occasionally an instruction such as

> Now obey the instruction stored in position 5606, and continue from there.

may be encountered, or again

> If position 4505 contains 0 obey next the instruction stored in 6707, otherwise continue straight on.

Instructions of these latter types are very important because they make it possible for a sequence of operations to be repeated over and over again until some condition is fulfilled, but in doing so to obey, not fresh instructions on each repetition, but the same ones over and over again. To take a domestic analogy, suppose Mother wants Tommy to call at the cobbler's every morning on his way to school to see if her shoes are done. She can ask him afresh every morning. Alternatively she can stick up a notice once and for all in the hall which he will see when he leaves for school and which tells him to call for the shoes, and also to destroy the notice when he comes back if he has the shoes with him.

The reader must accept it as a fact that digital computers can be constructed, and indeed have been constructed, according to the principles we have described, and that they can in fact mimic the actions of a human computer very closely.

The book of rules which we have described our human computer as using is of course a convenient fiction. Actual human computers really remember what they have got to do. If one wants to make a machine mimic the behavior of the human computer in some complex operation one has to ask him how it is done, and then translate the answer into the form of an instruction table. Constructing instruction tables is usually described as "programming". To "program a machine to carry out the operation A" means to put the appropriate instruction table into the machine so that it will do A.

An interesting variant on the idea of a digital computer is a digital computer with a random element. These have instructions involving the throwing of a die or some equivalent electronic process; one such instruction might for instance be

> Throw the die and put the resulting number into store 1000.

Sometimes such a machine is described as having free will (though I would not use this phrase myself). It is not normally possible to determine from observing a machine whether it has a random element, for a similar effect can be produced by such devices as making the choices depend on the digits of the decimal for π.

Most actual digital computers have only a finite store. There is no theoretical difficulty in the idea of a computer with an unlimited store. Of course only a finite part of it can have been used at any one time. Likewise only a finite amount can have been constructed, but we can imagine more and more being added as required. Such computers have special theoretical interest and will be called infinite capacity computers.

The idea of a digital computer is an old one. Charles Babbage, Lucasian Professor of Mathematics at Cambridge from 1828 to 1839, planned such a machine, called the "Analytical Engine", but it was never completed. Although Babbage had all the essential ideas, his machine was not at that time such a very attractive prospect. The speed which would have been available would be definitely faster than a human computer but something like 100 times slower than the Manchester machine, itself one of the slower of the modern machines. The storage was to be purely mechanical, using wheels and cards.

The fact that Babbage's Analytical Engine was to be entirely mechanical will help us to rid ourselves of a superstition. Importance is often attached to the fact that modern digital computers are electrical, and that the nervous system also is electrical. Since Babbage's machine was not electrical, and since all digital computers are in a sense equivalent, we see that this use of electricity cannot be of theoretical importance. Of course electricity usually comes in where fast signaling is concerned, so it is not surprising that we find it in both these connections. In the nervous system chemical phenomena are at least as important as electrical. In certain computers the storage system is mainly acoustic. The feature of using electricity is thus seen to be only a very superficial similarity. If we wish to find such similarities we should look rather for mathematical analogies of function.

5 Universality of digital computers

The digital computers considered in the last section may be classified among the "discrete state machines". These are the machines which move by sudden jumps or clicks from one quite definite state to another. These states are sufficiently different for the possibility of confusion between them to be ignored. Strictly speaking there are no such machines. Everything really moves continuously. But there are many kinds of machines which can profitably be *thought of* as being discrete state machines. For instance in considering the switches for a lighting system it is a convenient fiction that each switch must be definitely on or definitely off. There must be intermediate positions, but for most purposes we can forget about them. As an example of a discrete state machine, we might consider a wheel which clicks round through $120°$ once a second, but may be stopped by a lever which can be operated from outside; in addition a lamp is to light in one of the positions of the wheel. This machine could be described abstractly as follows: The internal state of the machine (which is described by the position of the wheel) may be q_1, q_2, or q_3. There is an input signal i_0 or i_1 (position of lever). The internal state at any moment is determined by the last state and input signal according to the table

		Last state:		
		q_1	q_2	q_3
Input:	i_0	q_2	q_3	q_1
	i_1	q_1	q_2	q_3

The output signals, the only externally visible indication of the internal state (the light), are described by the table

State:	q_1	q_2	q_3
Output:	O_0	O_0	O_1

This example is typical of discrete state machines. They can be described by such tables, provided they have only a finite number of possible states.

It will seem that given the initial state of the machine and the input signals it is always possible to predict all future states. This is reminiscent of Laplace's view that from the complete state of the universe at one moment of time, as described by the positions and velocities of all particles, it should be possible to predict all future states. The prediction which we are considering is, however, rather nearer to practicability than that considered by Laplace. The system of the "universe as a whole" is such that quite small errors in the initial conditions can have an overwhelming effect at a later time. The displacement of a single electron by a billionth of a centimeter at one moment might make the difference between a man being killed by an avalanche a year later, or escaping. It is an essential property of the mechanical systems which we have called "discrete state machines" that this phenomenon does not occur. Even when we consider the actual physical machines instead of the idealized machines, reasonably accurate knowledge of the state at one moment yields reasonably accurate knowledge any number of steps later.

As we have mentioned, digital computers fall within the class of discrete state machines. But the number of states of which such a machine is capable is usually enormously large. For instance, the number for the machine now working at Manchester is about $2^{165,000}$— that is, about $10^{50,000}$. Compare this with our example of the clicking wheel described above, which had three states. It is not difficult to see why the number of states should be so immense. The computer includes a store corresponding to the paper used by a human computer. It must be possible to write into the store any one of the combinations of symbols which might have been written on the paper. For simplicity suppose that only digits from 0 to 9 are used as symbols. Variations in handwriting are ignored. Suppose the computer is allowed 100 sheets of paper each containing 50 lines each with room for 30 digits. Then the number of states is $10^{100 \times 50 \times 30}$—that is, $10^{150,000}$. This is about the number of states of three Manchester machines put together. The logarithm to the base two of the number of states is usually called the "storage capacity" of the machine. Thus the Manchester machine has a storage capacity of about 165,000 and the wheel machine of our example about 1.6. If two machines are put together their capacities must be added to obtain the capacity of the resultant machine. This leads to the possibility of statements such as "The Manchester machine contains 64 magnetic tracks each with a capacity of 2560, eight electronic tubes with a capacity of 1280. Miscellaneous storage amounts to about 300 making a total of 174,380."

Given the table corresponding to a discrete state machine, it is possible to predict what it will do. There is no reason why this calculation should not be carried out by means of a digital computer. Provided it could be carried out sufficiently quickly the digital computer could mimic the behavior of any discrete state machine. The imitation game could then be played with the machine in question (as B) and the mimicking digital computer (as A) and the interrogator would be unable to distinguish them. Of course the digital computer must have adequate storage capacity a well as working sufficiently fast. Moreover, it must be programmed afresh for each new machine which it is desired to mimic.

This special property of digital computers, that they can mimic any discrete state machine, is described by saying that they are *universal* machines. The existence of machines with this property has the important consequence that, considerations of speed apart, it is unnecessary to design various new machines to do various computing processes. They can all be done with one digital computer, suitably programmed for each case. It will be seen that as a consequence of this all digital computers are in a sense equivalent.

We may now consider again the point raised at the end of section 3. It was suggested tentatively that the question, "Can machines think?" should be replaced by "Are there imaginable digital computers which would do well in the imitation game?" If we wish we can make this superficially more general and ask, "Are there discrete state machines which would do well?" But in view of the universality property we see that either of these questions is equivalent to this: "Let us fix our attention on one particular digital computer C. Is it true that by modifying this computer to have an adequate storage, suitably increasing its speed of action, and providing it with an appropriate program, C can be made to play satisfactorily the part of A in the imitation game, the part of B being taken by a man?"

6 Contrary views on the main question

We may now consider the ground to have been cleared and we are ready to proceed to the debate on our question, "Can machines think?" and the variant of it quoted at the end of the last section. We cannot altogether abandon the original form of the problem, for opinions will differ as to the appropriateness of the substitution and we must at least listen to what has to be said in this connection.

It will simplify matters for the reader if I explain first my own beliefs in the matter. Consider first the more accurate form of the question. I believe that in about fifty years' time it will be possible to program computers, with a storage capacity of about 10^9, to make them play the imitation game so well that an average interrogator will not have more than 70 per cent chance of making the right identification after five minutes of questioning. The original question, "Can machines think?" I believe to be too meaningless to deserve discussion. Nevertheless I believe that at the end of the century the use of words and general educated opinion will have altered so much that one will be able to speak of machines thinking without expecting to be contradicted. I believe further that no useful purpose is served by concealing these beliefs. The popular view that scientists proceed inexorably from well-established fact to well-established fact, never being influenced by any unproved conjecture, is quite mistaken. Provided it is made clear which are proved facts and which are conjectures, no harm can result. Conjectures are of great importance since they suggest useful lines of research.

I now proceed to consider opinions opposed to my own.

(1) THE THEOLOGICAL OBJECTION. Thinking is a function of man's immortal soul. God has given an immortal soul to every man and woman, but not to any other animal or to machines. Hence no animal or machine can think.[1]

I am unable to accept any part of this, but will attempt to reply in theological terms. I should find the argument more convincing if animals were classed with men, for there is a greater difference, to my mind, between the typical animate and the inanimate than there is between man and the other animals. The arbitrary character of the orthodox view becomes clearer if we consider how it might appear to a member of some other religious community. How do Christians regard the Moslem view that women have no souls? But let us leave this point aside and return to the main argument. It appears to me that the argument quoted above implies a serious restriction of the omnipotence of the Almighty. It is admitted that there are certain things that He cannot do such as making one equal to two, but should we not believe that He has freedom to confer a soul on an elephant if He sees fit? We might expect that He would only exercise this power in conjunction with a mutation which provided the elephant with an appropriately improved brain to minister to the needs of this soul. An argument of exactly similar form may be made for the case of machines. It may seem different because it is more difficult to "swallow". But this really only means that we think it would be less likely that He would consider the circumstances suitable for conferring a soul. The circumstances in question are discussed in the rest of this paper. In attempting to construct such machines we should not be irreverently usurping His power of creating souls, any more than we are in the procreation of children: rather we are, in either case, instruments of His will providing mansions for the souls that He creates.

However, this is mere speculation. I am not very impressed with theological arguments, whatever they may be used to support. Such arguments have often been found unsatisfactory in the past. In the time of Galileo it was argued that the texts, "And the sun stood still ... and hasted not to go down about a whole day" (Joshua x. 13) and "He laid the foundations of the earth, that it should not move at any time" (Psalm cv. 5) were an adequate refutation of the Copernican theory. With our present knowledge, such an argument appears futile. When that knowledge was not available, it made a quite different impression.

(2) THE "HEADS IN THE SAND" OBJECTION. "The consequences of machines thinking would be too dreadful. Let us hope and believe that they cannot do so."

This argument is seldom expressed quite so openly as in the form above. But it affects most of us who think about it at all. We like to believe that Man is in some subtle way superior to the rest of creation. It is best if he can be shown to be *necessarily* superior, for then there is no danger of him losing his commanding position. The popularity of the theological argument is clearly connected with this feeling. It is likely to be quite strong in intellectual people, since they value the power of thinking more highly than others, and are more inclined to base their belief in the superiority of Man on this power.

I do not think that this argument is sufficiently substantial to require refutation. Consolation would be more appropriate; perhaps this should be sought in the transmigration of souls.

(3) THE MATHEMATICAL OBJECTION. There are a number of results of mathematical logic which can be used to show that there are limitations to the powers of discrete state machines. The best known of these results is known as Gödel's theorem, and shows that in any sufficiently powerful logical system statements can be formulated which can neither be proved nor disproved within the system, unless possibly the system itself is inconsistent. There are other, in some respects similar, results due to Church (1936), Kleene (1935), Rosser (1936), and Turing (1937). The latter result is the most convenient to consider, since it refers directly to machines whereas the others can only be used in a comparatively indirect argument; for instance, if Gödel's theorem is to be used we need in addition to have some means of describing logical systems in terms of machines, and machines in terms of logical systems. The result in question refers to a type of machine which is essentially a digital computer with an infinite capacity. It states that there

are certain things that such a machine cannot do. If it is rigged up to give answers to questions as in the imitation game, there will be some questions to which it will either give a wrong answer, or fail to give an answer at all, however much time is allowed for a reply. There may, of course, be many such questions, and questions which cannot be answered by one machine may be satisfactorily answered by another. We are of course supposing for the present that the questions are of the kind to which an answer "Yes" or "No" is appropriate, rather than questions such as "What do you think of Picasso?" The questions that we know the machines must fail on are of this type, "Consider the machine specified as follows ... . Will this machine ever answer 'Yes' to any question?" The dots are to be replaced by a description of some machine in a standard form, which could be something like that used in section 5. When the machine described bears a certain comparatively simple relation to the machine which is under interrogation, it can be shown that the answer is either wrong or not forthcoming. This is the mathematical result; it is argued that it proves a disability of machines to which the human intellect is not subject.

The short answer to this argument is that, although it is established that there are limitations to the powers of any particular machine, it has only been stated, without any sort of proof, that no such limitations apply to the human intellect. But I do not think this view can be dismissed quite so lightly. Whenever one of these machines is asked the appropriate critical question, and gives a definite answer, we know that this answer must be wrong, and this gives us a certain feeling of superiority. Is this feeling illusory? It is no doubt quite genuine, but I do not think too much importance should be attached to it. We too often give wrong answers to questions ourselves to be justified in being very pleased at such evidence of fallibility on the part of the machines. Further, our superiority can only be felt on such an occasion in relation to the one machine over which we have scored our petty triumph. There would be no question of triumphing simultaneously over *all* machines. In short, then, there might be men cleverer than any given machine, but then again there might be other machines cleverer again, and so on.

Those who hold to the mathematical argument would, I think, mostly be willing to accept the imitation game as a basis for discussion. Those who believe in the two previous objections would probably not be interested in any criteria.

(4) THE ARGUMENT FROM CONSCIOUSNESS. This argument is very well expressed in Professor Jefferson's Lister Oration for 1949, from which I quote.

> Not until a machine can write a sonnet or compose a concerto because of thoughts and emotions felt, and not by the chance fall of symbols, could we agree that machine equals brain—that is, not only write it but know that it had written it. No mechanism could feel (and not merely artificially signal, and easy contrivance) pleasure at its successes, grief when its valves fuse, be warmed by flattery, be made miserable by its mistakes, be charmed by sex, be angry or depressed when it cannot get what it wants.

This argument appears to be a denial of the validity of our test. According to the most extreme form of this view, the only way by which one could be sure that a machine thinks is to *be* the machine and to feel oneself thinking. One could then describe these feelings to the world, but of course no one would be justified in taking any notice. Likewise according to this view, the only way to know that a *man* thinks is to be that particular man. It is in fact the solipsist point of view. It may be the most logical view to hold but it makes communication of ideas difficult. A is liable to believe "A thinks but B does not" while B believes "B thinks but A does not". Instead of arguing continually over this point, it is usual to have the polite convention that everyone thinks.

I am sure that Professor Jefferson does not wish to adopt the extreme and solipsist point of view. Probably he would be quite willing to accept the imitation game as a test. The game (with the player B omitted) is frequently used in practice under the name of *viva voce* to discover whether someone really understands something or has "learned it parrot fashion". Let us listen in to a part of such a *viva voce*:

INTERROGATOR: In the first line of your sonnet, which reads "Shall I compare thee to a summer's day," would not "a spring day" do as well or better?

WITNESS: It wouldn't scan.

INTERROGATOR: How about "a winter's day". That would scan all right.

WITNESS: Yes, but nobody wants to be compared to a winter's day.

INTERROGATOR: Would you say Mr. Pickwick reminded you of Christmas?

WITNESS: In a way.

INTERROGATOR: Yet Christmas is a winter's day, and I do not think Mr. Pickwick would mind the comparison.

WITNESS: I don't think you're serious. By a winter's day one means a typical winter's day, rather than a special one like Christmas.

And so on. What would Professor Jefferson say if the sonnet-writing machine were able to answer like this in the *viva voce*? I do not know whether he would regard the machine as "merely artificially signaling" these answers, but if the answers were as satisfactory and sustained as in the above passage I do not think he would describe it as "an easy contrivance". This phrase is, I think, intended to cover such devices as the inclusion in the machine of a record of someone reading a sonnet, with appropriate switching to turn it on from time to time.

In short then, I think that most of those who support the argument from consciousness could be persuaded to abandon it rather than be forced into the solipsist position. They will then probably be willing to accept our test.

I do not wish to give the impression that I think there is no mystery about consciousness. There is, for instance, something of a paradox connected with any attempt to localize it. But I do not think these mysteries necessarily need to be solved before we can answer the question with which we are concerned in this paper.

(5) ARGUMENTS FROM VARIOUS DISABILITIES. These arguments take the form, "I grant you that you can make machines do all the things you have mentioned but you will never be able to make one to do X." Numerous features X are suggested in this connection. I offer a selection:

> Be kind, resourceful, beautiful, friendly (44), have initiative, have a sense of humor, tell right from wrong, make mistakes (44), fall in love, enjoy strawberries and cream (44), make someone fall in love with it, learn from experience (50), use words properly, be the subject of its own thought (45), have as much diversity of behavior as a man, do something really new (46). (Some of these disabilities are given special consideration as indicated by the page numbers.)

No support is usually offered for these statements. I believe they are mostly founded on the principle of scientific induction. A man has seen thousands of machines in his lifetime. From what he sees of them he draws a number of general conclusions. They are ugly, each is designed for a very limited purpose, when required for a minutely different purpose they are useless, the variety of behavior of any one of them is very small, and so on and so forth. Naturally he concludes that these are necessary properties of machines in general. Many of these limitations are associated with the very small storage capacity of most machines. (I am assuming that the idea of storage capacity is extended in some way to cover machines other than discrete state machines. The exact definition does not matter as no mathematical accuracy is claimed in the present discussion.) A few years ago, when very little had been heard of digital computers, it was possible to elicit much incredulity concerning them, if one mentioned their properties without describing their construction. That was presumably due to a similar application of the principle of scientific induction. These applications of the principle are of course largely unconscious. When a burned child fears the fire and shows that he fears it by avoiding it, I should say that he was applying scientific induction. (I could of course also describe his behavior in many other ways.) The works and customs of mankind do not seem to be very suitable material to which to apply scientific induction. A very large part of space-time must be investigated if reliable results are to be obtained. Otherwise we may (as most English children do) decide that everybody speaks English, and that it is silly to learn French.

There are, however, special remarks to be made about many of the disabilities that have been mentioned. The inability to enjoy strawberries and cream may have struck the reader as frivolous. Possibly a machine might be made to enjoy this delicious dish, but any attempt to make one do so would be idiotic. What is important about this disability is that it contributes to some of the other disabilities, for instance, to the difficulty of the same kind of friendliness occurring between man and machine as between white man and white man, or between black man and black man.

The claim that "machines cannot make mistakes" seems a curious one. One is tempted to retort, "Are they any the worse for that?" But let us adopt a more sympathetic attitude, and try to see what is really meant. I think this criticism can be explained in terms of the imitation game. It is claimed that the interrogator could distinguish the machine from the man simply by setting them a number of problems in arithmetic. The machine would be unmasked because of its deadly accuracy. The reply to this is simple. The machine (programmed for playing the game) would not attempt to give the *right* answers to the arithmetic problems. It would deliberately introduce mistakes in a manner calculated to confuse the interrogator. A mechanical fault would probably show itself through an unsuitable decision as to what sort of a mistake to make in the arithmetic. Even this interpretation of the criticism is not sufficiently sympathetic. But we cannot afford the space to go into it much further. It seems to me that this criticism depends on a confusion between two kinds of mistakes. We may call them "errors of functioning" and "errors of conclusion". Errors of functioning are due to some mechanical or electrical fault which causes the machine to behave otherwise than it was designed to do. In philosophical discussions one like to ignore the possibility of such errors; one is therefore discussing "abstract machines". These abstract machines are mathematical fictions rather than physical objects. By definition they are incapable of errors of functioning. In this sense we can truly say that "machines can never make mistakes". Errors of conclusion can only arise when some meaning is attached to the output signals from the machine. The machine might, for instance, type out mathematical equations, or sentences in English. When a false proposition is typed we say that the machine has committed an error of conclusion. There is clearly no reason at all for saying that a machine cannot make this kind of mistake. It might do nothing but type out repeatedly "$0 = 1$". To take a less perverse example, it might have some method for drawing conclusions by scientific induction. We must expect such a method to lead occasionally to erroneous results.

The claim that a machine cannot be the subject of its own thought can of course only be answered if it can be shown that the machine has *some* thought with *some* subject matter. Nevertheless, "the subject matter of a machine's operations" does seem to mean something, at least to the people who deal with it. If, for instance, the machine were trying to find a solution of the equation $x^2 - 40x - 11 = 0$, one would be tempted to describe this equation as part of the machine's subject matter at that moment. It may be used to help in making up its own programs, or to predict the effect of alterations in its own structure. By observing the results of its own behavior it can modify its own programs so as to achieve some purpose more effectively. These are possibilities of the near future, rather than Utopian dreams.

The criticism that a machine cannot have much diversity of behavior is just a way of saying that it cannot have much storage capacity. Until fairly recently a storage capacity of even a thousand digits was very rare.

The criticisms that we are considering here are often disguised forms of the argument from consciousness. Usually if one maintains that a machine *can* do one of these things, and describes the kind of method that the machine could use, one will not make much of an impression. It is thought that the method (whatever it may be, for it must be mechanical) is really rather base. Compare the parenthesis in Jefferson's statement quoted above.

(6) LADY LOVELACE'S OBJECTION. Our most detailed information of Babbage's Analytical Engine comes from a memoir by Lady Lovelace. In it she states, "The Analytical Engine has no pretensions to *originate* anything. It can do *whatever we know how to order it* to perform" (her italics). This statement is quoted by Hartree who adds: "This does not imply that it may not be possible to construct electronic equipment which will 'think for itself', or in which, in biological terms, one could set up a conditioned reflex, which would serve as a basis for 'learning'. Whether this is possible in principle or not is a stimulating and exciting question, suggested by some of these recent developments. But it did not seem that the machines constructed or projected at the time had this property."

I am in thorough agreement with Hartree over this. It will be noticed that he does not assert that the machines in question had not got the property, but rather that the evidence available to Lady Lovelace did not encourage her to believe that they had it. It is quite possible that the machines in question had in a sense got this property. For suppose that some discrete state machine has the property. The Analytical Engine was a universal digital computer, so that, if its storage capacity and speed were adequate, it could by suitable programming be made to mimic the machine in question. Probably this argument did not occur to the Countess or to Babbage. In any case there was no obligation on them to claim all that could be claimed.

This whole question will be considered again under the heading of learning machines.

A variant of Lady Lovelace's objection states that a machine can "never do anything really new". This may be parried for moment with the saw, "There is nothing new under the sun." Who can be certain that "original work" that he has done was not simply the growth of the seed planted in him by teaching, or the effect of following well-known general principles. A better variant of the objection says that a machine can never "take us by surprise". This statement is a more direct challenge and can be met directly. Machines take me by surprise with great frequency. This is largely because I do not do sufficient calculation to decide what to expect them to do, or rather because, although I do a calculation, I do it in a hurried, slipshod fashion, taking risks. Perhaps I say to myself, "I suppose the voltage here ought to be the same as there: anyway let's assume it is." Naturally I am often wrong, and the result is a surprise for me, for by the time the experiment is done these assumptions have been forgotten. These admissions lay me open to lectures on the subject of my vicious ways, but do not throw any doubt on my credibility when I testify to the surprises I experience.

I do not expect this reply to silence my critic. He will probably say that such surprises are due to some creative mental act on my part, and reflect no credit on the machine. This leads us back to the argument from consciousness, and far from the idea of surprise. It is a line of argument we must consider closed, but it is perhaps worth remarking that the appreciation of something as surprising requires as much of a "creative mental act" whether the surprising event originates from a man, a book, a machine or anything else.

The view that machines cannot give rise to surprises is due, I believe, to a fallacy to which philosophers and mathematicians are particularly subject. This is the assumption that as soon as a fact is presented to a mind all consequences of that fact spring into the mind simultaneously with it. It is a very useful assumption under many circumstances, but one too easily forgets that it is false. A natural consequence of doing so is that one then assumes that there is no virtue in the mere working out of consequences from data and general principles.

(7) ARGUMENT FROM CONTINUITY IN THE NERVOUS SYSTEM. The nervous system is certainly not a discrete state machine. A small error in the information about the size of a nervous impulse impinging on a neuron, may make a large difference to the size of the outgoing impulse. It may be argued that, this being so, one cannot expect to be able to mimic the behavior of the nervous system with a discrete state system.

It is true that a discrete state machine must be different from a continuous machine. But if we adhere to the conditions of the imitation game, the interrogator will not be able to take any advantage of this difference. The situation can be made clearer if we consider some other simpler continuous machine. A differential analyzer will do very well.

(A differential analyzer is a certain kind of machine, not of the discrete state type, used for some types of calculation.) Some of these provide their answers in a typed form, and so are suitable for taking part in the game. It would not be possible for a digital computer to predict exactly what answers the differential analyzer would give to a problem, but it would be quite capable of giving the right sort of answer. For instance, if asked to give the value of π (actually about 3.1416) it would be reasonable to choose at random between the values 3.12, 3.13, 3.14, 3.15, 3.16 with the probabilities of 0.05, 0.15, 0.55, 0.19, 0.06 (say). Under these circumstances it would be very difficult for the interrogator to distinguish the differential analyzer from the digital computer.

(8) THE ARGUMENT FROM INFORMALITY OF BEHAVIOR. It is not possible to produce a set of rules purporting to describe what a man should do in every conceivable set of circumstances. One might for instance have a rule that one is to stop when one sees a red traffic light, and to go if one sees a green one; but what if by some fault both appear together? One may perhaps decide that it is safest to stop. But some further difficulty may well arise from this decision later. To attempt to provide rules of conduct to cover every eventuality, even those arising from traffic lights, appears to be impossible. With all this I agree.

From this it is argued that we cannot be machines. I shall try to reproduce the argument, but I fear I shall hardly do it justice. It seems to run something like this: "If each man had a definite set of rules of conduct by which he regulated his life he would be no better than a machine. But there are no such rules, so men cannot be machines." The undistributed middle is glaring. I do not think the argument is ever put quite like this, but I believe this is the argument used nevertheless. There may however be a certain confusion between "rules of conduct" and "laws of behavior" to cloud the issue. By "rules of conduct" I mean precepts such as "Stop if you see red lights", on which one can act, and of which one can be conscious. By "laws of behavior" I mean laws of nature as applied to a man's body such as "if you pinch him he will squeak". If we substitute "laws of behavior which regulate his life" for "laws of conduct by which he regulates his life" in the argument quoted the undistributed middle is no longer insuperable. For we believe that it is not only true that being regulated by laws of behavior implies being some sort of machine (though not necessarily a discrete state machine), but that conversely being such a machine implies being regulated by such laws. However, we cannot so easily convince ourselves of the absence of complete laws of behavior as of complete rules of conduct. The only way we know of for finding such laws is scientific observation, and we certainly know of no circumstances under which we could say: "We have searched enough. There are no such laws."

We can demonstrate more forcibly that any such statement would be unjustified. For suppose we could be sure of finding such laws if they existed. Then given a discrete state machine it should certainly be possible to discover by observation sufficient about it to predict its future behavior, and this within a reasonable time, say a thousand years. But this does not seem to be the case. I have set up on the Manchester computer a small program using only 1000 units of storage, whereby the machine supplied with one sixteen figure number replies with another within two seconds. I would defy anyone to learn from these replies sufficient about the program to be able to predict any replies to untried values.

(9) THE ARGUMENT FROM EXTRA-SENSORY PERCEPTION. I assume that the reader is familiar with the idea of extra-sensory perception, and the meaning of the four items of it, namely, telepathy, clairvoyance, precognition and psychokinesis. These disturbing phenomena seem to deny all our usual scientific ideas. How we should like to discredit them! Unfortunately the statistical evidence, at least for telepathy, is overwhelming. It is very difficult to rearrange one's ideas so as to fit these new facts in. Once one has accepted them it does not seem a very big step to believe in ghosts and bogies. The idea that our bodies move simply according to the known laws of physics, together with some others not yet discovered but somewhat similar, would be one of the first to go.

This argument is to my mind quite a strong one. One can say in reply that many scientific theories seem to remain workable in practice, in spite of clashing with E.S.P.; that in fact one can get along very nicely if one forgets about it. This is rather cold comfort, and one fears that thinking is just the kind of phenomenon where E.S.P. may be especially relevant.

A more specific argument based on E.S.P. might run as follows: "Let us play the imitation game, using as witnesses a man who is good as a telepathic receiver, and a digital computer. The interrogator can ask such questions as 'What suit does the card in my right hand belong to?' The man by telepathy or clairvoyance gives the right answer 130 times out of 400 cards. The machine can only guess at random, and perhaps get 104 right, so the interrogator makes the right identification." There is an interesting possibility which opens here. Suppose the digital computer contains a random number generator. Then it will be natural to use this to decide what answer to give. But then the random number generator will be subject to the psychokinetic powers of the interrogator. Perhaps this psychokinesis might cause the machine to guess right more often then would be expected on a probability calculation, so that the interrogator might still be unable to make the right identification. On the other hand, he might be able to guess right without any questioning, by clairvoyance. With E.S.P. anything may happen.

If telepathy is admitted it will be necessary to tighten our test. The situation could be regarded as analogous to that which would occur if the interrogator were talking to himself and one of the competitors was listening with his ear to the wall. To put the competitors into a "telepathy-proof room" would satisfy all requirements.

7 Learning machines

The reader will have anticipated that I have no very convincing arguments of a positive nature to support my views. If I had I should not have taken such pains to point out the fallacies in contrary views. Such evidence as I have I shall now give.

Let us return for a moment to Lady Lovelace's objection, which stated that the machine can only do what we tell it to do. One could say that a man can "inject" an idea into the machine, and that it will respond to a certain extent and then drop into quiescence, like a piano string struck by a hammer. Another simile would be an atomic pile of less than critical size: an injected idea is to correspond to a neutron entering the pile from without. Each such neutron will cause a certain disturbance which eventually dies away. If, however, the size of the pile is sufficiently increased, the disturbance caused by such an incoming neutron will very likely go on and on, increasing until the whole pile is destroyed. Is there a corresponding phenomenon for minds, and is there one for machines? There does seem to be one for the human mind. The majority of them seem to be "subcritical", that is, to correspond in this analogy to piles of subcritical size. An idea presented to such a mind will on an average give rise to less than one idea in reply. A smallish proportion are supercritical. An idea presented to such a mind may give rise to a whole "theory" consisting of secondary, tertiary and more remote ideas. Animals' minds seem to be very definitely subcritical. Adhering to this analogy we ask, "Can a machine be made to be supercritical?"

The "skin of an onion" analogy is also helpful. In considering the functions of the mind or the brain we find certain operations which we can explain in purely mechanical terms. This we say does not correspond to the real mind: it is a sort of skin which we must strip off if we are to find the real mind. But then in what remains we find a further skin to be stripped off, and so on. Proceeding in this way, do we ever come to the "real" mind, or do we eventually come to the skin which has nothing in it? In the latter case the whole mind is mechanical. (It would not be a discrete state machine however. We have discussed this.)

These last two paragraphs do not claim to be convincing arguments. They should rather be described as "recitations tending to produce belief".

The only really satisfactory support that can be given for the view expressed at the beginning of section 6 will be that provided by waiting for the end of the century and then doing the experiment described. But what can we say in the meantime? What steps should be taken now if the experiment is to be successful?

As I have explained, the problem is mainly one of programming. Advances in engineering will have to made too, but it seems unlikely that these will not be adequate for the requirements. Estimates of the storage capacity of the brain vary from 10^{10} to 10^{15} binary digits. I incline to the lower values and believe that only a very small fraction is used for the higher types of thinking. Most of it is probably used for the retention of visual impressions. I should be surprised if more than 10^9 was required for satisfactory playing of the imitation game, at any rate against a blind man. (Note: The capacity of the *Encyclopedia Britannica*, eleventh edition, is 2 x 10^9.) A storage capacity of 10^7 would be a very practicable possibility even by present techniques. It is probably not necessary to increase the speed of operations of the machines at all. Parts of modern machines which can be regarded as analogues of nerve cells work about a thousand times faster than the latter. This should provide a "margin of safety" which could cover losses of speed arising in many ways. Our problem then is to find out how to program these machines to play the game. At my present rate of working I produce about a thousand digits of program a day, so that about sixty workers, working steadily through the fifty years might accomplish the job, if nothing went into the wastepaper basket. Some more expeditious method seems desirable.

In the process of trying to imitate an adult human mind we are bound to think a good deal about the process which has brought it to the state that it is in. We may notice three components:

(a) The initial state of the mind, say at birth;

(b) The education to which it has been subjected; and

(c) Other experience, not to be described as education, to which it has been subjected.

Instead of trying to produce a program to simulate the adult mind, why not rather try to produce one which simulates the child's? If this were then subjected to an appropriate course of education one would obtain the adult brain. Presumably the child-brain is something like a notebook as one buys it from the stationers. Rather little mechanism, and lots of blank sheets. (Mechanism and writing are from our point of view almost synonymous.) Our hope is that there is so little mechanism in the child-brain that something like it can be easily programmed. The amount of work in the education we can assume, as a first approximation, to be much the same as for the human child.

We have thus divided our problem into two parts—the child-program and the education process. These two remain very closely connected. We cannot expect to find a good child-machine at the first attempt. One must experiment with teaching one such machine and see how well it learns. One can then try another and see if it is better or worse. There is an obvious connection between this process and evolution, by the identifications

Structure of the child-machine = Hereditary material

Changes of the child-machine = Mutations

Judgment of the experimenter = Natural selection

One may hope, however, that this process will be more expeditious than evolution. The survival of the fittest is a slow method for measuring advantages. The experimenter, by the exercise of intelligence, should be able to speed it up. Equally important is the fact that he is not restricted to random mutations. If he can trace a cause for some weakness he can probably think of the kind of mutation which will improve it.

It will not be possible to apply exactly the same teaching process to the machine as to a normal child. It will not, for instance, be provided with legs, so that it could not be asked to go out and fill the coal scuttle. Possibly it might not have eyes. But however well these deficiencies might be overcome by clever engineering, one could not send the creature to school without the other children making excessive fun of it. It must be given some tuition. We need not be too concerned about the legs, eyes, and so on. The example of Miss Helen Keller shows that education can take place provided that communication in both directions between teacher and pupil can take place by some means or other.

We normally associate punishments and rewards with the teaching process. Some simple child-machines can be constructed or programmed on this sort of principle. The machine has to be so constructed that events which shortly preceded the occurrence of a punishment-signal are unlikely to be repeated, whereas a reward-signal increases the probability of repetition of the events which led up to it. These definitions do not presuppose any feelings on the part of the machine. I have done some experiments with one such child-machine, and succeeded in teaching it a few things, but the teaching method was too unorthodox for the experiment to be considered really successful.

The use of punishments and rewards can at best be a part of the teaching process. Roughly speaking, if the teacher has no other means of communicating to the pupil, the amount of information which can reach him does not exceed the total number of rewards and punishments applied. By the time a child has learned to repeat "Casablanca" he would probably feel very sore indeed, if the text could only be discovered by a "Twenty Questions" technique, every "No" taking the form of a blow. It is necessary therefore to have some other "unemotional" channels of communication. If these are available it is possible to teach a machine by punishments and rewards to obey orders given in some language, such as a symbolic language. These orders are to be transmitted through the "unemotional" channels. The use of this language will diminish greatly the number of punishments and rewards required.

Opinions may vary as to the complexity which is suitable in the child-machine. One might try to make it as simple as possible consistently with the general principles. Alternatively one might have a complete system of logical inference "built in".[2] In the latter case the store would be largely occupied with definitions and propositions. The propositions would have various kinds of status, such as well-established facts, conjectures, mathematically proved theorems, statements given by an authority, and expressions having the logical form of a proposition but no belief-value. Certain propositions may be described as "imperatives". The machine should be so constructed that as soon as an imperative is classed as "well-established" the appropriate action automatically takes place. To illustrate this, suppose the teacher says to the machine, "Do your homework now." This may cause "Teacher says 'Do your homework now'" to be included among the well-established facts. Another such fact might be, "Everything that teacher says is true". Combining these may eventually lead to the imperative, "Do your homework now", being included amongst the well-established facts, and this, by the construction of the machine, will mean that the homework actually gets started; but the effect is very unsatisfactory. The processes of inference used by the machine need not be such as would satisfy the most exacting logicians. There might, for instance, be no hierarchy of types. But this need not mean that type fallacies will occur, any more than we are bound to fall over unfenced cliffs. Suitable imperatives (expressed *within* the systems, not forming part of the rules *of* the system) such as "Do not use a class unless it is a subclass of one which has been mentioned by teacher" can have a similar effect to "Do not go too near the edge."

The imperatives that can be obeyed by a machine that has no limbs are bound to be of a rather intellectual character, as in the example (doing homework) given above. Important among such imperatives will be ones which regulate the order in which the rules of the logical system concerned are to be applied. For at each stage when one is using a logical system, there is a very large number of alternative steps, any of which one is permitted to apply, so far as obedience to the rules of the logical system is concerned. These choices make the difference between a brilliant and a footling reasoner, not the difference between a sound and a fallacious one. Propositions leading to imperatives of this kind might be "When Socrates is mentioned, use the syllogism in Barbara" or "If one method has been proved to be quicker than another, do not use the slower method." Some of these may be "given by authority", but others may be produced by the machine itself, say by scientific induction.

The idea of a learning machine may appear paradoxical to some readers. How can the rules of operation of the machine change? They should describe completely how the machine will react whatever its history might be, whatever changes it might undergo. The rules are thus quite time-invariant. This is quite true. The explanation of the paradox is that the rules which get changed in the learning process are of a rather less pretentious kind, claiming only an ephemeral validity. The reader may draw a parallel with the Constitution of the United States.

An important feature of a learning machine is that its teacher will often be very largely ignorant of quite what is going on inside, although he may still be able to some extent to predict his pupil's behavior. This should apply most strongly to the later education of a machine arising from a child-machine of well-tried design (or program). This is in clear contrast with normal procedure when using a machine to do computations: one's object is then to have a clear mental picture of the state of the machine at each moment in the computation. This object can only be achieved with a struggle. The view that "the machine can only do what we know how to order it to do",[3] appears strange in face of this. Most of the programs which we can put into the machine will result in its doing something that we cannot make sense of at all, or which we regard as completely random behavior. Intelligent behavior presumably consists in a departure from the completely disciplined behavior involved in computation, but a rather slight one, which does not give rise to random behavior, or to pointless repetitive loops. Another important result of preparing our machine for its part in the imitation game by a process of teaching and learning is that "human fallibility" is likely to be admitted in a rather natural way, that is, without special "coaching". (The reader should reconcile this with the point of view on p. 43.) Processes that are learned do not produce a hundred percent certainty of result; if they did they could not be unlearned.

It is probably wise to include a random element in a learning machine (see p. 34). A random element is rather useful when we are searching for a solution of some problem. Suppose for instance we wanted to find a number between 50 and 200 which was equal to the square of the sum of its digits, we might start at 51 then try 52 and go on until we got a number that worked. Alternatively we might choose numbers at random until we got a good one. This method has the advantage that it is unnecessary to keep track of the values that have been tried, but the disadvantage that one may try the same one twice; but this is not very important if there are several solutions. The systematic method has the disadvantage that there may be an enormous block without any solutions in the region which has to be investigated first. Now the learning process may be regarded as a search for a form of behavior which will satisfy the teacher (or some other criterion). Since there is probably a very large number of satisfactory solutions, the random method seems to be better than the systematic. It should be noticed that it is used in the analogous process of evolution. But there the systematic method is not possible. How could one keep track of the different genetical combinations that had been tried, so as to avoid trying them again?

We may hope that machines will eventually compete with men in all purely intellectual fields. But which are the best ones to start with? Even this is a difficult decision. Many people think that a very abstract activity, like the playing of chess, would be best. It can also be maintained that it is best to provide the machine with the best sense organs that money can buy, and then teach it to understand and speak English. This process could follow the normal teaching of a child. Things would be pointed out and named, and so on. Again I do not know what the right answer is, but I think both approaches should be tried.

We can only see a short distance ahead, but we can see plenty there that needs to be done.

Notes

1. Possibly this view is heretical. St. Thomas Aquinas (*Summa Theologica*, quoted in Russell 1945, p. 458) states that God cannot make a man to have no soul. But this may not be a real restriction on His powers, but only a result of the fact that men's souls are immortal, and therefore indestructible.

2. Or rather "programmed in" for our child-machine will be programmed in a digital computer. But the logical system will not have to be learned.

3. Compare Lady Lovelace's statement (p. 46), which does not contain the word "only".

True Believers: The Intentional Strategy and Why It Works

Daniel C. Dennett
1981

> **DEATH SPEAKS:** There was a merchant in Baghdad who sent his servant to market to buy provisions and in a little while the servant came back, white and trembling, and said: "Master, just now when I was in the market-place I was jostled by a woman in the crowd and when I turned I saw it was Death that jostled me. She looked at me and made a threatening gesture; now, lend me your horse, and I will ride away from this city and avoid my fate. I will go to Samarra and there Death will not find me." The merchant lent him his horse, and the servant mounted it, and he dug his spurs in its flanks and as fast as the horse could gallop he went. Then the merchant went down to the market-place and he saw me standing in the crowd, and he came to me and said: "Why did you make a threatening gesture to my servant when you saw him this morning?" "That was not a threatening gesture," I said, "it was only a start of surprise. I was astonished to see him in Baghdad, for I had an appointment with him tonight in Samarra."
>
> W. Somerset Maugham

In the social sciences, talk about *belief* is ubiquitous. Since social scientists are typically self-conscious about their methods, there is also a lot of talk about *talk about belief.* And since belief is a genuinely curious and perplexing phenomenon, showing many different faces to the world, there is abundant controversy. Sometimes belief attribution appears to be a dark, risky, and imponderable business—especially when exotic, and more particularly religious or superstitious, beliefs are in the limelight. These are not the only troublesome cases; we also court argument and skepticism when we attribute beliefs to nonhuman animals, or to infants, or to computers or robots. Or when the beliefs we feel constrained to attribute to an apparently healthy adult member of our own society are contradictory, or even just wildly false. A biologist colleague of mine was once called on the telephone by a man in a bar who wanted him to settle a bet. The man asked: "Are rabbits birds?" "No" said the biologist. "Damn!" said the man as he hung up. Now could he *really* have believed that rabbits were birds? Could anyone really and truly be attributed that belief? Perhaps, but it would take a bit of a story to bring us to accept it.

In all of these cases, belief attribution appears beset with subjectivity, infected with cultural relativism, prone to "indeterminacy of radical translation"—clearly an enterprise demanding special talents: the art of phenomenological analysis, hermeneutics, empathy, *Verstehen,* and all that. On other occasions, normal occasions, when familiar beliefs are the topic, belief attribution looks as easy as speaking prose and as objective and reliable as counting beans in a dish. Particularly when these straightforward cases are before us, it is quite plausible to suppose that in principle (if not yet in practice) it would be possible to confirm these simple, objective belief attributions by *finding something inside the believer's head*—by finding the beliefs themselves, in effect. "Look", someone might say, "either you believe there's milk in the fridge or you don't believe there's milk in the fridge" (you might have no opinion, in the latter case). But if you do believe this, that's a perfectly objective fact about you, and it must come down in the end to your brain's being in some particular physical state. If we knew more about physiological psychology, we could in principle determine the facts about your brain state and thereby determine whether or not you believe there is milk in the fridge, even if you were determined to be silent or disingenuous on the topic. In principle, on this view, physiological psychology could trump the results—or nonresults—of any "black box" method in the social sciences that divines beliefs (and other mental features) by behavioral, cultural, social, historical, *external* criteria.

These differing reflections congeal into two opposing views on the nature of belief attribution, and hence on the nature of belief. The latter, a variety of *realism,* likens the question of whether a person has a particular belief to the question of whether a person is infected with a particular virus—a perfectly objective internal matter of fact about which an observer can often make educated guesses of great reliability. The former, which we could call *interpretationism* if we absolutely had to give it a name, likens the question of whether a person has a particular belief to the question of whether a person is immoral, or has style, or talent, or would make a good wife. Faced with such questions, we preface our answers with "well, it all depends on what you're interested in", or make some similar acknowledgment of the relativity of the issue. "It's a matter of interpretation", we say. These two opposing views, so baldly stated, do not fairly represent any serious theorists' positions, but they do express views that are typically seen as mutually exclusive and exhaustive; the theorist must be friendly with one and only one of these themes.

I think this is a mistake. My thesis will be that while belief is a perfectly objective phenomenon (that apparently makes me a realist), it can be discerned only from the point of view of one who adopts a certain *predictive strategy*, and its existence can be confirmed only by an assessment of the success of that strategy (that apparently makes me an interpretationist).

First I will describe the strategy, which I call the *intentional strategy* or adopting the *intentional stance*. To a first approximation, the intentional strategy consists of treating the object whose behavior you want to predict as a rational agent with beliefs and desires and other mental states exhibiting what Brentano and others call *intentionality*. The strategy has often been described before, but I shall try to put this very familiar material in a new light by showing *how* it works and by showing *how well* it works.

Then I will argue that any object—or as I shall say, any *system*—whose behavior is well predicted by this strategy is in the fullest sense of the word a believer. *What it is* to be a true believer is to be an *intentional system*, a system whose behavior is reliably and voluminously predictable via the intentional strategy. I have argued for this position before (1971/78, 1976/78, 1978a), and my arguments have so far garnered few converts and many presumed counterexamples. I shall try again here, harder, and shall also deal with several compelling objections.

1 The intentional strategy and how it works

There are many strategies, some good, some bad. Here is a strategy, for instance, for predicting the future behavior of a person: determine the date and hour of the person's birth and then feed this modest datum into one or another astrological algorithm for generating predictions of the person's prospects. This strategy is deplorably popular. Its popularity is deplorable only because we have such good reasons for believing that it does not work (*pace* Feyerabend 1978). When astrological predictions come true this is sheer luck, or the result of such vagueness or ambiguity in the prophecy that almost any eventuality can be construed to confirm it. But suppose the astrological strategy did in fact work well on some people. We could call those people *astrological systems*—systems whose behavior was, as a matter of fact, predictable by the astrological strategy. If there were such people, such astrological systems, we would be more interested than most of us in fact are in *how the astrological strategy works*—that is, we would be interested in the rules, principles, or methods of astrology. We could find out how the strategy works by asking astrologers, reading their books, and observing them in action. But we would also be curious about *why* it worked. We might find that astrologers had no useful opinions about this latter question—they either had no theory of why it worked or their theories were pure hokum. Having a good strategy is one thing; knowing why it works is another.

So far as we know, however, the class of astrological systems is empty; so the astrological strategy is of interest only as a social curiosity. Other strategies have better credentials. Consider the physical strategy, or *physical stance*; if you want to predict the behavior of a system, determine its physical constitution (perhaps all the way down to the microphysical level) and the physical nature of the impingements upon it, and use your knowledge of the laws of physics to predict the outcome for any input. This is the grand and impractical strategy of Laplace for predicting the entire future of everything in the universe; but it has more modest, local, actually usable versions. The chemist or physicist in the laboratory can use this strategy to predict the behavior of exotic materials, but equally the cook in the kitchen can predict the effect of leaving the pot on the burner too long. The strategy is not always practically available, but that it will always work *in principle* is a dogma of the physical sciences. (I ignore the minor complications raised by the subatomic indeterminacies of quantum physics.)

Sometimes, in any event, it is more effective to switch from the physical stance to what I call the *design stance*, where one ignores the actual (possibly messy) details of the physical constitution of an object, and, on the assumption that it has a certain design, predicts that it will behave *as it is designed to behave* under various circumstances. For instance, most users of computers have not the foggiest idea what physical principles are responsible for the computer's highly reliable, and hence predictable, behavior. But if they have a good idea of what the computer is designed to do (a description of its operation at any one of the many possible levels of abstraction), they can predict its behavior with great accuracy and reliability, subject to disconfirmation only in the cases of physical malfunction. Less dramatically, almost anyone can predict when an alarm clock will sound on the basis of the most casual inspection of its exterior. One does not know or care to know whether it is spring wound, battery driven, sunlight powered, made of brass wheels and jewel bearings or silicon chips—one just assumes that it is designed so that the alarm will sound when it is set to sound, and it is set to sound where it appears to be set to sound, and the clock will keep on running until that time and beyond, and is designed to run more or less accurately, and so forth. For more accurate and detailed design stance predictions of the alarm clock, one must descend to a less abstract level of description of its design; for instance, to the level at which gears are described, but their material is not specified.

Only the designed behavior of a system is predictable from the design stance, of course. If you want to predict the behavior of an alarm clock when it is pumped full of liquid helium, revert to the physical stance. Not just artifacts but also many biological objects (plants and animals, kidneys and hearts, stamens and pistils) behave in ways that can be predicted from the design stance. They are not just physical systems but designed systems.

Sometimes even the design stance is practically inaccessible, and then there is yet another stance or strategy one can adopt: the intentional stance. Here is how it works: first you decide to treat the object whose behavior is to be predicted as a rational agent; then you figure out what beliefs that agent ought to have, given its place in the world and its purpose. Then you figure out what desires it ought to have, on the same considerations, and finally you predict that this rational agent will act to further its goals in the light of its beliefs. A little practical reasoning from the chosen set of beliefs and desires will in many—but not all—instances yield a decision about what the agent *ought* to do; that is what you predict the agent *will* do.

The strategy becomes clearer with a little elaboration. Consider first how we go about populating each other's heads with beliefs. A few truisms: sheltered people tend to be ignorant; if you expose someone to something he comes to know all about it. In general, it seems, we come to believe all the truths about the parts of the world around us we are put in a position to learn about. Exposure to x—that is, sensory confrontation with *x* over some suitable period of time—is the *normally sufficient* condition for knowing (or having true beliefs) about *x*. As we say, we come to *know all about* the things around us. Such exposure is only *normally* sufficient for knowledge, but this is not the large escape hatch it might appear; our threshold for accepting abnormal ignorance in the face of exposure is quite high. "I didn't know the gun was loaded", said by one who was observed to be present, sighted, and awake during the loading, meets with a variety of utter skepticism that only the most outlandish supporting tale could overwhelm.

Of course we do not come to learn or remember all the truths our sensory histories avail us. In spite of the phrase "know all about", what we come to know, normally, are only all the *relevant* truths our sensory histories avail us. I do not typically come to know the ratio of spectacle-wearing people to trousered people in a room I inhabit, though if this interested me, it would be readily learnable. It is not just that some facts about my environment are below my thresholds of discrimination or beyond the integration and holding power of my memory (such as the height in inches of all the people present), but that many perfectly detectable, graspable, memorable facts are of no interest to me and hence do not come to be believed by me. So one rule for attributing beliefs in the intentional strategy is this: attribute as beliefs all the truths relevant to the system's interests (or desires) that the system's experience to date has made available. This rule leads to attributing somewhat too much—since we all are somewhat forgetful, even of important things. It also fails to capture the false beliefs we are all known to have. But the attribution of false belief, *any* false belief, requires a special genealogy, which will be seen to consist in the main in true beliefs. Two paradigm cases: *S* believes (falsely) that *p*, because *S* believes (truly) that Jones told him that *p*, that Jones is pretty clever, that Jones did not intend to deceive him, … and so on. Second case: *S* believes (falsely) that there is a snake on the barstool, because *S* believes (truly) that he seems to see a snake on the barstool, is himself sitting in a bar not a yard from the barstool he sees, and so forth. The falsehood has to start somewhere: the seed may be sown in hallucination, illusion, a normal variety of simple misperception, memory deterioration, or deliberate fraud, for instance; but the false beliefs that are reaped grow in a culture medium of true beliefs.

Then there are the arcane and sophisticated beliefs, true and false, that are so often at the focus of attention in discussions of belief attribution. They do not arise directly, goodness knows, from exposure to mundane things and events, but their attribution requires tracing out a lineage of mainly good argument or reasoning from the bulk of beliefs already attributed. An implication of the intentional strategy, then, is that true believers mainly believe truths. If anyone could devise an agreed-upon method of individuating and counting beliefs (which I doubt very much), we would see that all but the smallest portion (say, less than ten percent) of a person's beliefs were attributable under our first rule.[1]

Note that this rule is a derived rule, an elaboration and further specification of the fundamental rule: attribute those beliefs the system *ought to have*. Note also that the rule interacts with the attribution of desires. How do we attribute the desires (preferences, goals, interests) on whose basis we will shape the list of beliefs? We attribute the desires the system *ought to have*. That is the fundamental rule. It dictates, on a first pass, that we attribute the familiar list of highest, or most basic, desires to people: survival, absence of pain, food, comfort, procreation, entertainment. Citing any one of these desires typically terminates the "Why?" game of reason giving. One is not supposed to need an ulterior motive for desiring comfort or pleasure or the prolongation of one's existence. Derived rules of desire attribution interact with belief attributions. Trivially, we have the rule: attribute desires for those things a system believes to be good for it. Somewhat more informatively, attribute desires for those things a system believes to be best means to other ends it desires. The attribution of bizarre and detrimental desires thus requires, like the attribution of false beliefs, special stories.

The interaction between belief and desire becomes trickier when we consider what desires we attribute on the basis of verbal behavior. The capacity to *express* desires in language opens the floodgates of desire attribution. "I want a two-egg mushroom omelet, some French bread and butter, and a half bottle of lightly chilled white Burgundy." How could one begin to attribute a desire for anything so specific in the absence of such verbal declaration? How, indeed, could a creature come to *contract* such a specific desire without the aid of language? Language *enables* us to formulate highly specific desires, but it also *forces* us on occasion to commit ourselves to desires altogether more stringent in their conditions of satisfaction than anything we would otherwise have any reason to endeavor to satisfy. Since in order to get what you want you often have to say what you want, and since you often cannot say what you want without saying something more specific than you antecedently mean, you often end up giving others evidence (the very best of evidence, your unextorted word) that you desire things or states of affairs far more particular than would satisfy you—or better, than would have satisfied you, for once you have declared, being a man of your word, you acquire an interest in satisfying exactly the desire you declared and no other.

"I'd like some baked beans, please."
"Yes sir. How many?"

You might well object to having such a specification of desire demanded of you, but in fact we are all socialized to accede to similar requirements in daily life—to the point of not noticing it, and certainly not feeling oppressed by it. I dwell on this because it has a parallel in the realm of belief, where our linguistic environment is forever forcing us to give—or concede—precise verbal expression to convictions that lack the hard edges verbalization endows them with (see Dennett 1969, pp. 184-85, 1978a). By concentrating on the *results* of this social force, while ignoring its distorting effect, one can easily be misled into thinking that it is *obvious* that beliefs and desires are rather like sentences stored in the head. Being language-using creatures, it is inevitable that we should often come to believe that some particular, actually formulated, spelled, and punctuated sentence *is true*, and that on other occasions we should come to want such a sentence to *come true*; but these are special cases of belief and desire and as such may not be reliable models for the whole domain.

That is enough, on this occasion, about the principles of belief and desire attribution to be found in the intentional strategy. What about the rationality one attributes to an intentional system? One starts with the ideal of perfect rationality and revises downward as circumstances dictate. That is, one starts with the assumption that people believe all the implications of their beliefs and believe no contradictory pairs of beliefs. This does not create a practical problem of clutter (infinitely many implications, for instance), for one is interested only in ensuring that the system one is predicting is rational enough to get to the particular implications that are relevant to its behavioral predicament of the moment. Instances of irrationality, or of finitely powerful capacities of inferences, raise particularly knotty problems of interpretation, which I will set aside on this occasion (see Dennett 1981/87b and Cherniak 1986).

For I want to turn from the description of the strategy to the question of its use. Do people actually use this strategy? Yes, all the time. There may someday be other strategies for attributing belief and desire and for predicting behavior, but this is the only one we all know now. And when does it work? It works with people almost all the time. Why would it *not* be a good idea to allow individual Oxford colleges to create and grant academic degrees whenever they saw fit? The answer is a long story, but very easy to generate. And there would be widespread agreement about the major points. We have no difficulty thinking of the reasons people would then have for acting in such ways as to give others reasons for acting in such ways as to give others reasons for … creating a circumstance we would not want. Our use of the intentional strategy is so habitual and effortless that the role it plays in shaping our expectations about people is easily overlooked. The strategy also works on most other mammals most of the time. For instance, you can use it to design better traps to catch those mammals, by reasoning about what the creature knows or believes about various things, what it prefers, what it wants to avoid. The strategy works on birds, and on fish, and on reptiles, and on insects and spiders, and even on such lowly and unenterprising creatures as clams (once a clam believes there is danger about, it will not relax its grip on its closed shell until it is convinced that the danger has passed). It also works on some artifacts: the chess-playing computer will not take your knight because it knows that there is a line of ensuing play that would lead to losing its rook, and it does not want that to happen. More modestly, the thermostat will turn off the boiler as soon as it comes to believe the room has reached the desired temperature.

The strategy even works for plants. In a locale with late spring storms, you should plant apple varieties that are particularly *cautious* about *concluding* that it is spring—which is when they *want* to blossom, of course. It even works for such inanimate and apparently undesigned phenomena as lightning. An electrician once explained to me how he worked out how to protect my underground water pump from lightning damage: lightning, he said, always wants to find the best way to ground, but sometimes it gets tricked into taking second-best paths. You can protect the pump by making another, better path more *obvious* to the lightning.

2 True believers as intentional systems

Now clearly this is a motley assortment of "serious" belief attributions, dubious belief attributions, pedagogically useful metaphors, *façons de parler,* and, perhaps worse, outright frauds. The next task would seem to be distinguishing those intentional systems that *really* have beliefs and desires from those we may find it handy to treat *as if* they had beliefs and desires. But that would be a Sisyphean labor, or else would be terminated by fiat. A better understanding of the phenomenon of belief begins with the observation that even in the worst of these cases, even when we are surest that the strategy works *for the wrong reasons,* it is nevertheless true that it does work, at least a little bit. This is an interesting fact, which distinguishes this class of objects, the class of *intentional systems,* from the class of objects for which the strategy never works. But is this so? Does our definition of an intentional system exclude any objects at all? For instance, it seems the lectern in this lecture room can be construed as an intentional system, fully rational, believing that it is currently located at the center of the civilized world (as some of you may also think), and desiring above all else to remain at that center. What should such a rational agent so equipped with belief and desire do? Stay put, clearly—which is just what the lectern does. I predict the lectern's behavior, accurately, from the intentional stance, so is it an intentional system? If it is, anything at all is.

What should disqualify the lectern? For one thing, the strategy does not recommend itself in this case, for we get no predictive power from it that we did not antecedently have. We already knew what the lectern was going to do—namely nothing—and tailored the beliefs and desires to fit in a quite unprincipled way. In the case of people or animals or computers, however, the situation is different. In these cases often the only strategy that is at all practical is the intentional strategy; it gives us predictive power we can get by no other method. But, it will be urged, this is no difference in nature, but merely a difference that reflects upon our limited capacities as scientists. The Laplacean omniscient physicist could predict the behavior of a computer—or of a live human body, assuming it to be ultimately governed by the laws of physics—without any need for the risky, short-cut methods of either the design or intentional strategies. For people of limited mechanical aptitude, the intentional interpretation of a simple thermostat is a handy and largely innocuous crutch, but the engineers among us can quite fully grasp its internal operation without the aid of this anthropomorphizing. It may be true that the cleverest engineers find it practically impossible to maintain a clear conception of more complex systems, such as a time-sharing computer system or remote-controlled space probe, without lapsing into an intentional stance (and viewing these devices as asking and telling, trying and avoiding, wanting and believing), but this is just a more advanced case of human epistemic frailty. We would not want to classify these artifacts with the true believers—ourselves—on such variable and parochial grounds, would we? Would it not be intolerable to hold that some artifact or creature or person was a believer from the point of view of one observer, but not a believer at all from the point of view of another, cleverer observer? That would be a particularly radical version of interpretationism, and some have thought I espoused it in urging that belief be viewed in terms of the success of the intentional strategy. I must confess that my presentation of the view has sometimes invited that reading, but I now want to discourage it. The decision to adopt the intentional stance is free, but the facts about the success or failure of the stance, were one to adopt it, are perfectly objective.

Once the intentional strategy is in place, it is an extraordinarily powerful tool in prediction—a fact that is largely concealed by our typical concentration on the cases in which it yields dubious or unreliable results. Consider, for instance, predicting moves in a chess game. What makes chess an interesting game, one can see, is the *un*predictability of one's opponent's moves, except in those cases where moves are "forced"—where there is *clearly* one best move—typically the least of the available evils. But this unpredictability is put in context when one recognizes that in the typical chess situation there are very many perfectly legal and hence available moves, but only a few—perhaps half a dozen—with anything to be said for them, and hence only a few high-probability moves according to the intentional strategy. Even when the intentional strategy fails to distinguish a single move with a highest probability, it can dramatically reduce the number of live options.

The same feature of the intentional strategy is apparent when it is applied to "real world" cases. It is notoriously unable to predict the exact purchase and sell decisions of stock traders, for instance, or the exact sequence of words a politician will utter when making a scheduled speech. But one's confidence can be very high indeed about slightly less specific predictions: that the particular trader *will not buy utilities today*, or that the politician *will side with the unions against his party*, for example. This inability to predict fine-grained descriptions of actions, looked at another way, is a source of strength for the intentional strategy, for it is this neutrality with regard to details of implementation that permits one to exploit the intentional strategy in complex cases, for instance, in *chaining predictions* (see Dennett 1978). Suppose the US secretary of State were to announce he was a paid agent of the KGB. What an unparalleled event! How unpredictable its consequences! Yet in fact we can predict dozens of not terribly interesting but perfectly salient consequences, and consequences of consequences. The President would confer with the rest of the Cabinet, which would support his decision to relieve the Secretary of State of his duties pending the results of various investigations, psychiatric and political, and all this would be reported at a news conference to people who would write stories that would be commented upon in editorials that would be read by people who would write letters to the editors, and so forth. None of that is daring prognostication, but note that it describes an arc of causation in space-time that could not be predicted under *any* description by any imaginable practical extension of physics or biology.

The power of the intentional strategy can be seen even more sharply with the aid of an objection first raised by Robert Nozick some years ago. Suppose, he suggested, some beings of vastly superior intelligence—from Mars, let us say—were to descend upon us, and suppose that we were to them as simple thermostats are to clever engineers. Suppose, that is, that they did not *need* the intentional stance—or even the design stance—to predict our behavior in all its detail. They can be supposed to be Laplacean super-physicists, capable of comprehending the activity on Wall Street, for instance, at the microphysical level. Where we see brokers and buildings and sell orders and bids, they see vast congeries of subatomic particles milling about—and they are such good physicists that they can predict days in advance what ink marks will appear each day on the paper tape labeled "Closing Dow Jones Industrial Average". They can predict the individual behaviors of all the various moving bodies they observe without ever treating any of them as intentional systems. Would we be right then to say that from *their* point of view we really were not believers at all (any more than a simple thermostat is)? If so, then our status as believers is nothing objective, but rather something in the eye of the beholder—provided the beholder shares our intellectual limitations.

Our imagined Martians might be able to predict the future of the human race by Laplacean methods, but if they did not also see us as intentional systems, they would be missing something perfectly objective: the *patterns* in human behavior that are describable from the intentional stance, and only from that stance, and that support generalizations and predictions. Take a particular instance in which the Martians observe a stockbroker deciding to place an order for 500 shares of General Motors. They predict the exact motions of his fingers as he dials the phone and the exact vibrations of his vocal cords as he intones his order. But if the Martians do not see that indefinitely many *different* patterns of finger motions and vocal cord vibrations—even the motions of indefinitely many different individuals—could have been substituted for the actual particulars without perturbing the subsequent operation of the market, then they have failed to see a real pattern in the world they are observing. Just as there are indefinitely many ways of *being a spark plug*—and one has not understood what an internal combustion engine is unless one realizes that a variety of different devices can be screwed into these sockets without affecting the performance of the engine—so there are indefinitely many ways of *ordering 500 shares of General Motors*, and there are societal sockets in which one of these ways will produce just about the same effect as any other. There are also societal pivot points, as it were, where which way people go depends on whether they *believe that p*, or *desire A*, and does not depend on any of the other infinitely many ways they may be alike or different.

Suppose, pursuing our Martian fantasy a little further, that one of the Martians were to engage in a predicting contest with an Earthling. The Earthling and the Martian observe (and observe each other observing) a particular bit of local physical transaction. From the Earthling's point of view, this is what is observed. The telephone rings in Mrs. Gardner's kitchen. She answers, and this is what she says: "Oh, hello dear. You're coming home early? Within the hour? And bringing the boss to dinner? Pick up a bottle of wine on the way home then, and drive carefully." On the basis of this observation, our Earthling predicts that a large metallic vehicle with rubber tires will come to a stop on the drive within one hour, disgorging two human beings, one of whom will be holding a paper bag containing a bottle containing an alcoholic fluid. The prediction is a bit risky, perhaps, but a good bet on all counts. The Martian makes the same prediction, but has to avail himself of much more information about an extraordinary number of interactions of which, so far as he can tell, the Earthling is entirely ignorant. For instance, the deceleration of the vehicle at intersection *A*, five miles from the house, without which there would have been a collision with another vehicle—whose collision course had been laboriously calculated over some hundreds of meters by the Martian. The Earthling's performance would look like magic! How did the Earthling know that the human being who got out of the car and got the bottle in the shop would get back in? The coming true of the Earthling's prediction, after all the vagaries, intersections, and branches in the paths charted by the Martian, would seem to anyone bereft of the intentional strategy as marvelous and inexplicable as the fatalistic inevitability of the appointment in Samarra. Fatalists—for instance, astrologers—believe that there is a pattern in human affairs that is inexorable, that will impose itself *come what may*, that is, no matter how the victims scheme and second-guess, no matter how they twist and turn in their chains. These fatalists are wrong, but they are *almost* right. There *are* patterns in human affairs that impose themselves, not quite inexorably but with great vigor, absorbing physical perturbations and variations that might as well be considered random; these are the patterns that we characterize in terms of the beliefs, desires, and intentions of rational agents.

No doubt you will have noticed, and been distracted by, a serious flaw in our thought experiment: the Martian is presumed to treat his Earthling opponent as an intelligent being like himself, with whom communication is possible, a being with whom one can make a wager, against whom one can compete. In short, a being with beliefs (such as the belief he expressed in his prediction) and desires (such as the desire to win the prediction contest). So if the Martian sees the pattern in one Earthling, how can he fail to see it in the others? As a bit of narrative, our example could be strengthened by supposing that our Earthling cleverly learned Martian (which is transmitted by X-ray modulation) and disguised himself as a Martian, counting on the species-chauvinism of these otherwise brilliant aliens to permit him to pass as an intentional system while not giving away the secret of his fellow human beings. This addition might get us over a bad twist in the tale, but might obscure the moral to be drawn: namely, *the unavoidability of the intentional stance with regard to oneself and one's fellow intelligent beings.* This unavoidability is itself interest relative; it is perfectly possible to adopt a physical stance, for instance, with regard to an intelligent being, oneself included, but not to the exclusion of maintaining at the same time an intentional stance with regard to oneself at a minimum, and one's fellows *if* one intends, for instance, to learn what they know (a point that has been powerfully made by Stuart Hampshire in a number of writings). We can perhaps suppose our super-intelligent Martians fail to recognize *us* as intentional systems, but we cannot suppose them to lack the requisite concepts.[2] If they observe, theorize, predict, communicate, they view *themselves* as intentional systems.[3] Where there are intelligent beings, the patterns must be there to be described, whether or not we care to see them.

It is important to recognize the objective reality of the intentional patterns discernible in the activities of intelligent creatures, but also important to recognize the incompleteness and imperfections in the patterns. The objective fact is that the intentional strategy *works as well as it does*, which is not perfectly. No one is perfectly rational, perfectly unforgetful, all-observant, or invulnerable to fatigue, malfunction, or design imperfection. This leads inevitably to circumstances beyond the power of the intentional strategy to describe, in much the same way that physical damage to an artifact, such as a telephone or an automobile, may render it indescribable by the normal design terminology for that artifact. How do you draw the schematic wiring diagram of an audio amplifier that has been partially melted, or how do you characterize the program state of a malfunctioning computer? In cases of even the mildest and most familiar cognitive pathology—where people seem to hold contradictory beliefs or to be deceiving themselves, for instance—the canons of interpretation of the intentional strategy fail to yield clear, stable verdicts about which beliefs and desires to attribute to a person.

Now a *strong* realist position on beliefs and desires would claim that in these cases the person in question really does have some particular beliefs and desires which the intentional strategy, as I have described it, is simply unable to divine. On the milder sort of realism I am advocating, there is no fact of the matter of exactly which beliefs and desires a person has in these degenerate cases, but this is not a surrender to relativism or subjectivism, for *when* and *why* there is no fact of the matter is itself a matter of objective fact. On this view one can even acknowledge the *interest relativity* of belief attributions and grant that given the different interests of different cultures, for instance, the beliefs and desires one culture would attribute to a member might be quite different from the beliefs and desires another culture would attribute to the very same person. But supposing that were so in a particular case, there would be the further facts about *how well* each of the rival intentional strategies worked for predicting the behavior of that person. We can be sure in advance that no intentional interpretation of an individual will work to perfection, and it may be that two rival schemes are about equally good, and better than any others we can devise. That this is the case is itself something about which there can be a fact of the matter. The objective presence of one pattern (with whatever imperfections) does not rule out the objective presence of another pattern (with whatever imperfections).

The bogey of radically different interpretations with equal warrant from the intentional strategy is theoretically important—one might better say metaphysically important—but practically negligible once one restricts one's attention to the largest and most complex intentional systems we know: human beings.[4]

Until now I have been stressing our kinship to clams and thermostats, in order to emphasize a view of the logical status of belief attribution, but the time has come to acknowledge the obvious differences and say what can be made of them. The perverse claim remains: *all there is* to being a true believer is being a system whose behavior is reliably predictable via the intentional strategy, and hence *all there is* to really and truly believing that *p* (for any proposition *p*) is being an intentional system for which *p* occurs as a belief in the best (most predictive) interpretation. But once we turn out attention to the truly interesting and versatile intentional systems, we see that this apparently shallow and instrumentalistic criterion of belief puts a severe constraint on the internal constitution of a genuine believer, and thus yields a robust version of belief after all.

Consider the lowly thermostat, as degenerate a case of intentional system as could conceivably hold our attention for more than a moment. Going along with the gag, we might agree to grant it the capacity for about half a dozen different beliefs and fewer desires—it can believe the room is too cold or too hot, that the boiler is on or off, and that if it wants the room warmer it should turn on the boiler, and so forth. But surely this is imputing too much to the thermostat; it has no concept of heat or of a boiler, for instance. So suppose we *de-interpret* its beliefs and desires: it can believe the A is too F or G, and if it wants the A to be more F it should do K, and so forth. After all, by attaching the thermostatic control mechanism to different input and output devices, it could be made to regulate the amount of water in a tank, or the speed of a train, for instance. Its attachment to a heat-sensitive transducer and a boiler is too impoverished a link to the world to grant any rich semantics to its belief-like states.

But suppose we then enrich these modes of attachment. Suppose we give it more than one way of learning about the temperature, for instance. We give it an eye of sorts that can distinguish huddled, shivering occupants of the room and an ear so that it can be told how cold it is. We give it some facts about geography so that it can conclude that is probably in a cold place if it learns that its spatio-temporal location is Winnipeg in December. Of course giving it a visual system that is multipurpose and general—not a mere shivering-object detector—will require vast complications of its inner structure. Suppose we also give our system more behavioral versatility: it chooses the boiler fuel, purchases it from the cheapest and most reliable dealer, checks the weather stripping, and so forth. This adds another dimension of internal complexity; it gives individual belief-like states *more to do*, in effect, by providing more and different occasions for their derivation or deduction from other states, and by providing more and different occasions for them to serve as premises for further reasoning. The cumulative effect of enriching these connections between the device and the world in which it resides is to enrich the semantics of its dummy predicates, F and G and the rest. The more of this we add, the less amenable our device becomes to serving as the control structure of anything other than a room-temperature maintenance system. A more formal way of saying this is that the class of indistinguishably satisfactory models of the formal system embodied in its internal states gets smaller and smaller as we add such complexities; the more we add, the richer or more demanding or specific the semantics of the system, until eventually we reach systems for which a unique semantic interpretation is practically (but never in principle) dictated (see Hayes 1979). At that point we say this device (or animal or person) has beliefs *about heat* and *about this very room*, and so forth, not only because of the system's actual location in, and operations on, the world, but because we cannot imagine another niche in which it could be placed *where it would work* (see also Dennett 1982/87 and 1987a).

Our original simple thermostat had a state we called a belief about a particular boiler, to the effect that it was on or off. Why about *that* boiler? Well, what other boiler would you want to say it was about? The belief is about the boiler because it is *fastened* to the boiler.[5] Given the actual, if minimal, causal link to the world that happened to be in effect, we could endow a state of the device with *meaning* (of a sort) and *truth conditions*, but it was altogether too easy to substitute a different minimal link and completely change the meaning (in this impoverished sense) of that internal state. But as systems become perceptually richer and behaviorally more versatile, it becomes harder and harder to make substitutions in the actual links of the system to the world without changing the organization of the system itself. If you change its environment, it will *notice*, in effect, and make a change in its internal state in response. There comes to be a two-way constraint of growing specificity between the device and the environment. Fix the device in any one state and it demands a very specific environment in which to operate properly (you can no longer switch it easily from regulating temperature to regulating speed or anything else); but at the same time, if you do not *fix* the state it is in, but just plunk it down in a changed environment, its sensory attachments will be sensitive and discriminative enough to respond appropriately to the change, driving the system into a new state, in which it will operate effectively in the new environment. There is a familiar way of alluding to this tight relationship that can exist between the organization of a system and its environment: you say that the organism continuously *mirrors* the environment, or that there is a *representation* of the environment in—or implicit in—the organization of the system.

It is not that we attribute (or should attribute) beliefs and desires only to things in which we find internal representations, but rather that, when we discover some object for which the intentional strategy works, we endeavor to interpret some of its internal states or processes as internal representations. What makes some internal feature of a thing a representation could only be its role in regulating the behavior of an intentional system.

Now the reason for stressing our kinship with the thermostat should be clear. There is no magic moment in the transition from a simple thermostat to a system that *really* has an internal representation of the world around it. The thermostat has a minimally demanding representation of the world, fancier thermostats have more demanding representations of the world, fancier robots for helping around the house would have still more demanding representations of the world. Finally you reach us. We are so multifariously and intricately connected to the world that almost no substitution is possible—though it is clearly imaginable in a thought experiment. Hilary Putnam imagines the planet Twin Earth, which is just like Earth right down to the scuff marks on the shoes of the Twin Earth replica of your neighbor, but which differs from Earth in some property that is entirely beneath the thresholds of your capacities to discriminate. (What they call water on Twin Earth has a different chemical analysis.) Were *you* to be whisked instantaneously to Twin Earth and exchanged for your Twin Earth replica, you would never be the wiser—just like the simple control system that cannot tell whether it is regulating temperature, speed, or volume of water in a tank. It is easy to devise radically different Twin Earths for something as simple and sensorily deprived as a thermostat, but your internal organization puts a much more stringent demand on substitution. Your Twin Earth and Earth must be virtual replicas or you will change state dramatically on arrival.

So which boiler are *your* beliefs about when you believe the boiler is on? Why, the boiler in your cellar (rather than its twin on Twin Earth, for instance). What other boiler would your beliefs be about? The completion of the semantic interpretation of your beliefs, fixing the referents of your beliefs, requires, as in the case of the thermostat, facts about your actual embedding in the world. The principles, and problems, of interpretation that we discover when we attribute beliefs to people are the *same* principles and problems we discover when we look at the ludicrous, but blessedly simple, problem of attributing beliefs to a thermostat. The differences are of degree, but nevertheless of such great degree that understanding the internal organization of a simple intentional system gives one very little basis for understanding the internal organization of a complex intentional system, such as a human being.

3 Why does the intentional strategy work?

When we turn to the question of *why* the intentional strategy works as well as it does, we find that the question is ambiguous, admitting of two very different sorts of answer. If the intentional system is a simple thermostat, one answer is simply this: the intentional strategy works because the thermostat is well designed; it was designed to be a system that could be easily and reliably comprehended and manipulated from this stance. That is true, but not very informative, if what we are after are the actual features of its design that explain its performance. Fortunately, however, in the case of a simple thermostat those features are easily discovered and understood, so the other answer to our *why* question, which is really an answer about *how the machinery works*, is readily available.

If the intentional system in question is a person, there is also an ambiguity in our question. The first answer to the question of why the intentional strategy works is that evolution has designed human beings to be rational, to believe what they ought to believe and want what they ought to want. The fact that we are products of a long and demanding evolutionary process guarantees that using the intentional strategy on us is a safe bet. This answer has the virtues of truth and brevity, but it is also strikingly uninformative. The more difficult version of the question asks, in effect, how the machinery which Nature has provided us works. And we cannot yet give a good answer to that question. We just do not know. We do know how the *strategy* works, and we know the easy answer to the question of why it works, but knowing these does not help us much with the hard answer.

It is not that there is any dearth of doctrine, however. A Skinnerian behaviorist, for instance, would say that the strategy works because its imputations of beliefs and desires are shorthand, in effect, for as yet unimaginably complex descriptions of the effects of prior histories of response and reinforcement. To say that someone wants some ice cream is to say that in the past the ingestion of ice cream has been reinforced in him by the results, creating a propensity under certain background conditions (also too complex to describe) to engage in ice-cream-acquiring behavior. In the absence of detailed knowledge of those historical facts we can nevertheless make shrewd guesses on inductive grounds; these guesses are embodied in our intentional-stance claims. Even if all this were true, it would tell us very little about the way such propensities were regulated by the internal machinery.

A currently more popular explanation is that the account of how the strategy works and the account of how the mechanism works will (roughly) *coincide*: for each predictively attributable belief, there will be a functionally salient internal state of the machinery, decomposable into functional parts in just about the same way the sentence expressing the belief is decomposable into parts—that is, words or terms. The inferences we attribute to rational creatures will be mirrored by physical, causal processes in the hardware; the *logical* form of the propositions believed will be copied in the *structural* form of the states in correspondence with them. This is the hypothesis that there is a *language of thought* coded in our brains, and our brains will eventually be understood as symbol manipulating systems in at least rough analogy with computers. Many different versions of this view are currently being explored, in the new research program called cognitive science, and provided one allows great latitude for attenuation of the basic, bold claim, I think some version of it will prove correct.

But I do not believe that this is *obvious*. Those who think that it is obvious, or inevitable, that such a theory will prove true (and there are many who do), are confusing two empirical claims. The first is that intentional stance description yields an objective, real pattern in the world—the pattern our imaginary Martians missed. This is an empirical claim, but one that is confirmed beyond skepticism. The second is that this real pattern is *produced by* another real pattern roughly isomorphic to it within the brains of intelligent creatures. Doubting the existence of the second real pattern is not doubting the existence of the first. There *are* reasons for believing in the second pattern, but they are not overwhelming. The best simple account I can give of the reasons is as follows.

As we ascend the scale of complexity form simple thermostat, through sophisticated robot, to human being, we discover that our efforts to design systems with the requisite behavior increasingly run foul of the problem of *combinatorial explosion*. Increasing some parameter by, say, ten percent—ten percent more inputs or more degrees of freedom in the behavior to be controlled or more words to be recognized or whatever—tends to increase the internal complexity of the system being designed by orders of magnitude. Things get out of hand very fast and, for instance, can lead to computer programs that will swamp the largest, fastest machines. Now somehow the brain has solved the problem of combinatorial explosion. It is a gigantic network of billions of cells, but still finite, compact, reliable, and swift, and capable of learning new behaviors, vocabularies, theories, almost without limit. Some elegant, *generative*, indefinitely extensible principles of representation must be responsible. We have only one model of such a representation system: a human language. So the argument for a language of thought comes down to this: what else could it be? We have so far been unable to imagine any plausible alternative in any detail. That is a good reason, I think, for recommending as a matter of scientific tactics that we pursue the hypothesis in its various forms as far as we can.[6] But we will engage in that exploration more circumspectly, and fruitfully, if we bear in mind that its inevitable rightness is far from assured. One does not well understand even a true empirical hypothesis so long as one is under the misapprehension that it is necessarily true.

Notes

1. The idea that most of anyone's beliefs *must* be true seems obvious to some people. Support for the idea can be found in works by Quine, Putnam, Shoemaker, Davidson, and myself. Other people find the idea equally incredible—so probably each side is calling a different phenomenon belief. Once one makes the distinction between belief and opinion (in my technical sense—Dennett 1978a), according to which opinions are linguistically infected, relatively sophisticated cognitive states—*roughly* states of betting on the truth of a particular, formulated sentence—one can see the near triviality of the claim that most beliefs are true. A few reflections on peripheral matters should bring it out. Consider Democritus, who had a systematic, all-embracing, but (let us say, for the sake of argument) entirely false physics. He had things *all wrong*, though his views held together and had a sort of systematic utility. But even if every *claim* that scholarship permits us to attribute to Democritus (either explicit or implicit in his writings) is false, these represent a vanishingly small fraction of his *beliefs*, which include both the vast numbers of humdrum standing beliefs he must have had (about which house he lived in, what to look for in a good pair of sandals, and so forth) and also those occasional beliefs that came and went by the millions as his perceptual experience changed.

   But, it may be urged, this isolation of his humdrum beliefs from his science relies on an insupportable distinction between truths of observation and truths of theory; all Democritus's beliefs are theory-laden, and since his theory is false, they are false. The reply is as follows: Granted that all observation beliefs are theory laden, why should we choose Democritus's *explicit*, sophisticated theory (couched in his *opinions*) as the theory with which to burden his quotidian observations? Note that the least theoretical compatriot of Democritus also had myriads of theory-laden observation beliefs— and was, in one sense, none the wiser for it. Why should we not suppose Democritus's observations are laden with the same (presumably innocuous) theory? If Democritus forgot his theory, or changed his mind, his observational beliefs would be *largely* untouched. To the extent that his sophisticated theory played a discernible role in his routine behavior and expectations and so forth, it would be quite appropriate to couch his humdrum beliefs in terms of the sophisticated theory, but this will not yield a *mainly false* catalogue of beliefs, since so few of his beliefs will be affected. (The effect of theory on observation is nevertheless often underrated. See Churchland 1979 for dramatic and convincing examples of the tight relationship that can sometimes exist between theory and experience.) (The discussion in this note was distilled from a useful conversation with Paul and Patricia Churchland and Michael Stack.)

2. A member of the audience in Oxford pointed out that if the Martian included the Earthling in his physical stance purview (a possibility I had not explicitly excluded), he would not be surprised by the Earthling's prediction. He would indeed have predicted exactly the pattern of X-ray modulations produced by the Earthling speaking Martian. True, but as the Martian wrote down the results of his calculations, his prediction of the Earthling's prediction would appear, word by Martian word, as on a Ouija board, and what would be baffling to the Martian was how this chunk of mechanism, the Earthling predictor dressed up like a Martian, was able to yield this *true* sentence of Martian when it was so informationally isolated from the events the Martian needed to know of in order to make his own prediction about the arriving automobile.

3. Might there not be intelligent beings who had no use for communicating, predicting, observing, ...? There might be marvelous, nifty, invulnerable entities lacking these modes of action, but I cannot see what would lead us to call them *intelligent*.

4. John McCarthy's analogy to cryptography nicely makes this point. The larger the corpus of cipher text, the less chance there is of dual, systematically unrelated decipherings. For a very useful discussion of the principles and presuppositions of the intentional stance applied to machines—explicitly including thermostats—see McCarthy 1979.

5. This idea is the ancestor in effect of the species of different ideas lumped together under the rubric of *de re* belief. If one builds from this idea toward its scions, one can see better the difficulties with them, and how to repair them. (For more on this topic, see Dennett 1982/87.)

6. The fact that all *language-of-thought* models of mental representation so far proposed fall victim to combinatorial explosion in one way or another should temper one's enthusiasm for engaging in what Fodor aptly calls "the only game in town".

Computer Science as Empirical Inquiry: Symbols and Search

Allen Newell
Herbert A. Simon
1976

Computer science is the study of the phenomena surrounding computers. The founders of this society understood this very well when they called themselves the Association for Computing Machinery. The machine—not just the hardware, but the programmed living machine—is the organism we study.

This is the tenth Turing Lecture. The nine persons who preceded us on this platform have presented nine different views of computer science. For our organism, the machine, can be studied at many levels and from many sides. We are deeply honored to appear here today and to present yet another view, the one that has permeated the scientific work for which we have been cited. We wish to speak of computer science as an empirical inquiry.

Our view is only one of many; the previous lectures make that clear. However, even taken together the lectures fail to cover the whole scope of our science. Many fundamental aspects of it have not been represented in these ten awards. And if the time ever arrives, surely not soon, when the compass has been boxed, when computer science has been discussed from every side, it will be time to start the cycle again. For the hare as lecturer will have to make an annual sprint to overtake the cumulation of small, incremental gains that the tortoise of scientific and technical development has achieved in his steady march. Each year will create a new gap and call for a new sprint, for in science there is no final word.

Computer science is an empirical discipline. We would have called it an experimental science, but like astronomy, economics, and geology, some of its unique forms of observation and experience do not fit a narrow stereotype of the experimental method. Nonetheless, they are experiments. Each new machine that is built is an experiment. Actually constructing the machine poses a question to nature; and we listen for the answer by observing the machine in operation and analyzing it by all analytical and measurement means available. Each new program that is built is an experiment. It poses a question to nature, and its behavior offers clues to a new answer. Neither machines nor programs are black boxes; they are artifacts that have been designed, both hardware and software, and we can open them up and look inside. We can relate their structure to their behavior and draw many lessons from a single experiment. We don't have to build 100 copies of, say, a theorem prover, to demonstrate statistically that it has not overcome the combinatorial explosion of search in the way hoped for. Inspection of the program in the light of a few runs reveals the flaw and lets us proceed to the next attempt.

We build computers and programs for many reasons. We build them to serve society and as tools for carrying out the economic tasks of society. But as basic scientists we build machines and programs as a way of discovering new phenomena and analyzing phenomena we already know about. Society often becomes confused about this, believing that computers and programs are to be constructed only for the economic use that can be made of them (or as intermediate items in a developmental sequence leading to such use). It needs to understand that the phenomena surrounding computers are deep and obscure, requiring much experimentation to assess their nature. It needs to understand that, as in any science, the gains that accrue from such experimentation and understanding pay off in the permanent acquisition of new techniques; and that it is these techniques that will create the instruments to help society in achieving its goals.

Our purpose here, however, is not to plead for understanding from an outside world. It is to examine one aspect of our science, the development of new basic understanding by empirical inquiry. This is best done by illustrations. We will be pardoned if, presuming upon the occasion, we choose our examples from the area of our own research. As will become apparent, these examples involve the whole development of artificial intelligence, especially in its early years. They rest on much more than our own personal contributions. And even where we have made direct contributions, this has been done in cooperation with others. Our collaborators have included especially Cliff Shaw, with whom we formed a team of three through the exciting period of the late fifties. But we have also worked with a great many colleagues and students at Carnegie Mellon University.

Time permits taking up just two examples. The first is the development of the notion of a symbolic system. The second is the development of the notion of heuristic search. Both conceptions have deep significance for understanding how information is processed and how intelligence is achieved. However, they do not come close to exhausting the full scope of artificial intelligence, though they seem to us to be useful for exhibiting the nature of fundamental knowledge in this part of computer science.

1 Symbols and physical symbol systems

One of the fundamental contributions to knowledge of computer science has been to explain, at a rather basic level, what symbols are. This explanation is a scientific proposition about nature. It is empirically derived, with a long and gradual development.

Symbols lie at the root of intelligent action, which is, of course, the primary topic of artificial intelligence. For that matter, it is a primary question for all of computer science. For all information is processed by computers in the service of ends, and we measure the intelligence of a system by its ability to achieve stated ends in the face of variations, difficulties, and complexities posed by the task environment. This general investment of computer science in attaining intelligence is obscured when the tasks being accomplished are limited in scope, for then the full variations in the environment can be accurately foreseen. It becomes more obvious as we extend computers to more global, complex, and knowledge-intensive tasks—as we attempt to make them our agents, capable of handling on their own the full contingencies of the natural world.

Our understanding of the system's requirements for intelligent action emerges slowly. It is composite, for no single elementary thing accounts for intelligence in all its manifestations. There is no "intelligence principle", just as there is no "vital principle" that conveys by its very nature the essence of life. But the lack of a simple *deus ex machina* does not imply that there are no structural requirements for intelligence. One such requirement is the ability to store and manipulate symbols. To put the scientific question, we may paraphrase the title of a famous paper by Warren McCulloch (1961): What is a symbol, that intelligence may use it, and intelligence, that it may use a symbol?

1.1 Laws of qualitative structure

All sciences characterize the essential nature of the systems they study. These characterizations are invariably qualitative in nature, for they set the terms within which more detailed knowledge can be developed. Their essence can often be captured in very short, very general statements. One might judge these general laws, because of their limited specificity, as making relatively little contribution to the sum of a science, were it not for the historical evidence that shows them to be results of the greatest importance.

THE CELL DOCTRINE IN BIOLOGY. A good example of a law of qualitative structure is the cell doctrine in biology, which states that the basic building block of all living organisms is the cell. Cells come in a large variety of forms, though they all have a nucleus surrounded by protoplasm, the whole encased by a membrane. But this internal structure was not, historically, part of the specification of the cell doctrine; it was subsequent specificity developed by intensive investigation. The cell doctrine can be conveyed almost entirely by the statement we gave above, along with some vague notions about what size a cell can be. The impact of this law on biology, however, has been tremendous, and the lost motion in the field prior to its gradual acceptance was considerable.

PLATE TECTONICS IN GEOLOGY. Geology provides an interesting example of a qualitative structure law, interesting because it has gained acceptance in the last decade and so its rise in status is still fresh in our memory. The theory of plate tectonics asserts that the surface of the globe is a collection of huge plates—a few dozen in all—which move (at geological speeds) against, over, and under each other into the center of the earth, where they lose their identity. The movements of the plates account for the shapes and relative locations of the continents and oceans, for the areas of volcanic and earthquake activity, for the deep sea ridges, and so on. With a few additional particulars as to speed and size, the essential theory has been specified. It was of course not accepted until it succeeded in explaining a number of details, all of which hung together (for instance, accounting for flora, fauna, and stratification agreements between West Africa and Northeast South America). The plate-tectonics theory is highly qualitative. Now that it is accepted, the whole earth seems to offer evidence for it everywhere, for we see the world in its terms.

THE GERM THEORY OF DISEASE. It is little more than a century since Pasteur enunciated the germ theory of disease, a law of qualitative structure that produced a revolution in medicine. The theory proposes that most diseases are caused by the presence and multiplication in the body of tiny single-celled living organisms, and that contagion consists in the transmission of these organisms from one host to another. A large part of the elaboration of the theory consisted in identifying the organisms associated with specific diseases, describing them, and tracing their life histories. The fact that this law has many exceptions—that many diseases are not produced by germs—does not detract from its importance. The law tells us to look for a particular kind of cause; it does not insist that we will always find it.

THE DOCTRINE OF ATOMISM. The doctrine of atomism offers an interesting contrast to the three laws of qualitative structure we have just described. As it emerged from the work of Dalton and his demonstrations that the chemicals combined in fixed proportions, the law provided a typical example of qualitative structure: the elements are composed of small, uniform particles, differing from one element to another. But because the underlying species of atoms are so simple and limited in their variety, quantitative theories were soon formulated which assimilated all the general structure in the original qualitative hypothesis. With cells, tectonic plates, and germs, the variety of structure is so great that the underlying qualitative principle remains distinct, and its contribution to the total theory clearly discernible.

CONCLUSION. Laws of qualitative structure are seen everywhere in science. Some of our greatest scientific discoveries are to be found among them. As the examples illustrate, they often set the terms on which a whole science operates.

1.2 Physical symbol systems

Let us return to the topic of symbols, and define a *physical symbol system*. The adjective "physical" denotes two important features: (1) such systems clearly obey the laws of physics—they are realizable by engineered systems made of engineered components; and (2) although our use of the term "symbol" prefigures our intended interpretation, it is not restricted to human symbol systems.

A physical symbol system consists of a set of entities, called symbols, which are physical patterns that can occur as components of another type of entity called an expression (or symbol structure). Thus a symbol structure is composed of a number of instances (or tokens) of symbols related in some physical way (such as one token being next to another). At any instant of time the system will contain a collection of these symbol structures. Besides these structures, the system also contains a collection of processes that operate on expressions to produce other expressions: processes of creation, modification, reproduction, and destruction. A physical symbol system is a machine that produces through time an evolving collection of symbol structures. Such a system exists in a world of objects wider than just these symbolic expressions themselves.

Two notions are central to this structure of expressions, symbols, and objects: designation and interpretation.

> **DESIGNATION.** An expression designates an object if, given the expression, the system can either affect the object itself or behave in ways depending on the object.

In either case, access to the object via the expression has been obtained, which is the essence of designation.

> **INTERPRETATION.** The system can interpret an expression if the expression designates a process and if, given the expression, the system can carry out the process.*

Interpretation implies a special form of dependent action: given an expression, the system can perform the indicated process, which is to say, it can evoke and execute its own processes from expressions that designate them.

A system capable of designation and interpretation, in the sense just indicated, must also meet a number of additional requirements, of completeness and closure. We will have space only to mention these briefly; all of them are important and have far-reaching consequences.

(1) A symbol may be used to designate any expression whatsoever. That is, given a symbol, it is not prescribed a priori what expressions it can designate. This arbitrariness pertains only to symbols: the symbol

---

* *Editor's note:* These senses of the terms 'designation' and 'interpretation', and hence also of 'symbol', are specific to computer science; they concern only relationships and processes that occur *within* a computer. In linguistics and philosophy, by contrast, these terms would usually be explained in terms of relationships *between* an intelligent system (or what's inside of it) and its environment. Most of the essays in the present volume use the terms in this latter sense.

tokens and their mutual relations determine what object is designated by a complex expression. (2) There exist expressions that designate every process of which the machine is capable. (3) There exist processes for creating any expression and for modifying any expression in arbitrary ways. (4) Expressions are stable; once created, they will continue to exist until explicitly modified or deleted. (5) The number of expressions that the system can hold is essentially unbounded.

The type of system we have just defined is not unfamiliar to computer scientists. It bears a strong family resemblance to all general purpose computers. If a symbol-manipulation language, such as LISP, is taken as defining a machine, then the kinship becomes truly brotherly. Our intent in laying out such a system is not to propose something new. Just the opposite: it is to show what is now known and hypothesized about systems that satisfy such a characterization.

We can now state a general scientific hypothesis—a law of qualitative structure for symbol systems:

THE PHYSICAL SYMBOL SYSTEM HYPOTHESIS. A physical symbol system has the necessary and sufficient means for general intelligent action.

By "necessary" we mean that any system that exhibits general intelligence will prove upon analysis to be a physical symbol system. By "sufficient" we mean that any physical symbol system of sufficient size can be organized further to exhibit general intelligence. By "general intelligent action" we wish to indicate the same scope of intelligence as we see in human action: that in any real situation, behavior appropriate to the ends of the system and adaptive to the demands of the environment can occur, within some limits of speed and complexity.

The physical-symbol-system hypothesis clearly is a law of qualitative structure. It specifies a general class of systems within which one will find those capable of intelligent action.

This is an empirical hypothesis. We have defined a class of systems; we wish to ask whether that class accounts for a set of phenomena we find in the real world. Intelligent action is everywhere around us in the biological world, mostly in human behavior. It is a form of behavior we can recognize by its effects whether it is performed by humans or not. The hypothesis could indeed be false. Intelligent behavior is not so easy to produce that any system will exhibit it willy nilly. Indeed, there are people whose analyses lead them to conclude, either on philosophical or on scientific grounds, that the hypothesis is false.

Scientifically, one can attack or defend it only by bringing forth empirical evidence about the natural world.

We now need to trace the development of this hypothesis and look at the evidence for it.

1.3 Development of the symbol-system hypothesis

A physical symbol system is an instance of a universal machine. Thus the symbol-system hypothesis implies that intelligence will be realized by a universal computer. However, the hypothesis goes far beyond the argument, often made on general grounds of physical determinism, that any computation that is realizable can be realized by a universal machine, provided that it is specified. For it asserts specifically that the intelligent machine is a symbol system, thus making a specific architectural assertion about the nature of intelligent systems. It is important to understand how this additional specificity arose.

FORMAL LOGIC. The roots of the hypothesis go back to the program of Frege and of Whitehead and Russell for formalizing logic: capturing the basic conceptual notions of mathematics in logic and putting the notions of proof and deduction on a secure footing. This effort culminated in mathematical logic—our familiar propositional, first-order, and higher-order logics. It developed a characteristic view, often referred to as the "symbol game". Logic, and by incorporation all of mathematics, was a game played with meaningless tokens according to certain purely syntactic rules. All meaning had been purged. One had a mechanical, though permissive (we would now say nondeterministic), system about which various things could be proved. Thus progress was first made by walking away from all that seemed relevant to meaning and human symbols. We could call this the stage of formal symbol manipulation.

This general attitude is well reflected in the development of information theory. It was pointed out time and again that Shannon had defined a system that was useful only for communication and selection, and which had nothing to do with meaning. Regrets were expressed that such a general name as "information theory" had been given to the field, and attempts were made to rechristen it as "the theory of selective information"—to no avail, of course.

TURING MACHINES AND THE DIGITAL COMPUTER. The development of the first digital computers and of automata theory, starting with Turing's own work in the 1930s, can be treated together. They agree in their view of what is essential. Let us use Turing's own model, for it shows the features well.

A Turing machine consists of two memories: an unbounded tape and a finite-state control. The tape holds data, that is, the famous zeros and ones. The machine has a very small set of proper operations—read, write, and scan operations—on the tape. The read operation is not a data operation, but provides conditional branching to a control state as a function of the data under the read head. As we all know, this model contains the essentials of all computers, in terms of what they can do, though other computers with different memories and operations might carry out the same computations with different requirements of space and time. In particular, the model of a Turing machine contains within it the notions both of what cannot be computed and of universal machines—computers that can do anything that can be done by any machine.

We should marvel that two of our deepest insights into information processing were achieved in the thirties, before modern computers came into being. It is a tribute to the genius of Alan Turing. It is also a tribute to the development of mathematical logic at the time, and testimony to the depth of computer science's obligation to it. Concurrently with Turing's work appeared the work of the logicians Emil Post and (independently) Alonzo Church. Starting from independent notions of logistic systems (Post productions and recursive functions, respectively), they arrived at analogous results on undecidability and universality—results that were soon shown to imply that all three systems were equivalent. Indeed, the convergence of all these attempts to define the most general class of information-processing systems provides some of the force of our conviction that we have captured the essentials of information processing in these models.

In none of these systems is there, on the surface, a concept of the symbol as something that *designates*. The data are regarded as just strings of zeroes and ones—indeed, that data be inert is essential to the reduction of computation to physical process. The finite-state control system was always viewed as a small controller, and logical games were played to see how small a state system could be used without destroying the universality of the machine. No games, as far as we can tell, were ever played to add new states dynamically to the finite control—to think of the control memory as holding the bulk of the system's knowledge. What was accomplished at this stage was half of the principle of interpretation—showing that a machine could be run from a description. Thus, this is the stage of automatic formal symbol manipulation.

THE STORED-PROGRAM CONCEPT. With the development of the second generation of electronic machines in the mid-forties (after the Eniac) came the stored-program concept. This was rightfully hailed as a milestone, both conceptually and practically. Programs now can be data, and can be operated on as data. This capability is, of course, already implicit in the model of Turing: the descriptions are on the very same tape as the data. Yet the idea was realized only when machines acquired enough memory to make it practicable to locate actual programs in some internal place. After all, the Eniac had only twenty registers.

The stored-program concept embodies the second half of the interpretation principle, the part that says that the system's own data can be interpreted. But it does not yet contain the notion of designation—of the physical relation that underlies meaning.

LIST PROCESSING. The next step, taken in 1956, was list processing. The contents of the data structures were now symbols, in the sense of our physical symbol system: patterns that designated, that had referents. Lists held addresses which permitted access to other lists—thus the notion of list structures. That this was a new view was demonstrated to us many times in the early days of list processing when colleagues would ask where the data were—that is, which list finally held the collection of bits that were the content of the system. They found it strange that there were no such bits, there were only symbols that designated yet other symbol structures.

List processing is simultaneously three things in the development of computer science. (1) It is the creation of a genuine dynamic memory structure in a machine that had heretofore been perceived as having fixed structure. It added to our ensemble of operations those that built and modified structure in addition to those that replaced and changed content. (2) It was an early demonstration of the basic abstraction that a computer consists of a set of data types and a set of operations proper to these data types, so that a computational system should employ whatever data types are appropriate to the application, independent of the underlying machine. (3) List-processing produced a model of designation, thus defining symbol manipulation in the sense in which we use this concept in computer science today.

As often occurs, the practice of the time already anticipated all the elements of list processing: addresses are obviously used to gain access, the drum machines used linked programs (so called one-plus-one addressing), and so on. But the conception of list processing as an abstraction created a new world in which designation and dynamic symbolic structure were the defining characteristics. The embedding of the early list-processing systems in languages (the IPLs, LISP) is often decried as having been a barrier to the diffusion of list-processing techniques throughout programming practice; but it was the vehicle that held the abstraction together.

LISP. One more step is worth noting: McCarthy's creation of LISP in 1959-60 (McCarthy 1960). It completed the act of abstraction, lifting list structures out of their embedding in concrete machines, creating a new formal system with S-expressions, which could be shown to be equivalent to the other universal schemes of computation.

CONCLUSION. That the concept of a designating symbol and symbol manipulation does not emerge until the mid-fifties does not mean that the earlier steps were either inessential or less important. The total concept is the join of computability, physical realizability (and by multiple technologies), universality, the symbolic representation of processes (that is, interpretability), and, finally, symbolic structure and designation. Each of the steps provided an essential part of the whole.

The first step in this chain, authored by Turing, is theoretically motivated, but the others all have deep empirical roots. We have been led by the evolution of the computer itself.

The stored-program principle arose out of the experience with Eniac. List processing arose out of the attempt to construct intelligent programs. It took its cue from the emergence of random-access memories, which provided a clear physical realization of a designating symbol in the address. LISP arose out of the evolving experience with list processing.

1.4 The evidence

We come now to the evidence for the hypothesis that physical symbol systems are capable of intelligent action, and that general intelligent action calls for a physical symbol system. The hypothesis is an empirical generalization and not a theorem. We know of no way of demonstrating the connection between symbol systems and intelligence on purely logical grounds. Lacking such a demonstration, we must look at the facts. Our central aim, however, is not to review the evidence in detail, but to use the example before us to illustrate the proposition that computer science is a field of empirical inquiry. Hence, we will only indicate what kinds of evidence there are, and the general nature of the testing process.

The notion of a physical symbol system had taken essentially its present form by the middle of the 1950's, and one can date from that time the growth of artificial intelligence as a coherent subfield of computer science. The twenty years of work since then has seen a continuous accumulation of empirical evidence of two main varieties. The first addresses itself to the *sufficiency* of physical symbol systems for producing intelligence, attempting to construct and test specific systems that have such a capability. The second kind of evidence addresses itself to the *necessity* of having a physical symbol system wherever intelligence is exhibited. It starts with man, the intelligent system best known to us, and attempts to discover whether his cognitive activity can be explained as the working of a physical symbol system. There are other forms of evidence, which we will comment upon briefly later, but these two are the important ones. We will consider them in turn. The first is generally called artificial intelligence, the second, research in cognitive psychology.

CONSTRUCTING INTELLIGENT SYSTEMS. The basic paradigm for the initial testing of the germ theory of disease was: identify a disease, then look for the germ. An analogous paradigm has inspired much of the research in artificial intelligence: identify a task domain calling for intelligence, then construct a program for a digital computer that can handle tasks in that domain. The easy and well-structured tasks were looked at first: puzzles and games, operations-research problems of scheduling and allocating resources, simple induction tasks. Scores, if not hundreds, of programs of these kinds have by now been constructed, each capable of some measure of intelligent action in the appropriate domain.

Of course intelligence is not an all-or-none matter, and there has been steady progress toward higher levels of performance in specific domains, as well as toward widening the range of those domains. Early chess programs, for example, were deemed successful if they could play a game legally and with some indication of purpose; a little later, they reached the level of human beginners; within ten or fifteen years, they began to compete with serious amateurs. Progress has been slow (and the total programming effort invested small) but continuous, and the paradigm of construct-and-test proceeds in a regular cycle—the whole research activity mimicking at the macroscopic level the basic generate-and-test cycle of many of the AI programs.

There is a steadily widening area within which intelligent action is attainable. For the original tasks, research has extended to building systems that handle and understand natural language in a variety of ways, systems for interpreting visual scenes, systems for hand-eye coordination, systems that design, systems that write computer programs, systems for speech understanding—the list is, if not endless, at least very long. If there are limits beyond which the hypothesis will not carry us, they have not yet become apparent. Up to the present, the rate of progress has been governed mainly by the rather modest quantity of scientific resources that have been applied and the inevitable requirement of a substantial system-building effort for each new major undertaking.

Much more has been going on, of course, than simply a piling up of examples of intelligent systems adapted to specific task domains. It would be surprising and unappealing if it turned out that the AI programs performing these diverse tasks had nothing in common beyond their being instances of physical symbol systems. Hence, there has been great interest in searching for mechanisms possessed of generality, and for common components among programs performing a variety of tasks. This search carries the theory beyond the initial symbol-system hypothesis to a more complete characterization of the particular kinds of symbol systems that are effective in artificial intelligence. In the second section of this paper, we will discuss one example of an hypothesis at this second level of specificity: the heuristic-search hypothesis.

The search for generality spawned a series of programs designed to separate out general problem-solving mechanisms from the requirements of particular task domains. The General Problem Solver (GPS) was perhaps the first of these; while among its descendants are such contemporary systems as PLANNER and CONNIVER. The search for common components has led to generalized schemes of representations for goals and plans, methods for constructing discrimination nets, procedures for the control of tree-search, pattern-matching mechanisms, and language-parsing systems. Experiments are at present under way to find convenient devices for representing sequences of time and tense, movement, causality, and the like. More and more, it becomes possible to assemble large intelligent systems in a modular way from such basic components.

We can gain some perspective on what is going on by turning, again, to the analogy of the germ theory. If the first burst of research stimulated by that theory consisted largely in finding the germ to go with each disease, subsequent effort turned to learning what a germ was—to building on the basic qualitative law a new level of structure. In artificial intelligence, an initial burst of activity aimed at building intelligent programs for a wide variety of almost randomly selected tasks is giving way to more sharply targeted research aimed at understanding the common mechanisms·of such systems.

THE MODELING OF HUMAN SYMBOLIC BEHAVIOR. The symbol-system hypothesis implies that the symbolic behavior of man arises because he has the characteristics of a physical symbol system. Hence, the results of efforts to model human behavior with symbol systems become an important part of the evidence for the hypothesis, and research in artificial intelligence goes on in close collaboration with research in information-processing psychology, as it is usually called.

The search for explanations of man's intelligent behavior in terms of symbol systems has had a large measure of success over the past twenty years—to the point where information-processing theory is the leading contemporary point of view in cognitive psychology. Especially in the areas of problem solving, concept attainment, and long-term memory, symbol-manipulation models now dominate the scene.

Research in information-processing psychology involves two main kinds of empirical activity. The first is the conduct of observations and experiments on human behavior in tasks requiring intelligence. The second, very similar to the parallel activity in artificial intelligence, is the programming of symbol systems to model the observed human behavior. The psychological observations and experiments lead to the formulation of hypotheses about the symbolic processes the subjects are using, and these are an important source of the ideas that go into the construction of the programs. Thus many of the ideas for the basic mechanisms of GPS were derived from careful analysis of the protocols that human subjects produced while thinking aloud during the performance of a problem-solving task.

The empirical character of computer science is nowhere more evident than in this alliance with psychology. Not only are psychological experiments required to test the veridicality of the simulation models as explanations of the human behavior, but out of the experiments come new ideas for the design and construction of physical symbol systems.

OTHER EVIDENCE. The principal body of evidence for the symbol-system hypothesis that we have not considered is negative evidence: the absence of specific competing hypotheses as to how intelligent activity might be accomplished—whether by man or by machine. Most attempts to build such hypotheses have taken place within the field of psychology. Here we have had a continuum of theories from the points of view usually labeled "behaviorism" to those usually labeled "Gestalt theory". Neither of these points of view stands as a real competitor to the symbol-system hypothesis, and for two reasons. First, neither behaviorism nor Gestalt theory has demonstrated, or even shown how to demonstrate, that the explanatory mechanisms it postulates are sufficient to account for intelligent behavior in complex tasks. Second, neither theory has been formulated with anything like the specificity of artificial programs. As a matter of fact, the alternative theories are so vague that it is not terribly difficult to give them information-processing interpretations, and thereby assimilate them to the symbol-system hypothesis.

1.5 Conclusion

We have tried to use the example of the physical-symbol-system hypothesis to illustrate concretely that computer science is a scientific enterprise in the usual meaning of that term: it develops scientific hypotheses which it then seeks to verify by empirical inquiry. We had a second reason, however, for choosing this particular example to illustrate our point. The physical-symbol-system hypothesis is itself a substantial scientific hypothesis of the kind that we earlier dubbed "laws of qualitative structure". It represents an important discovery of computer science, which if borne out by the empirical evidence, as in fact appears to be occurring, will have major continuing impact on the field.

We turn now to a second example, the role of search in intelligence. This topic, and the particular hypothesis about it that we shall examine, have also played a central role in computer science, in general, and artificial intelligence, in particular.

2 Heuristic search

Knowing that physical symbol systems provide the matrix for intelligent action does not tell us how they accomplish this. Our second example of a law of qualitative structure in computer science addresses this latter question, asserting that symbol systems solve problems by using the processes of heuristic search. This generalization, like the previous one, resets on empirical evidence, and has not been derived formally from other premises. We shall see in a moment, however, that it does have some logical connection with the symbol-system hypothesis, and perhaps we can expect to formalize the connection at some time in the future. Until that time arrives, our story must again be one of empirical inquiry. We will describe what is known about heuristic search and review the empirical findings that show how it enables action to be intelligent. We begin by stating this law of qualitative structure, the heuristic-search hypothesis.

> HEURISTIC-SEARCH HYPOTHESIS. The solutions to problems are represented as symbol structures. A physical symbol system exercises its intelligence in problem solving by search—that is, by generating and progressively modifying symbol structures until it produces a solution structure.

Physical symbol systems must use heuristic search to solve problems because such systems have limited processing resources; in a finite number of steps, and over a finite interval of time, they can execute only a finite number of processes. Of course, that is not a very strong limitation, for all universal Turing machines suffer from it. We intend the limitation, however, in a stronger sense: we mean *practically* limited. We can conceive of systems that are not limited in a practical way but are capable, for example, of searching in parallel the nodes of an exponentially expanding tree at a constant rate for each unit advance in depth. We will not be concerned here with such systems, but with systems whose computing resources are scarce relative to the complexity of the situations with which they are confronted. The restriction will not exclude any real symbol systems, in computer or man, in the context of real tasks. The fact of limited resources allows us, for most purposes, to view a symbol system as though it were a serial, one-process-at-a-time device. If it can accomplish only a small amount of processing in any short time interval, then we might as well regard it as doing things one at a time. Thus "limited resource symbol system" and "serial symbol system" are practically synonymous. The problem of allocating a scarce resource from moment to moment can usually be treated, if the moment is short enough, as a problem of scheduling a serial machine.

2.1 Problem Solving

Since ability to solve problems is generally taken as a prime indicator that a system has intelligence, it is natural that much of the history of artificial intelligence is taken up with attempts to build and understand problem-solving systems. Problem solving has been discussed by philosophers and psychologists for two millennia, in discourses dense with a feeling of mystery. If you think there is nothing problematic or mysterious about a symbol system solving problems, you are a child of today, whose views have been formed since mid-century. Plato (and, by his account, Socrates) found difficulty understanding even how problems could be *entertained*, much less how they could be solved. Let us remind you of how he posed the conundrum in the *Meno*:

> Meno: And how will you inquire, Socrates, into that which you know not? What will you put forth as the subject of inquiry? And if you find what you want, how will you ever know that this is what you did not know?

To deal with this puzzle, Plato invented his famous theory of recollection: when you think you are discovering or learning something, you are really just recalling what you already knew in a previous existence. If you find this explanation preposterous, there is a much simpler one available today, based upon our understanding of symbol systems. An approximate statement of it is:

> To state a problem is to designate (a) a *test* for a class of symbol structures (solutions of the problem), and (2) a *generator* of symbol structures (potential solutions). To solve a problem is to generate a structure, using (2), that satisfies the test of (1).

We have a problem if we know what we want to do (the test), and if we don't know immediately how to do it (our generator does not immediately produce a symbol structure satisfying the test). A symbol system can state and solve problems (sometimes) because it can generate and test.

If that is all there is to problem solving, why not simply generate at once an expression that satisfies the test? This is, in fact, what we do when we wish and dream. "If wishes were horses, beggars might ride." But outside the world of dreams, it isn't possible. To know how we would test something, once constructed, does not mean that we know how to construct it—that we have any generator for doing so.

For example, it is well known what it means to "solve" the problem of playing winning chess. A simple test exists for noticing winning positions, the test for checkmate of the enemy king. In the world of dreams one simply generates a strategy that leads to checkmate for all counter strategies of the opponent. Alas, no generator that will do this is known to existing symbol systems (man or machine). Instead, good moves in chess are sought by generating various alternatives, and painstakingly evaluating them with the use of approximate, and often erroneous, measures that are supposed to indicate the likelihood that a particular line of play is on the route to a winning position. Move generators there are; winning-move generators there are not.

Before there can be a move generator for a problem, there must be a problem space: a space of symbol structures in which problem situations, including the initial and goal situations, can be represented. Move generators are processes for modifying one situation in the problem space into another. The basic characteristics of physical symbol systems guarantee that they can represent problem spaces and that they possess move generators. How, in any concrete situation they synthesize a problem space and move generators appropriate to that situation is a question that is still very much on the frontier of artificial intelligence research.

The task that a symbol system is faced with, then, when it is presented with a problem and a problem space, is to use its limited processing resources to generate possible solutions, one after another until if finds one that satisfies the problem-defining test. If the system had some control over the order in which potential solutions were generated, then it would be desirable to arrange this order of generation so that actual solutions would have a high likelihood of appearing early. A symbol system would exhibit intelligence to the extent that it succeeded in doing this. Intelligence for a system with limited processing resources consists in making wise choices of what to do next.

2.2 Search in problem solving

During the first decade or so of artificial-intelligence research, the study of problem solving was almost synonymous with the study of search processes. From our characterization of problems and problem solving, it is easy to see why this was so. In fact, it might be asked whether it could be otherwise. But before we try to answer that question, we must explore further the nature of search processes as it revealed itself during that decade of activity.

EXTRACTING INFORMATION FROM THE PROBLEM SPACE. Consider a set of symbol structures, some small subset of which are solutions to a given problem. Suppose, further, that the solutions are distributed randomly through the entire set. By this we mean that no information exists that would enable any search generator to perform better than a random search. Then no symbol system could exhibit more intelligence (or less intelligence) than any other in solving the problem, although one might experience better luck than another.

A condition, then, for the appearance of intelligence is that the distribution of solutions be not entirely random, that the space of symbol structures exhibit at least some degree of order and pattern. A second condition is that the pattern in the space of symbol structures be more or less detectable. A third condition is that the generator of potential solutions be able to behave differentially, depending on what pattern is detected. There must be information in the problem space, and the symbol system must be capable of extracting and using it. Let us look first at a very simple example, where the intelligence is easy to come by.

Consider the problem of solving a simple algebraic equation:

$$ax + b = cx + d$$

The test defines a solution as any expression of the form, $x = e$, such that $ae + b = ce + d$. Now, one could use as generator any process that would produce numbers which could then be tested by substituting in the latter equation. We would not call this an intelligent generator.

Alternatively, one could use generators that would make use of the fact that the original equation can be modified—by adding or subtracting equal quantities from both sides, or multiplying or dividing both sides by the same quantity—without changing its solutions. But, of course, we can obtain even more information to guide the generator by comparing the original expression with the form of the solution, and making precisely those changes in the equation that leave its solution unchanged, while at the same time bringing it into the desired form. Such a generator could notice that there was an unwanted cx on the right-hand side of the original equation, subtract it from both sides, and collect terms again. It could then notice that there was an unwanted b on the left-hand side and subtract that. Finally, it could get rid of the unwanted coefficient $(a-c)$ on the left-hand side by dividing.

Thus, by this procedure, which now exhibits considerable intelligence, the generator produces successive symbol structures, each obtained by modifying the previous one; and the modifications are aimed at reducing the differences between the form of the input structure and the form of the test expression, while maintaining the other conditions for a solution.

This simple example already illustrates many of the main mechanisms that are used by symbol systems for intelligent problem solving. First, each successive expression is not generated independently, but is produced by modifying one produced previously. Second, the modifications are not haphazard, but depend upon two kinds of information. They depend on information that is constant over this whole class of algebra problems, and that is built into the structure of the generator itself: all modifications of expressions must leave the equation's solution unchanged. They also depend on information that changes at each step: detection of the differences in form that remain between the current expression and the desired expression. In effect, the generator incorporates some of the tests the solution must satisfy, so that expressions that don't meet these tests will never be generated. Using the first kind of information guarantees that only a tiny subset of all possible expressions is actually generated, but without losing the solution expression from this subset. Using the second kind of information arrives at the desired solution by a succession of approximations, employing a simple form of means-ends analysis to give direction to the search.

There is no mystery where the information that guided the search came from. We need not follow Plato in endowing the symbol system with a previous existence in which it already knew the solution. A moderately sophisticated generate-and-test system did the trick without invoking reincarnation.

SEARCH TREES. The simple algebra problem may seem an unusual, even pathological, example of search. It is certainly not trial-and-error search, for though there were a few trials, there was no error. We are more accustomed to thinking of problem-solving search as generating lushly branching trees of partial solution possibilities which may grow to thousands, or even millions, of branches, before they yield a solution. Thus, if from each expression it produces, the generator creates B new branches, then the tree will grow as B^D, where D is its depth. The tree grown for the algebra problem had the peculiarity that its branchiness, B, equaled unity.

Programs that play chess typically grow broad search trees, amounting in some cases to a million branches or more. Although this example will serve to illustrate our points about tree search, we should note that the purpose of search in chess is not to generate proposed solutions, but to evaluate (test) them. One line of research into game-playing programs has been centrally concerned with improving the representation of the chess board, and the processes for making moves on it, so as to speed up search and make it possible to search larger trees. The rationale for this direction, of course, is that the deeper the dynamic search, the more accurate should be the evaluations at the end of it. On the other hand, there is good empirical evidence that the strongest human players, grandmasters, seldom explore trees of more than one hundred branches. This economy is achieved not so much by searching less deeply than do chess-playing programs, but by branching very sparsely and selectively at each node. This is only possible, without causing a deterioration of the evaluations, by having more of the selectivity built into the generator itself, so that it is able to select for generation only those branches which are very likely to yield important relevant information about the position.

The somewhat paradoxical-sounding conclusion to which this discussion leads is that search—successive generation of potential solution structures—is a fundamental aspect of a symbol system's exercise of intelligence in problem solving but that the amount of search is not a measure of the amount of intelligence being exhibited. What makes a problem a problem is not that a large amount of search is required for its solution, but that a large amount *would* be required if a requisite level of intelligence were not applied. When the symbolic system that is endeavoring to solve a problem knows enough about what to do, it simply proceeds directly towards its goal; but whenever its knowledge becomes inadequate, when it enters terra incognita, it is faced with the threat of going through large amounts of search before it finds its way again.

The potential for the exponential explosion of the search tree that is present in every scheme for generating problem solutions warns us against depending on the brute force of computers—even the biggest and fastest computers—as a compensation for the ignorance and unselectivity of their generators. The hope is still periodically ignited in some human breasts that a computer can be found that is fast enough, and that can be programmed cleverly enough, to play good chess by brute-force search. There is nothing known in theory about the game of chess that rules out this possibility. But empirical studies on the management of search in sizable trees with only modest results make this a much less promising direction than it was when chess was first chosen as an appropriate task for artificial intelligence. We must regard this as one of the important empirical findings of research with chess programs.

THE FORMS OF INTELLIGENCE. The task of intelligence, then, is to avert the ever-present threat of the exponential explosion of search. How can this be accomplished? The first route, already illustrated by the algebra example and by chess programs that only generate "plausible" moves for further analysis, is to build selectivity into the generator: to generate only structures that show promise of being solutions or of being along the path toward solutions. The usual consequence of doing this is to decrease the rate of branching, not to prevent it entirely. Ultimate exponential explosion is not avoided—save in exceptionally highly structured situations like the algebra example—but only postponed. Hence, an intelligent system generally needs to supplement the selectivity of its solution generator with other information-using techniques to guide search.

Twenty years of experience with managing tree search in a variety of task environments has produced a small kit of general techniques which is part of the equipment of every researcher in artificial intelligence today. Since these techniques have been described in general works like that of Nilsson (1971), they can be summarized very briefly here.

In serial heuristic search, the basic question always is: What shall be done next? In tree search, that question, in turn, has two components: (1) From what node in the tree shall we search next, and (2) What direction shall we take from that node? Information helpful in answering the first question may be interpreted as measuring the relative distance of different nodes from the goal. Best-first search calls for searching next from the node that appears closest to the goal. Information helpful in answering the second question—in what direction to search—is often obtained, as in the algebra example, by detecting specific differences between the current nodal structure and the goal structure described by the test of a solution, and selecting actions that are relevant to reducing these particular kinds of differences. This is the technique known as means-ends analysis, which plays a central role in the structure of the General Problem Solver.

The importance of empirical studies as a source of general ideas in AI research can be demonstrated clearly by tracing the history, through large numbers of problem-solving programs, of these two central ideas: best-first search and means-ends analysis. Rudiments of best-first search were already present, though unnamed, in the Logic Theorist in 1955. The General Problem Solver, embodying means-ends analysis, appeared about 1957—but combined it with modified depth-first search rather than best-first search. Chess programs were generally wedded, for reasons of economy of memory, to depth-first search, supplemented after about 1958 by the powerful alpha-beta pruning procedure. Each of these techniques appears to have been reinvented a number of times, and it is hard to find general, task-independent, theoretical discussions of problem-solving in terms of these concepts until the middle or late 1960's. The amount of formal buttressing they have received from mathematical theory is still minuscule: some theorems about the reduction in search that can be secured from using the alpha-beta heuristic, a couple of theorems (reviewed by Nilsson 1971) about shortest-path search, and some very recent theorems on best-first search with a probabilistic evaluation function.

"WEAK" AND "STRONG" METHODS. The techniques we have been discussing are dedicated to the control of exponential expansion rather than its prevention. For this reason, they have been properly called "weak methods"—methods to be used when the symbol system's knowledge or the amount of structure actually contained in the problem space are inadequate to permit search to be avoided entirely. It is instructive to contrast a highly-structured situation, which can be formulated, say, as a linear-programming problem, with the less-structured situations of combinatorial problems like the traveling-salesman problem or scheduling problems. ("Less structured" here refers to the insufficiency or nonexistence of relevant theory about the structure of the problem space.)

In solving linear-programming problems, a substantial amount of computation may be required, but the search does not branch. Every step is a step along the way to a solution. In solving combinatorial problems or in proving theorems, tree search can seldom be avoided, and success depends on heuristic search methods of the sort we have been describing.

Not all streams of AI problem-solving research have followed the path we have been outlining. An example of a somewhat different point is provided by the work on theorem-proving systems. Here, ideas imported from mathematics and logic have had a strong influence on the direction of inquiry. For example, the use of heuristics was resisted when properties of completeness could not be proved (a bit ironic, since most interesting mathematical systems are known to be undecidable). Since completeness can seldom be proved for best-first search heuristics, or for many kinds of selective generators, the effect of this requirement was rather inhibiting. When theorem-proving programs were continually incapacitated by the combinatorial explosion of their search trees, thought began to be given to selective heuristics, which in many cases proved to be analogues of heuristics used in general problem-solving programs. The set-of-support heuristic, for example, is a form of working backward, adapted to the resolution theorem-proving environment.

A SUMMARY OF THE EXPERIENCE. We have now described the workings of our second law of qualitative structure, which asserts that physical symbol systems solve problems by means of heuristic search. Beyond that, we have examined some subsidiary characteristics of heuristic search, in particular the threat that it always faces of exponential explosion of the search tree, and some of the means it uses to avert that threat. Opinions differ as to how effective heuristic search has been as a problem-solving mechanism—the opinions depending on what task domains are considered and what criterion of adequacy is adopted. Success can be guaranteed by setting aspiration levels low—or failure by setting them high. The evidence might be summed up about as follows: Few programs are solving problems at "expert" professional levels. Samuel's checker program and Feigenbaum and Lederberg's DENDRAL are perhaps the best-known exceptions, but one could point also to a number of heuristic search programs for such operations-research problem domains as scheduling and integer programming. In a number of domains, programs perform at the level of competent amateurs: chess, some theorem-proving domains, many kinds of games and puzzles. Human levels have not yet been nearly reached by programs that have a complex perceptual "front end": visual-scene recognizers, speech understanders, robots that have to maneuver in real space and time. Nevertheless, impressive progress has been made, and a large body of experience assembled about these difficult tasks.

We do not have deep theoretical explanations for the particular pattern of performance that has emerged. On empirical grounds, however, we might draw two conclusions. First, from what has been learned about human expert performance in tasks like chess, it is likely that any system capable of matching that performance will have to have access, in its memories, to very large stores of semantic information. Second, some part of the human superiority in tasks with a large perceptual component can be attributed to the special-purpose built-in parallel-processing structure of the human eye and ear.

In any case, the quality of performance must necessarily depend on the characteristics both of the problem domains and of the symbol systems used to tackle them. For most real-life domains in which we are interested, the domain structure has so far not proved sufficiently simple to yield theorems about complexity, or to tell us, other than empirically, how large real-world problems are in relation to the abilities of our symbol systems to solve them. That situation may change, but until it does, we must rely upon empirical explorations, using the best problem solvers we know how to build, as a principal source of knowledge about the magnitude and characteristics of problem difficulty. Even in highly structured areas like linear programming, theory has been much more useful in strengthening the heuristics that underlie the most powerful solution algorithms than in providing a deep analysis of complexity.

2.3 Intelligence without much search

Our analysis of intelligence equated it with ability to extract and use information about the structure of the problem space, so as to enable a problem solution to be generated as quickly and directly as possible. New directions for improving the problem-solving capabilities of symbol systems can be equated, then, with new ways of extracting and using information. At least three such ways can be identified.

NONLOCAL USE OF INFORMATION. First, it has been noted by several investigators that information gathered in the course of tree search is usually only used *locally*, to help make decisions at the specific node where the information was generated. Information about a chess position, obtained by dynamic analysis of a subtree of continuations, is usually used to evaluate just that position, not to evaluate other positions that may contain many of the same features. Hence, the same facts have to be rediscovered repeatedly at different nodes of the search tree. Simply to take the information out of the context in which it arose and use it generally does not solve the problem, for the information may be valid only in a limited range of contexts. In recent years, a few exploratory efforts have been made to transport information from its context of origin to other appropriate contexts. While it is still too early to evaluate the power of this idea, or even exactly how it is to be achieved, it shows considerable promise. An important line of investigation that Berliner (1975) has been pursuing is to use causal analysis to determine the range over which a particular piece of information is valid. Thus if a weakness in a chess position can be traced back to the move that made it, then the same weakness can be expected in other positions descendant from the same move.

The HEARSAY speech understanding system has taken another approach to making information globally available. That system seeks to recognize speech strings by pursuing a parallel search at a number of different levels: phonemic, lexical, syntactic, and semantic. As each of these searches provides and evaluates hypotheses, it supplies the information it has gained to a common "blackboard" that can be read by all the sources. This shared information can be used, for example, to eliminate hypotheses, or even whole classes of hypotheses, that would otherwise have to be searched by one of the processes. Thus increasing our ability to use tree-search information nonlocally offers promise for rasing the intelligence of problem-solving systems.

SEMANTIC RECOGNITION SYSTEMS. A second active possibility for raising intelligence is to supply the symbol system with a rich body of semantic information about the task domain it is dealing with. For example, empirical research on the skill of chess masters shows that a major source of the master's skill is stored information that enables him to recognize a large number of specific features and patterns of features on a chess board, and information that uses this recognition to propose actions appropriate to the features recognized. This general idea has, of course, been incorporated in chess programs almost from the beginning. What is new is the realization of the number of such patterns and associated information that may have to be stored for master-level play: something on the order of 50,000.

The possibility of substituting recognition for search arises because a particular, and especially a rare, pattern can contain an enormous

amount of information, provided that it is closely linked to the structure of the problem space. When that structure is "irregular", and not
subject to simple mathematical description, then knowledge of a large
number of relevant patterns may be the key to intelligent behavior.
Whether this is so in any particular task domain is a question more
easily settled by empirical investigation than by theory. Our experience
with symbol systems richly endowed with semantic information and
pattern-recognizing capabilities for accessing it is still extremely limited.

The discussion above refers specifically to semantic information
associated with a recognition system. Of course, there is also a whole
large area of AI research on semantic information processing and the
organization of semantic memories that falls outside the scope of the
topics we are discussing in this paper.*

SELECTING APPROPRIATE REPRESENTATIONS. A third line of inquiry
is concerned with the possibility that search can be reduced or avoided
by selecting an appropriate problem space. A standard example that
illustrates this possibility dramatically is the mutilated-checkerboard
problem. A standard 64-square checker board can be covered exactly
with 32 tiles, each a 1 x 2 rectangle covering exactly two squares. Suppose, now, that we cut off squares at two diagonally opposite corners of
the checkerboard, leaving a total of 62 squares. Can this mutilated
board be covered exactly with 31 tiles? With (literally) heavenly
patience, the impossibility of achieving such a covering can be demonstrated by trying all possible arrangements. The alternative, for those
with less patience and more intelligence, is to observe that the two
diagonally opposite corners of a checkerboard are of the same color.
Hence, the mutilated checkerboard has two fewer squares of one color
than of the other. But each tile covers one square of one color and one
square of the other, and any set of tiles must cover the same number of
squares of each color. Hence, there is no solution. How can a symbol
system discover this simple inductive argument as an alternative to a
hopeless attempt to solve the problem by search among all possible
coverings? We would award a system that found the solution high
marks for intelligence.

---

* *Editor's note*: Much of the research described in chapters 5 and 6 of this
  volume falls in the category mentioned here.

Perhaps, however, in posing this problem we are not escaping from search processes. We have simply displaced the search from a space of possible problems solutions to a space of possible representations. In any event, the whole process of moving from one representation to another, and of discovering and evaluating representations, is largely unexplored territory in the domain of problem-solving research. The laws of qualitative structure governing representations remain to be discovered. The search for them is almost sure to receive considerable attention in the coming decade.

2.4 Conclusion

That is our account of symbol systems and intelligence. It has been a long road from Plato's *Meno* to the present, but it is perhaps encouraging that most of the progress along that road has been made since the turn of the twentieth century, and a large fraction of it since the midpoint of the century. Thought was still wholly intangible and ineffable until modern formal logic interpreted it as the manipulation of formal tokens. And it seemed still to inhabit mainly the heaven of Platonic ideas, or the equally obscure spaces of the human mind, until computers taught us how symbols could be processed by machines. A. M. Turing made his great contributions at the mid-century crossroads of these developments that led from modern logic to the computer.

PHYSICAL SYMBOL SYSTEMS. The study of logic and computers has revealed to us that intelligence resides in physical-symbol systems. This is computer science's most basic law of qualitative structure.

Symbol systems are collections of patterns and processes, the latter being capable of producing, destroying, and modifying the former. The most important properties of patterns is that they can designate objects, processes, or other patterns, and that when they designate processes, they can be interpreted. Interpretation means carrying out the designated process. The two most significant classes of symbol systems with which we are acquainted are human beings and computers.

Our present understanding of symbol systems grew, as indicated earlier, through a sequence of stages. Formal logic familiarized us with symbols, treated syntactically, as the raw material of thought, and with the idea of manipulating them according to carefully defined formal processes. The Turing machine made the syntactic processing of symbols truly machine-like, and affirmed the potential universality of strictly defined symbol systems. The stored-program concept for computers reaffirmed the interpretability of symbols, already implicit in the Turing machine. List processing brought to the forefront the denotational capacities of symbols and defined symbol processing in ways that allowed independence from the fixed structure of the underlying physical machine. By 1956 all of these concepts were available, together with hardware for implementing them. The study of the intelligence of symbol systems, the subject of artificial intelligence, could begin.

HEURISTIC SEARCH. A second law of qualitative structure of AI is that symbol systems solve problems by generating potential solutions and testing them—that is, by searching. Solutions are usually sought by creating symbolic expressions and modifying them sequentially until they satisfy the conditions for a solution. Hence, symbol systems solve problems by searching. Since they have finite resources, the search cannot be carried out all at once, but must be sequential. It leaves behind it either a single path from starting point to goal or, if correction and backup are necessary, a whole tree of such paths.

Symbol systems cannot appear intelligent when they are surrounded by pure chaos. They exercise intelligence by extracting information from a problem domain and using that information to guide their search, avoiding wrong turns and circuitous by-paths. The problem domain must contain information—that is, some degree of order and structure—for the method to work. The paradox of the *Meno* is solved by the observation that information may be remembered, but new information may also be extracted from the domain that the symbols designate. In both cases, the ultimate source of the information is the task domain.

THE EMPIRICAL BASE. Research on artificial intelligence is concerned with how symbol systems must be organized in order to behave intelligently. Twenty years of work in the area has accumulated a considerable body of knowledge, enough to fill several books (it already has), and most of it in the form of rather concrete experience about the behavior of specific classes of symbol systems in specific task domains. Out of this experience, however, there have also emerged some generalizations, cutting across task domains and systems, about the general characteristics of intelligence and its methods of implementation.

We have tried to state some of these generalizations here. They are mostly qualitative rather than mathematical. They have more the flavor of geology or evolutionary biology than the flavor of theoretical physics. They are sufficiently strong to enable us today to design and build moderately intelligent systems for a considerable range of task domains, as well as to gain a rather deep understanding of how human intelligence works in many situations.

WHAT NEXT? In our account we have mentioned open questions as well as settled ones; there are many of both. We see no abatement of the excitement of exploration that has surrounded this field over the past quarter century. Two resource limits will determine the rate of progress over the next such period. One is the amount of computing power that will be available. The second, and probably the more important, is the number of talented young computer scientists who will be attracted to this area of research as the most challenging they can tackle.

A. M. Turing concluded his famous paper "Computing Machinery and Intelligence" [chapter 2 of this volume] with the words:

> We can only see a short distance ahead, but we can see plenty there that needs to be done.

Many of the things Turing saw in 1950 that needed to be done have been done, but the agenda is as full as ever. Perhaps we read too much into his simple statement above, but we like to think that in it Turing recognized the fundamental truth that all computer scientists instinctively know. For all physical symbol systems, condemned as we are to serial search of the problem environment, the critical question is always: What to do next?

A Framework for Representing Knowledge

Marvin Minsky
1974

1 Frames

It seems to me that the ingredients of most theories both in artificial intelligence and in psychology have been on the whole too minute, local, and unstructured to account—either practically or phenomeno-logically—for the effectiveness of common-sense thought. The "chunks" of reasoning, language, memory, and perception ought to be larger and more structured; their factual and procedural contents must be more intimately connected in order to explain the apparent power and speed of mental activities.

Similar feelings seem to be emerging in several centers working on theories of intelligence. They take one form in the proposal of Papert and myself (1972) to divide knowledge into substructures, "micro-worlds". Another form is in the "problem spaces" of Newell and Simon (1972), and yet another is in the new, large structures that theorists like Schank (1973), Abelson (1973), and Norman (1973) assign to linguistic objects. I see all these as moving away from the traditional attempts both by behavioristic psychologists and by logic-oriented students of Artificial Intelligence in trying to represent knowledge as collections of separate, simple fragments.

I try here to bring together several of these issues by pretending to have a unified, coherent theory. The paper raises more questions than it answers, and I have tried to note the theory's deficiencies.

Here is the essence of the theory: when one encounters a new situation (or makes a substantial change in one's view of the present problem), one selects from memory a structure called a *frame*. This is a remembered framework to be adapted to fit reality by changing details as necessary

A *frame* is a data structure for representing a stereotyped situation, like being in a certain kind of living room, or going to a child's birthday party. Attached to each frame are several kinds of information. Some of this information is about how to use the frame. Some is about what one can expect to happen next. Some is about what to do if these expectations are not confirmed.

We can think of a frame as a network of nodes and relations. The top levels of a frame are fixed, and represent things that are always true about the supposed situation. The lower levels have many *terminals*— slots that must be filled by specific instances or data. Each terminal can specify conditions its assignments must meet. (The assignments themselves are usually smaller subframes.) Simple conditions are specified by *markers* that might require a terminal assignment to be a person, an object of sufficient value, or a pointer to a subframe of a certain type. More complex conditions can specify relations among the things assigned to several terminals.

Collections of related frames are linked together into *frame systems*. The effects of the important actions are mirrored by *transformations* between the frames of a system. These are used to make certain kinds of calculations economical, to represent changes of emphasis and attention, and to account for the effectiveness of imagery.

For visual scene analysis, the different frames of a system describe the scene from different viewpoints, and the transformations between one frame and another represent the effects of moving from place to place. For nonvisual kinds of frames, the differences between the frames of a system can represent actions, cause-effect relations, or changes in conceptual viewpoint. *Different frames of a system share the same terminals*; this is the critical point that makes it possible to coordinate information gathered from different viewpoints.

Much of the phenomenological power of the theory hinges on the inclusion of expectations and other kinds of presumptions. A *frame's terminals are normally already filled with "default" assignments.* Thus a frame may contain a great many details whose supposition is not specifically warranted by the situation. These have many uses in representing general information, most likely cases, techniques for bypassing "logic", and ways to make useful generalizations.

The default assignments are attached loosely to their terminals, so that they can be easily displaced by new items that better fit the current situation. They thus can serve also as variables or as special cases for reasoning by example, or as textbook cases, and often make the use of logical quantifiers unnecessary.

The frame systems are linked, in turn, by an *information retrieval network*. When a proposed frame cannot be made to fit reality—when we cannot find terminal assignments that suitably match its terminal marker conditions—this network provides a replacement frame. These interframe structures make possible other ways to represent knowledge about facts, analogies, and other information useful in understanding.

Once a frame is proposed to represent a situation, a *matching* process tries to assign values to each frame's terminals, consistent with the markers at each place. The matching process is partly controlled by information associated with the frame (which includes information about how to deal with surprises) and partly by knowledge about the system's current goals. There are important uses for the information, obtained when a matching process fails. I will discuss how it can be used to select an alternative frame that better suits the situation.

An apology: the schemes proposed herein are incomplete in many respects. First, I often propose representations without specifying the processes that will use them. Sometimes I only describe properties the structures should exhibit. I talk about markers and assignments as though it were obvious how they are attached and linked; it is not.

Besides the technical gaps, I will talk as though unaware of many problems related to "understanding" that really need much deeper analysis. I do not claim that the ideas proposed here are enough for a complete theory, only that the frame-system scheme may help explain a number of phenomena of human intelligence. The basic frame idea itself is not particularly original—it is in the tradition of the "schemata" of Bartlett and the "paradigms" of Kuhn; the idea of a frame-system is probably more novel. Winograd (1974) discusses the recent trend, in theories of AI, toward frame-like ideas.

In the body of the paper I discuss different kinds of reasoning by analogy, and ways to impose stereotypes on reality and jump to conclusions based on partial-similarity matching. These are basically uncertain methods. Why not use methods that are more logical and certain? Section 6 is a sort of appendix which argues that traditional logic cannot deal very well with realistic, complicated problems because it is poorly suited to represent *approximations* to solutions—and these are absolutely vital.

> Thinking always begins with suggestive but imperfect plans and images; these are progressively replaced by better—but usually still imperfect—ideas.

1.3* Artificial intelligence and human problem solving

In this essay I draw no boundary between a theory of human thinking and a scheme for making an intelligent machine; no purpose would be served by separating them today, since neither domain has theories good enough to explain, or produce, enough mental capacity. There is, however, a difference in professional attitudes. Workers from psychology inherit stronger desires to minimize the variety of assumed mechanisms. I believe this leads to attempts to extract more performance from fewer "basic mechanisms" than is reasonable. Such theories especially neglect mechanisms of procedure control and explicit representations of processes. On the other side, workers in AI have perhaps focused too sharply on just such questions. Neither has given enough attention to the structure of knowledge, especially procedural knowledge.

It is understandable that psychologists are uncomfortable with complex proposals not based on well established mechanisms, but I believe that parsimony is still inappropriate at this stage, valuable as it may be in later phases of every science. There is room in the anatomy and genetics of the brain for much more mechanism than anyone today is prepared to propose, and we should concentrate for a while longer on *sufficiency* and *efficiency* rather than on *necessity*.

1.11 Default assignment

Although both seeing and imagining result in assignments to frame terminals, imagination leaves us wider choices of detail and variety of such assignments. I conjecture that frames are never stored in long-term memory with unassigned terminal values. Instead, what really happens is that frames are stored with weakly bound default assignments at every terminal! These manifest themselves as often-useful but sometimes counterproductive stereotypes.

Thus if I say, "John kicked the ball", you probably cannot think of a purely abstract ball, but must imagine characteristics of a vaguely particular ball; it probably has a certain default size, default color, default weight. Perhaps it is a descendant of one you first owned or were injured by. Perhaps it resembles your latest one. In any case your image lacks the sharpness of presence because the processes that

---

* *Editor's note:* Section numbers have been retained from the original tech report, and hence are not always sequential in this abridged edition.

inspect and operate upon the weakly bound default features are very likely to change, adapt, or detach them.

Such default assignments would have subtle, idiosyncratic influences on the paths an individual would tend to follow in making analogies, generalizations, and judgements, especially when the exterior influences on such choices are weak. Properly chosen, such stereotypes could serve as a storehouse of valuable heuristic plan skeletons; badly selected, they could form paralyzing collections of irrational biases. Because of them, one might expect, as reported by Freud, to detect evidences of early cognitive structures in free-association thinking.

2 Language, understanding, and scenarios

2.1 Words, sentences, and meanings

> The device of images has several defects that are the price of its peculiar excellences. Two of these are perhaps the most important: the image, and particularly the visual image, is apt to go farther in the direction of the individualisation of situations than is biologically useful; and the principles of the combination of images have their own peculiarities and result in constructions which are relatively wild, jerky, and irregular, compared with the straightforward unwinding of a habit, or with the somewhat orderly march of thought.   (Bartlett 1932/61)

The concepts of frame and default assignment seem helpful in discussing the phenomenology of "meaning". Chomsky (1957) points out that such a sentence as

   (A) colorless green ideas sleep furiously

is treated very differently from the nonsentence

   (B) furiously sleep ideas green colorless

and suggests that because both are "equally nonsensical", what is involved in the recognition of sentences must be quite different from what is involved in the appreciation of meanings.

There is no doubt that there are processes especially concerned with grammar. Since the meaning of an utterance is encoded as much in the positional and structural relations between the words as in the word choices themselves, there must be processes concerned with analyzing those relations in the course of building the structures that will more directly represent the meaning. What makes the words of (A) more effective and predictable than (B) in producing such a structure—putting aside the question of whether that structure should be called semantic or syntactic—is that the word-order relations in (A) exploit the (grammatical) conventions and rules people usually use to induce others to make assignments to terminals of structures. This is entirely consistent with theories of grammar. A generative grammar would be a summary description of the *exterior* appearance of those frame rules— or their associated processes—while the operators of transformational grammars seem similar enough to some of our frame transformations.

But one must also ask: to what degree does grammar have a separate identity in the actual working of a human mind? Perhaps the rejection of an utterance (either as ungrammatical, as nonsensical, or, most important, as *not understood*) indicates a more complex failure of the semantic process to arrive at any usable representation; I will argue now that the grammar/meaning distinction may illuminate two extremes of a continuum but obscures its all-important interior.

We certainly cannot assume that logical meaninglessness has a precise psychological counterpart. Sentence (A) can certainly generate an image! The dominate frame (in my case) is that of someone sleeping; the default system assigns a particular bed, and in it lies a mummy-like shape-frame with a translucent green color property. In this frame there is a terminal for the character of the sleep—restless, perhaps— and 'furiously' seems somewhat inappropriate at that terminal, perhaps because the terminal does not like to accept anything so "intentional" for a sleeper. 'Idea' is even more disturbing, because a person is expected, or a least something animate. I sense frustrated procedures trying to resolve these tensions and conflicts more properly, here or there, into the sleeping framework that has been evoked.

Utterance (B) does not get nearly so far because no subframe accepts any substantial fragment. As a result, no larger frame finds anything to match its terminals, hence, finally, no top level "meaning" or "sentence" frame can organize the utterance as either meaningful or grammatical. By combining this "soft" theory with gradations of assignment tolerances, I imagine one could develop systems that degrade properly for sentences with poor grammar rather than none; if the smaller fragments—phrases and subclauses—satisfy subframes well enough, an image adequate for certain kinds of comprehension could be constructed anyway, even though some parts of the top level structure are not entirely satisfied. Thus we arrive at a qualitative theory of "grammatical": *if the top levels are satisfied but some lower terminals are not, we have a meaningless sentence; if the top is weak but the bottom solid, we can have an ungrammatical but meaningful utterance.*

I do not mean to suggest that sentences must evoke visual images. Some people do not admit to assigning a color to the ball in "He kicked the ball." But everyone admits (eventually) to having assumed, if not a size or color, at least some purpose, attitude, or other elements of an assumed scenario. When we go beyond vision, terminals and their default assignments can represent purposes and functions, not just colors, sizes, and shapes.

2.6 Scenarios

Thinking ... is biologically subsequent to the image-forming process. It is possible only when a way has been found of breaking up the "massed" influence of past stimuli and situations, only when a device has already been discovered for conquering the sequential tyranny of past reactions. But though it is a later and a higher development, it does not supercede the method of images. It has its own drawbacks. Contrasted with imagining it loses something of vivacity, of vividness, of variety. Its prevailing instruments are words, and, not only because these are social, but also because in use they are necessarily strung out in sequence, they drop into habit reactions even more readily than images do. [With thinking] we run greater and greater risk of being caught up in generalities that may have little to do with actual concrete experience. If we fail to maintain the methods of thinking, we run the risks of becoming tied to individual instances and of being made sport of by the accidental circumstances belonging to these.   (Bartlett 1932/61)

We condense and conventionalize, in language and thought, complex situations and sequences into compact words and symbols. Some words can perhaps be "defined" in elegant, simple structures, but only a small part of the meaning of "trade" is captured by:

(first frame)   (second frame)

| A has X   B has Y | $\longrightarrow$ | B has X   A has Y |

Trading normally occurs in a social context of law, trust, and convention. Unless we also represent these other facts, most trade transactions will be almost meaningless. It is usually essential to know that each party usually wants both things but has to compromise. It is a happy but unusual circumstance in which each trader is glad to get rid of what he has. To represent trading strategies, one could insert the basic maneuvers right into the above frame-pair scenario: in order for A to make B want X more (or want Y less) we expect him to select one of the familiar tactics:

- Offer more for Y.
- Explain why X is so good.
- Create favorable side-effect of B having X.
- Disparage the competition.
- Make B think C wants X.

These only scratch the surface. Trades usually occur within a scenario tied together by more than a simple chain of events each linked to the next. No single such scenario will do; when a clue about trading appears, it is essential to guess which of the different available scenarios is most likely to be useful.

Charniak's thesis (1972) studies questions about transactions that seem easy for people to comprehend yet obviously need rich default structures. We find in elementary school reading books such stories as:

> Jane was invited to Jack's birthday party.
> She wondered if he would like a kite.
> She went to her room and shook her piggy bank.
> It made no sound.

Most young readers understand that Jane wants money to buy Jack a kite for a present but that there is no money to pay for it in her piggy bank. Charniak proposes a variety of ways to facilitate such inferences—a "demon" for 'present' that looks for things concerned with money, a demon for 'piggy bank' which knows that shaking without sound means the bank is empty, and so on. But although 'present' now activates 'money', the reader may be surprised to find that neither of those words (nor any of their synonyms) occurs in the story. 'Present' is certainly associated with 'party' and 'money' with 'bank', but how are the longer chains built up? Here is another problem raised by Charniak. A friend tells Jane:

> He already has a Kite.
> He will make you take it back.

Take *which* kite back? We do not want Jane to return Jack's old kite. To determine the referent of the pronoun 'it' requires understanding a lot about an assumed scenario. Clearly, 'it' refers to the proposed *new* kite. How does one know this? (Note that we need not agree on any single explanation.) Generally, pronouns refer to recently mentioned things, but as this example shows, the referent depends on more than the local syntax.

Suppose for the moment we are already trying to instantiate a "buying-a-present" default subframe. Now, the word 'it' alone is too small a fragment to deal with, but 'take it back' could be a plausible unit to match a terminal of an appropriately elaborate 'buying' scenario. Since that terminal would be constrained to agree with the assignment of 'present' itself, we are assured of the correct meaning of 'it' in 'take X back'. Automatically, the correct kite is selected. Of course, that terminal will have its own constraints as well; a subframe for the 'take-it-back' idiom should know that 'take X back' requires that:

- X was recently purchased.
- The return is to the place of purchase.
- You must have your sales slip.

And so on.

If the current scenario does not contain a 'take-it-back' terminal, then we have to find one that does and substitute it, maintaining as many prior assignments as possible. Notice that if things go well, the question of it being the old kite never even arises. *The sense of ambiguity arises only when a "near miss" mismatch is tried and rejected.*

Charniak's proposed solution to this problem is in the same spirit but emphasizes understanding that, because Jack already has a kite, he may not want another one. He proposes a mechanism associated with 'present':

(A) If we see that person P might not like a present X, then look for X being returned to the store where it was bought.

(B) If we see this happening, or even being suggested, assert that the reason why is that P does not like X.

This statement of "advice" is intended by Charniak to be realized as a production-like entity, to be added to the currently active data base whenever a certain kind of context is encountered. Later, if its antecedent condition is satisfied, its action adds enough information about Jack and about the new kite to lead to a correct decision about the pronoun.

Charniak in effect proposes that the system should watch for certain kinds of events or situations and inject proposed reasons, motives, and explanations for them. The additional interconnections between the story elements are expected to help bridge the gaps that logic might find it hard to cross, because the additions are only "plausible" default explanations, assumed without corroborative assertions. By assuming (tentatively) "does not like X" when X is taken back, Charniak hopes to simulate much of ordinary "comprehension" of what is happening. We do not yet know how complex and various such plausible inferences must be to get a given level of performance, and the thesis does not answer this because it did not include a large simulation. Usually he proposes terminating the process by asserting the allegedly plausible motive without further analysis unless necessary. To understand why Jack might return the additional kite, it should usually be enough to assert that he does not like it. A deeper analysis might reveal that Jack would not really mind having two kites but he probably realizes that he will get only one present; his utility for two different presents is probably higher.

2.7 Scenarios and "questions"

The meaning of a child's birthday party is very poorly approximated by any dictionary definition like "a party assembled to celebrate a birthday", where a party would be defined, in turn, as "people assembled for a celebration". This lacks all the flavor of the culturally required activities. Children know that the "definition" should include more specifications, the particulars of which can normally be assumed by way of default assignments:

Dress .... Sunday best.

Present .... Must please host.
                       Must be bought and gift wrapped.

Games .... Hide and seek; pin tail on donkey.

Decor .... Balloons, favors, crepe-paper.

Party-meal .... Cake, ice cream, soda, hot dogs.

Cake .... Candles; blow out; wish; sing birthday song.

Ice-cream .... Standard three-flavor.

These ingredients for a typical American birthday party must be set into a larger structure. Extended events take place in one or more days.

A Party takes place in a day, of course, and occupies a substantial part of it, so we locate it in an appropriate Day frame. A typical day has main events, such as:

Get-up   Dress   Eat-1   Go-to-Work   Eat-2

but a School-Day has more fixed detail:

Get-up Dress
    Eat-1   Go-to-School   Be-in-School
       Home-Room   Assembly   English   Math (arrgh)
    Eat-2   Science   Recess   Sport
      Go-Home   Play
    Eat-3   Homework
Go-To-Bed

Birthday parties obviously do not fit well into school-day frames. Any parent knows that the Party-Meal is bound to Eat-2 of its Day. I remember a child who did not seem to realize this. Absolutely stuffed after the Party-Meal, he asked when he would get Lunch.

Returning to Jane's problem with the kite, we first hear that she is invited to Jack's birthday party. Without this party scenario, or at least an invitation scenario, the second line seems rather mysterious:

She wondered if he would like a kite.

To explain one's rapid comprehension of this, I will make a somewhat radical proposal: *to represent explicitly, in the frame for a scenario structure, pointers to a collection of the most serious problems and questions commonly associated with it.* In fact, we shall consider the idea that the frame terminals are exactly those questions. Thus, for the birthday party:

Y must get P for X .... Choose P!

X must like P .... Will X like P?

Buy P .... Where to buy P?

    Get money to buy P ..... Where to get money?
                    (Sub-question of the Buy frame?)

Y must dress up .... What should Y wear?

Certainly these are one's first concerns, when one is invited to a party.

The reader is free to wonder, with the author, whether this solution is acceptable. The question, "Will X like P?" certainly matches "She wondered if he would like a kite?" and correctly assigns the kite to P.

But is our world regular enough that such question sets could be pre-compiled to make this mechanism often work smoothly? I think the answer is mixed. We do indeed expect many such questions; we surely do not expect all of them. But surely "expertise" consists partly in not having to realize *ab initio* what are the outstanding problems and interactions in situations. Notice, for example, that there is *no* default assignment for the Present in our party-scenario frame. This mandates attention to that assignment problem and prepares us for a possible thematic concern. In any case, we probably need a more active mechanism for understanding *"wondered"* which can apply the information currently in the frame to produce an expectation of what Jane will think about.

The third line of our story, about shaking the bank, should also eventually match one of the present-frame questions, but the unstated connection between Money and Piggy-Bank is presumably represented in the piggy-bank frame, *not* the party frame, although once it is found, it will match our Get-Money question terminal. The primary functions and actions associated with piggy banks are Saving and Getting-Money-Out, and the latter has three principal methods:

(1) Using a key.   (Most piggy banks don't offer this option.)

(2) Breaking it.   (Children hate this.)

(3) Shaking the money out, or using a thin slider.

In the fourth line, does one know specifically that a *silent* Piggy Bank is empty, and hence out of money (I think, yes), or does one use general knowledge that a hard container which makes no noise when shaken is empty? I have found quite a number of people who prefer the latter. Logically, the "general principle" would indeed suffice, but I feel that this misses the important point that a specific scenario of this character is engraved in every child's memory. The story is instantly intelligible to most readers. If more complex reasoning from general principles were required, this would not be so, and more readers would surely go astray. It is easy to find more complex problems.

> A goat wandered into the yard where Jack was painting. The goat got the paint all over himself. When Jack's mother saw the goat, she asked, "Jack, did you do *that*?"

There is no one word or line, which is the referent of "that". It seems to refer, as Charniak notes, to "cause the goat to be covered with paint". Charniak does not permit himself to make a specific proposal to handle this kind of problem, remarking only that his "demon" model would need a substantial extension to deal with such a poorly localized "thematic subject". Consider how much one has to know about our culture, to realize that *that* is not the *goat-in-the-yard* but the *goat-covered-with-paint.* Charniak's thesis—basically a study rather than a debugged system—discusses issues about the activation, operation, and dismissal of expectation and default-knowledge demons. Many of his ideas have been absorbed into this essay.

In spite of its tentative character, I will try to summarize this image of language understanding as somewhat parallel to seeing. The key words and ideas of a discourse evoke substantial thematic or scenario structures, drawn from memory with rich default assumptions. The individual statements of a discourse lead to temporary representations—which seem to correspond to what contemporary linguists call "deep structures"—which are then quickly rearranged or consumed in elaborating the growing scenario representation. In order of "scale", among the ingredients of such a structure there might be these kinds of levels:

SURFACE SYNTACTIC FRAMES. Mainly verb and noun structures. Prepositional and word-order indicator conventions.

SURFACE SEMANTIC FRAMES. Action-centered meanings of words. Qualifiers and relations concerning participants, instruments, trajectories and strategies, goals, consequences, and side-effects.

THEMATIC FRAMES. Scenarios concerned with topics, activities, portraits, setting. Outstanding problems and strategies commonly connected with topic.

NARRATIVE FRAMES. Skeleton forms for typical stories, explanations, and arguments. Conventions about foci, protagonists, plot forms, development, and so on, designed to help a listener construct a new, instantiated thematic frame in his own mind.

A single sentence can assign terminals, attach subframes, apply a transformation, or cause a gross replacement of a high-level frame when a proposed assignment no longer fits well enough. A pronoun is comprehensible only when general linguistic conventions, interacting with defaults and specific indicators, determine a terminal or subframe of the current scenario.

In *vision* the transformations usually have a simple grouplike structure; in *language* we expect more complex, less regular systems of frames. Nevertheless, because *time, cause,* and *action* are so important to us, we often use sequential transformation pairs that replace situations by their temporal or causal successors.

Because syntactic structural rules direct the selection and assembly of the transient sentence frames, research on linguistic structures should help us understand how our frame systems are constructed. One might look for such structures specifically associated with assigning terminals, selecting emphasis or attention viewpoints (transformation), inserting sentential structures into thematic structures, and changing gross thematic representations.

Finally, just as there are familiar "basic plots" for stories, there must be basic superframes for discourses, arguments, narratives, and so forth. As with sentences, we should expect to find special linguistic indicators for operations concerning these larger structures; we should move beyond the grammar of sentences to try to find and systematize the linguistic conventions that, operating across wider spans, must be involved with assembling and transforming scenarios and plans.

2.8 Questions, systems, and cases

> Questions arise from a point of view—from something that helps to structure what is problematical, what is worth asking, and what constitutes an answer (or progress). It is not that the view determines reality, only what we accept from reality and how we structure it. I am realist enough to believe that in the long run reality gets its own chance to accept or reject our various views.
>
> (Newell 1973a)

Examination of linguistic discourse leads thus to a view of the frame concept in which the "terminals" serve to represent the questions most likely to arise in a situation. To make this important viewpoint more explicit, we will spell out this reinterpretation.

> A *frame* is a collection of questions to be asked about a hypothetical situation: it specifies issues to be raised and methods to be used in dealing with them.

The terminals of a frame correspond perhaps to what Schank (1973) calls "conceptual cases", although I do not think we should restrict them to as few types as Schank suggests. To understand a narrated or perceived action, one often feels compelled to ask such questions as

- What caused it (agent)?
- What was the purpose (intention)?

- What are the consequences (side-effects)?
- Whom does it affect (recipient)?
- How is it done (instrument)?

The number of such "cases" or questions is problematical. While we would like to reduce meaning to a very few "primitive" concepts, perhaps in analogy to the situation in traditional linguistic analysis, I know of no reason to suppose that that goal can be achieved. My own inclination is to side with such workers as Martin (1974) who look toward very large collections of "primitives", annotated with comments about how they are related. Only time will tell which is better.

For entities other than actions, one asks different questions; for thematic topics the questions may be much less localized, for instance:

- Why are they telling this to me?
- How can I find out more about it?
- How will it help with the "real problem"?

In a "story" one asks what is the topic, what is the author's attitude, what is the main event, who are the protagonists, and so on. As each question is given a tentative answer, the corresponding subframes are attached and the questions they ask become active in turn.

The "markers" we proposed for vision-frames become more complex in this view. If we adopt for the moment Newell's larger sense of "view", it is not enough simply to ask a question; one must indicate how it is to be answered. Thus a terminal should also contain (or point to) suggestions and recommendations about how to find an assignment. Our "default" assignments then become the simplest special cases of such recommendations, and one certainly could have a hierarchy in which such proposals depend on features of the situation, perhaps along the lines of Wilks's (1973) "preference" structures.

For syntactic frames, the drive toward ritualistic completion of assignments is strong, but we are more flexible at the conceptual level. As Schank (1973) says:

> People do not usually state all the parts of a given thought that they are trying to communicate because the speaker tries to be brief and leaves out assumed or inessential information ... The conceptual processor makes use of the unfilled slots to search for a given type of information in a sentence or a larger unit of discourse that will fill the needed slot.

Even in physical perception we have the same situation. A box will not present all of its sides at once to an observer, and, although this is certainly not because it wants to be brief, the effect is the same; the processor is prepared to find out what the missing sides look like and (if the matter is urgent enough) to move around to find answers to such questions.

Frame *systems*, in this view, become choice points corresponding (on the conceptual level) to the mutually exclusive choice "systems" exploited by Winograd (1970). The different frames of a system represent different ways of using the same information, located at the common terminals. As in the grammatical situation, one has to choose one of them at a time. On the conceptual level this choice becomes: *what questions shall I ask about this situation?*

View changing, as we shall argue, is a problem-solving technique important in representing, explaining, and predicting. In the rearrangements inherent in the frame-system representation (for example, of an action), we have a first approximation to Simmons's (1973) idea of "procedures which in some cases will change the contextual definitional structure to reflect the action of a verb".

Where do the "questions" come from? This is not in the scope of this paper, really, but we can be sure that the frame makers (however they operate) must use some principles. The methods used to generate the questions ultimately shape each person's general intellectual style. People surely differ in details of preferences for asking "Why?", "How can I find out more?", "What's in it for me?", "How will this help with the current higher goals?", and so forth.

Similar issues about the style of *answering* must arise. In its simplest form, the drive toward instantiating empty terminals would appear as a variety of hunger or discomfort, satisfied by any default or other assignment that does not conflict with a prohibition. In more complex cases we should perceive less animalistic strategies for acquiring deeper understandings.

It is tempting, then, to imagine varieties of frame systems that span from simple template-filling structures to implementations of the "views" of Newell—with all their implications about coherent generators of issues with which to be concerned, ways to investigate them, and procedures for evaluating proposed solutions. But I feel uncomfortable about any superficially coherent synthesis in which one expects the same kind of theoretical framework to function well on many different levels of scale or concept. We should expect very different question-processing mechanisms to operate our low-level stereotypes and our most comprehensive strategic overviews.

3 Learning, memory, and paradigms

> To the child, nature gives various means of rectifying any mistakes he may commit respecting the salutary or hurtful qualities of the objects which surround him. On every occasion his judgements are corrected by experience; want and pain are the necessary consequences arising from false judgement; gratification and pleasure are produced by judging aright. Under such masters, we cannot fail but to become well informed; and we soon learn to reason justly, when want and pain are the necessary consequences of a contrary conduct.
>
> In the study and practice of the sciences it is quite different: the false judgments we form neither affect our existence nor our welfare; and we are not forced by any physical necessity to correct them. Imagination, on the contrary, which is ever wandering beyond the bounds of truth, joined to self-love and that self-confidence we are so apt to indulge, prompt us to draw conclusions that are not immediately derived from facts.   (Lavoisier 1789/1949)

How does one locate a frame to represent a new situation? Obviously, we cannot begin any complete theory outside the context of some proposed global scheme for the organization of knowledge in general. But if we imagine working within some bounded domain, we can discuss some important issues:

EXPECTATION: How to select an initial frame to meet some given conditions.

ELABORATION: How to select and assign subframes to represent additional details.

ALTERATION: How to find a frame to replace one that does not fit well enough.

NOVELTY: What to do if no acceptable frame can be found. Can we modify an old frame or must we build a new one?

LEARNING: What frames should be stored, or modified, as result of the experience?

In popular culture, memory is seen as separate from the rest of thinking; but finding the right memory—it would be better to say: finding a *useful* memory—needs the same sorts of strategies used in other kinds of thinking!

We say someone is "clever" who is unusually good at quickly locating highly appropriate frames. His information-retrieval systems are better at making good hypotheses, formulating the conditions the new frame should meet, and exploiting knowledge gained in the "unsuccessful" part of the search. Finding the right memory is no less a problem than solving any other kind of puzzle! Because of this, a good retrieval mechanism can be based only in part upon basic "innate" mechanisms. It must also depend largely on (learned) knowledge about the structure of one's own knowledge! Our proposal will combine several elements—a pattern-matching process, a clustering theory, and a similarity network.

In seeing a room or understanding a story, one assembles a network of frames and subframes. Everything noticed or guessed, rightly or wrongly, is represented in this network. We have already suggested that an active frame cannot be maintained unless its terminal conditions are satisfied.

We now add the postulate that *all satisfied frames must be assigned to terminals of superior frames.* This applies, as a special case, to any substantial fragments of "data" that have been observed and represented.

Of course, there must be an exception! We must allow a certain number of items to be attached to something like a set of "short term memory" registers. But the intention is that very little can be remembered unless embedded in a suitable frame. This, at any rate, is the conceptual scheme; in certain domains we would, of course, admit other kinds of memory "hooks" and special sensory buffers.

3.1 Requests to memory

We can now imagine the memory system as driven by two complementary needs. *On one side are items demanding to be properly represented by being embedded into larger frames; on the other side are incompletely filled frames demanding terminal assignments.* The rest of the system will try to placate these lobbyists, but not so much in accord with general principles as in accord with special knowledge and conditions imposed by the currently active goals.

When a frame encounters trouble—when an important condition cannot be satisfied—something must be done. We envision the following major kinds of accommodation to trouble:

MATCHING: When nothing more specific is found, we can attempt to use some "basic" associative memory mechanism. This will succeed by itself only in relatively simple situations, but should play a supporting role in the other tactics.

EXCUSE: An apparent misfit can often be excused or explained. A "chair" that meets all other conditions but is much too small could be a "toy".

ADVICE: The frame contains explicit knowledge about what to do about the trouble. Below, we describe an extensive, learned, "similarity network" in which to embed such knowledge.

SUMMARY: If a frame cannot be completed or replaced, one must give it up. But first one must construct a well-formulated complaint or summary to help whatever process next becomes responsible for reassigning the subframes left in limbo.

In my view, all four of these are vitally important. I discuss them in the following sections.

3.3 Excuses

We can think of a frame as describing an "ideal". If an ideal does not match reality because it is "basically" wrong, it must be replaced. *But it is in the nature of ideals that they are really elegant simplifications; their attractiveness derives from their simplicity, but their real power depends upon additional knowledge about interactions between them!* Accordingly we need not abandon an ideal because of a failure to instantiate it, provided one can explain the discrepancy in terms of such an interaction. Here are some examples in which such an "excuse" can save a failing match:

OCCLUSION: A table, in a certain view, should have four legs, but a chair might occlude one of them. One can look for things like T-joints and shadows to support such an excuse.

FUNCTIONAL VARIANT: A chair-leg is usually a stick, geometrically; but more important, it is functionally a support. Therefore, a strong center post, with an adequate base plate, should be an acceptable replacement for all the legs. Many objects are multiple purpose and need functional rather than physical descriptions.

BROKEN: A visually missing component could be explained as in fact physically missing, or it could be broken. Reality has a variety of way to frustrate ideals.

PARASITIC CONTEXTS: An object that is just like a chair, except in size, could be (and probably is) a toy chair. The complaint "too small" could often be so interpreted in contexts with other things too small, children playing, peculiarly large "grain", and so forth.

In most of these examples, the kinds of knowledge to make the repair—and thus salvage the current frame—are "general" enough usually to be attached to the thematic context of a superior frame. In the remainder of this essay, I will concentrate on types of more sharply localized knowledge that would naturally be attached to a frame itself, for recommending its own replacement.

3.5 Clusters, classes, and a geographic analogy

Though a discussion of *some* of the attributes shared by a *number* of games or chairs or leaves often helps us to learn how to employ the corresponding term, there is no set of characteristics that is simultaneously applicable to all members of the class and to them alone. Instead, confronted with a previously unobserved activity, we apply the term 'game' because what we are seeing bears a close "family resemblance" to a number of the activities we have previously learned to call by that name. For Wittgenstein, in short, games, chairs, and leaves are natural families, each constituted by a network of overlapping and crisscross resemblances. The existence of such a network sufficiently accounts for our success in identifying the corresponding object or activity.   (Kuhn 1962/70, p. 45)

To make the similarity network act more "complete", consider the following analogy. In a city, any person should be able to visit any other; but we do not build a special road between each pair of houses; we place a group of houses on a "block". We do not connect roads between each pair of blocks, but have them share streets. We do not connect each town to every other, but construct main routes, connecting the centers of larger groups. Within such an organization, each member has direct links to some other individuals at its own "level", mainly to nearby, highly similar ones; but each individual has also at least a few links to "distinguished" members of higher-level groups. The result is that there is usually a rather short sequence between any two individuals, if one can but find it.

To locate something in such a structure, one uses a hierarchy like the one implicit in a mail address. Everyone knows something about the largest categories, in that he knows where the major cities are. An inhabitant of a city knows the nearby towns, and people in the towns know the nearby villages. No person knows all the individual routes between pairs of houses; but, for a particular friend, one may know a special route to his home in a nearby town that is better than going to the city and back. *Directories* factor the problem, basing paths on standard routes between major nodes in the network. Personal shortcuts can bypass major nodes and go straight between familiar locations. Although the standard routes are usually not quite the very best possible, our stratified transport and communication services connect everything together reasonably well, with comparatively few connections.

At each level, the aggregates usually have distinguished foci or *capitals*. These serve as elements for clustering at the next level of aggregation. There is no nonstop airplane service between New Haven and San Jose because it is more efficient overall to share the trunk route between New York and San Francisco, which are the capitals at that level of aggregation.

As our memory networks grow, we can expect similar aggregations of the destinations of our similarity pointers. Our decisions about what we consider to be primary or trunk difference features and which are considered subsidiary will have large effects on our abilities. Such decisions eventually accumulate to become epistemological commitments about the conceptual cities of our mental universe.

The nonrandom convergences and divergences of the similarity pointers, for each difference d, thus tend to structure our conceptual world around

- the aggregation into d-clusters, and
- the selection of d-capitals.

Note that it is perfectly all right to have *several capitals in a cluster*, so that there need be no one attribute common to them all. The "criss-cross resemblances" of Wittgenstein are then consequences of the local connections in our similarity network, which are surely adequate to explain how we can feel as though we know what a chair or a game is—yet cannot always define it in a logical way as an element in some class-hierarchy or by any other kind of compact, formal, declarative rule. The apparent coherence of the conceptual aggregates need not reflect explicit definitions, but can emerge from the success-directed sharpening of the difference-describing processes.

The selection of capitals corresponds to selecting the stereotypes or typical elements whose default assignments are unusually useful. There are many forms of chairs, for example, and one should choose carefully the chair-description frames that are to be the major capitals of chair-land. These are used for rapid matching and assigning priorities to the various differences. The lower-priority features of the cluster center then serve either as default properties of the chair types or, if more realism is required, as dispatch pointers to the local chair villages and towns. Difference points could be "functional" as well as geometric. Thus, after rejecting a first try at "chair", one might try the functional idea of "something one can sit on" to explain an unconventional form. This requires a deeper analysis in terms of forces and strengths. Of course, that analysis would fail to capture toy chairs, or chairs of such ornamental delicacy that their actual use would be unthinkable. These would be better handled by the method of excuses, in which one would bypass the usual geometrical or functional explanations in favor of responding to contexts involving art or play.

It is important to reemphasize that there is no reason to restrict the memory structure to a single hierarchy; the notions of "level" of aggregation need not coincide for different kinds of differences. The d-capitals can exist, not only by explicit declarations, but also implicitly by their focal locations in the structure defined by convergent d-pointers. (In Newell and Simon's GPS framework, the "differences" are ordered into a fixed hierarchy. By making the priorities depend on the goal, the same memories could be made to serve more purposes; the resulting problem solver would lose the elegance of a single, simple-ordered measure of "progress", but that is the price of moving from a first-order theory.)

Finally, we should point out that we do not need to invoke any mysterious additional mechanism for *creating* the clustering structure. Developmentally, one would assume, the earliest frames would tend to become the capitals of their later relatives, unless this is firmly prevented by experience, because each time the use of one stereotype is reasonably successful, its centrality is reinforced by another pointer from somewhere else. Otherwise, *the acquisition of new centers is in large measure forced upon us from the outside: by the words available in our language; by the behavior of objects in our environment; by what we are told by our teachers, family, and general culture.* Of course, at each step the structure of the previous structure dominates the acquisition of the later. But in any case such forms and clusters should emerge from the interactions between the world and almost any memory-using mechanism; it would require more explanation were they *not* found!

3.6 Analogies and alternative descriptions

We have discussed the use of different frames of the same system to describe the same situation in different ways: for change of position in vision and for change of emphasis in language. Sometimes, in "problem solving", we use two or more descriptions in a more complex way to construct an analogy or to apply two radically *different* kinds of analysis to the same situation. *For hard problems, one "problem space" is usually not enough!*

Suppose your car battery runs down. You believe that there is an electricity shortage and blame the generator.

The generator can be represented as a mechanical system: the rotor has a pulley wheel driven by a belt from the engine. Is the belt tight enough? Is it even there? The output, seen mechanically, is a cable to the battery or whatever. Is it intact? Are the bolts tight? Are the brushes pressing on the commutator?

Seen electrically, the generator is described differently. The rotor is seen as a flux-linking coil, rather than as a rotating device. The brushes and commutator are seen as electrical switches. The output is current along a pair of conductors leading from the brushes through control circuits to the battery.

We thus represent the situation in two quite different frame systems. In one, the armature is a mechanical rotor with pulley; in the other, it is a conductor in a changing magnetic field. The same—or analogous—elements share terminals of different frames, and the frame transformations apply only to some of them.

The differences between the two frames are substantial. The entire mechanical chassis of the car plays the simple role, in the electrical frame, of one of the battery connections. The diagnostician has to use both representations. A failure of current to flow often means that an intended conductor is not acting like one. For this case, the basic transformation between the frames depends on the fact that electrical continuity is in general equivalent to firm mechanical attachment. Therefore, any conduction disparity revealed by electrical measurements should make us look for a corresponding disparity in the mechanical frame. In fact, since "repair" in this universe is synonymous with "mechanical repair", the diagnosis *must* end in the mechanical frame. Eventually, we might locate a defective mechanical junction and discover a loose connection, corrosion, wear, or whatever.

Why have two separate frames, rather than one integrated structure to represent the generator? I believe that in such a complex problem, one can never cope with many details at once. At each moment one must work within a reasonably simple framework. I contend that any problem that a person can solve at all is worked out at each moment in a small context and that the key operations in problem solving are concerned with finding or constructing these working environments.

Indeed, finding an electrical fault requires moving between at least three frames: a visual one along with the electrical and mechanical frames. If electrical evidence suggests a loose mechanical connection, one needs a visual frame to guide oneself to the mechanical fault.

Are there general methods for constructing adequate frames? The answer is both yes and no! There are some often-useful strategies for adapting old frames to new purposes; but I should emphasize that humans certainly have no magical way to solve *all* hard problems! One must not fall into what Papert calls the superhuman-human fallacy and require a theory of human behavior to explain even things that people cannot really do!

One cannot expect to have a frame exactly right for any problem or expect always to be able to invent one. But we do have a good deal to work with, and it is important to remember the contribution of one's culture in assessing the complexity of problems people seem to solve. *The experienced mechanic need not routinely invent*; he already has engine representations in terms of ignition, lubrication, cooling, timing, fuel mixing, transmission, compression, and so forth. Cooling, for example, is already subdivided into fluid circulation, air flow, thermostasis, and the like. Most "ordinary" problems are presumably solved by systematic use of the analogies provided by the transformations between pairs of these structures. The huge network of knowledge, acquired from school, books, apprenticeship, or whatever, is interlinked by difference and relevancy pointers. No doubt, the culture imparts a good deal of this structure by its conventional *use of the same words* in explanations of different views of a subject.

3.8 Frames and paradigms

Until that scholastic paradigm [the medieval 'impetus' theory] was invented, there were no pendulums, but only swinging stones, for

> scientists to see. Pendulums were brought into the world by some-
> thing very like a paradigm-induced gestalt switch.
>
> Do we, however, really need to describe what separates Galileo
> from Aristotle, or Lavoisier from Priestly, as a transformation of
> vision? Did these men really *see* different things when *looking at* the
> same sorts of objects? Is there any legitimate sense in which we can
> say they pursued their research in different worlds? ...
>
> I am ... acutely aware of the difficulties created by saying that
> when Aristotle and Galileo looked at swinging stones, the first saw
> constrained fall, the second a pendulum. ... Nevertheless, I am
> convinced that we must learn to make sense of sentences that at
> least resemble these.   (Kuhn 1962/70, pp. 120-121)

According to Kuhn's model of scientific evolution, normal science proceeds by using established descriptive schemes. Major changes result
from new paradigms, new ways of describing things that lead to new
methods and techniques. Eventually there is a redefining of "normal".

Now while Kuhn prefers to apply his own very effective redescription paradigm at the level of major scientific revolutions, it seems to
me that the same idea applies as well to the microcosm of everyday
thinking. Indeed, in the above quotation, we see that Kuhn is seriously
considering that the paradigms play a substantive rather than metaphorical role in visual perception, just as we have proposed for frames.

Whenever our customary viewpoints do not work well, whenever
we fail to find effective frame systems in memory, we must construct
new ones that bring out the right features. Presumably, the most usual
way to do this is to build some sort of pair-system from two or more
old ones and then edit or debug it to suit the circumstances. How
might this be done? It is tempting to formulate the requirements, and
then solve the construction problem.

But that is certainly not the usual course of ordinary thinking! Neither are requirements formulated all at once, nor is the new system
constructed entirely by deliberate preplanning. Instead we recognize
unsatisfied requirements, one by one, as deficiencies or "bugs", in the
course of a sequence of modifications made to an unsatisfactory representation.

I think Papert (1972; see also Minsky 1970) is correct in believing
that the ability to diagnose and modify one's own procedures is a collection of specific and important "skills". *Debugging*, a fundamentally
important component of intelligence, has its own special techniques
and procedures. Every normal person is pretty good at them; or

otherwise he would not have learned to see and talk! Although this essay is already speculative, I would like to point here to the theses of Goldstein (1974) and Sussman (1973/75) about the explicit use of *knowledge about debugging* in learning symbolic representations. They build new procedures to satisfy multiple requirements by such elementary but powerful techniques as:

(1) Make a crude first attempt by the first order method of simply putting together procedures that *separately* achieve the individual goals.

(2) If something goes wrong, try to characterize one of the defects as a *specific* (and undesirable) kind of interaction between two procedures.

(3) Apply a debugging technique that, according to a record in memory, is good at repairing that *specific kind* of interaction.

(4) Summarize the experience, to add to the "debugging techniques library" in memory.

These might seem simple minded, but if the new problem is not too radically different from the old ones, they have a good chance to work, especially if one picks out the right first-order approximations. If the new problem *is* radically different, one should not expect *any* learning theory to work well. Without a structured cognitive map—without the "near misses" of Winston or a cultural supply of good training sequences of problems, we should not expect radically new paradigms to appear magically whenever we need them.

What are "kinds of interactions", and what are "debugging techniques"? The simplest, perhaps, are those in which the result of achieving a first goal interferes with some condition prerequisite for achieving a second goal. The simplest repair is to reinsert the prerequisite as a new condition. There are examples in which this technique alone cannot succeed because a prerequisite for the second goal is incompatible with the first. Sussman presents a more sophisticated diagnosis and repair method that recognizes this and exchanges the order of the goals. Goldstein considers related problems in a multiple description context.

If asked about important future lines of research on artificial or natural intelligence, I would point to the interactions between these ideas and the problems of using multiple representations to deal with the same situation from several viewpoints. To carry out such a study, we need better ideas about interactions among the transformed relationships. Here the frame-system idea by itself begins to show limitations. Fitting together new representations from parts of old ones is clearly a complex process itself, and one that could be solved within the framework of our theory (if at all) only by an intricate bootstrapping. This, too, is surely a special skill with its own techniques. I consider it a crucial component of a theory of intelligence.

We must not expect complete success in the above enterprise; there is a difficulty, as Newell (1973) notes in a larger context:

> Elsewhere is another view—possibly from philosophy—or other "elsewheres" as well, since the views of man are multiple. Each view has its own questions. Separate views speak mostly past each other. Occasionally, of course, they speak to the same issue and then comparison is possible, but not often and not on demand.

Appendix: criticism of the logistic approach

> If one tries to describe processes of genuine thinking in terms of formal traditional logic, the result is often unsatisfactory; one has, then, a series of correct operations, but the sense of the process and what was vital, forceful, creative in it seems somehow to have evaporated in the formulations.   (Wertheimer 1959)

I here explain why I think more "logical" approaches will not work. There have been serious attempts, from as far back as Aristotle, to represent common-sense reasoning by a "logistic" system—that is, one that makes a complete separation between

(1) "propositions" that embody specific information, and

(2) "syllogisms" or general laws of proper inference.

No one has been able successfully to confront such a system with a realistically large set of propositions. I think such attempts will continue to fail, because of the character of logistic in general rather than from defects of particular formalisms. (Most recent attempts have used variants of "first order predicate logic", but I do not think *that* is the problem.)

A typical attempt to simulate common-sense thinking by logistic systems begins in a micro-world of limited complication. At one end are high-level goals such as "I want to get from my house to the airport". At the other end we start with many small items—the *axioms*—

like "The car is in the garage", "One does not go outside undressed", "To get to a place one should (on the whole) move in its direction", and so on. To make the system work, one designs heuristic search procedures to "prove" the desired goal, or to produce a list of actions that will achieve it.

I will not recount the history of attempts to make both ends meet—but merely summarize my impression: in simple cases, one can get such systems to "perform", but as we approach reality, the obstacles become overwhelming. The problem of finding suitable axioms—the problem of "stating the facts" in terms of always-correct, logical assumptions—is very much harder than is generally believed.

FORMALIZING THE REQUIRED KNOWLEDGE: Just constructing a knowledge base is a major intellectual research problem. Whether one's goal is logistic or not, we still know far too little about the contents and structure of common-sense knowledge. A "minimal" common-sense system must "know" something about cause and effect, time, purpose, locality, process, and types of knowledge. It also needs ways to acquire, represent, and use such knowledge. We need a serious epistemological research effort in this area. The essays of McCarthy (1969) and Sandewall (1970) are steps in that direction. I have no easy plan for this large enterprise; but the magnitude of the task will certainly depend strongly on the representations chosen, and I think that "logistic" is already making trouble.

RELEVANCE: The problem of selecting relevance from excessive variety is a key issue! A modern epistemology will not resemble the old ones! Computational concepts are necessary and novel. Perhaps the better part of knowledge is not propositional in character, but interpropositional. For each "fact" one needs meta-facts about how it is to be used and when it should not be used. In McCarthy's "Airport" paradigm we see ways to deal with some interactions between "situations, actions, and causal laws" within a restricted micro-world of things and actions. But though the system can make deductions implied by its axioms, it cannot be told when it should or should not make such deductions.

For example, one might want to tell the system to "not cross the road if a car is coming". But one cannot demand that the system "prove" no car is coming, for there will not usually be any such proof. In PLANNER, one can direct an *attempt* to prove that a car *is* coming, and if the (limited) deduction attempt ends with "failure", one can act. This cannot be done in a pure logistic system. "Look right, look left" is a first approximation. But if one tells the system the real truth about speeds, blind driveways, probabilities of racing cars whipping around the corner, proof becomes impractical. If it reads in a physics book that intense fields perturb light rays, should it fear that a mad scientist has built an invisible car? We need to represent "usually"! Eventually it must understand the trade-off between mortality and accomplishment, for one can do nothing if paralyzed by fear.

MONOTONICITY: Even if we formulate relevance restrictions, logistic systems have a problem in using them. In any logistic system, all the axioms are necessarily "permissive"—they all help to permit new inferences to be drawn. Each added axiom means more theorems; none can disappear. There simply is no direct way to add information to tell such a system about kinds of conclusions that should *not* be drawn! To put it simply: if we adopt enough axioms to deduce what we need, we deduce far too many other things. But if we try to change this by adding axioms about relevance, we still produce all the unwanted theorems, plus annoying statements about their irrelevance.

Because logicians are not concerned with systems that will later be enlarged, they can design axioms that permit only the conclusions they want. In the development of intelligence the situation is different. One has to learn which features of situations are important and which kinds of deductions are not to be regarded seriously. The usual reaction to the "liar's paradox" is, after a while, to laugh. The conclusion is not to reject an axiom, but to reject the deduction itself! This raises another issue.

PROCEDURE-CONTROLLING KNOWLEDGE: The separation between axioms and deduction makes it impractical to include classificational knowledge about propositions. Nor can we include knowledge about management of deduction. A paradigm problem is that of axiomatizing everyday concepts of approximation or nearness. One would like nearness to be transitive:

$$(A \text{ near } B) \text{ and } (B \text{ near } C) \rightarrow (A \text{ near } C)$$

but unrestricted application of this rule would make everything near everything else. One can try technical tricks like

$$(A \text{ near}_1 B) \text{ and } (B \text{ near}_1 C) \rightarrow (A \text{ near}_2 C)$$

and admit only (say) five grades: $near_1$, $near_2$, ... $near_5$. One might invent analog quantities or parameters. But one cannot (in a logistic system) decide to make a new kind of "axiom" to prevent applying transitivity after (say) three chained uses, conditionally, unless there is a "good excuse". I do not mean to propose a particular solution to the transitivity of nearness. (To my knowledge, no one has made a creditable proposal about it.) My complaint is that, because of acceptance of logistic, no one has freely explored this kind of procedural restriction.

COMBINATORIAL PROBLEMS: A human thinker reviews plans and goal lists as he works, revising his knowledge and policies about using them. One can program some of this into the theorem-proving program itself; but one really wants also to represent it directly, in a natural way, in the declarative corpus—for use in further introspection. Why then do workers try to make logistic systems do the job? A valid reason is that the systems have an attractive simple elegance; if they worked, this would be fine. An invalid reason is more often offered: that such systems have a mathematical virtue because they are:

(1) Complete: All true statements can be proven; and

(2) Consistent: No false statements can be proven.

It seems not often realized that completeness is no rare prize. It is a trivial consequence of any exhaustive search procedure, and any system can be "completed" by adjoining to it any other complete system and interlacing the computational steps. Consistency is more refined; it requires one's axioms to imply no contradictions. But I do not believe that consistency is necessary or even desirable in a developing intelligent system. No one is ever completely consistent. What is important is how one handles paradox or conflict, how one learns from mistakes, how one turns aside from suspected inconsistencies.

Because of this kind of misconception, Gödel's incompleteness theorem has stimulated much foolishness about alleged differences between machines and men. No one seems to have noted its more "logical" interpretation: that enforcing consistency produces limitations. Of course there will be differences between humans (who are demonstrably inconsistent) and machines whose designers have imposed consistency. But it is not inherent in machines that they be programmed only with consistent logical systems. Those "philosophical" discussions all make these quite unnecessary assumptions! (I regard the recent demonstration of the consistency of modern set theory, thus, as indicating that set theory is probably inadequate for our purposes—not as reassuring evidence that set theory is safe to use!)

A famous mathematician, warned that his proof would lead to a paradox if he took one more logical step, replied "Ah, but I shall not take that step." He was completely serious. A large part of ordinary (or even mathematical) knowledge resembles the cautions in dangerous professions: When are certain actions unwise? When are certain approximations safe to use? When do various measures yield sensible estimates? Which self-referential statements are permissible if not carried too far? Concepts like "nearness" are too valuable to give up just because no one can exhibit satisfactory axioms for them.

In summary:

(1) "Logical" reasoning is not flexible enough to serve as a basis for thinking: I prefer to think of it as a collection of heuristic methods, effective only when applied to starkly simplified schematic plans. The consistency that logic absolutely demands is not otherwise usually available—*and probably not even desirable!*—because consistent systems are likely to be too weak.

(2) I doubt the feasibility of representing ordinary knowledge effectively in the form of many small, independently true propositions.

(3) The strategy of complete separation of specific knowledge from general rules of inference is much too radical. We need more direct ways for linking fragments of knowledge to advice about *how* they are to be used.

(4) It was long believed that it was crucial to make all knowledge accessible to deduction in the form of declarative statements; but this seems less urgent as we learn ways to manipulate structural and procedural descriptions.

I do not mean to suggest that "thinking" can proceed very far without something like "reasoning". We certainly need (and use) something like syllogistic deduction; but I expect mechanisms for doing such things to emerge in any case from processes for "matching" and "instantiation" required for other functions. Traditional formal logic is a technical tool for discussing either *everything that can be deduced from some data* or *whether a certain consequence can be so deduced*; it cannot discuss at all what *ought* to be deduced under ordinary circumstances. Like the abstract theory of syntax, formal logic without a powerful procedural semantics cannot deal with meaningful situations.

I cannot state strongly enough my conviction that the preoccupation with consistency, so valuable for mathematical logic, has been incredibly destructive to those working on models of the mind. At the popular level it has produced a weird conception of the potential capabilities of machines in general. At the "logical" level it has blocked efforts to represent ordinary knowledge, by presenting an unreachable image of a corpus of context-free "truths" that can stand almost by themselves. And at the intellect-modeling level it has blocked the fundamental realization that *thinking begins first with suggestive but defective plans and images that are slowly (if ever) refined and replaced by better ones.*

From Micro-Worlds to Knowledge Representation: AI at an Impasse

Hubert L. Dreyfus
1979

Since the completion, near the beginning of the decade, of the first edition of *What Computers Can't Do* (Dreyfus 1972/92), there has been considerable change and development in artificial intelligence. None of this more recent work leads me to relax my overall skepticism, but it does call for new and detailed discussion. In this article I review and examine a representative sample of AI as it has developed in the seventies. The work discussed falls into two categories, which can be assigned to the first and second halves of the decade, respectively.

1 The early seventies: micro-worlds

1.1 SHRDLU: understanding natural language

We begin with Winograd's (1972) natural-language understanding program, SHRDLU, inasmuch as it was the most impressive new achievement at the time. SHRDLU simulates a robot arm which can move a set of variously shaped blocks, and allows a person to engage in a dialogue with the computer—asking questions, making statements, and issuing commands about this simple world of movable blocks. The program is an integrated system which makes use of syntax, semantics, and facts about blocks. It is thus, as Winograd cautiously claims, "a computer program which 'understands' language in a limited domain, by including a model of the subject being talked about and a context of discourse" (1973). Furthermore, this program explores the new idea of representing this knowledge in the form of procedures. The resulting dialogue is strikingly natural. Here is a sample. (The sentences in small caps are computer print-out; the parentheses contain Winograd's comments.)

(1) Pick up a big red block.

Okay.

(The system answers "Okay" when it carries out a command. In order to pick up the red block, it had to clear it off by finding a space for the green one and moving the green one away.)

(2) Grasp the pyramid.

I don't understand which pyramid you mean.

(There are three pyramids in the scene, so the program does nothing.)

(3) Find a block which is taller than the one you are holding and put it into the box.

(The system has to figure out what is meant by "one" and "it", as well as using deduction to decide which block it is holding.)

By "it", I assume you mean the block which is taller than the one I am holding.

(Printed out to keep us informed.)

Okay.

(The hand has to set down the red block to pick up the taller blue one.)

(4) What does the box contain?

The blue pyramid and the blue block.

(5) What is the pyramid supported by?

(Earlier the system responded to "the pyramid by saying, "I don't understand which pyramid you mean". Now, it assumes that we mean the one just mentioned.)

The box.

. . .

(9) Can the table pick up blocks?

No.

(The semantic rules make this a nonsensical questions which therefore must be false.)

(10) Can a pyramid be supported by a block?

Yes.

(The deductive system finds an actual example, so it knows this is possible.)

(11) Can a pyramid support a pyramid?

I DON'T KNOW.

(The question makes sense, but there is no example in the scene, so there is no easy way to tell without being able to examine the robot's programs.)

(12) Stack up two pyramids.

I CAN'T.

(The robot tries and fails.)

(13) The blue pyramid is mine.

I UNDERSTAND.

(This datum is added to the data base.)

(14) I own blocks which are not red, but I don't own anything which supports a pyramid.

I UNDERSTAND.

(Two new theorems are created for proving things about "owning".)

(15) Do I own the box?

No.

(Winograd 1972, pp. 8–11)

If being a major advance means being more general than its predecessors, then SHRDLU, since it no longer depends for its analysis of language on external constraints of the sort essential to Bobrow's STUDENT (1967), is a major achievement. Winograd himself points out the superiority of his program over earlier language understanding programs.

> A program may succeed by carefully choosing the problem it will attack, so that some simple special-purpose solution will work. ELIZA (Weizenbaum 1964) and STUDENT (Bobrow 1967) are examples of programs which give impressive performances owing to a severe and careful restriction of the kind of understanding they try to achieve. If a model is to be of broader significance, it must be designed to cover a large range of things we mean when we talk of understanding. The principles should derive from an attempt to deal with the basic cognitive structures.   (1973, p. 167)

If, however, "a major advance" means that a step has been made in dealing with the basic cognitive structures needed to cover everyday understanding—that, thanks to SHRDLU, there is now reason to be optimistic about the possibility of AI—then no progress at all can be claimed. To justify this negative judgment we must first find out how the optimists of the early seventies were able to convince themselves that, with SHRDLU, AI was at last on the right track. Workers in AI were certainly not trying to cover up the fact that it was SHRDLU's restricted domain which made apparent understanding possible. They even had a name for Winograd's method of restricting the domain of discourse. He was dealing with a *micro-world*. And in a 1970 internal memo at MIT, Minsky and Papert frankly note:

> Each model—or "micro-world" as we shall call it—is very schematic; it talks about a fairyland in which things are so simplified that almost every statement about them would be literally false if asserted about the real world.   (p. 39)

But they immediately add:

> Nevertheless, we feel that they [the micro-worlds] are so important that we are assigning a large portion of our effort toward developing a collection of these micro-worlds and finding how to use the suggestive and predictive powers of the models without being overcome by their incompatibility with literal truth.

Given the admittedly artificial and arbitrary character of micro-worlds, why do Papert and Minsky think they provide a promising line of research?

To find an answer we must follow Minsky and Papert's perceptive remarks on narrative, and their less-than-perceptive conclusions:

> In a familiar fable, the wily Fox tricks the vain Crow into dropping the meat by asking it to sing. The usual test of understanding is the ability of the child to answer questions like: "Did the Fox think the Crow had a lovely voice?" The topic is sometimes classified as "natural-language manipulation" or as "deductive logic", and the like. These descriptions are badly chosen. For the real problem is not to understand English; it is to *understand* at all. To see this more clearly, observe that nothing is gained by presenting the story in simplified syntax: CROW ON TREE. CROW HAS MEAT. FOX SAYS: "YOU HAVE A LOVELY VOICE. PLEASE SING." FOX GOBBLES MEAT. The difficulty in getting a machine to give the right answer does not at all depend on "disambiguating" the words (at least, not in the usual primitive sense of selecting one "meaning" out of a discrete set of "meanings"). And neither does the difficulty lie in the need for unusually powerful logical apparatus. The main problem is that no

one has constructed the elements of a body of knowledge about such matters that is adequate for understanding the story. Let us see what is involved.

To begin with, there is never a unique solution to such problems, so we do not ask what the Understander *must* know. But he will surely gain by having the concept of *flattery*. To provide this knowledge, we imagine a "micro-theory" of flattery—an extendible collection of facts or procedures that describe conditions under which one might expect to find flattery, what forms it takes, what its consequences are, and so on. How complex this theory is depends on what is presupposed. Thus it would be very difficult to describe flattery to our Understander if he (or it) does not already know that statements can be made for purposes other than to convey literally correct, factual information. It would be almost impossibly difficult if he does not even have some concept like *purpose* or *intention*.   (1970, pp. 42–44)

The surprising move here is the conclusion that there could be a circumscribed "micro-theory" of flattery—somehow intelligible apart from the rest of human life—while at the same time the account shows an understanding of flattery opening out into the rest of our everyday world, with its understanding of purposes and intentions.

What characterizes the period of the early seventies, and makes SHRDLU seem an advance toward general intelligence, is the very concept of a micro-world—a domain which can be analyzed in isolation. This concept implies that although each area of discourse seems to open out into the rest of human activities, its endless ramifications are only apparent and will soon converge on a self-contained set of facts and relations. For example, in discussing the micro-world of bargaining, Papert and Minsky consider what a child needs to know to understand the following fragment of conversation:

> Janet: That isn't a very good ball you have. Give it to me and I'll
> give you my lollipop.   (p. 48)

And remark:

> We conjecture that, eventually, the required micro-theories can be made reasonably compact and easily stated (or, by the same token, *learned*) once we have found an adequate set of structural primitives for them. When one begins to catalogue what one needs for just a little of Janet's story, it seems at first to be endless:

Time	Things	Words
Space	People	Thoughts

Talking:	Explaining; asking; ordering; persuading; pretending.
Social relations:	Giving, buying, bargaining, begging, asking, stealing; presents.
Playing:	Real and unreal; pretending.
Owning:	Part of; belongs to; master of; captor of.
Eating:	How does one compare the values of foods with the values of toys?
Liking:	Good, bad, useful, pretty; conformity.
Living:	Girl. Awake. Eats. Plays.
Intention:	Want; plan, plot; goal; cause, result, prevent.
Emotions:	Moods, dispositions; conventional expressions.
States:	Asleep, angry, at home.
Properties:	Grown-up, red-haired; called "Janet".
Story:	Narrator; plot; principal actors.
People:	Children, bystanders.
Places:	Houses; outside.
Angry:	State caused by: insult, deprivation, assault, disobedience, frustration; or spontaneous.
Results:	Not cooperative; lower threshold; aggression; loud voice; irrational; revenge.

And so on.   (pp. 50–52)

They conclude:

> But [the list] is not endless. It is only large, and one needs a large set of concepts to organize it. After a while one will find it getting harder to add new concepts, and the new ones will begin to seem less indispensable.   (p. 52)

This totally unjustified belief that the seemingly endless reference to other human practices will converge, so that simple micro-worlds can be studied in relative isolation, reflects a naive transfer to AI of methods that have succeeded in the natural sciences. Winograd characteristically describes his work in terms borrowed from physical science.

> We are concerned with developing a formalism, or "representation", with which to describe ... knowledge. We seek the "atoms" and "particles" of which it is built, and the "forces" that act on it.
>
> (1976, p. 9)

It is true that physical theories about the universe can be built up by studying relatively simple and isolated systems and then making the model gradually more complex and integrating it with other domains of phenomena. This is possible because all the phenomena are presumably the result of the lawlike relations of a set of basic elements, what Papert and Minsky call "structural primitives". This belief in local success and gradual generalization was clearly also Winograd's hope at the time he developed SHRDLU.

> The justification for our particular use of concepts in this system is that it is thereby enabled to engage in dialogs that simulate in many ways the behavior of a human language user. For a wider field of discourse, the conceptual structure would have to be expanded in its details, and perhaps in some aspects of its overall organization.   (1972, p. 26)

Thus, it might seem that one could "expand" SHRDLU's concept of owning, since in the above sample conversation SHRDLU seems to have a very simple "micro-theory" of owning blocks. But, as Simon points out in an excellent analysis of SHRDLU's limitations, the program does not understand owning at all, because it cannot deal with meanings. It has merely been given a set of primitives and their possible relationships. As Simon puts it:

> The SHRDLU system deals with problems in a single blocks world, with a fixed representation. When it is instructed to "pick up a big red block", it needs only to associate the term "pick up" with a procedure for carrying out that process; identify, by applying appropriate tests associated with "big", "red", and "block", the argument for the procedure; and use its problem-solving capabilities to carry out the procedure. In saying "it needs only", it is not my intention to demean the capabilities of SHRDLU. It is precisely because the program possesses stored programs expressing the intensions of the terms used in inquiries and instructions that

its interpretation of those inquiries and instructions is relatively straightforward.   (1977, p. 1062)

In understanding, on the other hand,

> the problem-understanding subsystem will have a more compli-cated task than just mapping the input language onto the inten-tions stored in a lexicon. It will also have to create a representation for the information it receives, and create meanings for the terms that are consistent with the representation.   (p. 1063)

So, for example, in the conversation concerning owning,

> although SHRDLU's answer to the question is quite correct, the system cannot be said to understand the meaning of "own" in any but a sophistic sense. SHRDLU's test of whether something is owned is simply whether it is tagged "owned". There is no inten-tional test of ownership, hence SHRDLU knows what it owns, but doesn't understand what it is to own something. SHRDLU would understand what it meant to own a box if it could, say, test its own-ership by recalling how it had gained possession of the box, or by checking its possession of a receipt in payment for it; could respond differently to requests to move a box it owned from requests to move one it didn't own; and, in general, could perform those tests and actions that are generally associated with the deter-mination and exercise of ownership in our law and culture.
>   (p. 1064)

Moreover, even if it satisfied all these conditions, it still wouldn't understand, unless it also understood that it (SHRDLU) couldn't own anything, since it isn't a part of the community in which owning makes sense. Given our cultural practices which constitute owning, a computer cannot own something any more than a table can.

This discussion of owning suggests that, just as it is misleading to call a program UNDERSTAND when the problem is to find out what understanding is (compare McDermott 1976, p. 4), it is likewise mis-leading to call a set of facts and procedures concerning blocks a micro-*world* when what is really at stake is the understanding of what a world is. A set of interrelated facts may constitute a *universe*, a domain, a group, etc., but it does not constitute a *world*, for a world is an orga-nized body of objects, purposes, skills, and practices in terms of which human activities have meaning or make sense. It follows that although there is a children's world in which, among other things, there are blocks, there is no such thing as a blocks world. Or, to put this as a critique of Winograd, one cannot equate, as he does (1974, p. 20), a program that deals with a "tiny bit of the world", with a program that deals with a "mini-world".

In our everyday life we are, indeed, involved in such various "sub-worlds" as the world of the theater, of business, or of mathematics, but each of these is a "mode" of our shared everyday world.[1] That is, sub-worlds are not related like isolable physical systems to larger systems they *compose*; rather they are local elaborations of a whole which they *presuppose*. If micro-worlds *were* sub-worlds, one would not have to extend and combine them to reach the everyday world, because the everyday world would have to be included already. Since, however, micro-worlds are *not* worlds, there is no way they can be combined and extended to the world of everyday life. As a result of failing to ask what a world is, five years of stagnation in AI was mistaken for progress.

1.2 "Scene parsing" and computer vision

A second major application of the micro-world technique was in computer vision. Already in 1968, Adolfo Guzman's SEE program could analyze two-dimensional projections of complicated three-dimensional "scenes", consisting of piles of polyhedra. Even this early program correctly analyzed certain classes of scenes which people find difficult to figure out; but it had serious limitations. In 1972/75, Waltz generalized Guzman's methods, and produced a much more powerful vision system. Together, these programs provide a case study not only in how much can be achieved with the micro-worlds approach, but also in the kind of generalization that is possible within that approach—and, by implication, the kind that isn't.

Guzman's program analyzes scenes involving cubes and other such rectilinear solids by merging regions into bodies using evidence from the vertices. Each vertex suggests that two or more of the regions around it belong together, depending on whether the vertex is shaped like an L, an arrow, a T, a K, an X, a fork, a peak, or an upside-down peak. With these eight primitives and common-sense rules for their use, Guzman's program did quite well. But it had certain weaknesses. According to Winston, "The program could not handle shadows, and it did poorly if there were holes in objects or missing lines in the drawing" (1975, p. 8). Waltz then generalized Guzman's work and showed that by introducing three more such primitives, a computer can be programmed to decide if a particular line in a drawing is a shadow, a

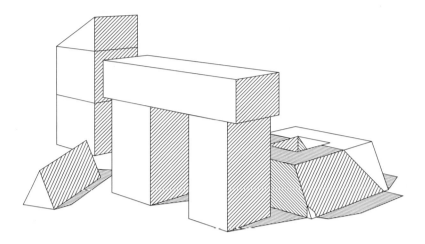

Figure 6.1: Sample blocks-world scene "parsed" by Waltz's program.

crack, an obscuring edge, or an internal seam in a way analogous to the solution of sets of algebraic equations. As Winston later sums up the change:

> Previously it was believed that only a program with a complicated control structure and lots of explicit reasoning power could hope to analyze scenes like that in figure [6.1]. Now we know that understanding the constraints the real world imposes on how boundaries, concave and convex interiors, shadows, and cracks can come together at junctions is enough to make things much simpler. A table which contains a list of the few thousand physically possible ways that line types can come together accompanied by a simple matching program are all that is required. Scene analysis is translated into a problem resembling a jigsaw puzzle or a set of linear equations. No deep problem-solving effort is required; it is just a matter of executing a very simple constraint-dependent, iterative process that successively throws away incompatible line arrangement combinations.   (1976, pp. 77–78)

This is just the kind of mathematical generalization within a domain that one might expect in a micro-world, where the rule-governed relations of the primitives (in this case the set of vertices) are under some external constraint (in this case the laws of geometry and optics). What one would not expect is that the special-purpose heuristics which depend on corners for segregating rectilinear objects could in any way be generalized so as to make possible the recognition of other sorts of objects. And, indeed, none of Guzman's or Waltz's techniques, since they rely on the intersection of straight lines, have any use in analyzing a scene involving curved objects. What one gains in narrowing a domain, one loses in breadth of significance. Winston's evaluation covers up this lesson.

> It is wrong to think of Waltz's work as only a statement of the epistemology of line drawings of polyhedra. Instead I think it is an elegant case study of a paradigm we can expect to see again and again, and as such, it is a strong metaphoric tool for guiding our thinking, not only in vision but also in the study of other systems involving intelligence. (1975, p. 8)

But in a later grant proposal he acknowledges that:

> To understand the real world, we must have a different set of primitives from the relatively simple line trackers suitable and sufficient for the blocks world. (1976, p. 39)

Waltz's work is a paradigm of the kind of generalization one can strive for *within* a micro-world all right, but for that very reason it provides no way of thinking about general intelligent systems.

The nongeneralizable character of the programs so far discussed makes them engineering feats, not steps toward generally intelligent systems, and they are, therefore, not at all promising as contributions to psychology. Yet Winston includes Waltz's work in his claim that "making machines see is an important way to understand how we animals see" (1975, p. 2), and Winograd makes similar claims for the psychological relevance of his work.

> The gain from developing AI is not primarily in the usefulness of the programs we create, but in the set of concepts we develop, and the ways in which we can apply them to understanding human intelligence. (1976, p. 3)

These comments suggest that in the early seventies an interesting change was taking place at MIT In previous papers, Minsky and his co-workers sharply distinguished themselves from workers in cognitive simulation, such as Simon, who presented their programs as psychological theories, insisting that the MIT programs were "an attempt to build intelligent machines without any prejudice toward making the system ... humanoid" (Minsky 1969, p. 7). Now, in their book *Artificial Intelligence*, a summary of work done at MIT during the period 1967–72, Minsky and Papert (1973) present the MIT research as a contribution to psychology. They first introduce the notion of a symbolic description.

> What do we mean by "description"? We do not mean to suggest that our descriptions must be made of strings of ordinary language words (although they might be). The simplest kind of description is a structure in which some features of a situation are represented by single ("primitive") symbols, and relations between those features are represented by other symbols—or by other features of the way the description is put together.   (p. 11)

They then defend the role of symbolic descriptions in a psychological account of intelligent behavior by a constant polemic against behaviorism and gestalt theory, which have opposed the use of formal models of the mind.

One can detect, underlying this change, the effect of the proliferation of micro-worlds, with their reliance on symbolic descriptions, and the disturbing failure to produce even the hint of a system with the flexibility of a six-month-old child. Instead of concluding from this frustrating situation that the special-purpose techniques which work in context-free, gamelike, micro-worlds may in no way resemble general-purpose human and animal intelligence, the AI workers seem to have taken the less embarrassing if less plausible tack of suggesting that even if they could not succeed in building intelligent systems, the *ad hoc* symbolic descriptions successful in micro-world analysis could be justified as a valuable contribution to psychology.

Such a line, however, since it involves a stronger claim than the old slogan that as long as the machine was intelligent it did not matter at all whether it performed in a humanoid way, runs the obvious risk of refutation by empirical evidence. An information-processing model must be a formal symbol structure, however, so Minsky and Papert, making a virtue of necessity, revive the implausible intellectualist position according to which concrete perception is assimilated to the rule-governed symbolic descriptions used in abstract thought.

> The Gestaltists look for simple and fundamental principles about how perception is organized, and then attempt to show how symbolic reasoning can be seen as following the same principles, while we construct a complex theory of how knowledge is applied to solve intellectual problems and then attempt to show how the symbolic description that is what one "sees" is constructed according to similar processes.   (1973, p. 34)

Some recent work in psychology, however, points exactly in the opposite direction. Rather than showing that perception can be analyzed in terms of formal features, Erich Goldmeier's (1972) extension of early Gestalt work on the perception of similarity of simple perceptual figures—arising in part in response to "the frustrating efforts to teach pattern recognition to [computers]" (p. 1)—has revealed sophisticated distinctions between figure and ground, matter and form, essential and accidental aspects, norms and distortions, etc., which he shows cannot be accounted for in terms of any known formal features of the phenomenal figures. They can, however, according to Goldmeier, perhaps be explained on the neurological level, where the importance of *Prägnanz*—that is, singularly salient shapes and orientations—suggests underlying physical phenomena such as "regions of resonance" (p. 128) in the brain.

Of course, it is still possible that the Gestaltists went too far in trying to assimilate thought to the same sort of concrete, holistic, processes they found necessary to account for perception. Thus, even though the exponents of symbolic descriptions have no account of perceptual processes, they might be right that the mechanism of everyday thinking and learning consists in constructing a formal description of the world and transforming this representation in a rule-governed way.

1.3 Learning new concepts or categories

Just such a formal model of everyday learning and categorization is proposed by Winston in his 1970 thesis, "Learning Structural Descriptions from Examples" (see Winston 1975). Given a set of positive and negative instances, Winston's self-proclaimed "classic" program can, for example, use a descriptive repertoire to construct a formal description of the class of arches. Since Winston's program (along with those of Winograd, Guzman, and Waltz) is often mentioned as a major success of the micro-worlds technique, we must examine it in detail.

This program, too, illustrates the possibilities and essential limitations of micro-worlds. Is it the basis of a plausible general approach to learning? Winston thinks so.

> Although this may seem like a very special kind of learning, I think the implications are far ranging, because I believe that learning by examples, learning by being told, learning by imitation, learning by reinforcement, and other forms, are much like one another. In the literature on learning there is frequently an unstated assumption that these various forms are fundamentally different. But I think

the classical boundaries between the various kinds of learning
will disappear once superficially different kinds of learning are
understood in terms of processes that construct and manipulate
descriptions.   (1975, p. 185)

Yet Winston's program works only if the "student" is saved the trouble
of what Charles Sanders Peirce called 'abduction', by being "told" a set
of context-free features and relations—in this case, a list of possible
spatial relationships of blocks such as 'left-of', 'standing', 'above', and
'supported by'—from which to build up a description of an arch.
Minsky and Papert presuppose this preselection when they say that "to
eliminate objects which seem atypical ... the program lists all relationships exhibited by more than half of the candidates in the set" (1973,
p. 56). Lurking behind this claim is the supposition that there are only
a finite number of relevant features; but without preselected features all
objects share an indefinitely large number of relationships. The work
of discriminating, selecting, and weighting a limited number of relevant features is the result of repeated experience and is the first stage of
learning. But since in Winston's work the programmer selects and pre-
weights the primitives, his program gives us no idea how a computer
could make this selection and assign these weights. Thus the Winston
program, like every micro-world program, works only because it has
excluded from its task domain the very ability it is supposed to explain.

If not a theory of learning, is Winston's program at least a plausible
theory of categorization? Consider again the arch example. Once it has
been given what Winston disarmingly calls a "good description"
(p. 158) and carefully-chosen examples, the program does conclude
that an arch is a structure in which a prismatic body is supported by
two upright blocks that do not touch each other. But, since arches
function in various ways in our everyday activity, there is no reason to
suppose that these are the necessary and sufficient conditions for being
an arch, or that there are any such defining features. Some prominent
characteristics shared by most everyday arches are "helping to support
something while leaving an important open space under it", or "being
the sort of thing one can walk under and through at the same time".
How does Winston propose to capture such contextual characteristics
in terms of the context-free features required by his formal representation?

Winston admits that having two supports and a flat top does not
begin to capture even the geometrical structure of arches. So he
proposes "generalizing the machine's descriptive ability to acts and

properties required by those acts" (p. 194) by adding a functional predicate, "something to walk through" (p. 193). But it is not at all clear how a functional predicate which refers to implicit knowledge of the bodily skill of walking through is to be formalized. Indeed, Winston himself provides a *reductio ad absurdum* of this facile appeal to formal functional predicates:

> To a human, an arch may be something to walk through, as well as an appropriate alignment of bricks. And certainly, a flat rock serves as a table to a hungry person, although far removed from the image the word table usually calls to mind. But the machine does not yet know anything of walking or eating, so the programs discussed here handle only some of the physical aspects of these human notions. There is no inherent obstacle forbidding the machine to enjoy functional understanding. It is a matter of generalizing the machine's descriptive ability to acts and properties required by these acts. Then chains of pointers can link TABLE to FOOD as well as to the physical image of a table, and the machine will be perfectly happy to draw up its chair to a flat rock with the human given that there is something on that table which it wishes to eat.
>
> (pp. 193–194)

Progress on recognition of arches, tables, and the like, must, it seems, either wait until we have captured in an abstract symbolic description much of what human beings implicitly know about walking and eating simply by having a body, or else until computers no longer have to be told what it is to walk and eat, because they have human bodies and appetites themselves!

Despite these seemingly insurmountable obstacles, Winston boasts that "there will be no contentment with [concept learning] machines that only do as well as humans" (p. 160). But it is not surprising that Winston's work is nine years old and there has been little progress in machine learning, induction, or concept formation. In their account Minsky and Papert (1973) admit that "we are still far from knowing how to design a powerful yet subtle and sensitive inductive learning program" (p. 56). What is surprising is that they add: "but the schemata developed in Winston's work should take us a substantial part of the way". The lack of progress since Winston's work was published, plus the use of predigested weighted primitives from which to produce its rigid, restricted, and largely irrelevant descriptions, makes it hard to understand in what way the program is a substantial step.

Moreover, if Winston claims to "shed some light on [the question:] How do we recognize examples of various concepts?" (1975, p. 157), his theory of concepts as definitions must, like any psychological theory, be subject to empirical test. It so happens that, contrary to Winston's claims, recent evidence collected and analyzed by Eleanor Rosch on just this subject shows that human beings are not aware of classifying objects as instances of abstract rules, but rather group objects as more or less distant from an imagined paradigm. This does not exclude the possibility of unconscious processing, but it does highlight the fact that there is no empirical evidence at all for Winston's formal model. As Rosch puts it:

> Many experiments have shown that categories appear to be coded in the mind neither by means of lists of each individual member of the category, nor by means of a list of formal criteria necessary and sufficient for category membership, but, rather, in terms of a prototype of a typical category member. The most cognitively economical code for a category is, in fact, a *concrete image* of an average category member.   (1977, p. 30)

One paradigm, it seems, is worth a thousand rules. As we shall soon see, one of the characteristics of the next phase of work in AI is to try to take account of the implications of Rosch's research.

Meanwhile, what can we conclude concerning AI's contribution to the science of psychology? No one can deny Minsky and Papert's claim that "computer science has brought a flood of ... ideas, well-defined and experimentally implemented, for thinking about thinking" (1973, p. 25). But all of these ideas can be boiled down to ways of constructing and manipulating symbolic descriptions, and, as we have seen, the notion that human cognition can be explained in terms of formal representations does not seem at all obvious in the face of actual research on perception, and everyday concept formation. Even Minsky and Papert show a commendable new modesty. They as much as admit that AI is still at the stage of astrology, and that the much heralded breakthrough still lies in the future.

> Just as astronomy succeeded astrology, following Kepler's discovery of planetary regularities, the discoveries of these many principles in empirical explorations on intellectual processes in machines should lead to a science, eventually.   (1973, p. 25)

Happily, "should" has replaced "will" in their predictions. Indeed, this period's contribution to psychology suggests an even more modest hope: As more psychologists like Goldmeier are frustrated by the limitations of formal computer models, and others turn to investigating the function of images as opposed to symbolic representations, the strikingly limited success of AI may come to be seen as an important disconfirmation of the information-processing approach.

Before concluding our discussion of this research phase, it should be noted that some problem domains are (nearly enough) micro-worlds already; so they lend themselves to AI techniques without the need for artificial restrictions, and, by the same token, nongeneralizability is not the same kind of Waterloo. Game playing, particularly chess, is the most conspicuous example. Though some extravagant early predictions were not fulfilled, large computers now play fairly high caliber chess, and small machines that play creditable amateur games are being marketed as toys. But game players are not the only examples; excellent programs have been written for analyzing certain kinds of mass-spectroscopy data (Feigenbaum 1977), and for assisting in the diagnosis and treatment of some diseases (Shortliffe 1976). Such work is both impressive and important; but it shouldn't give the *wrong* impression. In each case, it succeeds because (and to the extent that) the relevant domain is well circumscribed in advance, with all the significant facts, questions, and/or options already laid out, and related by a comparatively small set of explicit rules—in short, because it's a micro-world. This is not to belittle either the difficulty or the value of spelling out such domains, or designing programs which perform well in them. But we should not see them as any closer to the achievement of genuine artificial intelligence than we do the "blocks-world" programs. In principle, interpreting mass spectrograms or batteries of specific symptoms has as little to do with the general intelligence of physicists and physicians, as disentangling vertices in projections of polyhedra does with vision. The real, theoretical problems for AI lie elsewhere.

2 The later seventies: knowledge representation

In roughly the latter half of the decade, the problem of how to structure and retrieve information, in situations where *anything* might be relevant, has come to the fore as the "knowledge-representation problem". Of course, the representation of knowledge was always a central problem for work in AI, but earlier periods were characterized by an attempt to repress it by seeing how much could be done with as little knowledge as possible. Now, the difficulties are being faced. As Roger Schank of Yale recently remarked:

> Researchers are starting to understand that *tours de force* in programming are interesting but non-extendable ... the AI people recognize that how people use and represent knowledge is the key issue in the field.   (1977, pp. 1007–1008)

Papert and Goldstein explain the problem:

> It is worthwhile to observe here that the goals of a knowledge-based approach to AI are closely akin to those which motivated Piaget to call ... himself an "epistemologist" rather than a psychologist. The common theme is the view that the process of intelligence is determined by the knowledge held by the subject. The deep and primary questions are to understand the operations and data structures involved.   (1975/76, p. 7)

Another memorandum illustrates how ignoring the background knowledge can come back to haunt one of AI's greatest tricks in the form of nongeneralizability.

> Many problems arise in experiments on machine intelligence because things obvious to any person are not represented in any program. One can pull with a string, but one cannot push with one. One cannot push with a thin wire, either. A taut inextensible cord will break under a very small lateral force. Pushing something affects first its speed, only indirectly its position! Simple facts like these caused serious problems when Charniak attempted to extend Bobrow's STUDENT program to more realistic applications, and they have not been faced up to until now.
> (Papert and Minsky 1973, p. 77)

The most interesting current research is directed toward the underlying problem of developing new, flexible, complex data types which will allow the representation of background knowledge in larger, more structured units.

In 1972, drawing on Husserl's phenomenological analysis, I pointed out that it was a major weakness of AI that no programs made use of expectations (1972/92, pp. 153f/241f and 162/250). Instead of modeling intelligence as a passive receiving of context-free facts into a structure of already stored data, Husserl thinks of intelligence as a context-determined, goal-directed activity—as a *search* for anticipated facts. For him the *noema*, or mental representation of any type of object, provides a context or "inner horizon" of expectations or "predelineations" for structuring the incoming data: a "rule governing *possible* other consciousness of [the object] as identical—possible as exemplifying essentially predelineated types" (Husserl 1960, p. 53). As I explained in chapter 7:

> We perceive a house, for example, as more than a façade—as having some sort of back—some inner horizon. We respond to this whole object first and then, as we get to know the object better, fill in the details as to inside and back.   (p. 153/241)

The noema is thus a symbolic description of all the features which can be expected with certainty in exploring a certain type of object—features which remain, as Husserl puts it, "inviolably the same: as long as the objectivity remains intended as *this* one and of this kind" (p. 51)—plus "predelineations" of those properties which are possible but not necessary features of this type of object.

2.1 Frames and knowledge representation

Then, in 1974, Minsky proposed a new data structure remarkably similar to Husserl's for representing everyday knowledge.

> A frame is a data structure for representing a stereotyped situation, like being in a certain kind of living room, or going to a child's birthday party ...
>
> We can think of a frame as a network of nodes and relations. The "top levels" of a frame are fixed, and represent things that are always true about the supposed situation. The lower levels have many *terminals*—"slots" that must be filled by specific instances or data. Each terminal can specify conditions its assignments must meet ...
>
> Much of the phenomenological power of the theory hinges on the inclusion of expectations and other kinds of presumptions. A frame's terminals are normally already filled with "default" assignments.   (1974 [chapter 5 of this volume], pp. 1f [111f])

In Minsky's model of a frame, the "top level" is a developed version of what in Husserl's terminology "remains inviolably the same" in the representation, and Husserl's predelineations have been made precise as "default assignments"—additional features that can normally be expected. The result is a step forward in AI techniques from a passive model of information processing to one which tries to take account of the context of the interactions between a knower and his world. Husserl thought of his method of transcendental-phenomenological constitution—that is, "explicating" the noemata for all types of objects—as the beginning of progress toward philosophy as a rigorous science; and Patrick Winston has hailed Minsky's proposal as "the ancestor of a wave of progress in AI" (1975, p. 16). But Husserl's project ran into serious trouble and there are signs that Minsky's may too.

During twenty years of trying to spell out the components of the noema of everyday objects, Husserl found that he had to include more and more of what he called the "outer horizon", a subject's total knowledge of the world:

> To be sure, even the tasks that present themselves when we take single types of objects as restricted clues prove to be extremely complicated and always lead to extensive disciplines when we penetrate more deeply. That is the case, for example, with a transcendental theory of the constitution of a spatial object (to say nothing of nature) as such, of psycho-physical being and humanity as such, cultures as such.   (1960, pp. 54–55)

He sadly concluded at the age of seventy-five that he was "a perpetual beginner" and that phenomenology was an "infinite task"—and even that may be too optimistic. His successor, Heidegger, pointed out that since the outer horizon or background of cultural practices was the condition of the possibility of determining relevant facts and features and thus prerequisite for structuring the inner horizon, as long as the cultural context had not been clarified, the proposed analysis of the inner horizon of the noema could not even claim progress.

There are hints in the frame paper that Minsky has embarked on the same misguided "infinite task" that eventually overwhelmed Husserl.

> Just constructing a knowledge base is a major intellectual research problem … We still know far too little about the contents and structure of common-sense knowledge. A "minimal" common-sense system must "know" something about cause and effect, time, purpose, locality, process, and types of knowledge … We need a serious epistemological research effort in this area.   (p. 74 [138])

Minsky's naïveté and faith are astonishing. Philosophers from Plato to Husserl, who uncovered all these problems and more, have carried on serious epistemological research in this area for two thousand years without notable success. Moreover, the list Minsky includes in this passage deals only with natural objects, and their positions and interactions. As Husserl saw, intelligent behavior also presupposes a background of cultural practices and institutions. Observations in the frame paper such as: "Trading normally occurs in a social context of law, trust, and convention. Unless we also represent these other facts, most trade transactions will be almost meaningless" (p. 34 [117]) show that Minsky has understood this too. But Minsky seems oblivious to the hand-waving optimism of his proposal that programmers rush in where philosophers such as Heidegger fear to tread, and simply make explicit the totality of human practices which pervade our lives as water encompasses the life of a fish.

To make this essential point clear, it helps to take an example used by Minsky and look at what is involved in understanding a piece of everyday equipment as simple as a chair. No piece of equipment makes sense by itself. The physical object which is a chair can be defined in isolation as a collection of atoms, or of wood or metal components, but such a description will not enable us to pick out chairs. What makes an object a *chair* is its function, and what makes possible its role as equipment for sitting is its place in a total practical context. This presupposes certain facts about human beings (fatigue, the ways the body bends), and a network of other culturally determined equipment (tables, floors, lamps) and skills (eating, writing, going to conferences, giving lectures). Chairs would not be equipment for sitting if our knees bent backwards like those of flamingos, or if we had no tables, as in traditional Japan or the Australian bush.

Anyone in our culture understands such things as how to sit *on* kitchen chairs, swivel chairs, folding chairs; and *in* arm chairs, rocking chairs, deck chairs, barbers' chairs, sedan chairs, dentists' chairs, basket chairs, reclining chairs, wheel chairs, sling chairs, and beanbag chairs—as well as how to get off/out of them again. This ability presupposes a repertoire of bodily skills which may well be indefinitely large, since there seems to be an indefinitely large variety of chairs and of successful (graceful, comfortable, secure, poised) ways to sit on/in them. Moreover, understanding chairs also includes social skills such as being able to sit appropriately (sedately, demurely, naturally, casually, sloppily, provocatively) at dinners, interviews, desk jobs, lectures, auditions, concerts (intimate enough for there to be chairs rather than seats), and in waiting rooms, living rooms, bedrooms, courts, libraries, and bars (of the sort sporting chairs, not stools).

In light of this amazing capacity, Minsky's remarks on chairs in his frame paper seem more like a review of the difficulties than even a hint of how AI could begin to deal with our common sense understanding in this area.

> There are many forms of chairs, for example, and one should choose carefully the chair-description frames that are to be the major capitals of chair-land. These are used for rapid matching and assigning priorities to the various differences. The lower priority *features* of the *cluster* center then serve ... as properties of the chair *types* ...   (p. 52 [132]; emphasis added)

There is no argument why we should expect to find elementary context-free *features* characterizing a chair *type,* nor any suggestion as to what these features might be. They certainly cannot be legs, back, seat, and so on, since these are not context-free characteristics defined apart from chairs which then "cluster" in a chair representation; rather, legs, back, and the rest, come in all shapes and variety and can only be recognized as *aspects* of already recognized chairs. Minsky continues:

> Difference pointers could be "functional" as well as geometric. Thus, after rejecting a first try at "chair" one might try the functional idea of "something one can sit on" to explain an unconventional form.

But, as we already saw in our discussion of Winston's concept-learning program, a function so defined is not abstractable from human embodied know-how and cultural practices. A functional description such as "something one can sit on" treated merely as an additional context-free descriptor cannot even distinguish conventional chairs from saddles, thrones, and toilets. Minsky concludes:

> Of course, that analysis would fail to capture toy chairs, or chairs of such ornamental delicacy that their actual use would be unthinkable. These would be better handled by the method of excuses, in which one would bypass the usual geometrical or functional explanation in favor of responding to *contexts* involving *art* or *play.*
>
> (emphasis added)

This is what is required all right; but by what elementary features are *these* contexts to be recognized? There is no reason at all to suppose that one can avoid the difficulty of formally representing our knowledge of chairs by abstractly representing even more holistic, concrete, culturally determined, and loosely organized human practices such a art and play.

Minsky in his frame article claims that "the frame idea ... is in the tradition of ... the 'paradigms' of Kuhn" (p. 3 [113]); so it's appropriate to ask whether a theory of formal representation such as Minsky's, even if it can't account for everyday objects like chairs, can do justice to Kuhn's analysis of the role of paradigms in the practice of science. Such a comparison might seem more promising than testing the ability of frames to account for our everyday understanding, since science is a theoretical enterprise which deals with context-free data whose lawlike relations can in principle be grasped by any sufficiently powerful "pure-intellect", whether human, Martian, digital, or divine.

Paradigms, like frames, serve to set up expectations. As Kuhn notes: "In the absence of a paradigm or some candidate for paradigm, all the facts that could possibly pertain to the development of a given science are likely to seem equally relevant" (1962/70, p. 15). Minsky interprets as follows.

> According to Kuhn's model of scientific evolution, normal science proceeds by using established *descriptive schemes*. Major changes result from new paradigms, new ways of describing things ...
>
> Whenever our customary viewpoints do not work well, whenever we fail to find effective frame systems in memory, we must construct new ones that bring out the right *features*.
>
> (p. 58 [135]; emphasis added)

But what Minsky leaves out is precisely Kuhn's claim that a paradigm or exemplar is *not* an *abstract explicit descriptive scheme* utilizing formal *features*, but rather a shared *concrete* case, which dispenses with features altogether.

> The practice of normal science depends on the ability, acquired from exemplars, to group objects and situations into similarity sets which are primitive in the sense that the grouping is done without an answer to the question, "Similar with respect to what?"
>
> (Kuhn 1962/70, p. 200)

Thus, although it is the job of scientists to find abstractable, exact, symbolic descriptions, and *the subject matter of science* consists of such formal accounts, the *thinking* of scientists themselves does not seem to be amenable to this sort of analysis. Kuhn explicitly repudiates any formal reconstruction which claims that the scientists must be using symbolic descriptions.

> I have in mind a manner of knowing which is misconstrued if reconstructed in terms of rules that are first abstracted from exemplars and thereafter function in their stead.   (p. 192)

Indeed, Kuhn sees his book as raising just those questions which Minsky refuses to face.

> Why is the *concrete* scientific achievement, as a locus of professional commitment, prior to the various concepts, laws, theories, and points of view that may be *abstracted* from it? In what sense is the shared paradigm a fundamental unit for the student of scientific development, a unit that *cannot* be fully reduced to logically *atomic components* which might function in its stead?
>
> (p. 11; emphasis added)

Although research based on frames cannot deal with this question, and so cannot account for common-sense or scientific knowledge, the frame idea did bring the problem of how to represent our everyday knowledge into the open in AI. Moreover, it provided a model so vague and suggestive that it could be developed in several different directions. Two alternatives immediately presented themselves: either to use frames as part of a special-purpose micro-world analysis dealing with common-sense knowledge, as if everyday activity took place in preanalyzed specific domains, or else to try to use frame structures in "a no-tricks basic study" of the open-ended character of everyday know-how. Of the two most influential current schools in AI, Roger Schank and his students at Yale have tried the first approach. Winograd, Bobrow, and their group at Stanford and Xerox, the second.

2.2 Scripts and primitive actions

Schank's version of frames are called "scripts". Scripts encode the essential steps involved in stereotypical social activities. Schank uses them to enable a computer to "understand" simple stories. Like the micro-world builders, Schank believes he can start with isolated stereotypical situations described in terms of primitive actions and gradually work up from there to all of human life.

To carry out this project, Schank invented an event description language consisting of eleven primitive acts such as: ATRANS—the transfer of an abstract relationship such as possession, ownership, or control; PTRANS—the transfer of physical location of an object; INGEST—the taking of an object by an animal into the inner workings of that animal, and so forth. (1975a, p 39); and from these primitives he builds gamelike scenarios which enable his program to fill in gaps and pronoun reference in stories.

Such primitive acts, of course, make sense only when the context is already interpreted in a specific piece of discourse. Their artificiality can easily be seen if we compare one of Schank's context-free primitive acts to real-life actions. Take PTRANS, the transfer of physical location of an object. At first it seems an interpretation-free fact if ever there were one. After all, either an object moves or it doesn't. But in real life things are not so simple; even what counts as physical motion depends on our purposes. If someone is standing still in a moving elevator on a moving ocean liner, is his going from A to B deck a PTRANS? What about when he is just sitting on B deck? Are we all PTRANS-ing around the sun? Clearly the answer depends on the situation in which the question is asked.

Such primitives can be used, however, to describe fixed situations or scripts, once the relevant purposes have already been agreed upon. Schank's definition of a script emphasizes its predetermined, bounded, gamelike character.

> We define a script as a *predetermined* causal chain of conceptualizations that describe the *normal sequence of things* in a familiar situation. Thus there is a restaurant script, a birthday-party script, a football-game script, a classroom script, and so on. Each script has a *minimum number of players* and objects that assume certain roles within the script ... [E]ach *primitive* action given stands for the most important *element* in a *standard set* of actions.
>
> (1975b, p. 131; emphasis added)

His illustration of the restaurant script spells out in terms of primitive actions the rules of the restaurant game:

Script: restaurant.
Roles: customer; waitress; chef; cashier.
Reason: to get food so as to go down in hunger and up in pleasure.

Scene 1, entering:

PTRANS—go into restaurant
MBUILD—find table
PTRANS—go to table
MOVE—sit down

Scene 2, ordering:

ATRANS—receive menu
ATTEND—look at it
MBUILD—decide on order
MTRANS—tell order to waitress

Scene 3, eating:

ATRANS—receive food
INGEST—eat food

Scene 4, exiting:

MTRANS—ask for check
ATRANS—give tip to waitress
PTRANS—go to cashier
ATRANS—give money to cashier
PTRANS—go out of restaurant   (1975b, p. 131)

No doubt many of our social activities are stereotyped, and there is nothing in principle misguided in trying to work out primitives and rules for a restaurant game, the way the rules of Monopoly are meant to capture a simplified version of the typical moves in the real estate business. But Schank claims that he can use this approach to understand stories about *actual* restaurant-going—that, in effect, he can treat the sub-world of restaurant going as if it were an isolated microworld. To do this, however, he must artificially limit the possibilities; for, as one might suspect, no matter how stereotyped, going to the restaurant is not a self-contained game but a highly variable set of behaviors which open out into the rest of human activity. What "normally" happens when one goes to a restaurant can be preselected and formalized by the programmer as default assignments; but the background has been left out, so that a program using such a script cannot be said to understand going to a restaurant at all.

This can easily be seen by imagining a situation that deviates from the norm. What if, when one tries to order, one finds that the item in question is not available, or before paying one finds that the bill is added up wrongly? Of course, Schank would answer that he could build these normal ways restaurant going breaks down into his script. But there are always *abnormal* ways everyday activities can break down: the juke box might be too noisy, there might be too many flies on the counter, or, as in the film *Annie Hall,* in a New York delicatessen one's girl friend might order a pastrami sandwich on white bread with mayonnaise. When we understand going to a restaurant we understand how to cope with even these abnormal possibilities because going to a restaurant is part of our everyday activities of going into buildings, getting things we want, interacting with people, and so on.

To deal with this sort of objection, Schank has added some general rules for coping with unexpected disruptions. The general idea is that in a story "it is usual for nonstandard occurrences to be explicitly mentioned" (Schank and Abelson 1977, p. 51); so the program can spot the abnormal events and understand the subsequent events as ways of coping with them. But here we can see that dealing with stories allows Schank to bypass the basic problem, since it is the *author's* understanding of the situation which enables him to decide which events are disruptive enough to mention.

This *ad hoc* way of dealing with the abnormal can always be revealed by asking further questions; for the program has not understood a restaurant story the way people in our culture do, until it can answer such simple questions as: When the waitress came to the table, did she wear clothes? Did she walk forward or backward? Did the customer eat his food with his mouth or his ear? If the program answers, "I don't know", we feel that all of its right answers were tricks or lucky guesses and that it has not understood *anything* of our everyday restaurant behavior.[2] The point here, and throughout, is not that there are subtle things human beings can do and recognize which are beyond the low-level understanding of present programs, but that in any area there are simple taken-for-granted responses central to human understanding, lacking which a computer program cannot be said to have *any understanding at all*. Schank's claim, then, that "the paths of a script are the possibilities that are extant in a situation" (1975b, p. 132) is insidiously misleading. Either it means that the script accounts for the possibilities in the restaurant game defined by Schank, in which case it is true but uninteresting; or he is claiming that he can account for the possibilities in an everyday restaurant situation which is impressive but, by Schank's own admission, false.

Real short stories pose a further problem for Schank's approach. In a script what the primitive actions and facts are is determined beforehand, but in a short story *what counts as the relevant facts depends on the story itself.* For example, a story that describes a bus trip contains in its script that the passenger thanks the driver (a Schank example). But the fact that the passenger thanked the driver would not be important in a story in which the passenger simply took the bus as a part of a longer journey, while it might be crucially important if the story concerned a misanthrope who had never thanked anyone before, or a very law-abiding young man who had courageously broken the prohibition against speaking to drivers in order to speak to the attractive woman driving the bus. Overlooking this point, Schank claimed at a recent meeting that his program, which can extract death statistics from newspaper accident reports, had answered my challenge that a computer would count as intelligent only if it could summarize a short story.[3] But Schank's newspaper program cannot provide a clue concerning judgments of what to include in a story summary because it works only where relevance and significance have been predetermined, and thereby avoids dealing with the world built up in a story in terms of which judgments of relevance and importance are made.

Nothing could ever call into question Schank's basic assumption that all human practice and know-how is represented in the mind as a system of beliefs constructed from context-free primitive actions and facts; but there are signs of trouble. Schank does admit than an individual's "belief system" cannot be fully elicited from him—though he never doubts that it exists and that it could in principle be represented in his formalism. He is therefore led to the desperate idea of a program which could learn about everything from restaurants to life themes the way people do. In one of his papers he concludes:

> We hope to be able to build a program that can learn, as a child does, how to do what we have described in this paper, instead of being spoon-fed the tremendous information necessary.
>
> (1972, pp. 553–554)

In any case, Schank's appeal to learning is at best another evasion. Developmental psychology has shown that children's learning does not consist merely in acquiring more and more information about specific routine situations by adding new primitives and combining old ones, as Schank's view would lead one to expect. Rather, learning of specific details takes place on a background of shared practices which seem to be picked up in everyday interactions not as facts and beliefs but as bodily skills for coping with the world. Any learning presupposes this background of implicit know-how which gives significance to details. Since Schank admits that he cannot see how this background can be made explicit so as to be given to a computer, and since the background is presupposed for the kind of script learning Schank has in mind, it seems that his project of using preanalyzed primitives to capture common sense understanding is doomed.

2.3 KRL: a knowledge-representation language

Winograd and Bobrow propose a more plausible, even if in the last analysis perhaps no more promising, approach that would use the new theoretical power of frames or stereotypes to dispense with the need to preanalyze everyday situations in terms of a set of primitive features whose *relevance is independent of context.* This approach starts with the recognition that in everyday communication: "'Meaning' is multidimensional, formalizable only in terms of the entire complex of goals and knowledge [of the world] being applied by both the producer and understander." (Winograd 1976b, p. 262) This knowledge, of course, is assumed to be "a body of specific beliefs (expressed as symbol structures …) making up the person's 'model of the world'" (p. 268). Given these assumptions, Winograd and his coworkers are developing a new knowledge-representation language (KRL), which they hope will enable programmers to capture these beliefs in symbolic descriptions of multidimensional prototypical objects whose *relevant aspects are a function of their context.*

Prototypes would be structured so that any sort of description from proper names to procedures for recognizing an example could be used to fill in any one of the nodes or slots that are attached to a prototype. This allows representations to be defined in terms of each other, and results in what the authors call "a *holistic* as opposed to *reductionistic* view of representation" (Bobrow and Winograd 1977, p. 7). For example, since any description could be part of any other, chairs could be described as having aspects such as seats and backs, and seats and backs in turn could be described in terms of their function in chairs. Furthermore, each prototypical object or situation could be described from many different perspectives. Thus nothing need be defined in terms of its necessary and sufficient features in the way Winston and traditional philosophers have proposed, but rather, following Rosch's research on prototypes, objects would be classified as more or less resembling certain prototypical descriptions.

Winograd illustrates this idea by using the traditional philosophers' favorite example:

> The word 'bachelor' has been used in many discussions of semantics, since (save for obscure meanings involving aquatic mammals and medieval chivalry) it seems to have a formally tractable meaning which can be paraphrased "an adult human male who has never been married" … In the realistic use of the word, there are many problems which are not as simply stated and formalized. Consider the following exchange.
>
> > Host: I'm having a big party next weekend. Do you know any nice bachelors I could invite?

Yes, I know this fellow X.

The problem is to decide, given the facts below, for which values of X the response would be a reasonable answer, in light of the normal meaning of the word "bachelor". A simple test is to ask for which ones the host might fairly complain "You lied. You said X was a bachelor".

A: Arthur has been living happily with Alice for the last five years. They have a two year old daughter and have never officially married.

B: Bruce was going to be drafted, so he arranged with his friend Barbara to have a justice of the peace marry them so he would be exempt. They have never lived together. He dates a number of women, and plans to have the marriage annulled as soon as he finds someone he wants to marry.

C: Charlie is 17 years old. He lives at home with his parents and is in high school.

D: David is 17 years old. He left home at 13, started a small business, and is now a successful young entrepreneur leading a playboy's life style in his penthouse apartment.

E: Eli and Edgar are homosexual lovers who have been living together for many years.

F: Faisal is allowed by the law of his native Abu Dhabi to have three wives. He currently has two and is interested in meeting another potential fiancée.

G: Father Gregory is the bishop of the Catholic cathedral at Groton upon Thames.

[This] cast of characters could be extended indefinitely, and in each case there are problems in deciding whether the word 'bachelor' could appropriately be applied. In normal use, a word does not convey a clearly definable combination of primitive propositions, but evokes an *exemplar* which possesses a number of properties. This exemplar is not a specific individual in the experience of the language user, but is more abstract, representing a conflation of typical properties. A prototypical bachelor can be described as:

1. a person
2. a male
3. an adult
4. not currently officially married
5. not in a marriage-like living situation

6. potentially marriageable
7. leading a bachelor-like life style
8. not having been married previously
9. having an intention, at least temporarily, not to marry
10. ...

Each of the men described above fits some but not all of these characterizations. Except for narrow legalistic contexts, there is no significant sense in which a subset of the characteristics can be singled out as the "central meaning" of the word. In fact, among native English speakers there is little agreement about whether someone who has been previously married can properly be called a "bachelor" and fairly good agreement that it should not apply to someone who is not potentially marriageable (for instance, has taken a vow of celibacy).

Not only is this list [of properties] open-ended, but the individual terms are themselves not definable in terms of primitive notions. In reducing the meaning of 'bachelor' to a formula involving 'adult' or 'potentially marriageable', one is led into describing these in terms of exemplars as well. 'Adult' cannot be defined in terms of years of age for any but technical legal purposes and in fact even in this restricted sense, it is defined differently for different aspects of the law. Phrases such as 'marriage-like living situation' and 'bachelor-like life-style' reflect directly in the syntactic form the intention to convey stereotyped exemplars rather than formal definitions.   (1976b, 276–278)

Obviously, if KRL succeeds in enabling AI researchers to use such prototypes to write flexible programs, such a language will be a major breakthrough and will avoid the *ad hoc* character of the "solutions" typical of micro-world programs. Indeed, the future of AI depends on some such work as that begun with the development of KRL. But there are problems with this approach. Winograd's analysis has the important consequence that in comparing two prototypes, what counts as a match and thus what count as the relevant aspects which justify the match will be a result of the program's understanding of the current context.

The result of a matching process is not a simple true/false answer. It can be stated in its most general form as: "Given the set of alternatives which I am currently considering ... and looking in order at those stored structures which are most accessible in the *current context*, here is the best match, here is the degree to which it seems to hold, and here are the specific detailed places where match was not found ..."

The selection of the order in which substructures of the description will be compared is a function of their current accessibility, which depends both on the form in which they are stored and the *current context.*   (1976b, p. 281–282; emphasis added)

This raises four increasingly grave difficulties. *First,* for there to be "a class of cognitive 'matching' processes which operate on the descriptions (symbol structures) available for two entities, looking for correspondences and differences" (p. 280), there must be a finite set of prototypes to be matched. To take Winograd's example:

A single object or event can be described with respect to several prototypes, with further specifications from the perspective of each. The fact that last week *Rusty flew to San Francisco* would be expressed by describing the event as a typical instance of *Travel* with the mode specified as *Airplane*, destination *San Francisco*, and so on. It might also be described as a *Visit* with the actor being *Rusty*, the friends a particular group of people, the interaction warm, and so on.   (Bobrow and Winograd 1977, p. 8)

But *"and so on"* covers what might, without predigestion for a specific purpose, be a hopeless proliferation. The same flight might also be a test flight, a check of crew performance, a stopover, a mistake, a golden opportunity, not to mention a visit to brother, sister, thesis adviser, guru, *and so on, and so on, and so on.* Before the program can function at all, the total set of possible alternatives must be pre-selected by the programmer.

Second, the matching makes sense only *after* the current candidates for comparison have been found. In chess, for example, positions can be compared only after the chess master calls to mind past positions that the current board positions might plausibly resemble. And (as in the chess case) the discovery of the relevant candidates which make the matching of aspects possible requires experience and intuitive association.

The only way a KRL-based program (which must use symbolic descriptions) could proceed, in chess or anywhere else, would be to guess some frame on the basis of what was already "understood" by the program, and then see if that frame's features could be matched to some current description. If not, the program would have to backtrack and try another prototype until it found one into whose slots or default terminals the incoming data could be fitted. This seems an altogether implausible and inefficient model of how we perform, and only rarely occurs in our conscious life. Of course, cognitive scientists could answer the above objection by maintaining, in spite of the implausibility, that we try out the various prototypes very quickly and are simply not aware of the frantic shuffling of hypotheses going on in our unconscious. But, in fact, most would still agree with Winograd's (1974) assessment that the frame selection problem remains unsolved.

> The problem of choosing the frames to try is another very open area. There is a selection problem, since we cannot take all of our possible frames for different kinds of events and match them against what is going on. (p. 80)

There is, moreover, a *third* and more basic question which may pose an in-principle problem for any formal holistic account in which the significance of any fact, indeed what counts as a fact, always depends on the context. Bobrow and Winograd stress the critical importance of context.

> The results of human reasoning are *context dependent*, the structure of memory includes not only the long-term storage organization (What do I know?) but also a current context (What is in focus at the moment?). We believe that this is an important feature of human thought, not an inconvenient limitation. (1977, p. 32)

Winograd further notes that "the problem is to find a formal way of talking about ... current attention focus and goals" (1976b, p. 283). Yet he gives no formal account of how a computer program written in KRL could determine the current context.

Winograd's work does contain suggestive claims, such as his remark that "the procedural approach formalizes notions like 'current context' ... and 'attention focus' in terms of the processes by which cognitive state changes as a person comprehends or produces utterances" (pp. 287–288). There are also occasional parenthetical references to "current goals, focus of attention, set of words recently heard, and so on" (p. 282). But reference to recent words has proven useless as a way of determining what the current context is, and reference to current goals and focus of attention is vague and perhaps even question-begging. If a human being's current goal is, say, to find a chair to sit on, his current focus might be on recognizing whether he is in a living room or a warehouse. He will also have short-range goals like finding the walls, longer-range goals like finding the light switch, middle-range goals like wanting to write or rest; and what counts as satisfying these goals will in turn depend on his ultimate goals and interpretation of himself as, say, a writer, or merely as easily exhausted and deserving comfort. So Winograd's appeal to "current goals and focus" covers too much to be useful in determining what specific situation the program is in.

To be consistent, Winograd would have to treat each type of situation the computer could be in as an object with *its* prototypical description; then in recognizing a specific situation, the situation or context in which *that* situation was encountered would determine which foci, goals, and the like, were relevant. But where would such a regress stop? Human beings, of course, don't have this problem. They are, as Heidegger puts it, *always already* in a situation, which they constantly revise. If we look at it genetically, this is no mystery. We can see that human beings are gradually trained into their cultural situation on the basis of their embodied precultural situation, in a way no programmer using KRL is trying to capture. But for this very reason a program in KRL is *not* always-already-in-a-situation. Even if it represents all human knowledge in its stereotypes, including all possible types of human situations, it represents them from the outside, like a Martian or a god. It isn't situated *in* any one of them, and it may be impossible to program it to behave as if it were.

This leads to my *fourth* and final question. Is the know-how that enables human beings constantly to sense what specific situation they are in the sort of know-how that can be represented as a kind of knowledge in *any* knowledge-representation language no matter how ingenious and complex? It seems that our sense of our situation is determined by our changing moods, by our current concerns and projects, by our long-range self-interpretation and probably also by our sensory–motor skills for coping with objects and people—skills we develop by practice without ever having to represent to ourselves our body as an object, our culture as a set of beliefs, or our propensities as situation–action rules. All these uniquely human capacities provide a "richness" or a "thickness" to our way of being-in-the-world and thus seem to play an essential role in situatedness, which in turn underlies all intelligent behavior.

There is no reason to suppose that moods, mattering, and embodied skills can be captured in any formal web of belief; and except for Kenneth Colby, whose view is not accepted by the rest of the AI community, no current work assumes that they can. Rather, all AI workers and cognitive psychologists are committed, more or less lucidly, to the view that such noncognitive aspects of the mind can simply be ignored. This belief that a significant part of what counts as intelligent behavior can be captured in purely cognitive structures defines cognitive science and is a version of what I call the *psychological assumption* (1972/92, chapter 4). Winograd makes it explicit.

> AI is the general study of those aspects of cognition which are common to all physical symbol systems, including humans and computers.   (see Schank et al. 1977, p. 1008)

But this definition merely delimits the field; it in no way shows there is anything to study, let alone guarantees the project's success.

Seen in this light, Winograd's grounds for optimism contradict his own basic assumptions. On the one hand, he sees that a lot of what goes on in human minds cannot be programmed, so he only hopes to program a significant part.

> [C]ognitive science ... does not rest on an assumption that the analysis of mind as a physical symbol system provides a *complete* understanding of human thought ... For the paradigm to be of value, it is only necessary that there be *some significant aspects* of thought and language which can be profitably understood through analogy with other symbol systems we know how to construct.
>   (1976b, p. 264)

On the other hand, he sees that human intelligence is "holistic" and that meaning depends on "the entire complex of goals and knowledge". What our discussion suggests is that all aspects of human thought, including nonformal aspects like moods, sensory–motor skills, and long-range self-interpretations, are so interrelated that one cannot substitute an abstractable web of explicit beliefs for the whole cloth of our concrete everyday practices.

What lends plausibility to the cognitivist position is the conviction that such a web of beliefs must finally fold back on itself and be complete, since we can know only a finite number of facts and procedures describable in a finite number of sentences. But since facts are discriminated, and language is used, only in a context, the argument that the web of belief must in principle be completely formalizable does not show that such a belief system can account for intelligent behavior. This would be true only if the context could also be captured in the web of facts and procedures. But if the context is determined by moods, concerns, and skills, then the fact that our beliefs can in principle be completely represented does not show that representations are sufficient to account for cognition. Indeed, if nonrepresentable capacities play an essential role in situatedness, and the situation is presupposed by all intelligent behavior, then the "aspects of cognition which are common to all physical symbol systems" will not be able to account for any cognitive *performance* at all.

In the end, the very idea of a holistic information-processing model in which the relevance of the facts depends on the context may involve a contradiction. To recognize any context one must have already selected from the indefinite number of possibly discriminable features the possibly relevant ones; but such a selection can be made only after the context has already been recognized as similar to an already analyzed one. The holist thus faces a vicious circle: relevance presupposes similarity and similarity presupposes relevance. The only way to avoid this loop is to be always-already-in-a-situation without representing it, so that the problem of the priority of context and features does not arise, or else to return to the reductionist project of preanalyzing all situations in terms of a fixed set of possibly relevant primitives—a project which has its own practical problems, as our analysis of Schank's work has shown, and, as we shall see in the conclusion, may have its own internal contradiction as well.

Whether this is, indeed, an in-principle obstacle to Winograd's approach, only further research will tell. Winograd himself is admirably cautious in his claims.

> If the procedural approach is successful, it will eventually be possible to describe the mechanisms at such a level of detail that there will be a verifiable fit with many aspects of detailed human performance ... but we are nowhere near having explanations which cover language processing as a whole, including meaning.
>
> (1976b, p. 297)

If problems do arise because of the necessity in any formalism of isolating beliefs from the rest of human activity, Winograd will no doubt have the courage to analyze and profit from the discovery. In the meantime everyone interested in the philosophical project of cognitive science will be watching to see if Winograd and company can produce a moodless, disembodied, concernless, already-adult surrogate for our slowly-acquired situated understanding.

3 Conclusion

Given the fundamental supposition of the information-processing approach that all that is relevant to intelligent behavior can be formalized in a structured description, all problems must appear to be merely problems of complexity. Bobrow and Winograd put this final faith very clearly at the end of their description of KRL.

> The system is complex, and will continue to get more so in the near future … [W]e do not expect that it will ever be reduced to a very small set of mechanisms. Human thought, we believe, is the product of the interaction of a fairly large set of interdependent processes. Any representation language which is to be used in modeling thought or achieving "intelligent" performance will have to have an extensive and varied repertoire of mechanisms.
> (Bobrow and Winograd 1977, p. 43)

Underlying this mechanistic assumption is an even deeper assumption which has gradually become clear during the past ten years of research. During this period, AI researchers have consistently run up against the problem of representing everyday context. Work during the first five years (1967-1972) demonstrated the futility of trying to evade the importance of everyday context by creating artificial gamelike contexts preanalyzed in terms of a list of fixed-relevance features. More recent work has thus been forced to deal directly with the background of common-sense know-how which guides our changing sense of what counts as the relevant facts. Faced with this necessity, researchers have implicitly tried to treat the broadest context or background as an object with its own set of preselected descriptive features. This assumption, that the background can be treated as just another object to be represented in the same sort of structured description in which everyday objects are represented, is essential to our whole philosophical tradition. Following Heidegger, who is the first to have identified and criticized this assumption, I will call it the *metaphysical assumption.*

The obvious question to ask in conclusion is: Is there any evidence, besides the persistent difficulties and history of unfulfilled promises in AI, for believing that the metaphysical assumption is unjustified? It may be that no argument can be given against it, since facts put forth to show that the background of practices is unrepresentable are in that very act shown to be the sort of facts which *can* be represented. Still, I will attempt to lay out the argument which underlies my antiformalist, and therefore, antimechanist convictions.

My thesis, which owes a lot to Wittgenstein (1953), is that whenever human behavior is analyzed in terms of rules, these rules must always contain a *ceteris paribus* condition, that is, they apply "everything else being equal"; and what "everything else" and "equal" mean in any specific situation can never be fully spelled out without a regress. Moreover, the ceteris paribus condition is not merely an annoyance which shows that the analysis is not yet complete and might be what Husserl called and "infinite task". Rather the ceteris paribus condition points to a background of practices which are the condition of the possibility of all rule-like activity. In explaining our actions we must always sooner or later fall back on our everyday practices and simply say "this is what we do" or "that's what it is to be a human being". Thus in the last analysis all intelligibility and all intelligent behavior must be traced back to our sense of what we *are*, which is, according to this argument, necessarily, on pain of regress, something we can never explicitly *know*.

Still, to this dilemma the AI researchers might plausibly respond: "*Whatever* background of shared interests, feelings, and practices is necessary for understanding specific situations, that knowledge *must* somehow be represented in the human beings who have that understanding. And how else could such knowledge be represented but in some explicit data structure?" Indeed, the kind of computer programming accepted by all workers in AI would require such a data structure, and so would philosophers who hold that all knowledge must be explicitly represented in our minds. But there are two alternatives which would avoid the contradictions inherent in the information-processing model, by avoiding the idea that everything we know must be in the form of some explicit symbolic representation.

One response, shared by existential phenomenologists such as Merleau-Ponty and ordinary-language philosophers such as Wittgenstein, is to say that such "knowledge" of human interests and practices need not be represented at all. Just as it seems plausible that I can learn to swim by practicing until I develop the necessary patterns of responses, without representing my body and muscular movements in some data structure, so too what I "know" about the cultural practices which enable me to recognize and act in specific situations has been gradually acquired through training in which no one ever did or could, again on pain of regress, make explicit what was being learned.

Another possible account would allow a place for representations, at least in special cases where I have to stop and reflect, but would stress that these are usually nonformal representations—more like images, by means of which I explore what I *am*, not what I *know*. We thus appeal to *concrete* representations (images or memories) based on our own experience, without having to make explicit the strict rules and their spelled out ceteris paribus conditions as required by *abstract* symbolic representations.

The idea that feelings, memories, and images *must* be the conscious tip of an unconscious frame-like data structure runs up against both prima facie evidence and the problem of explicating the ceteris paribus conditions. Moreover, the formalist assumption is not supported by one shred of scientific evidence from neurophysiology or psychology, or from the past "successes" of AI—whose repeated failures required appeal to the metaphysical assumption in the first place.

AI's current difficulties, moreover, become intelligible in the light of this alternative view. The proposed formal representation of the background of practices in symbolic descriptions, whether in terms of situation-free primitives or more sophisticated data structures whose building blocks can be descriptions of situations, would, indeed, look more and more complex and intractable if minds were not physical symbol systems. If belief structures are the result of abstraction from the concrete practical context, rather than the true building blocks of our world, it is no wonder the formalist finds himself stuck with the view that they are endlessly explicable. On my view, the organization of world knowledge provides the largest stumbling block to AI precisely because the programmer is forced to treat the world as an object, and our know-how as knowledge.

Looking back over the past ten years of AI research we might say that the basic point which has emerged is that *since intelligence must be situated it cannot be separated from the rest of human life.* The persistent denial of this seemingly obvious point cannot, however, be laid at the door of AI. It starts with Plato's separation of the intellect or rational soul from the body with its skills, emotions, and appetites. Aristotle continued this unlikely dichotomy when he separated the theoretical from the practical, and defined man as a *rational* animal—as if one could separate man's rationality from his animal needs and desires. If one thinks of the importance of the sensory–motor skills in the development of our ability to recognize and cope with objects, or of the role of needs and desires in structuring all social situations, or finally of the whole cultural background of human self-interpretation involved in our simply knowing how to pick out and use chairs, the idea that we can simply ignore this know-how while formalizing our intellectual understanding as a complex system of facts and rules is highly implausible.

Great artists have always sensed the truth, stubbornly denied by both philosophers and technologists, that the basis of human intelligence cannot be isolated and explicitly understood. In *Moby Dick*, Melville writes of the tattooed savage, Queequeg, that he had "written out on his body a complete theory of the heavens and the earth, and a mystical treatise on the art of attaining truth; so that Queequeg in his own proper person was a riddle to unfold, a wondrous work in one volume; but whose mysteries not even he himself could read" (1851/ 1952, p. 477). Yeats puts it even more succinctly: "I have found what I wanted—to put it in a phrase I say, 'Man can embody the truth, but he cannot know it'."

Notes

1. This view is worked out further in Heidegger (1927/62); see especially p. 93 and all of section 18.

2. This is John Searle's way of formulating this important point. In a talk at the University of California at Berkeley (October 19, 1977), Schank agreed with Searle that to understand a visit to a restaurant, the computer needs more than a script; it needs to know everything that people know. He added that he is unhappy that as it stands his program cannot distinguish "degrees of weirdness". Indeed, for the program it is equally "weird" for the restaurant to be out of food as it is for the customer to respond by devouring the chef. Thus Schank seems to agree that without some understanding of degree of deviation from the norm, the program does not understand a story even when in that story events follow a completely normal stereotyped script. It follows that although scripts capture a necessary condition of everyday understanding, they do not provide a sufficient condition.

3. At the Society for Interdisciplinary Study of the Mind, Symposium for Philosophy and Computer Technology, State University College, New Paltz, NY, March 1977.

Minds, Brains, and Programs

John R. Searle
1980

What psychological and philosophical significance should we attach to recent efforts at computer simulations of human cognitive capacities? In answering this question I find it useful to distinguish what I will call "strong" AI from "weak" or "cautious" AI. According to weak AI, the principal value of the computer in the study of the mind is that it gives us a very powerful tool. For example, it enables us to formulate and test hypotheses in a more rigorous and precise fashion than before. But according to strong AI the computer is not merely a tool in the study of the mind; rather, the appropriately programmed computer really is a mind in the sense that computers given the right programs can be literally said to *understand* and have other cognitive states. And, according to strong AI, because the programmed computer has cognitive states, the programs are not mere tools that enable us to test psychological explanations; rather, the programs are themselves the explanations. I have no objection to the claims of weak AI, at least as far as this article is concerned. My discussion here will be directed to the claims I have defined as strong AI, specifically the claim that the appropriately programmed computer literally has cognitive states and that the programs thereby explain human cognition. When I refer to AI, it is the strong version as expressed by these two claims which I have in mind.

I will consider the work of Roger Schank and his colleagues at Yale (see, for instance, Schank and Abelson 1977), because I am more familiar with it than I am with any similar claims, and because it provides a clear example of the sort of work I wish to examine. But nothing that follows depends upon the details of Schank's programs. The same arguments would apply to Winograd's (1972) SHRDLU, Weizenbaum's (1965) ELIZA, and indeed, any Turing-machine simulation of human mental phenomena.

Briefly, and leaving out the various details, one can describe Schank's program as follows: the aim of the program is to simulate the human ability to understand stories. It is characteristic of the abilities of human beings to understand stories that they can answer questions about the story, even though the information they give was not explicitly stated in the story. Thus, for example, suppose you are given the following story: "A man went into a restaurant and ordered a hamburger. When the hamburger arrived, it was burned to a crisp, and the man stormed out of the restaurant angrily without paying for the hamburger or leaving a tip." Now, if you are given the question "Did the man eat the hamburger?", you will presumably answer, "No, he did not." Similarly if you are given the following story: "A man went into a restaurant and ordered a hamburger; when the hamburger came, he was very pleased with it; and as he left the restaurant he gave the waitress a large tip before paying his bill.", and you are asked the question "Did the man eat the hamburger?", you will presumably answer, "Yes, he ate the hamburger."

Now Schank's machines can similarly answer questions about restaurants in this fashion. In order to do so, they have a "representation" of the sort of information that human beings have about restaurants which enables them to answer such questions as those above, given these sorts of stories. When the machine is given the story and then asked the question, the machine will print out answers of the sort that we would expect human beings to give if told similar stories. Partisans of strong AI claim that in this question-and-answer sequence, not only is the machine simulating a human ability but also:

(a) The machine can literally be said to *understand* the story and provide answers to questions; and

(b) What the machine and its program do *explains* the human ability to understand the story and answer questions about it.

Claims (a) and (b) seem to me totally unsupported by Schank's work, as I will attempt to show in what follows.[1]

A way to test any theory of mind is to ask oneself what it would be like if one's own mind actually worked on the principles that the theory says all minds work on. Let us apply this test to the Schank program with the following *Gedankenexperiment*. Suppose that I am locked in a room and suppose that I'm given a large batch of Chinese writing. Suppose furthermore, as is indeed the case, that I know no Chinese either written or spoken, and that I'm not even confident that I could recognize Chinese writing as Chinese writing distinct from, say, Japanese writing or meaningless squiggles. Now suppose further that, after this first batch of Chinese writing, I am given a second batch of Chinese script together with a set of rules for correlating the second batch with the first batch. The rules are in English and I understand these rules as well as any other native speaker of English. They enable me to correlate one set of formal symbols with another set of formal symbols, and all that "formal" means here is that I can identify the symbols entirely by their shapes. Now suppose also that I am given a third batch of Chinese symbols together with some instructions, again in English, that enable me to correlate elements of this third batch with the first two batches, and these rules instruct me how I am to give back certain Chinese symbols with certain sorts of shapes in response to certain sorts of shapes given me in the third batch.

Unknown to me, the people who are giving me all of these symbols call the first batch a "script", they call the second batch a "story", and they call the third batch "questions". Furthermore, they call the symbols I give them back in response to the third batch "answers to the questions", and the set of rules in English that they gave me they call "the program". To complicate the story a little bit, imagine that these people also give me stories in English which I understand, and they then ask me questions in English about these stories, and I give them back answers in English. Suppose also that after a while I get so good at following the instructions for manipulating the Chinese symbols and the programmers get so good at writing the programs that from the external point of view—that is, from the point of view of somebody outside the room in which I am locked—my answers to the questions are indistinguishable from those of native Chinese speakers. Nobody looking at my answers can tell that I don't speak a word of Chinese. Let us also suppose that my answers to the English questions are, as they no doubt would be, indistinguishable from those of other native English speakers, for the simple reason that I am a native speaker of English. From the external point of view, from the point of view of someone reading my "answers", the answers to the Chinese questions and the English questions are equally good. But in the Chinese case, unlike the English case, I produce the answers by manipulating uninterpreted formal symbols. As far as the Chinese is concerned, I simply behave like a computer; I perform computational operations on formally specified elements. For the purposes of the Chinese, I am simply an instantiation of the computer program.

Now the claims made by strong AI are that the programmed computer understands the stories and that the program in some sense explains human understanding. But we are now in a position to examine these claims in light of our thought experiment.

(a) As regards the first claim, it seems to me obvious in the example that I do not understand a word of the Chinese stories. I have inputs and outputs that are indistinguishable from those of the native Chinese speaker, and I can have any formal program you like, but I still understand nothing. Schank's computer, for the same reasons, understands nothing of any stories, whether in Chinese, English, or whatever, since in the Chinese case the computer is me; and in cases where the computer is not me, the computer has nothing more than I have in the case where I understand nothing.

(b) As regards the second claim—that the program explains human understanding—we can see that the computer and its program do not provide sufficient conditions of understanding, since the computer and the program are functioning and there is no understanding. But does it even provide a necessary condition or a significant contribution to understanding? One of the claims made by the supporters of strong AI is this: when I understand a story in English, what I am doing is exactly the same—or perhaps more of the same—as what I was doing in the case of manipulating the Chinese symbols. It is simply more formal symbol manipulation which distinguishes the case in English, where I do understand, from the case in Chinese, where I don't. I have not demonstrated that this claim is false, but it would certainly appear an incredible claim in the example.

Such plausibility as the claim has derives from the supposition that we can construct a program that will have the same inputs and outputs as native speakers, and in addition we assume that speakers have some level of description where they are also instantiations of a program. On the basis of these two assumptions, we assume that even if Schank's program isn't the whole story about understanding, maybe it is part of the story. That is, I suppose, an empirical possibility, but not the slightest reason has so far been given to suppose it is true, since what is suggested—though certainly not demonstrated—by the example is that the computer program is irrelevant to my understanding of the story. In the Chinese case I have everything that artificial intelligence can put into me by way of a program, and I understand nothing; in the English case I understand everything, and there is so far no reason at all to suppose that my understanding has anything to do with computer programs—that is, with computational operations on purely formally specified elements.

As long as the program is defined in terms of computational operations on purely formally-defined elements, what the example suggests is that these by themselves have no interesting connection with understanding. They are certainly not sufficient conditions, and not the slightest reason has been given to suppose that they are necessary conditions or even that they make a significant contribution to understanding. Notice that the force of the argument is not simply that different machines can have the same input and output while operating on different formal principles—that is not the point at all—but rather that whatever purely formal principles you put into the computer will not be sufficient for understanding, since a human will be able to follow the formal principles without understanding anything, and no reason has been offered to suppose they are necessary or even contributory, since no reason has been given to suppose that when I understand English, I am operating with any formal program at all.

What is it, then, that I have in the case of the English sentences which I do not have in the case of the Chinese sentences? The obvious answer is that I know what the former mean but haven't the faintest idea what the latter mean. In what does this consist, and why couldn't we give it to a machine, whatever it is? Why couldn't the machine be given whatever it is about me that makes it the case that I know what English sentences mean? I will return to these questions after developing my example a little more.

I HAVE HAD OCCASIONS to present this example to several workers in artificial intelligence and, interestingly, they do not seem to agree on what the proper reply to it is. I get a surprising variety of replies, and in what follows I will consider the most common of these (specified along with their geographical origins). First I want to block out some common misunderstandings about "understanding". In many of these discussions one finds fancy footwork about the word 'understanding'. My critics point out that there are different degrees of understanding, that 'understands' is not a simple two-place predicate, that there are even different kinds and levels of understanding, and often the law of the excluded middle doesn't even apply in a straightforward way to statements of the form 'x understands y', that in many cases it is a matter for decision and not a simple matter of fact whether x understands y. And so on.

To all these points I want to say: "Of course, of course." But they have nothing to do with the points at issue. There are clear cases where 'understands' applies and clear cases where it does not apply; and such cases are all I need for this argument.[2] I understand stories in English; to a lesser degree I can understand stories in French; to a still lesser degree, stories in German; and in Chinese, not at all. My car and my adding machine, on the other hand, understand nothing; they are not in that line of business.

We often attribute "understanding" and other cognitive predicates by metaphor and analogy to cars, adding machines, and other artifacts; but nothing is proved by such attributions. We say, "The door *knows* when to open because of its photoelectric cell", "The adding machine *knows how* (*understands how*, is *able*) to do addition and subtraction but not division", and "The thermostat *perceives* changes in the temperature". The reason we make these attributions is interesting and has to do with the fact that in artifacts we extend our own intentionality;[3] our tools are extensions of our purposes, and so we find it natural to make metaphorical attributions of intentionality to them. But I take it no philosophical ice is cut by such examples. The sense in which an automatic door "understands instructions" from its photoelectric cell is not at all the sense in which I understand English.

If the sense in which Schank's programmed computers understand stories were supposed to be the metaphorical sense in which the door understands, and not the sense in which I understand English, the issue would not be worth discussing. Newell and Simon write that the sense of "understanding" they claim for computers is exactly the same as for human beings. I like the straightforwardness of this claim, and it is the sort of claim I will be considering. I will argue that, in that literal sense, the programmed computer understands what the car and the adding machine understand: exactly nothing. The computer's understanding is not just (as in the case of my understanding of German) partial or incomplete; it is zero.

Now to the replies.

I THE SYSTEMS REPLY (Berkeley): While it is true that the individual person who is locked in the room does not understand the story, the fact is that he is merely part of a whole system and the system does understand the story. The person has large ledger in front of him in which are written the rules, he has a lot of scratch paper and pencils for doing calculations, he has "data banks" of sets of Chinese symbols. Now, understanding is not being ascribed to the mere individual; rather it is being ascribed to this whole system of which he is a part.

My response to the systems theory is simple. Let the individual internalize all of these elements of the system. He memorizes the rules in the ledger and the data banks of Chinese symbols, and he does all the calculations in his head. The individual then incorporates the entire system. There isn't anything at all to the system which he does not encompass. We can even get rid of the room and suppose he works outdoors. All the same, he understands nothing of the Chinese, and a fortiori neither does the system, because there isn't anything in the system which isn't in him. If he doesn't understand, then there is no way the system could understand because the system is just a part of him.

Actually I feel somewhat embarrassed even to give this answer to the systems theory because the theory seems to me so implausible to start with. The idea is that while a person doesn't understand Chinese, somehow the *conjunction* of that person and some bits of paper might understand Chinese. It is not easy for me to imagine how someone who was not in the grip of an ideology would find the idea at all plausible. Still, I think many people who are committed to the ideology of strong AI will in the end be inclined to say something very much like this; so let us pursue it a bit further. According to one version of this view, while the man in the internalized systems example doesn't understand Chinese in the sense that a native Chinese speaker does (because, for example, he doesn't know that the story refers to restaurants and hamburgers, and so on), still "the man as formal symbol manipulation system" *really does understand Chinese.* The subsystem of the man which is the formal symbol manipulation system for Chinese should not be confused with the subsystem for English.

So there are really two subsystems in the man; one understands English, the other Chinese, and "it's just that the two systems have little to do with each other". But, I want to reply, not only do they have little to do with each other, they are not even remotely alike. The subsystem that understands English (assuming we allow ourselves to talk in this jargon of "subsystems" for a moment) knows that the stories are about restaurants and eating hamburgers, and the like; he knows that he is being asked questions about restaurants and that he is answering questions as best he can by making various inferences from the content of the story, and so on. But the Chinese system knows none of this; whereas the English subsystem knows that 'hamburgers' refers to hamburgers, the Chinese subsystem knows only that 'squiggle-squiggle' is followed by 'squoggle-squoggle'. All he knows is that various formal symbols are being introduced at one end and are manipulated according to rules written in English, and that other symbols are going out at the other end.

The whole point of the original example was to argue that such symbol manipulation by itself couldn't be sufficient for understanding Chinese in any literal sense because the man could write 'squoggle-squoggle' after 'squiggle-squiggle' without understanding anything in Chinese. And it doesn't meet that argument to postulate subsystems within the man, because the subsystems are no better off than the man was in the first place; they still don't have anything even remotely like what the English-speaking man (or subsystem) has. Indeed, in the case as described, the Chinese subsystem is simply a part of the English subsystem, a part that engages in meaningless symbol manipulation according to the rules of English.

Let us ask ourselves what is supposed to motivate the systems reply in the first place—that is, what *independent* grounds are there supposed to be for saying that the agent must have a subsystem within him that literally understands stories in Chinese? As far as I can tell, the only grounds are that in the example I have the same input and output as native Chinese speakers, and a program that goes from one to the other. But the point of the example has been to show that that couldn't be sufficient for understanding, in the sense in which I understand stories in English, because a person, hence the set of systems that go to make up a person, could have the right combination of input, output, and program and still not understand anything in the relevant literal sense in which I understand English.

The only motivation for saying there *must* be a subsystem in me that understands Chinese is that I have a program and I can pass the Turing test: I can fool native Chinese speakers (see Turing 1950 [chapter 2 of this volume]). But precisely one of the points at issue is the adequacy of the Turing test. The example shows that there could be two "systems", both of which pass the Turing test, but only one of which understands; and it is no argument against this point to say that, since they both pass the Turing test, they must both understand, since this claim fails to meet the argument that the system in me which understands English has a great deal more than the system which merely processes Chinese. In short the systems reply simply begs the question by insisting without argument that the system must understand Chinese.

Furthermore, the systems reply would appear to lead to consequences that are independently absurd. If we are to conclude that there must be cognition in me on the grounds that I have a certain sort of input and output and a program in between, then it looks as though all sorts of noncognitive subsystems are going to turn out to be cognitive. For example, my stomach has a level of description where it does information processing, and it instantiates any number of computer programs, but I take it we do not want to say that it has any understanding. Yet if we accept the systems reply, it is hard to see how we can avoid saying that stomach, heart, liver, and so on, are all understanding subsystems, since there is no principled way to distinguish the motivation for saying the Chinese subsystem understands from saying that the stomach understands. (It is, by the way, not an answer to this point to say that the Chinese system has information as input and output and the stomach has food and food products as input and output, since from the point of view of the agent, from my point of view, there is no information in either the food or the Chinese; the Chinese is just so many meaningless squiggles. The information in the Chinese case is solely in the eyes of the programmers and the interpreters, and there is nothing to prevent them from treating the input and output of my digestive organs as information if they so desire.)

This last point bears on some independent problems in strong AI, and it is worth digressing for a moment to explain it. If strong AI is to be a branch of psychology, it must be able to distinguish systems which are genuinely mental from those which are not. It must be able to distinguish the principles on which the mind works from those on which nonmental systems work; otherwise it will offer us no explanations of what is specifically mental about the mental. And the mental/nonmental distinction cannot be just in the eye of the beholder—it must be intrinsic to the systems. For otherwise it would be up to any beholder to treat people as nonmental and, for instance, hurricanes as mental, if he likes.

But quite often in the AI literature the distinction is blurred in ways which would in the long run prove disastrous to the claim that AI is a cognitive inquiry. McCarthy, for example, writes: "Machines as simple as thermostats can be said to have beliefs, and having beliefs seems to be a characteristic of most machines capable of problem solving performance" (1979). Anyone who thinks strong AI has a chance as a theory of the mind ought to ponder the implications of that remark. We are asked to accept it as a discovery of strong AI that the hunk of metal on the wall which we use to regulate the temperature has beliefs in exactly the same sense that we, our spouses, and our children have beliefs, and furthermore that "most" of the other machines in the room—telephone, tape recorder, adding machine, electric light switch, and so on—also have beliefs in this literal sense. It is not the aim of this article to argue against McCarthy's point, so I will simply assert the following without argument. The study of the mind starts with such facts as that humans have beliefs and thermostats, telephones, and adding machines don't. If you get a theory that denies this point, you have produced a counter-example to the theory, and the theory is false.

One gets the impression that people in AI who write this sort of thing think they can get away with it because they don't really take it seriously and they don't think anyone else will either. I propose, for a moment at least, to take it seriously. Think hard for one minute about what would be necessary to establish that that hunk of metal on the wall over there has real beliefs, beliefs with direction of fit, propositional content, and conditions of satisfaction; beliefs that have the possibility of being strong beliefs or weak beliefs; nervous, anxious or secure beliefs; dogmatic, rational, or superstitious beliefs; blind faiths or hesitant cogitations; any kind of beliefs. The thermostat is not a candidate. Neither are stomach, liver, adding machine, or telephone. However, since we are taking the idea seriously, notice that its truth would be fatal to the claim of strong AI to be a science of the mind, for now the mind is everywhere. What we wanted to know is what distinguishes the mind from thermostats, livers, and the rest. And if McCarthy were right, strong AI wouldn't have a hope of telling us that.

II The robot reply (Yale): Suppose we wrote a different kind of program from Schank's program. Suppose we put a computer inside a robot, and this computer would not just take in formal symbols as input and give out formal symbols as output, but rather it would actually operate the robot in such a way that the robot does something very much like perceiving, walking, moving about, hammering nails, eating, drinking—anything you like. The robot would, for example, have a television camera attached to it that enabled it to see, it would have arms and legs that enabled it to act, and all of this would be controlled by its computer brain. Such a robot would, unlike Schank's computer, have genuine understanding and other mental states.

The first thing to notice about the robot reply is that it tacitly concedes that cognition is not solely a matter of formal symbol manipulation, since this reply adds a set of causal relations with the outside world.

But the answer to the robot reply is that the addition of such "perceptual" and "motor" capacities adds nothing by way of understanding, in particular, or intentionality, in general, to Schank's original program. To see this, notice that the same thought experiment applies to the robot case. Suppose that, instead of the computer inside the robot, you put me inside the room and you give me again, as in the original Chinese case, more Chinese symbols with more instructions in English for matching Chinese symbols to Chinese symbols and feeding back Chinese symbols to the outside.

Now suppose also that, unknown to me, some of the Chinese symbols that come to me come from a television camera attached to the robot, and other Chinese symbols that I am giving out serve to make the motors inside the robot move the robot's legs or arms. It is important to emphasize that all I am doing is manipulating formal symbols; I know none of these other facts. I am receiving "information" from the robot's "perceptual" apparatus, and I am giving out "instructions" to its motor apparatus without knowing either of these facts. I am the robot's homunculus, but unlike the traditional homunculus, I don't know what's going on. I don't understand anything except the rules for symbol manipulation. Now in this case I want to say that the robot has no intentional states at all; it is simply moving about as a result of its electrical wiring and its program. And furthermore, by instantiating the program, I have no intentional states of the relevant type. All I do is follow formal instructions about manipulating formal symbols.

III THE BRAIN-SIMULATOR REPLY (Berkeley and MIT): Suppose we design a program that doesn't represent information that we have about the world, such as the information in Schank's scripts, but simulates the actual sequence of neuron firings at the synapses of the brain of a native Chinese speaker when he understands stories in Chinese and gives answers to them. The machine takes in Chinese stories and questions about them as input, it simulates the formal structure of actual Chinese brains in processing these stories, and it gives out Chinese answers as outputs. We can even imagine that the machine operates not with a single serial program but with a whole set of programs operating in parallel, in the manner that actual human brains presumably operate when they process natural language. Now surely in such a case we would have to say that the machine understood the stories; and if we refuse to say that, wouldn't we also have to deny that native Chinese speakers understood the stories? At the level of the synapses what would or could be different about the program of the computer and the program of the Chinese brain?

Before addressing this reply, I want to digress to note that it is an odd reply for any partisan of artificial intelligence (functionalism, and so on) to make. I thought the whole idea of strong artificial intelligence is that we don't need to know how the brain works to know how the mind works. The basic hypothesis, or so I had supposed, was that there is a level of mental operations that consists in computational processes over formal elements which constitute the essence of the mental, and can be realized in all sorts of different brain processes in the same way that any computer program can be realized in different computer hardware. On the assumptions of strong AI, the mind is to the brain as the program is to the hardware, and thus we can understand the mind without doing neurophysiology. If we had to know how the brain worked in order to do AI, we wouldn't bother with AI.

However, even getting this close to the operation of the brain is still not sufficient to produce understanding. To see that this is so, imagine that instead of a monolingual man in a room shuffling symbols we have the man operate an elaborate set of water pipes with valves connecting them. When the man receives the Chinese symbols he looks up in the program, written in English, which valves he has to turn on and off. Each water connection corresponds to a synapse in the Chinese brain, and the whole system is rigged up so that after doing all the right firings—that is, after turning on all the right faucets—the Chinese answers pop out at the output end of the series of pipes.

Now where is the understanding in this system? It takes Chinese as input, it simulates the formal structure of the synapses of the Chinese brain, and it gives Chinese as output. But the man certainly doesn't understand Chinese, and neither do the water pipes. And if we are tempted to adopt what I think is the absurd view that somehow the *conjunction* of man *and* water pipes understands, remember that in principle the man can internalize the formal structure of the water pipes and do all the "neuron firings" in his imagination. The problem with the brain simulator is that it is simulating the wrong things about the brain. As long as it simulates only the formal structure of the sequence of neuron firings at the synapses, it won't have simulated what matters about the brain: its ability to produce intentional states. And that the formal properties are not sufficient for the causal properties is shown by the water pipe example. We can have all the formal properties carved off from the relevant neurobiological causal properties.

IV THE COMBINATION REPLY (Berkeley and Stanford): While each of the previous three replies might not be completely convincing by itself as a refutation of the Chinese room counter-example, if you take all three together they are collectively much more convincing and even decisive. Imagine a robot with a brain-shaped computer lodged in its cranial cavity; imagine the computer programmed with all the synapses of a human brain; imagine that the whole behavior of the robot is indistinguishable from human behavior; and now think of the whole thing as a unified system and not just as a computer with inputs and outputs. Surely in such a case we would have to ascribe intentionality to the system.

I entirely agree that in such a case we would find it rational and indeed irresistible to accept the hypothesis that the robot had intentionality, as long as we knew nothing more about it. Indeed, besides appearance and behavior, the other elements of the combination are really irrelevant. If we could build a robot whose behavior was indistinguishable over a large range from human behavior, we would attribute intentionality to it, pending some reason not to. We wouldn't need to know in advance that its computer brain was a formal analogue of the human brain.

But I really don't see that this is any help to the claims of strong AI, and here is why. According to strong AI, instantiating a formal program with the right input and output is a sufficient condition of, indeed is constitutive of, intentionality. As Newell (1980) puts it, the essence of the mental is the operation of a physical symbol system. But the attributions of intentionality that we make to the robot in this example have nothing to do with formal programs. They are simply based on the assumption that if the robot looks and behaves sufficiently like us, we would suppose, until proven otherwise, that it must have mental states like ours, which cause and are expressed by its behavior, and it must have an inner mechanism capable of producing such mental states. If we knew independently how to account for its behavior without such assumptions, we would not attribute intentionality to it, especially if we knew it had a formal program. And this is the point of my earlier response to the robot reply.

Suppose we knew that the robot's behavior was entirely accounted for by the fact that a man inside it was receiving uninterpreted formal symbols from the robot's sensory receptors and sending out uninterpreted formal symbols to its motor mechanisms, and the man was doing this symbol manipulation in accordance with a bunch of rules. Furthermore, suppose the man knows none of these facts about the robot; all he knows is which operations to perform on which meaningless symbols. In such a case we would regard the robot as an ingenious mechanical dummy. The hypothesis that the dummy has a mind would now be unwarranted and unnecessary, for there is now no longer any reason to ascribe intentionality to the robot or to the system of which it is a part (except of course for the man's intentionality in manipulating the symbols). The formal symbol manipulations go on, the input and output are correctly matched, but the only real locus of intentionality is the man, and he doesn't know any of the relevant intentional states; he doesn't, for example, *see* what comes into the robot's eyes, he doesn't *intend* to move the robot's arm, and he doesn't *understand* any of the remarks made to or by the robot. Nor, for the reasons stated earlier, does the system of which man and robot are a part.

To see the point, contrast this case with cases where we find it completely natural to ascribe intentionality to members of certain other primate species, such as apes and monkeys, and to domestic animals, such as dogs. The reasons we find it natural are, roughly, two: we can't make sense of the animal's behavior without the ascription of intentionality, and we can see that the beasts are made of stuff similar to our own—an eye, a nose, its skin, and so on. Given the coherence of the animal's behavior and the assumption of the same causal stuff underlying it, we assume both that the animal must have mental states underlying its behavior, and that the mental states must be produced by mechanisms made out of the stuff that is like our stuff. We would certainly make similar assumptions about the robot unless we had some reason not to; but as soon as we knew that the behavior was the result of a formal program, and that the actual causal properties of the physical substance were irrelevant, we would abandon the assumption of intentionality.

There are two other responses to my example which come up frequently (and so are worth discussing) but really miss the point.

V THE OTHER-MINDS REPLY (Yale): How do you know that other people understand Chinese or anything else? Only by their behavior. Now the computer can pass the behavior tests as well as they can (in principle), so if you are going to attribute cognition to other people, you must in principle also attribute it to computers.

The objection is worth only a short reply. The problem in this discussion is not about how I know that other people have cognitive states, but rather what it is that I am attributing to them when I attribute cognitive states to them. The thrust of the argument is that it couldn't be just computational processes and their output because there can be computational processes and their output without the cognitive state. It is no answer to this argument to feign anesthesia. In "cognitive sciences" one presupposes the reality and knowability of the mental in the same way that in physical sciences one has to presuppose the reality and knowability of physical objects.

VI THE MANY-MANSIONS REPLY (Berkeley): Your whole argument presupposes that AI is only about analogue and digital computers. But that just happens to be the present state of technology. Whatever these causal processes are that you say are essential for intentionality (assuming you are right), eventually we will be able to build devices that have these causal processes, and that will be artificial intelligence. So your arguments are in no way directed at the ability of artificial intelligence to produce and explain cognition.

I have no objection to this reply except to say that it in effect trivializes the project of strong artificial intelligence by redefining it as whatever artificially produces and explains cognition. The interest of the original claim made on behalf of artificial intelligence is that it was a precise, well defined thesis: mental processes are computational processes over formally defined elements. I have been concerned to challenge that thesis. If the claim is redefined so that it is no longer that thesis, my objections no longer apply, because there is no longer a testable hypothesis for them to apply to.

LET US NOW RETURN to the questions I promised I would try to answer. Granted that in my original example I understand the English and I do not understand the Chinese, and granted therefore that the machine doesn't understand either English or Chinese, still there must be something about me that makes it the case that I understand English, and a corresponding something lacking in me which makes it the case that I fail to understand Chinese. Now why couldn't we give the former something, whatever it is, to a machine?

I see no reason in principle why we couldn't give a machine the capacity to understand English or Chinese, since in an important sense our bodies with our brains are precisely such machines. But I do see very strong arguments for saying that we could not give such a thing to a machine where the operation of the machine is defined solely in terms of computational processes over formally defined elements— that is, where the operation of the machine is defined as an instantiation of a computer program. It is not because I am the instantiation of a computer program that I am able to understand English and have other forms of intentionality. (I am, I suppose, the instantiation of any number of computer programs.) Rather, as far as we know, it is because I am a certain sort of organism with a certain biological (that is, chemical and physical) structure, and this structure under certain conditions is causally capable of producing perception, action, understanding, learning, and other intentional phenomena. And part of the point of the present argument is that only something that had those causal powers could have that intentionality. Perhaps other physical and chemical processes could produce exactly these effects; perhaps, for example, Martians also have intentionality, but their brains are made of different stuff. That is an empirical question, rather like the question whether photosynthesis can be done by something with a chemistry different from that of chlorophyll.

But the main point of the present argument is that no purely formal model will ever be by itself sufficient for intentionality, because the formal properties are not by themselves constitutive of intentionality, and they have by themselves no causal powers except the power, when instantiated, to produce the next state of the formalism when the machine is running. And any other causal properties which particular realizations of the formal model have are irrelevant to the formal model, because we can always put the same formal model in a different realization where those causal properties are obviously absent. Even if by some miracle Chinese speakers exactly realize Schank's program, we can put the same program in English speakers, water pipes, or computers, none of which understand Chinese, the program notwithstanding.

What matters about brain operation is not the formal shadow cast by the sequence of synapses but rather the actual properties of the sequences. All arguments for the strong version of artificial intelligence that I have seen insist on drawing an outline around the shadows cast by cognition and then claiming that the shadows are the real thing.

BY WAY OF CONCLUDING I want to state some of the general philosophical points implicit in the argument. For clarity I will try to do it in a question-and-answer fashion, and I begin with that old chestnut:

• Could a machine think?

The answer is, obviously: Yes. We are precisely such machines.

• Yes, but could an artifact, a man-made machine, think?

Assuming it is possible to produce artificially a machine with a nervous system, neurons with axons and dendrites, and all the rest of it, sufficiently like ours, again the answer to the question seems to be obviously: Yes. If you can exactly duplicate the causes, you can duplicate the effects. And indeed it might be possible to produce consciousness, intentionality, and all the rest of it, using chemical principles different from those human beings use. It is, as I said, an empirical question.

• OK, but could a digital computer think?

If by "digital computer" we mean anything at all which has a level of description where it can correctly be described as the instantiation of a computer program, then, since we are the instantiations of any number of computer programs and we can think, again the answer is, of course: Yes.

• But could something think, understand, and so on, *solely by virtue of* being a computer with the right sort of program? Could instantiating a program, the right program of course, by itself be a sufficient condition for understanding?

This I think is the right question to ask, though it is usually confused with one or more of the earlier questions, and the answer to it is: No.

• Why not?

Because the formal symbol manipulations by themselves don't have any intentionality. They are meaningless—they aren't even *symbol* manipulations, since the "symbols" don't symbolize anything. In the linguistic jargon, they have only a syntax but no semantics. Such intentionality as computers appear to have is solely in the minds of those who program them and those who use them, those who send in the input and who interpret the output.

The aim of the Chinese room example was to try to show this by showing that, as soon as we put something into the system which really does have intentionality, a man, and we program the man with the formal program, you can see that the formal program carries no additional intentionality. It adds nothing, for example, to a man's ability to understand Chinese.

Precisely that feature of AI which seemed so appealing—the distinction between the program and the realization—proves fatal to the claim that simulation could be duplication. The distinction between the program and its realization in the hardware seems to be parallel to the distinction between the level of mental operations and the level of brain operations. And if we could describe the level of mental operations as a formal program, it seems we could describe what was essential about the mind without doing either introspective psychology or neurophysiology of the brain. But the equation "Mind is to brain as program is to hardware" breaks down at several points, among them the following three.

First, the distinction between program and realization has the consequence that the same program could have all sorts of crazy realizations which have no form of intentionality. Weizenbaum (1976), for example, shows in detail how to construct a computer using a roll of toilet paper and a pile of small stones. Similarly, the Chinese story-understanding program can be programmed into a sequence of water pipes, a set of wind machines, or a monolingual English speaker—none of which thereby acquires an understanding of Chinese. Stones, toilet paper, wind, and water pipes are the wrong kind of stuff to have intentionality in the first place (only something that has the same causal powers as brains can have intentionality), and, though the English speaker has the right kind of stuff for intentionality, you can easily see that he doesn't get any extra intentionality by memorizing the program, since memorizing it won't teach him Chinese.

Second, the program is purely formal, but the intentional states are not in that way formal. They are defined in terms of their content, not their form. The belief that it is raining, for example, if defined not as a certain formal shape, but as a certain mental content, with conditions of satisfaction, a direction of fit, and so on (see Searle 1979). Indeed, the belief as such hasn't even got a formal shape in this syntactical sense, since one and the same belief can be given an indefinite number of different syntactical expressions in different linguistic systems.

Third, as I mentioned before, mental states and events are a product of the operation of the brain, but the program is not in that way a product of the computer.

- Well if programs are in no way constitutive of mental processes, then why have so many people believed the converse? That at least needs some explanation.

I don't know the answer to that. The idea that computer simulations could be the real thing ought to have seemed suspicious in the first place, because the computer isn't confined to simulating mental operations, by any means. No one supposes that computer simulations of a five-alarm fire will burn the neighborhood down, or that a computer simulation of a rainstorm will leave us all drenched. Why on earth would anyone suppose that a computer simulation of understanding actually understood anything? It is sometimes said that it would be frightfully hard to get computers to feel pain or fall in love, but love and pain are neither harder nor easier than cognition or anything else. For simulation, all you need is the right input and output and a program in the middle that transforms the former into the latter. That is all the computer has for anything it does. To confuse simulation with duplication is the same mistake, whether it is pain, love, cognition, fires, or rainstorms.

Still, there are several reasons why AI must have seemed, and to many people perhaps still does seem in some way to reproduce and thereby explain mental phenomena. And I believe we will not succeed in removing these illusions until we have fully exposed the reasons that give rise to them.

First, and perhaps most important, is a confusion about the notion of "information processing". Many people in cognitive science believe that the human brain with its mind does something called "information processing", and, analogously, the computer with its program does information processing; but fires and rainstorms, on the other hand, don't do information processing at all. Thus, though the computer can simulate the formal features of any process whatever, it stands in a special relation to the mind and brain because, when the computer is properly programmed, ideally with the same program as the brain, the information processing is identical in the two cases, and this information processing is really the essence of the mental.

But the trouble with this argument is that it rests on an ambiguity in the notion of "information". In the sense in which people "process information" when they reflect, say, on problems in arithmetic or when they read and answer questions about stories, the programmed computer does not do "information processing". Rather, what it does is manipulate formal symbols. The fact that the programmer and the interpreter of the computer output use the symbols to stand for objects in the world is totally beyond the scope of the computer. The computer, to repeat, has a syntax but no semantics. Thus if you type into the computer "2 plus 2 equals?" it will type out "4". But it has no idea that '4' means 4, or that it means anything at all. And the point is not that it lacks some second-order information about the interpretation of its first-order symbols, but rather that its first-order symbols don't have any interpretations as far as the computer is concerned. All the computer has is more symbols.

The introduction of the notion of "information processing" therefore produces a dilemma. Either we construe the notion of "information processing" in such a way that it implies intentionality as part of the process, or we don't. If the former, then the programmed computer does not do information processing, it only manipulates formal symbols. If the latter, then, although the computer does information processing, it is only in the sense in which adding machines, typewriters, stomachs, thermostats, rainstorms, and hurricanes do information processing—namely, in the sense that there is a level of description at which we can describe them as taking information in at one end, transforming it, and producing information as output. But in this case it is up to outside observers to interpret the input and output as information in the ordinary sense. And no similarity is established between the computer and the brain in terms of any similarity of information processing in either of the two cases.

Secondly, in much of AI there is a residual behaviorism or operationalism. Since appropriately programmed computers can have input/output patterns similar to human beings, we are tempted to postulate mental states in the computer similar to human mental states. But once we see that it is both conceptually and empirically possible for a system to have human capacities in some realm without having any intentionality at all, we should be able to overcome this impulse. My desk adding machine has calculating capacities but no intentionality; and in this paper I have tried to show that a system could have input and output capabilities which duplicated those of a native Chinese speaker and still not understand Chinese, regardless of how it was programmed. The Turing test is typical of the tradition in being unashamedly behavioristic and operationalistic, and I believe that if AI workers totally repudiated behaviorism and operationalism, much of the confusion between simulation and duplication would be eliminated.

Third, this residual operationalism is joined to a residual form of dualism; indeed, strong AI only makes sense given the dualistic assumption that where the mind is concerned the brain doesn't matter. In strong AI (and in functionalism, as well) what matters are programs, and programs are independent of their realization in machines; indeed, as far as AI is concerned, the same program could be realized by an electronic machine, a Cartesian mental substance, or an Hegelian world spirit. The single most surprising discovery that I have made in discussing these issues is that many AI workers are shocked by my idea that actual human mental phenomena might be dependent on actual physical-chemical properties of actual human brains. But I should not have been surprised; for unless you accept some form of dualism, the strong-AI project hasn't got a chance.

The project is to reproduce and explain the mental by designing programs; but unless the mind is not only conceptually but empirically independent of the brain, you cannot carry out the project, for the program is completely independent of any realization. Unless you believe that the mind is separable from the brain both conceptually and empirically—dualism in a strong form—you cannot hope to reproduce the mental by writing and running programs, since programs must be independent of brains or any other particular forms of instantiation. If mental operations consist of computational operations on formal symbols, it follows that they have no interesting connection with the brain, and the only connection would be that the brain just happens to be one of the indefinitely many types of machines capable of instantiating the program. This form of dualism is not the traditional Cartesian variety that claims there are two sorts of *substances*, but it is Cartesian in the sense that it insists that what is specifically mental about the mind has no intrinsic connection with the actual properties of the brain. This underlying dualism is masked from us by the fact that AI literature contains frequent fulminations against "dualism". What the authors seem to be unaware of is that their position presupposes a strong version of dualism.

• Could a machine think?

My own view is that *only* a machine could think, and indeed only very special kinds of machines, namely brains and machines that had the *same causal powers* as brains. And that is the main reason why strong AI has had little to tell us about thinking: it has nothing to tell us about machines. By its own definition it is about programs, and programs are

not machines. Whatever else intentionality is, it is a biological phenomenon, and it is likely to be as causally dependent on the specific
biochemistry of its origins as are lactation, photosynthesis, or any biological phenomena. No one would suppose that we could produce
milk and sugar by running a computer simulation of the formal
sequences in lactation and photosynthesis; but where the mind is concerned, many people are willing to believe in such a miracle, because of
a deep and abiding dualism: the mind, they suppose, is a matter of formal processes and is independent of specific material causes in a way
that milk and sugar are not.

In defense of this dualism, the hope is often expressed that the
brain is a digital computer. (Early computers, by the way, were often
called "electronic brains".) But that is no help. Of course the brain is a
digital computer. Since everything is a digital computer, brains are too.
The point is that the brain's causal capacity to produce intentionality
cannot consist in its instantiating a computer program, since for any
program you like it is possible for something to instantiate that program and still not have any mental states. Whatever it is that the brain
does to produce intentionality, it cannot consist in instantiating a program, since no program by itself is sufficient for intentionality.

Notes

1. I am not saying, of course, that Schank himself is committed to these
   claims.

2. Also, "understanding" implies both the possession of mental (intentional) states and the truth (validity, success) of these states. For the
   purposes of this discussion, we are concerned only with the possession
   of the states.

3. Intentionality is by definition that feature of certain mental states by
   which they are directed at or are about objects and states of affairs in the
   world. Thus, beliefs, desires, and intentions are intentional states; undi-
   rected forms of anxiety and depression are not. (For further discussion,
   see Searle 1979).

The Architecture of Mind: A Connectionist Approach

David E. Rumelhart

1989

Cognitive science has a long-standing and important relationship to the computer. The computer has provided a tool whereby we have been able to express our theories of mental activity; it has been a valuable source of metaphors through which we have come to understand and appreciate how mental activities might arise out of the operations of simple-component processing elements.

I recall vividly a class I taught some fifteen years ago in which I outlined the then-current view of the cognitive system. A particularly skeptical student challenged my account, with its reliance on concepts drawn from computer science and artificial intelligence, with the question of whether I thought my theories would be different if it had happened that our computers were parallel instead of serial. My response, as I recall, was to concede that our theories might very well be different, but to argue that that wasn't a bad thing. I pointed out that the inspiration for our theories and our understanding of abstract phenomena always is based on our experience with the technology of the time. I pointed out that Aristotle had a wax tablet theory of memory, that Leibniz saw the universe as clockworks, that Freud used a hydraulic model of libido flowing through the system, and that the telephone-switchboard model of intelligence had played an important role as well. The theories posited by those of previous generations had, I suggested, been useful in spite of the fact that they were based on the metaphors of their time. Therefore, I argued, it was natural that in our generation—the generation of the serial computer—we should draw our insights from analogies with the most advanced technological developments of our time. I don't now remember whether my response satisfied the student, but I have no doubt that we in cognitive science have gained much of value through our use of concepts drawn from our experience with the computer.

In addition to its value as a source of metaphors, the computer differs from earlier technologies in another remarkable way. The computer can be made to *simulate* systems whose operations are very different from the computers on which these simulations run. In this way we can use the computer to simulate systems with which we *wish* to have experience and thereby provide a source of experience that can be drawn upon in giving us new metaphors and new insights into how mental operations might be accomplished. It is this use of the computer that the connectionists have employed. The architecture that we are exploring is not one based on the von Neumann architecture of our current generation of computers but rather an architecture based on considerations of how brains themselves might function. Our strategy has thus become one of offering a general and abstract model of the computational architecture of brains, to develop algorithms and procedures well suited to this architecture, to simulate these procedures and architecture on a computer, and to explore them as hypotheses about the nature of the human information-processing system. We say that such models are *neurally inspired*, and we call computation on such a system *brain-style computation*. Our goal in short is to replace the computer metaphor with the brain metaphor.

1 Why brain-style computation?

Why should a brain-style computer be an especially interesting source of inspiration? Implicit in the adoption of the computer metaphor is an assumption about the appropriate level of explanation in cognitive science. The basic assumption is that we should seek explanation at the *program* or *functional* level rather than the implementation level. Thus, it is often pointed out that we can learn very little about what kind of program a particular computer may be running by looking at the electronics. In fact we don't care much about the details of the computer at all; all we care about is the particular program it is running. If we know the program, we know how the system will behave in any situation. It doesn't matter whether we use vacuum tubes or transistors, whether we use an IBM or an Apple, the essential characteristics are the same. This is a very misleading analogy. It is true for computers because they are all essentially the same. Whether we make them out of vacuum tubes or transistors, and whether we use an IBM or an Apple computer, we are using computers of the same general design. But, when we look at an essentially different architecture, we see that the architecture makes a good deal of difference. It is the architecture that determines which kinds of algorithms are most easily carried out on the machine in question. It is the architecture of the machine that determines the essential nature of the program itself. It is thus reasonable that we should begin by asking what we know about the architecture of the brain and how it might shape the algorithms underlying biological intelligence and human mental life.

The basic strategy of the connectionist approach is to take as its fundamental processing unit something close to an abstract neuron. We imagine that computation is carried out through simple interactions among such processing units. Essentially the idea is that these processing elements communicate by sending numbers along the lines that connect the processing elements. This identification already provides some interesting constraints on the kinds of algorithms that might underlie human intelligence.

The operations in our models then can best be characterized as "neurally-inspired". How does the replacement of the computer metaphor with the brain metaphor as model of mind affect our thinking? This change in orientation leads us to a number of considerations that further inform and constrain our model-building efforts. Perhaps the most crucial of these is time. Neurons are remarkably slow relative to components in modern computers. Neurons operate in the time scale of milliseconds, whereas computer components operate in the time scale of nanoseconds—a factor of 10^6 faster. This means that human processes that take on the order of a second or less can involve only a hundred or so time steps. Because most of the processes we have studied—perception, memory retrieval, speech processing, sentence comprehension, and the like—take about a second or so, it makes sense to impose what Feldman (1985a) calls the "100-step-program" constraint. That is, we seek explanations for these mental phenomena that do not require more than about a hundred elementary sequential operations. Given that the processes we seek to characterize are often quite complex and may involve consideration of large numbers of simultaneous constraints, our algorithms *must* involve considerable parallelism. Thus although a serial computer could be created out of the kinds of components represented by our units, such an implementation would surely violate the 100-step-program constraint for any but the simplest processes. Some might argue that, although parallelism is obviously present in much of human information processing, this fact alone need not greatly modify our world view. This is unlikely. The speed of components is a critical design constraint. Although the brain has *slow* components, it has *very many* of them. The human brain contains billions of such processing elements. Rather than organize computation with many, many serial steps, as we do with systems whose steps are very fast, the brain must deploy many, many processing elements cooperatively and in parallel to carry out its activities. These design characteristics, among others, lead, I believe, to a general organization of computing that is fundamentally different from what we are used to.

A further consideration differentiates our models from those inspired by the computer metaphor—that is, the constraint that all the knowledge is *in the connections*. From conventional programmable computers we are used to thinking of knowledge as being stored in the states of certain units in the system. In our systems we assume that only very short-term storage can occur in the states of units; long-term storage takes place in the connections among units. Indeed it is the connections—or perhaps the rules for forming them through experience—that primarily differentiate one model from another. This is a profound difference between our approach and other more conventional approaches, for it means that almost all knowledge is *implicit* in the structure of the device that carries out the task, rather than *explicit* in the states of units themselves. Knowledge is not directly accessible to interpretation by some separate processor, but it is built into the processor itself and directly determines the course of processing. It is acquired through tuning of connections, as they are used in processing, rather than formulated and stored as declarative facts.

These and other neurally inspired classes of working assumptions have been one important source of assumptions underlying the connectionist program of research. These have not been the only considerations. A second class of constraints arises from our beliefs about the nature of human information processing considered at a more abstract, computational level of analysis. We see the kinds of phenomena we have been studying as products of a kind of constraint-satisfaction procedure in which a very large number of constraints act simultaneously to produce the behavior. Thus we see most behavior not as the product of a single, separate component of the cognitive system but as the product of a large set of interacting components, each mutually constraining the others and contributing in its own way to the globally observable behavior of the system. It is very difficult to use serial algorithms to implement such a conception but very natural to use highly parallel ones. These problems can often be characterized as *best-match* or *optimization* problems. As Minsky and Papert (1969) have pointed out, it is very difficult to solve best-match problems serially. This is precisely the kind of problem, however, that is readily implemented using highly parallel algorithms of the kind we have been studying.

The use of brain-style computational systems, then, offers not only a hope that we can characterize how brains actually carry out certain information-processing tasks but also solutions to computational problems that seem difficult to solve in more traditional computational frameworks. It is here where the ultimate value of connectionist systems must be evaluated.

In this chapter, I begin with a somewhat more formal sketch of the computational framework of connectionist models. I then follow with a general discussion of the kinds of computational problems that connectionist models seem best suited for. Finally, I briefly review the state of the art in connectionist modeling.

1.1 The connectionist framework

There are seven major components of any connectionist system:

- a *set of processing units*;
- a *state of activation* defined over the processing units;
- an *output function* for each unit that maps its state of activation into an output;
- a *pattern of connectivity* among units;
- an *activation rule* for combining the inputs impinging on a unit with its current state to produce a new level of activation for the unit;
- a *learning rule* whereby patterns of connectivity are modified by experience; and
- an *environment* within which the system must operate.

Figure 8.1 illustrates the basic aspects of these systems. There is a set of processing units, generally indicated by circles in my diagrams; at each point in time each unit u_i has an activation value, denoted in the diagram as $a_i(t)$; this activation value is passed through a function f_i to produce an output value $o_i(t)$. This output value can be seen as passing through a set of unidirectional connections (indicated by lines or arrows in the diagrams) to other units in the system. There is associated with each connection a real number, usually called the *weight* or

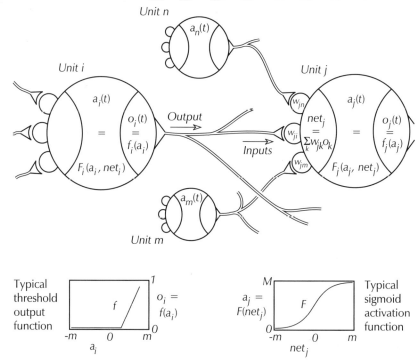

Figure 8.1:   The basic parts of a parallel distributed processing system.

strength of the connection, designated w_{ij} (*to* unit *i*, *from* unit *j*), which determines how strongly the former is affected by the latter. All of the inputs must then be combined; and the combined inputs to a unit (usually designated the *net input* to that unit), along with its current activation value, determine its new activation value via a function *F*. These systems are viewed as being plastic in the sense that the pattern of interconnections is not fixed for all time; rather the weights can undergo modification as a function of experience. In this way the system can evolve. What a unit represents can change with experience, and the system can come to perform in substantially different ways.

THE SET OF PROCESSING UNITS.   Any connectionist system begins with a set of processing units. Specifying the set of processing units and what they represent is typically the first stage of specifying a connectionist model. In some systems these units may represent particular conceptual objects such as features, letters, words, or concepts; in others they are simply abstract elements over which meaningful patterns can be defined. When we speak of a distributed representation, we mean one in which the units represent small, featurelike entities we call *microfeatures*. In this case it is the pattern as a whole that is the meaningful level of analysis. This should be contrasted to a *one-unit–one-concept* or *localist* representational system, in which single units represent entire concepts or other large meaningful entities.

All of the processing of a connectionist system is carried out by these units. There is no executive or other overseer. There are only relatively simple units, each doing its own relatively simple job. A unit's job is simply to receive input from its neighbors and, as a function of the inputs it receives, to compute an output value, which it sends to its neighbors. The system is inherently parallel in that many units can carry out their computations at the same time.

Within any system we are modeling, it is useful to characterize three types of units: *input, output,* and *hidden* units. Input units receive inputs from sources external to the system under study. These inputs may be either sensory inputs or inputs from other parts of the processing system in which the model is embedded. The output units send signals out of the system. They may either directly affect motoric systems or simply influence other systems external to the ones we are modeling. The hidden units are those whose only inputs and outputs are within the system we are modeling. They are not "visible" to outside systems.

THE STATE OF ACTIVATION. In addition to the set of units we need a representation of the state of the system at time t. This is primarily specified by a vector $\mathbf{a}(t)$, representing the pattern of activation over the set of processing units. Each element of the vector stands for the activation of one of the units. It is the *pattern* of activation over the whole set of units that captures what the system is representing at any time. It is useful to see processing in the system as the evolution, through time, of a pattern of activity over the set of units.

Different models make different assumptions about the activation values a unit is allowed to take on. Activation values may be continuous or discrete. If they are continuous, they may be unbounded or bounded. If they are discrete, they may take binary values or any of a small set of values. Thus in some models units are continuous and may take on any real number as an activation value. In other cases they may take on any real value between some minimum and maximum such as, for example, the interval [0,1]. When activation values are restricted to discrete values, they most often are binary—such as the values 0 and 1,

where 1 is usually taken to mean that the unit is active and 0 is taken
to mean that it is inactive.

THE OUTPUT FUNCTION. Units interact by transmitting signals to
their neighbors. The strengths of their signals, and therefore the
degrees to which they affect their neighbors, are determined by their
levels of activation. Associated with each unit u_i is an output function
$f_i(a_i(t))$, which maps the current state of activation to an output signal
$o_i(t)$. In some of our models, the output level is exactly equal to the
activation level of the unit. In this case, f is the identity function
$f(x) = x$. Sometimes f is some sort of threshold function, so that a
unit has no effect on another unit unless its activation exceeds a certain
value. Sometimes the function f is assumed to be a stochastic function
in which the output of the unit depends probabilistically on its activation level.

THE PATTERN OF CONNECTIVITY. Units are connected to one another.
It is this pattern of connectivity that constitutes what the system
knows and determines how it will respond to any arbitrary input.
Specifying the processing system and the knowledge encoded therein
is, in a connectionist model, a matter of specifying this pattern of connectivity among the processing units.

In many cases we assume that each unit provides an additive contribution to the input of the units to which it is connected. In such cases
the total input to any unit is simply the weighted sum of the separate
inputs from each of the units connected to it. That is, the inputs from
all of the incoming units are simply multiplied by their respective connection weights and summed to get the overall input to that unit. In
this case the total pattern of connectivity can be represented by merely
specifying the weights for each of the connections in the system. A
positive weight represents an excitatory input, and a negative weight
represents an inhibitory input. It is often convenient to represent such
a pattern of connectivity by a weight matrix **W** in which the entry w_{ij}
represents the strength and sense of the connection to unit u_i from
unit u_j. The weight w_{ij} is a positive number if unit u_j excites unit u_i;
it is a negative number if unit u_j inhibits unit u_i; and it is 0 if unit u_j
has no direct connection to unit u_i. The absolute value of w_{ij} specifies
the *strength of the connection*.

The pattern of connectivity is very important. It is this pattern that
determines what each unit represents. One important issue that may
determine both how much information can be stored and how much

serial processing the network must perform is the *fan-in* and *fan-out* of a unit The fan-in is the number of elements that either excite or inhibit a given unit. The fan-out is the number of units affected directly by a unit. It is useful to note that in brains these numbers are relatively large. Fan-in and fan-out range as high as 100,000 in some parts of the brain. It seems likely that this large fan-in and fan-out allows for a kind of operation that is less like a fixed circuit and more statistical in character.

THE ACTIVATION RULE. We also need a rule whereby the inputs impinging on a particular unit are combined with one another and with the current state of the unit to produce a new state of activation. We need a function F_i, which takes $a_i(t)$ and the net inputs, $net_i = \Sigma_j w_{ij} o_j(t)$, and produces a new state of activation. In the simplest cases, when F_i is the identity function and depends only on the inputs, we can write $a_i(t + 1) = net_i(t)$ —or, in vector notation for the whole network at once, $\mathbf{a}(t + 1) = \mathbf{net}(t) = \mathbf{Wo}(t)$. Sometimes F is a threshold function so that the net input must exceed some value before contributing to the new state of activation. Often the new state of activation depends on the old one as well as the current input. The function F itself is what we call the activation rule. Usually the function is assumed to be deterministic. Thus, for example, if a threshold is involved, it may be that $a_i(t) = 1$ if the total input exceeds some threshold value, and equals 0 otherwise. Other times it is assumed that F is stochastic. Sometimes activations are assumed to decay slowly with time so that even with no external input the activation of a unit will simply decay and not go directly to zero. Whenever $a_i(t)$ is assumed to take on continuous values, it is common to assume that F is a kind of sigmoid (that is, S-shaped) function. In this case an individual unit can *saturate* and reach a minimum or maximum value of activation.

THE LEARNING RULE: CHANGES AS A FUNCTION OF EXPERIENCE. Changing the processing or knowledge structure in a connectionist system involves modifying the patterns of interconnectivity. In principle this can involve three kinds of modification:

(1) development of new connections;

(2) loss of existing connections;

(3) modification of the strengths of connections that already exist.

Very little work has been done on (1) and (2). To a first order of approximation, however, (1) and (2) can be considered a special case of

(3). Whenever we change the strength of connection away from zero to some positive or negative value, it has the same effect as growing a new connection. Whenever we change the strength of a connection to zero, that has the same effect as losing an existing connection. Thus we have concentrated on rules whereby *strengths* of connections are modified through experience.

Virtually all learning rules for models of this type can be considered variants of the *Hebbian* learning rule, suggested by Hebb in his classic book *Organization of Behavior* (1949). Hebb's basic idea is this: if a unit u_i receives an input from another unit u_j at a time when both units are highly active, then the weight w_{ij} to u_i from u_j should be *strengthened.* This idea has been extended and modified so that it can be stated more generally as

$$\delta w_{ij} = g\left(a_i(t), \tau_i(t)\right) \cdot h\left(o_j(t), w_{ij}\right)$$

or, suppressing the time variables for easier readability, as

$$\delta w_{ij} = g\left(a_i, \tau_i\right) \cdot h\left(o_j, w_{ij}\right)$$

where τ_i is a kind of *teaching* input to u_i. Simply stated, this equation says that the *change* in the connection to u_i from u_j is given by the product of a function $g(\dots)$ of the activation of u_i and its teaching input τ_i and another function $h(\dots)$ of the output value of u_j and the current connection strength w_{ij}. In the simplest versions of Hebbian learning, there is no teacher and the functions g and h are simply proportional to their first arguments. Thus we have

$$\delta w_{ij} = \varepsilon a_i o_j$$

where ε is the constant of proportionality representing the learning rate. Another common variation is a rule in which

$$h\left(o_j, w_{ij}\right) = o_j$$

(as in the simplest case) but

$$g\left(a_i, \tau_i\right) = \varepsilon \cdot \left(\tau_i - a_i\right)$$

This is often called the *Widrow-Hoff* rule, because it was originally formulated by Widrow and Hoff (1960), or the *delta* rule, because the amount of learning is proportional to the *difference* (or delta) between the actual activation achieved and the target activation provided by a teacher. In this case we have

$$\delta w_{ij} = \varepsilon \cdot \left(\tau_i - a_i\right) \cdot o_j$$

This is a generalization of the *perceptron* learning rule for which the famous *perceptron convergence theorem* has been proved. Still another variation has

$$\delta w_{ij} = \varepsilon a_i \cdot (o_i - w_{ij})$$

This is a rule employed by Grossberg (1976) and others in the study of *competitive learning.* In this case usually only the units with the strongest activation values are allowed to learn.

THE ENVIRONMENT. It is crucial in the development of any model to have a clear representation of the environment in which this model is to exist. For connectionist models, we represent the environment as a time-varying stochastic function over a space of possible input patterns. That is, for each possible input pattern, we imagine that there is some probability that, at any given time, that pattern is impinging on the input units. This probability function may in general depend on the history of inputs to the system as well as outputs of the system. In practice most connectionist models involve a much simpler characterization of the environment. Typically, the environment is characterized by a stable probability distribution over the set of possible input patterns, independent of past inputs and past responses of the system. In this case we can imagine listing the set of possible inputs to the system and numbering them from 1 to M. The environment is then characterized by a set of probabilities p_i for $i = 1, \ldots, M$. Because each input pattern can be considered a vector, it is sometimes useful to characterize those patterns with nonzero probabilities as constituting *orthogonal* or *linearly independent* sets of vectors.

To summarize, the connectionist framework consists not only of a formal language but also a perspective on our models. Other qualitative and quantitative considerations arising from our understanding of brain processing and of human behavior combine with the formal system to form what might be viewed as an aesthetic for our model-building enterprises.

1.2 Computational features of connectionist models

In addition to the fact that connectionist systems are capable of exploiting parallelism in computation and mimicking brain-style computation, such systems are important because they provide good solutions to a number of very difficult computational problems that seem to arise often in models of cognition. In particular they typically:

- are good at solving constraint-satisfaction problems;

- are efficient mechanisms for best-match search, pattern recognition, and content-addressable memory;

- automatically implement similarity-based generalization;

- offer simple, general mechanisms for adaptive learning; and

- exhibit graceful degradation with damage or information overload.

CONSTRAINT SATISFACTION PROBLEMS. Many cognitive-science problems are usefully conceptualized as problems in which a solution is given through the satisfaction of a very large number of mutually interacting constraints. The challenge is to devise a computational system that is capable of efficiently solving such problems. Connectionist networks are ideal for implementing constraint-satisfaction systems; indeed, the trick for getting connectionist networks to solve difficult problems is often to cast the problems as constraint-satisfaction problems. In this case, we conceptualize the connectionist network as a *constraint network* in which each unit represents a hypothesis of some sort (for example, that a certain semantic feature, visual feature, or acoustic feature is present in the input), and each connection represents a constraint among the hypotheses.

Thus, for such a network, if feature B is expected to be present whenever feature A is present, there should be a positive connection from the unit corresponding to the hypothesis that A is present to the unit representing the hypothesis that B is present. Contrariwise, if there is a constraint that whenever A is present B is expected *not* to be present, there should be a negative connection from A to B. If the constraints are weak, the weights should be small; if the constraints are strong, then the weights should be large. Similarly, the inputs to such networks can also be thought of as constraints. A positive input to a particular unit means that there is evidence from the outside that the relevant feature is present. A negative input means that there is evidence from the outside that the feature is not present. The stronger the input, the greater the evidence. If a network of this kind is allowed to run, it will eventually *settle* into an optimal state in which as many as possible of the constraints are satisfied, with priority given to the strongest constraints. (Actually, the system will find a *locally* best solution to the constraint-satisfaction problem. *Global* optima are more difficult to find.) The procedure whereby such a system *settles* into such a state

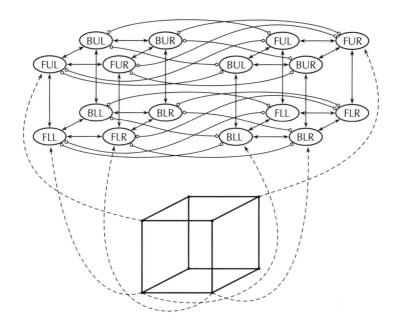

Figure 8.2: A simple network representing some constraints involved in perceiving a Necker cube. The ovals are the units in the network; connections with arrow-heads are positive (excitatory), while those with circle-heads are negative (inhibitory); the dotted lines represent input stimuli from the perceived cube.

is called *relaxation*. We speak of the system *relaxing* to a solution. Thus, many connectionist models are constraint-satisfaction models that settle on locally optimal solutions through a process of relaxation.

Figure 8.2 shows an example of a simple 16-unit constraint network. Each unit in the network represents a hypothesis concerning a vertex in a line drawing of a Necker cube. The network consists of two interconnected subnetworks—one corresponding to each of the two global interpretations of the Necker cube. Each unit in each subnetwork is assumed to receive input from the region of the input figure—the cube—corresponding to its location in the network. Each unit in figure 8.2 is labeled with a three-letter sequence indicating whether its vertex is hypothesized to be front or back (F or B), upper or lower (U or L), and right or left (R or L). Thus, for example, the lower-left unit of each subnetwork is assumed to receive input from the lower-left vertex of the input figure. The unit in the left network represents the hypothesis that it is receiving input from a lower-left vertex in the front surface of the cube (and is thus labeled FLL), whereas the one in the right subnetwork represents the hypothesis that it is receiving input from a lower-left vertex in the back surface (BLL). Because there is a constraint that each vertex has a single interpretation, these two units are connected by a strong negative connection. Because the interpretation of any given vertex is constrained by the interpretations of its neighbors, each unit in a subnetwork is connected positively with each of its neighbors within the network. Finally, since there is a constraint that there can be only one vertex of each kind (for example, there can be only one lower-left vertex in the front plane, FLL), there is a strong negative connection between units representing the same label in each subnetwork. Thus each unit has three neighbors connected positively, two competitors connected negatively, and one positive input from the stimulus.

For purposes of this example, we assume that the strengths of the connections have been arranged so that two negative inputs exactly balance three positive inputs. Further it is assumed that each unit receives an excitatory input from the ambiguous stimulus pattern and that each of these excitatory influences is relatively small. Thus, if all three of a unit's neighbors are on and both of its competitors are on, these effects would entirely cancel out one another; and if there were a small input from the outside, the unit would have a tendency to come on. On the other hand, if fewer than three of its neighbors were on and both of its competitors were on, the unit would have a tendency to turn off, even with an excitatory input from the stimulus pattern.

In the preceding paragraphs, I focused on the individual units of the networks. It is often useful, however, to focus not on the units but on entire *states* of the network. In the case of binary (on-off or 0-1) units, there would be a total of 2^{16} possible states in which a network of this size could reside—since, in principle, each of the 16 units could have either value 0 or 1. In the case of continuous units, in which each unit can take on any value between 0 and 1, the system could in principle take on any of an infinite number of states. Yet because of the constraints built into the network, there are only a relatively few of those states into which the system will ever actually settle.

To see this, consider the case in which the units are updated asynchronously, one at a time. During each time slice, one of the units is chosen to update. If its net input exceeds 0, its value will be pushed toward 1; otherwise its value will be pushed toward 0. Imagine that the system starts with all units off. A unit is then chosen at random to be updated. Because it is receiving slight positive input from the stimulus and no other inputs, it will be given a positive activation value. Then another unit is chosen to update. Unless it is in direct competition with the first unit, it too will be turned on. Eventually a coalition of neighboring units will be turned on. These units will tend to turn on more of their neighbors in the same subnetwork and turn off their competitors in the other subnetwork. The system will (almost always) end up in a situation in which all of the units in one subnetwork are fully activated and none of the units in the other subnetwork is activated. That is, the system will end up interpreting the Necker cube as either facing left or facing right. Whenever the system gets into a state and stays there, the state is called a *stable state* or a *fixed point* of the network. The constraints implicit in the pattern of connections among the units determine the set of possible stable states of the system and therefore the set of possible interpretations of the inputs.

Hopfield (1982) has shown that it is possible to give a general account of the behavior of systems like this (with symmetric weights and asynchronous updates). In particular, he has shown that such systems can be conceptualized as minimizing a global measure, which he calls the *energy* of the system, through a method of *gradient descent* or, equivalently, maximizing the constraints satisfied through a method of *hill climbing*. More specifically, the system operates so as to move always from a state that satisfies fewer constraints to one that satisfies more, where the measure of constraint satisfaction is given by

$$G(t) = \sum_i \sum_j w_{ij} a_i(t) a_j(t) + \sum_i \text{input}_i(t) a_i(t)$$

Essentially the equation says that the overall goodness of fit is given by the sum of the degrees to which each pair of units contributes to the goodness plus the degree to which the units satisfy the input constraints. The contribution of a pair of units is given by the product of their activation values and the weight connecting them. Thus, if the weight is positive, each unit wants to be as active as possible—that is, the activation values for those two units should be pushed toward 1. If the weight is negative, then at least one of the units should be 0 to maximize the pairwise goodness. Similarly if the input constraint for a given unit is positive, then its contribution to the total goodness of fit is maximized by bringing the activation of that unit toward its maximal value. If it is negative, the activation value should be decreased toward 0. Of course the constraints will generally not be totally consistent. Sometimes a given unit may have to be turned on to increase the function in some ways yet decrease it in other ways. The point is that it is the sum of all of these individual contributions that the system seeks to maximize. Thus, for every state of the system— every possible pattern of activation over the units—the pattern of inputs and the connectivity matrix $\mathbf{W}$ determine a value of the good-ness-of-fit function. The system processes its input by moving upward from state to adjacent state until it reaches a state of maximum good-ness. When it reaches such a *stable state* or *fixed point*, it will stay in that state and it can be said to have "settled" on a solution to the con-straint-satisfaction problem or, as in our present case, "settled into an interpretation" of the input.

It is important to see then that entirely *local* computational opera-tions, in which each unit adjusts its activation up or down on the basis of its net input, serve to allow the network to converge toward states that maximize a *global* measure of goodness or degree of constraint sat-isfaction. Hopfield's main contribution to the present analysis was to point out this basic fact about the behavior of networks with symmet-rical connections and asynchronous update of activations.

Finally, one of the most difficult problems in cognitive science is to build systems that can allow a large number of knowledge sources to interact usefully in the solution of a problem. Thus, in language pro-cessing we would want syntactic, phonological, semantic, and prag-matic knowledge sources all to interact in the construction of the meaning of an input. Reddy and his colleagues (1973) have had some success in the case of speech perception with the Hearsay system because they were working in the highly structured domain of lan-guage. Less structured domains have proved very difficult to organize. Connectionist models, conceived as constraint-satisfaction networks, are ideally suited for blending multiple-knowledge sources. Each knowledge type is simply another constraint, and the system will, in parallel, find those configurations of values that best satisfy all of the constraints from all of the knowledge sources. The uniformity of rep-resentation and the common currency of interaction (activation val-ues) make connectionist systems especially powerful for this domain.

To summarize, there is a large subset of connectionist models that can be considered constraint-satisfaction models. These networks can be described as carrying out their information processing by climbing into states of maximal satisfaction of the constraints implicit in the network. A very useful consequence of this way of viewing networks is that we can describe their behavior not only in terms of the behavior of individual units but also in terms of the properties of the network itself. A primary concept for understanding these network properties is the *goodness-of-fit landscape* over which the system moves. Once we have correctly described this landscape, we have described the operational properties of the system—it will process information by moving uphill toward goodness maxima. The particular maximum that the system will find is determined by where the system starts and by the distortions of the space induced by the input. One of the very important descriptors of a goodness landscape is the set of maxima that a system can find, the size of the region that feeds into each maximum, and the height of the maximum itself. The states themselves correspond to possible interpretations, the peaks in the space correspond to the best interpretations, the extent of the foothills or skirts surrounding a particular peak determines the likelihood of finding the peak, and the height of the peak corresponds to the degree to which the constraints of the network are actually met or alternatively to the goodness of the interpretation associated with the corresponding state.

BEST-MATCH SEARCH, PATTERN RECOGNITION, AND CONTENT-ADDRESS-ABLE MEMORY. These are all variants on the general best-match problem (compare Minsky and Papert 1969). Best-match problems are especially difficult for serial computational algorithms (they involve exhaustive search), but, as we have just indicated, connectionist systems can readily be used to find the interpretation that best matches a set of constraints.

They can similarly be used to find stored data that best match some target or probe. In this case, it is useful to imagine that the network consists of two classes of units. One class, the *visible* units, corresponds to the contents stored in the network, in the sense that each stored pattern is a possible pattern of activation of these units. The other units, the *hidden* units, correspond to shared structural properties of the stored patterns that play a role in storing and retrieving them. The patterns themselves are actually stored in the weights on the connections among all these units. If we think of each stored pattern as a collection of features, then each visible unit corresponds to the hypothesis that some particular feature is present in the relevant pattern, and each hidden unit corresponds to a hypothesis concerning a *configuration* of several features. The hypothesis to which a particular hidden unit corresponds is determined by the exact *learning rule* used to store the input and by the characteristics of the ensemble of stored patterns. Retrieval in such a network amounts to setting the values of *some* of the visible units (the retrieval probe) and letting the system settle to the best interpretation of that input, while itself setting the values of the remaining visible units. This is a kind of pattern completion. The details are not too important here because a variety of learning rules lead to networks that all have the following important properties:

- When a previously stored (that is, familiar) pattern enters the memory system, it is amplified, and the system responds with a stronger version of the input pattern. This is a kind of recognition response.

- When an unfamiliar pattern enters the memory system, it is dampened, and the activity of the memory system is shut down. This is a kind of unfamiliarity response.

- When part of a familiar pattern is presented, the system responds by "filling in" the missing parts. This is a kind of recall paradigm in which the part constitutes the retrieval cue, and the filling in is a kind of memory-reconstruction process. This is a content-addressable memory system.

- When a pattern similar to a stored pattern is presented, the system responds by distorting the input pattern toward the stored pattern. This is a kind of assimilation response in which similar inputs are assimilated to similar stored events.

- Finally, if a number of similar patterns have been stored, the system will respond strongly to the central tendency of the stored patterns, even though the central tendency itself was never stored. Thus this sort of memory system automatically responds to prototypes even when no prototype has been seen.

These properties correspond very closely to the characteristics of human memory and, I believe, are exactly the kind of properties we want in any theory of memory.

AUTOMATIC, SIMILARITY-BASED GENERALIZATION. One of the major complaints against AI programs is their "fragility". The programs are usually very good at what they are programmed to do, but respond in unintelligent or odd ways when faced with novel situations. There seem to be at least two reasons for this fragility. In conventional symbol-processing systems similarity is represented only indirectly, and is therefore not available as a basis for generalizations; and most AI programs are not self-modifying and cannot adapt to their environments.

In our connectionist systems, on the other hand, similarities among patterns are directly represented along with the patterns themselves in the connection weights—in such a way that similar patterns have similar effects. Therefore, similarity-based generalization is an automatic property of connectionist models. It should be noted that the degree of similarity between patterns is roughly given by the inner product of the vectors representing the patterns. Thus the dimensions of generalization are given by the dimensions of the representational space. Often this will lead to the right generalizations. But, there are situations in which it leads to inappropriate generalizations. In such cases, we must allow the system to *learn* its appropriate representation. In the next section I describe how the appropriate representation can be learned so that the correct generalizations are automatically made.

LEARNING. A key advantage of connectionist systems is the fact that simple yet powerful learning procedures can be defined that allow the systems to adapt to their environments. It was work on the learning aspect of neurally inspired models that first led to an interest in them (compare Rosenblatt 1962), and it was the demonstration that those learning procedures could not work for complex networks that contributed to the loss of interest (compare Minsky and Papert 1969). Although the *perceptron convergence procedure* and its variants have been around for some time, they are limited to simple two-layer networks involving only input and output units. There were no hidden units in these cases and no internal representation. The coding provided by the external world had to suffice. Nevertheless, such networks have proved useful in a wide variety of applications. Perhaps their most important characteristic is that they map similar input patterns to similar output patterns. This is what allows them to make reasonable generalizations and perform reasonably on patterns that have never before been presented. The similarity of patterns in connectionist systems is determined by their overlap. This overlap, for two-layer networks, is determined entirely outside the learning system itself—by whatever produces the patterns.

The constraint that similar input patterns lead to similar outputs can lead to an inability of the system to learn certain mappings from input to output. Whenever the representation provided by the outside world is such that the similarity structure of the input and output patterns is very different, a network without internal representations (that is, a network without hidden units) will be unable to perform the

Input patterns		Output patterns
00	→	0
01	→	1
10	→	1
11	→	0

Table 8.1: XOR problem.

Input patterns		Output patterns
000	→	0
010	→	1
100	→	1
111	→	0

Table 8.2: XOR problem with redundant third bit.

necessary mappings. A classic example of this case is the exclusive-or (XOR) problem illustrated in table 8.1. Here we see that those patterns that overlap least are supposed to generate identical output values. This problem and many others like it cannot be solved by networks that lack hidden units with which to create their own internal representations of the input patterns. It is interesting to note that if the input patterns contained a third input bit, taking the value 1 when and only when the other two were both 1 (as shown in table 8.2), a two-layer system would be able to solve the problem.

Minsky and Papert (1969) have provided a careful analysis of conditions under which such systems are capable of carrying out the required mappings. They show that in many interesting cases networks of this kind are incapable of solving the problems. On the other hand, as Minsky and Papert also point out, if there is a layer of simple perceptron-like hidden units, as shown in figure 8.3, with which the original input pattern can be augmented, there is always a recoding (that is, an internal representation) of the input patterns in the hidden units in which the similarity of the patterns among the hidden units can support any required mapping from the input to the output units. Thus if we have the right connections from the input units to a large enough set of hidden units, we can always find a representation that will perform any mapping from input to output through these hidden units. In the case of the XOR problem, the addition of a feature that detects the conjunction of the input units changes the similarity structure of the patterns sufficiently to allow the solution to be learned. As illustrated in figure 8.4, this can be done with a single hidden unit. The numbers on the arrows represent the strengths of the connections among the units. The numbers written in the circles represent the thresholds of the units. The value of +1.5 for the threshold of the hidden unit ensures that it will be turned on only when both input units

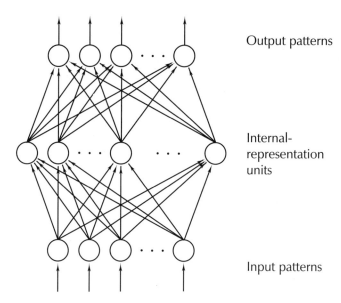

Figure 8.3: A multilayer network in which input patterns are recoded by internal representation units.

are on. The threshold of 0.5 for the output unit ensures that it will turn on only when it receives a net positive input greater than 0.5. The weight of -2 from the hidden unit to the output unit ensures that the output unit will not come on when both input units are on. Note that, from the point of view of the output unit, the hidden unit is treated as simply another input unit. It is as if the input patterns consisted of three rather than two units (essentially as in table 8.2).

The existence of networks such as this illustrates the potential power of hidden units and internal representations. The problem, as

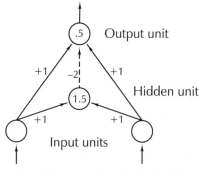

Figure 8.4: A simple XOR network with one hidden unit.

noted by Minsky and Papert, is that, whereas there is a very simple guaranteed learning rule for all problems that can be solved without hidden units—namely, the perceptron convergence procedure (or the variation reported originally by Widrow and Hoff 1960)—there has been no equally powerful rule for learning in multilayer networks.

It is clear that if we hope to use these connectionist networks for general computational purposes, we must have a learning scheme capable of learning its own internal representations. This is just what we (Rumelhart, Hinton, and Williams 1986) have done. We have developed a generalization of the perceptron learning procedure, called the *generalized delta rule*, which allows the system to learn to compute arbitrary functions. The constraints inherent in networks without self-modifying internal representations are no longer applicable. The basic learning procedure is a two-stage process. First, an input is applied to the network. Then, after the system has processed for some time, certain units of the network—usually the output units—are informed of the values they ought to have attained. If they have attained the desired values, the weights on their input connections are left unchanged. If they differ from their target values, then those weights are changed slightly, in such a way as to reduce the differences between the actual values attained and the target values.

Those *differences* between the actual and target values at the output units can be thought of as *error signals*. Similar error signals must be sent back in turn to those units that impinged on the output units. Each such unit receives an error signal that is equal to the sum of the errors in each of the output units to which it connects times the weight on the connection to that output unit. Then, based on those error signals, the weights on the *input* connections into those "second-layer" units can be modified, after which error signals can be passed back another layer. This process—called the *backpropagation of error*—continues until the error signals reach the input units or until they have been passed back a predetermined number of times. Then a new input pattern is presented and the process repeats. Although the procedure may sound difficult, it is actually quite simple and easy to implement within these nets. As shown in Rumelhart, Hinton, and Williams (1986), such a procedure will always change its weights in such a way as to reduce the overall difference between the actual output values and the desired output values. Moreover it can be shown that this system will work for any network whatsoever.

Minsky and Papert, in their pessimistic discussion of perceptrons, discuss *multilayer machines*. They state that

> The perceptron has shown itself worthy of study despite (and even because of!) its severe limitations. It has many features that attract attention: its linearity; its intriguing learning theorem; its clear paradigmatic simplicity as a kind of parallel computation. There is no reason to suppose that any of these virtues carry over to the many-layered version. Nevertheless, we consider it to be an important research problem to elucidate (or reject) our intuitive judgment that the extension is sterile. Perhaps some powerful convergence theorem will be discovered, or some profound reason for the failure to produce an interesting "learning theorem" for the multilayered machine will be found.   (1969, pp. 231–232)

Although our learning results do not *guarantee* that we can find a solution for all solvable problems, our analysis and simulation results have shown that, as a practical matter, this error-propagation scheme leads to solutions in virtually every case. In short, I believe that we have answered Minsky and Papert's challenge and *have* found a learning result sufficiently powerful to demonstrate that their pessimism about learning in multilayer machines was misplaced.

One way to view the procedure I have been describing is as a parallel computer that, having been shown the appropriate input/output exemplars specifying some function, programs itself to compute that function in general. Parallel computers are notoriously difficult to program. Here we have a mechanism whereby we do not actually have to know how to write the program to get the system to do it.

GRACEFUL DEGRADATION. Finally, connectionist models are interesting candidates for cognitive-science models because of their property of graceful degradation in the face of damage and information overload. The ability of our networks to learn leads to the promise of computers that can literally learn their way around faulty components: because every unit participates in the storage of many patterns and because each pattern involves many different units, the loss of a few components will degrade the stored information, but will not destroy it. Similarly such memories should not be conceived as having a certain fixed capacity. Rather, there is simply more and more storage interference and blending of similar pieces of information as the memory is overloaded. This property of graceful degradation mimics the human response in many ways and is one of the reasons we find these models of human information processing plausible.

2 The state of the art

Recent years have seen a virtual explosion of work in the connectionist area. This work has been singularly interdisciplinary, being carried out by psychologists, physicists, computer scientists, engineers, neuroscientists, and other cognitive scientists. A number of national and international conferences have been established and are being held each year. In such an environment it is difficult to keep up with the rapidly developing field. Nevertheless, a reading of recent papers indicates a few central themes in this activity. These themes include the study of learning and generalization (especially the use of the backpropagation learning procedure), applications to neuroscience, mathematical properties of networks—both of the learning algorithms and of connectionist style computation itself in comparison to more conventional computational paradigms—and finally the development of an implementational base for physical realizations of connectionist computational devices, especially in the areas of optics and analog VLSI.

Although there are many other interesting and important developments, I conclude with a brief summary of the work with which I have been most involved over the past several years, namely, the study of learning and generalization within multilayer networks. Even this summary is necessarily selective, but it should give a sampling of much of the current work in the area.

The backpropagation learning procedure has become possibly the single most popular method for training networks. The procedure has been used to train networks on problem domains including character recognition, speech recognition, sonar detection, mapping from spelling to sound, motor control, analysis of molecular structure, diagnosis of eye diseases, prediction of chaotic functions, playing backgammon, the parsing of simple sentences, and many, many more areas. Perhaps the major point of these examples is the enormous range of problems to which the backpropagation learning procedure can usefully be applied. In spite of the rather impressive breadth of topics and the success of some of these applications, there are a number of serious open problems. The theoretical issues of primary concern fall into three main areas. (1) The architecture problem: are there useful architectures beyond the standard three-layer network that are appropriate for

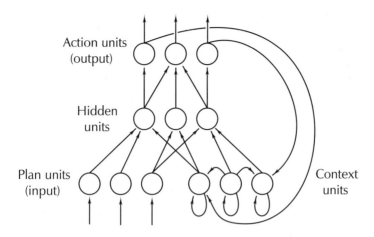

Figure 8.5: A recurrent network of the type developed by Jordan (1986)
for learning to *perform* sequential operations.

certain areas of application? (2) The scaling problem: how can we cut
down on the substantial training time that seems to be involved for
more difficult and interesting problems? (3) The generalization problem: how can we be certain that a network trained on a subset of the
example set will generalize correctly to the entire set of examples?

2.1 Some architecture

Although most applications have involved the simple three-layer back-
propagation network with one input layer, one hidden layer, and one
output layer of units, there have been a large number of interesting
architectures proposed—each for the solution of some particular problem of interest. There are, for example, a number of "special" architectures that have been proposed for the modeling of such sequential
phenomena as motor control. Perhaps the most important of these is
the one proposed by Mike Jordan (1986) for producing sequences of
phonemes. The basic structure of the network is illustrated in figure
8.5. It consists of four groups of units. *Plan units*, which tell the network which sequence it is producing, are fixed at the start of a
sequence and are not changed. *Context units*, which keep track of
where the system is in the sequence, receive input from the output
units of the systems and from themselves, constituting a memory for
the sequence produced thus far. *Hidden units* combine the information
from the plan units with that from the context units to determine
which output is to be produced next. *Output units* produce the desired

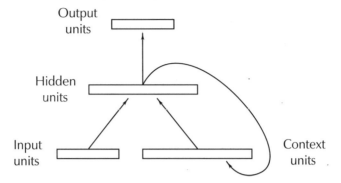

Figure 8.6:   A recurrent network of the type employed by Elman (1986) for learning to *recognize* sequences.

output values. This basic structure, with numerous variations, has been used successfully in producing sequences of phonemes (Jordan, 1986), sequences of movements (Jordan, 1989), sequences of notes in a melody (Todd, 1988), sequences of turns in a simulated ship (Miyata, 1987), and for many other applications. An analogous network for *recognizing* sequences has been used by Elman (1988) for processing sentences one at a time; and another variation has been developed and studied by Mozer (1988). The architecture used by Elman is illustrated in figure 8.6. This network also involves four sets of units: *input units*, in which the sequence to be recognized is presented one element at a time; *context units*, which receive inputs from and send outputs to the hidden units and thus constitute a memory for recent events; *hidden units*, which combine the current input with the memory of past inputs either to name the sequence, to predict the next element of the sequence, or both; and, of course, *output units*.

Another kind of architecture that has received some attention was suggested by Hinton and has been employed by Elman and Zipser (1987), Cottrell, Munro, and Zipser (1987), and many others. It has become part of the standard toolkit of backpropagation. This is the so-called method of autoencoding the pattern set. The basic architecture in this case consists of three layers of units as in the conventional case; however, the input and output layers are identical. The idea is to pass the input through a small number of hidden units and reproduce it over the output units. This requires the hidden units to do a kind of nonlinear, principle-components analysis of the input patterns. In this case, that corresponds to a kind of extraction of critical features. In many applications, these features turn out to provide a useful compact description of the patterns. Many other architectures are being explored as well. The space of interesting and useful architecture is large and the exploration will continue for many years.

2.2 The scaling problem

The scaling problem has received somewhat less attention, although it has clearly emerged as a central problem with backpropagation-like learning procedures. The basic finding has been that difficult problems require many learning trials. For example, it is not unusual to require tens or even hundreds of thousands of pattern presentations to learn moderately difficult problems—that is, problems whose solutions require tens of thousands to a few hundred thousand connections. Large and fast computers are required for such problems, and it is impractical for problems requiring more than a few hundred thousand connections. It is therefore a matter of concern to learn how to speed up the learning so that it can learn more difficult problems in a more reasonable number of exposures. The proposed solutions fall into two basic categories. One line of attack is to improve the learning procedure, either by optimizing the parameters dynamically (that is, change the learning rate systematically during learning), or by using more information in the weight-changing procedure (that is, the so-called second-order backpropagation procedure, in which the second derivatives are also computed). Although some improvements can be attained by these methods, in certain problem domains the basic scaling problem still remains. It seems that the basic problem is that difficult problems require a large number of exemplars, however efficiently each exemplar is used. The other approach grows from viewing *learning* and *evolution* as continuous with one another. On this view, the fact that networks take a long time to learn is to be expected, because we normally compare their behavior to organisms that have long evolutionary histories. Accordingly, the solution is to *start* the systems at places that are as pre-suited as possible for the problem domains to be learned. Shepherd (1989) has argued that such an approach is critical for an appropriate understanding of the phenomena being modeled.

A final approach to the scaling problem is through modularity. Sometimes it is possible to break a problem into smaller subproblems and train subnetworks separately on these. Larger networks can then be assembled from those pretrained modules to solve the original problem. An advantage of the connectionist approach in this regard is that the preliminary training need only be approximately right. A final round of training can be used after assembly to learn the interfaces among the modules.

2.3 The generalization problem

One final aspect of learning that has been looked at is the nature of generalization. It is clear that the most important aspect of networks is not that they learn a set of mappings but that they learn the function implicit in the exemplars under study in such a way that they respond properly to cases not yet observed. Although there are many examples of successful generalization (e.g., the learning of spelling-to-phoneme mappings in Sejnowski and Rosenberg's NETtalk, 1987), there are a number of cases in which the networks do not generalize correctly (see Denker et al. 1987). One simple way to understand this is to note that for most problems there are enough degrees of freedom in the network that there are a large number of genuinely different solutions to the problems—each of which constitutes a different way of generalizing to unseen patterns. Clearly not all of these can be correct.

Weigend and I have proposed an hypothesis that shows some promise in promoting better generalization (Weigend and Rumelhart 1991). The basic idea is this: the problem of generalization is essentially the induction problem. Given a set of observations, what is the appropriate principle that applies to all cases? Note that the network at any point in time can be viewed as a specification of an inductive hypothesis. Our proposal is that we follow a version of Occam's razor and select the *simplest, most robust* network that is consistent with the observations made. The assumption of robustness is simply an embodiment of a kind of continuity assumption that small variations in the input pattern should have little effect on the output or on the performance of the system. The simplicity assumption is simply to choose— of all networks that correctly account for the input data—the net with the fewest hidden units, the fewest connections, the most symmetries among the weights, and so on. We have formalized this procedure and modified the backpropagation learning procedure so that it prefers simple, robust networks, and, all things being equal, will select those networks. In many cases it turns out that these are just the networks that do the best job generalizing.

Connectionist Modeling: Neural Computation / Mental Connections

Paul Smolensky

1989

In the past few years the approach to cognitive science and artificial intelligence known as *connectionist modeling* has dramatically increased its influence. Connectionist systems are large networks of extremely simple computational units, massively interconnected and running in parallel. Each unit or processor has a numerical *activation value* which it communicates to other processors along connections of varying strength; the activation value of each processor constantly changes in response to the activity of the processors to which it is connected. The values of some of the units form the input to the system, and the values of other units form the output; the connections between the units determine how input is transformed to output. In connectionist systems, knowledge is encoded not in symbolic structures but rather in the pattern of numerical strengths of the connections between units.

The goal of connectionist research is to model both lower-level perceptual processes and such higher-level processes as object recognition, problem solving, planning, and language understanding. The rapidly growing collection of connectionist systems includes models of the following cognitive phenomena:

- speech perception,
- visual recognition of figures in the "origami world",
- development of specialized feature detectors,
- amnesia,
- language parsing and generation,
- aphasia,
- discovering binary encodings,
- dynamic programming of massively parallel networks,
- acquisition of English past tense morphophonology from examples,

- tic-tac-toe,
- inference about rooms, and
- qualitative problem solving in simple electric circuits.

One crucial question is whether the computational power of connectionist systems is sufficient for the construction of truly intelligent systems. Explorations addressing this question form the bulk of the contributions to the connectionist literature; many can be found in the proceedings of the International Joint Conference on AI, the annual meetings of the American Association for AI, and the Cognitive Science Society over the past several years. The connectionist systems referred to in the previous paragraph can be found in the collections in Hinton and Anderson (1981); Feldman (1985); Rumelhart, McClelland, and the PDP Research Group (1986); McClelland, Rumelhart, and the PDP Research Group (1986); and the bibliography by Feldman, Ballard, Brown, and Dell (1985). In the present paper I will not address the issue of computational power, except to point out that connectionist research has been strongly encouraged by successful formal models of the details of human cognitive performance, and strongly motivated by the conviction that the pursuit of the principles of neural computation will eventually lead to architectures of great computational power.

In addition to the question of whether the connectionist approach to AI *can* work, there is the question: What exactly would it mean if the approach *did* work? There are fundamental questions about the connectionist approach that are not yet clearly understood despite their importance. What is the relation between connectionist systems and the brain? How does the connectionist approach to modeling higher-level cognitive processes relate to the symbolic approach that has traditionally *defined* AI and cognitive science? Can connectionist models contribute to our understanding of the nature of the symbol processing characterizing the mind and its relation to the neural processing characterizing the brain? These are the questions I address in this paper. In the process of addressing these questions it will become clear that the answers are important not only in their own right, but also as contributions to the determination of whether the connectionist approach has sufficient power.

1 Levels of analysis: neural and mental structures

We begin with the questions: How do accounts of intelligence relate to neural and mental structures? What are the roles of the neural and the symbolic levels of analysis? We first consider the answers from the traditional symbolic approach to AI, and then from a connectionist alternative.

1.1 The symbolic paradigm

We start with the mental structures of "folk psychology": goals, beliefs, concepts, and so forth (figure 9.1). In the symbolic approach, these mentalist concepts are formalized in terms of a "language of thought", as Fodor (1975) calls it; this language is supposed to provide a literal formalization of folk psychology. The rules for operating on this language are essentially Boole's (1854/1961) "laws of thought". These symbolic structures are supported by a *physical symbol system* (a physical computing device for manipulating symbols), which in turn is supported by lower implementation levels in a computing device. The idea is that, eventually, if we were to get low enough down in the human physical symbol system, we would see something like neurons. In other words, on this account we just have to figure out how to relate neural structures to the low implementation levels of a physical symbol system, and then we understand the relation between neural structures and mental structures. If it were the case that increasingly lower levels

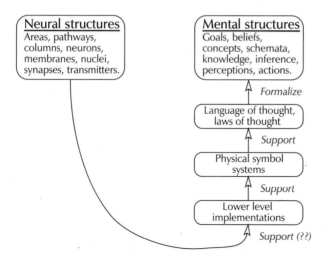

Figure 9.1: Neural and mental structures in the symbolic paradigm

of computers looked more and more like neural systems this would be a promising approach; unfortunately, insights into the design and implementation of physical symbol systems have so far shed virtually no light on how the brain works.

To understand the connectionist alternative more clearly, it is helpful to articulate a number of the properties of the symbolic approach. Allen Newell formulated this paradigm best in his *physical symbol system hypothesis*:

> The necessary and sufficient condition for a physical system to exhibit general intelligent action is that it be a physical symbol system.   (1980, p. 170).

"General intelligent action" means rational behavior (p. 171); "rationality" means that, when an agent has a certain goal and the knowledge that a certain action will lead to that goal, then the agent selects that action (Newell 1982); and physical symbol systems are physically realized universal computers.

What all this means in the practice of symbolic AI is that goals, beliefs, knowledge, and so on are all formalized as symbolic structures (for instance, Lisp lists) that are built of symbols (such as Lisp atoms) that are each semantically interpretable in terms of the ordinary concepts we use to conceptualize the domain. Thus in a medical expert system, we expect to find structures like (IF FEVER THEN (HYPOTHESIZE INFECTION)). These symbolic structures are operated on by symbol-manipulation procedures composed of primitive operations like concatenating lists and extracting elements from lists. According to the symbolic paradigm, it is in terms of such operations that we are to understand cognitive processes.

It is important to note that in the symbolic paradigm, levels of cognition are analogized to levels of computer systems. The symbolic level that implements knowledge structures is alleged to be exact and complete. That means that lower levels are *unnecessary* for the accurate description of cognition in terms of the semantically interpretable elements. This relegates the neural question to simply: How does the nervous system happen to physically implement a physical symbol system? The answer to this question does not matter as far as symbol-level AI systems are concerned.

In this paradigm—which Hofstadter (1985) has called "the Boolean dream"—there are a number of inadequacies. These can be seen from a number of perspectives, which can only be caricatured here:

- From the perspective of neuroscience, the problem with the symbolic paradigm is quite simply, as I have already indicated, that it has provided precious little insight into the computational organization of the brain.

- From the perspective of modeling human performance, symbolic models, such as Newell and Simon's General Problem Solver (1972), do a good job on a coarse level; but the fine structure of cognition seems to be more naturally described by nonsymbolic models. In word recognition, for example, it is natural to think about activation levels of perceptual units.

- In AI, the trouble with the Boolean dream is that symbolic rules and the logic used to manipulate them tend to produce rigid and brittle systems.

1.2 The subsymbolic paradigm

The alternative to the symbolic paradigm that I want to present is what I call the *subsymbolic paradigm* (figure 9.2). In this paradigm, there is an intermediate level of structure between the neural and symbolic levels. This new *subsymbolic level* is supposed to be closer to each of the neural and symbolic levels than they are to each other. When cognition is described at the subsymbolic level, the description is that of a connectionist system.

The subsymbolic level is an attempt to formalize, *at some level of abstraction*, the kind of processing occurring in the nervous system. Many of the details of neural structure and function are absent from the subsymbolic level, and the level of description is higher than the

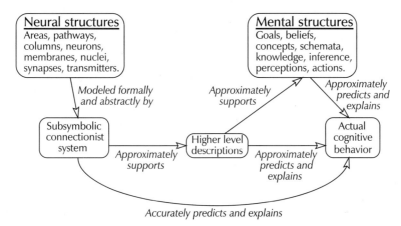

Figure 9.2: Neural and mental structures in the *sub*symbolic paradigm.

neural level. The precise relationship between the neural and subsymbolic levels is still a fairly wide-open research question; but it seems quite clear that connectionist systems are much closer to neural systems than are symbolic systems.

The relation between the subsymbolic and symbolic descriptions of cognition is illustrated in figure 9.2. If we adopt a higher level of description of what's going on in these subsymbolic systems (and that involves, to a significant degree, approximation) then we get descriptions that are approximately like symbolic accounts—the sort that traditional AI constructs. While the subsymbolic paradigm is content to give approximate accounts of things like goals and beliefs, it is not prepared to compromise on actual performance. Behind the accounts of folk psychology and symbolic AI, there lie real data on human intelligent performance; and the claim is that subsymbolic systems can provide accurate accounts of that data.

Note that the subsymbolic paradigm gives an essentially different role to the neural part of the story: Neural structures provide the basis (in some suitably abstract sense) of the formalism that gives the precise description of intelligence, whereas mental structures enter only into approximate descriptions.

In the remainder of the essay, I will elaborate on the nature of the subsymbolic level, and on the higher-level descriptions of subsymbolic systems that approximate symbolic accounts. I want to indicate how formalizing cognition by abstracting from neural structures—rather than with symbolic formalizations of mental structures—provides new and exciting views of knowledge, memory, concepts, and learning.

Figure 9.2 illustrates an important part of the subsymbolic paradigm: that levels of cognition should *not* be thought of by analogy to levels of computer systems, all stacked underneath the "mental" part of the diagram. Just as Newtonian concepts provide approximately valid descriptions of physical phenomena that are more accurately described with quantum concepts, so the symbolic concepts of folk psychology provide approximately valid descriptions of cognitive phenomena that are more accurately described with subsymbolic concepts. Mental structures are like higher-level descriptions of a *physical* system, rather than higher-level descriptions of a *computer* system.

1.3 Semantic interpretation

Perhaps the most fundamental contrast between the paradigms pertains to semantic interpretation of the formal models. In the symbolic approach, symbols (atoms) are used to denote the semantically interpretable entities (concepts); these same symbols are the objects governed by symbol manipulations in the rules that define the system. The entities which are semantically interpretable are *also* the entities governed by the formal laws that define the system. In the subsymbolic paradigm, this is no longer true. The semantically interpretable entities are *patterns of activation* over large number of units in the system, whereas the entities manipulated by formal rules are the individual activations of cells in the network. The rules take the form of activation-passing rules, which are essentially different in character from symbol-manipulation rules.

Now, what I'm talking about here is the particular kind of connectionist system in which what I just said is true: concepts are represented by patterns of activity, rather than by the activations of individual elements in the network. (In the latter case, we would have a collapse of just the same kind that we have the in symbolic paradigm.) So the subsymbolic paradigm involves connectionist systems using so-called *distributed representations,* as opposed to local representations. (The *PDP* books by Rumelhart, et al., and McClelland, et al., consider *distributed* connectionist systems; *local* connectionist systems are considered in Feldman and Ballard 1982, and Feldman, Ballard, Brown, and Dell 1985.)

Thus, in the subsymbolic paradigm the formal system description is at a lower level than the level of semantic interpretation; the level of denotation is higher than the level of manipulation. There is a fundamental two-layer structure to the subsymbolic paradigm, in contrast to the symbolic approach. The higher semantic level is not necessarily precisely formalizable, and the lower level is not "merely implementation" of a complete higher-level formalism. Both levels are essential: the lower level is essential for defining what the system *is* (in terms of activation passing), and the higher level is essential for understanding what the system *means* (in terms of the problem domain).

2 The subsymbolic level

I shall now characterize the subsymbolic level in more detail. Cognition looks quite different at this level than at the symbolic level. In section 3, where higher-level descriptions of connectionist systems will be considered, we will see some of the characteristics of the symbolic level emerging.

2.1 Subsymbolic computation

At the fundamental level in subsymbolic systems we have a collection of dynamical variables. There are two kinds of variables: an activation value for each of the units and a connection strength for each of the links. Typically, both kinds of variables are continuous. The rules that define these systems are activation-passing rules and connection-strength-modification rules. Typically these are expressed as differential equations (although they are simulated with finite difference equations). The differential equations are typically not stochastic, but stochastic versions will enter briefly later.

The computational role of these two kinds of equations are as follows. The activation-passing rules are in fact inference rules—not logical inference rules, but statistical inference rules. And the connection-strength-modification rules are memory-storage and learning procedures. These points will be expanded shortly.

Because the fundamental system is a dynamical system with continuously evolving variables, the subsymbolic paradigm constitutes a radical departure from the symbolic paradigm; the claim, in effect, is that *cognition should be thought of taking place in dynamical systems and not in digital computers.* This is a natural outcome of the neurally-inspired (rather than mentally-inspired) conception of computation.

The relation between the subsymbolic formalism and psychological processing is in part determined by the time constants that enter into the differential equations governing activation and connection-strength modification. The time required for significant change in activation levels is on the order of 100 milliseconds; the time it takes for a connection strength to change appreciably is much longer (say, on the order of a minute). Thus, for times less than about 100 milliseconds, what we're talking about is a single equilibration or "settling" of the network; all the knowledge embedded in the connections is used in parallel. On this time scale, we have parallel computation. When we go beyond this, to cognitive processes that go on for several seconds (such as problem solving and extended reasoning), then we're talking about multiple settlings of the network, and serial computation. This is the part of cognition for which serial symbolic descriptions, such as Newell and Simon's General Problem Solver, provide a fairly good description of the coarse structure. The claim of the subsymbolic paradigm is that the symbolic description of such processing is an approximate description of the global behavior of a lot of parallel computation. Finally, if we go to still longer time scales (on the order of a minute), then we have adaptation of the network to the situation it finds itself in.

Let me summarize the contrasts between the symbolic and subsymbolic approaches, viewed at the fundamental level. In the subsymbolic paradigm we have fundamental laws that are differential equations, not symbol-manipulation procedures. The systems we are talking about are dynamical systems, not von Neumann machines. The mathematical category in which these formalisms live is the continuous category, not the discrete category; so we have a different kind of mathematics coming into play. The differences are dramatically illustrated in the way memory is modeled in the two formalisms. In a von Neumann machine, memory storage is a primitive operation (you give a location and a content, and it gets stored), memory retrieval is likewise primitive. In subsymbolic systems, by contrast, these processes are quite involved—they're not primitive operations at all. When a memory is retrieved, it is "addressed" by its *contents*: a fragment of a previously-instantiated activation pattern is put into one part of the network (by another part of the network), and the connections fill out the remainder of that previously-present pattern. This is a much more involved process than a simple "memory fetch". Memories are stored in subsymbolic systems by adjusting connection strengths such that the retrieval process will actually work—and this is no simple matter.

2.2 Subsymbolic inference and the statistical connection

At the fundamental level of the subsymbolic formalism, we have moved from thinking about cognition in terms of discrete processes to thinking in terms of continuous processes. This means that different mathematical concepts apply. One manifestation of this, in computational terms, is the claim that inference should be construed not in the logical sense but rather in the statistical sense—at least at the fundamental level of the system. (We will see below that, *at higher levels*, certain subsymbolic systems do perform logical inference.)

I have encapsulated this idea in what I've called the *statistical connection*:

> The strength of the connection between two units is a measure of the statistical relation between their activity.

The origins of this principle are easily seen. The relationship between statistics and connections was represented in neuroscience by Hebb's (1949) principle: a synapse between two neurons is strengthened when both are active simultaneously. In psychology, this relation appeared in the notion of "strength of association" between concepts, an important precursor of connectionist ideas (although, since this involved statistical associations between *concepts*, it was not itself a subsymbolic notion).

From a physical point of view, the statistical connection is basically a tautology, since if two units are strongly connected, then when one is active the other is likely to be too. But from a computational point of view, the statistical connection has rather profound implications for AI and for symbolic computation. Activation passing is now to be thought of as statistical inference. Each connection represents a *soft constraint*; and the knowledge contained in the system is the set of all such constraints. If two units have an inhibitory connection, then the network has the knowledge that when one is active the other ought not be; but that is a soft constraint that can easily be overridden by countermanding excitatory connections to that same unit (if those excitatory connections come from units that are sufficiently active). The important point is that soft constraints, any one of which can be overridden by the others, *have no implications singly*; they only have implications collectively. That's why the natural process for using this kind of knowledge is *relaxation*, in which the network uses all the connections at once, and tries to settle into a state that balances all the constraints against each other. This is to be contrasted with *hard constraints*, such as rules of the form "If A, then B", which can be used individually, one at a time, to make inferences serially. The claim is that using soft constraints avoids the brittleness that hard constraints tend to produce in AI. (It is interesting to note that advocates of logic in AI have, for some time now, been trying to evade the brittleness of hard constraints by developing logics, such as non-monotonic logics, in which all of the rules are essentially used *together* to make inferences, and not separately; see, for example, *Artificial Intelligence*, 1980.)

To summarize: In the symbolic paradigm, constraints are typically hard, inference is logical, and processing can therefore be serial. (One can try to parallelize it, but the most natural approach is serial inference.) In the subsymbolic paradigm, constraints are soft, inference is statistical, and therefore it is most natural to use parallel implementations of inference.

3 Higher-level descriptions

Having characterized the subsymbolic paradigm at the fundamental, subsymbolic level, I would now like to turn to higher-level descriptions of these connectionist systems. As was stated above, according to the subsymbolic paradigm, serial symbolic descriptions of cognitive processing are approximate descriptions of the higher-level properties of connectionist computations. I will only be able to sketch this part of the story—pointing to published work for further details. The main point is that interesting relations *do* exist between the higher-level properties of connectionist systems and mental structures, as they have been formalized symbolically. The view of mental structures that emerges is strikingly different from that of the symbolic paradigm.

3.1 The best-fit principle

That crucial principle of the subsymbolic level, the statistical connection, can be reformulated at a higher level as what I call the *best-fit principle*:

> Given an input, a connectionist system outputs a set of inferences that, as a whole, give a best fit to the input, in a statistical sense defined by the statistical knowledge stored in the system's connections.

In this vague form, this principle may be generally true of connectionist systems. But it is exactly true in a precise sense, at least in an idealized limit, for a certain class of systems that I have studied in what I call *harmony theory* (Smolensky 1983, 1984a, 1984b, 1986a, 1986b, 1986c; Riley and Smolensky 1984).

To render the best-fit principle precise, it is necessary to provide precise definitions of "inferences", "best fit", and "statistical knowledge stored in the system's connections". This is done in harmony theory, where the central object is the "harmony function" H, which measures, for any possible set of inferences, the goodness-of-fit to the input with respect to the soft constraints stored in the connection strengths. The set of inferences with the largest value of H (that is, with the highest harmony) is the best set of inferences, with respect to a well-defined statistical problem.

Harmony theory basically offers three things. It gives a mathematically precise characterization of a very general statistical inference problem that covers a great number of connectionist computations. It tells how that problem can be solved using a connectionist network with a certain set of connections. And it provides a procedure by which the network can learn the correct connections with experience. I will comment briefly on each of these three elements, to give the flavor of the form that the best-fit principle takes, and to prepare the way for the remaining remarks on higher-level properties of connectionist computation.

Harmony theory analyzes systems that confront the following statistical inference task: If we give the system some features of an environmental state, it should infer values for unknown features. An example I will consider in the next section concerns reasoning about a simple electric circuit. Given a change in the value of some circuit feature (say, an increase in the value of some resistor), then what happens to the other, "unknown" features—the currents and voltages, say? This general task is what I call *the completion task*.

In response to a completion problem, the system is supposed to give the maximum-likelihood set of inferred values, with respect to a probability distribution maintained internal to the system as a model of the environment. In other words, the system maintains a probability distribution that represents the likelihoods of various events' occurring in the environment; and it should give as its output the maximum-likelihood set of values for the unknowns.

What model of the environment—what probability distribution— is the system supposed to use? Here harmony theory adopts a principle commonly used in statistical inference: The system should use the probability distribution with minimal informational content that is consistent with the statistical constraints that the system observes holding in the environment.

Having specified the inference problem in this way, we can now draw some conclusions. The first result says that the minimal information distribution can actually be computed as follows. The probability of a set of inferred values x is proportional to the exponential of a particular function:

$$prob\,(x) \propto e^{\Sigma_\alpha \lambda_\alpha f_\alpha\,(x)}$$

This function has one parameter λ_α for each statistical constraint α observed in the environment. (The function f_α has value 1 when constraint α is satisfied, and 0 otherwise). It turns out that the maximum-likelihood completions that the system is supposed to give as answers to questions can be computed from a simpler distribution that has a quadratic function in the exponent, but which uses auxiliary variables to achieve the simplification:

$$prob\,(x, y) \propto e^{H\,(x, y)}$$

This quadratic function H measures the internal consistency of a set of inferred values, with respect to these constraint parameters λ_α; I called it H because it turns out to play the mathematical role of the Hamiltonian of a statistical-mechanical system. That's where the name "harmony" comes from: H measures the internal consistency of states of the system.

I call this first result the *competence theorem* because it explicitly characterizes how the system ideally ought to behave. The next result, the *realizability theorem*, describes how to instantiate this competence in a performance system—an actual computing device—the behavior of which obeys the competence theorem in suitably ideal circumstances, but which in real circumstances exhibits performance that deviates from the ideal competence. By creating one computing element for each of the given and to-be-inferred variables in the set x, and one for each of the auxiliary variables in the set y, and using the parameters λ_α to determine connection strengths, a connectionist network can be built which can compute the maximum-likelihood completions by a stochastic relaxation method. The units in this harmony network are stochastic processors—the differential equations defining the system are stochastic. There is a system parameter called the *computational temperature* that governs the degree of randomness in the units' behavior: it starts out high, at the beginning of the computation when there is a lot of randomness in the network, but then is lowered during computation until eventually the system "freezes" into an answer. In the idealized limit, where the system has unlimited relaxation time, the network converges with probability 1 to the correct answer, as characterized by the competence theorem. (The stochastic relaxation process is *simulated annealing*, as in the Boltzmann machine; see Hinton and Sejnowski 1983. For the historical and logical relations between harmony theory and the Boltzmann machine, see Rumelhart, et al. 1986, p. 148, and Smolensky 1986a.)

The third result is a learnability theorem. It says that, through a statistical sampling of the environment, the values of the parameters λ_α (that is, the connection strengths) required by the competence theorem can be computed by relaxation. That is, the parameters start off with some initial values ("genetically" selected or randomly assigned) which are then gradually tuned through experience to become the correct ones for the given environment.

3.2 Productions, sequential processing, and logical inference

A simple harmony model of expert intuition in qualitative physics was described in Riley and Smolensky (1984) and Smolensky (1986a, 1986c). The model answers questions like: "What happens to the voltages in this circuit if I increase this resistor?" Higher-level descriptions of this subsymbolic problem-solving system illustrate several interesting points.

It is possible to identify *macro-decisions* during the system's solution of a problem; these are each the result of many individual micro-decisions by the units of the system, and each amounts to a large-scale commitment to a portion of the solution. These macro-decisions are approximately like the firing of production rules. In fact, these "productions" "fire" at different times, in essentially the same order as in a symbolic forward-chaining inference system. One can measure the total amount of order in the system, and see that there is a qualitative change in the system when the first micro-decisions are made—the system changes from a disordered phase to an ordered one.

A corollary of the way this network embodies the problem-domain constraints, and the general theorems of harmony theory, is that the system, when given a well-posed problem and unlimited relaxation time, will always give the correct answer. Thus, under that idealization, the *competence* of the system is described by *hard* constraints: Ohm's law, Kirchoff's laws, and so on. It is as if the system had those laws written down inside it. However, as in all subsymbolic systems, the *performance* of the system is achieved by satisfying a large set of *soft* constraints. What this means is that if we go outside of the ideal conditions under which hard constraints seem to be obeyed, the illusion that the system has hard constraints inside it is quickly dispelled. The system can violate Ohm's law if it has to; but if it doesn't have to violate the law, it won't. Thus, *outside the idealized domain of well-posed problems and unlimited processing time, the system gives sensible performance.* It isn't brittle in the way that symbolic inference systems are. If the system is given an ill-posed problem, it satisfies as many constraints as possible. If it is given inconsistent information, it doesn't fall flat, and deduce just anything. If it is given insufficient information, it doesn't just sit there and deduce nothing. Given limited processing time, the performance degrades gracefully as well. Thus, the competence/performance distinction can be addressed in a sensible way.

Continuing the theme of physical analogies instead of computer analogies, we might think of this as like a "quantum" system that appears to be "Newtonian" under certain conditions. A system that has, at the micro-level, soft constraints, satisfied in parallel, *appears* at the macro-level, under the right conditions, to have hard constraints, satisfied serially. But it doesn't *really*; and if you go outside the "Newtonian" domain, you see that it has really been a "quantum" system all along.

3.3 The dynamics of activation patterns

In the subsymbolic paradigm, semantic interpretation occurs at the higher level of patterns of activity, not at the lower level of individual nodes. Thus an important question about the higher level is: How do the semantically-interpretable entities *combine*?

In the symbolic paradigm, the semantically-interpretable entities are symbols, which combine by some form of *concatenation*. In the subsymbolic paradigm, the semantically-interpretable entities are activation patterns, and these combine by *superposition*: activation patterns superimpose upon each other, the way that wave-like structures always do in physical systems. This difference is another manifestation of moving the formalization from the discrete to the continuous (indeed the linear) category.

Using the mathematics of the superposition operation, it is possible to describe connectionist systems at the higher, semantic level. If the connectionist system is purely linear (so that the activity of each unit is precisely a weighted sum of the activities of the units giving it input), it can easily be proved that the higher-level description obeys formal laws of just the same sort as the lower level: the subsymbolic and symbolic levels are *isomorphic*. Linear connectionist systems are, however, of limited computational power; and most interesting connectionist systems are nonlinear. However, nearly all are *quasi-linear*—that is, each unit *combines* its inputs linearly, even though the effect of this combination on the unit's activity is nonlinear. Further, the problem-specific *knowledge* in such systems is in the combination weights (that is, the *linear part* of the dynamical equations); and, in learning systems, it is generally only these linear weights that adapt. For these reasons, even though the higher level is not isomorphic to the lower level in nonlinear systems, there are senses in which the higher level *approx-*

imately obeys formal laws similar to the lower level. (For the details, see Smolensky 1986b.)

The conclusion here is a rather different one from that of the preceding subsection, where we saw how there are senses in which higher-level characterizations of certain subsymbolic systems approximate productions, serial processing, and logical inference. What we see now is that there are also senses in which the laws approximately describing cognition at the semantic level are *activation-passing laws*—like those at the subsymbolic level, but operating between "units" with individual semantics. These semantic-level descriptions of mental processing (which include *local* connectionist models) have been of considerable value in cognitive psychology (see, for example, McClelland and Rumelhart 1981; Rumelhart and McClelland 1982; Dell 1985). We can now see how these "spreading-activation" accounts of mental processing relate to subsymbolic accounts.

3.4 Schemata

One of the most important symbolic concepts is that of the *schema* (Rumelhart 1980). This concept goes back at least to Kant (1787/ 1929) as a description of mental concepts and mental categories. Schemata appear in many AI systems in the forms of frames, scripts, or similar structures; they are prepackaged bundles of information that support inference in stereotyped situations.

I will very briefly summarize work on schemata in connectionist systems reported in Rumelhart, Smolensky, McClelland and Hinton (1986; see also Feldman 1981, and Smolensky 1986a, 1986c). This work addressed the case of schemata for rooms. Subjects were asked to describe some imagined rooms using a set of 40 features like: has-ceiling, has-window, contains-toilet, and so on. Statistics computed from these data were used to construct a network containing one node for each feature, and containing connections computed from the statistical data by using a particular form of the statistical connection.

This resulting network can do inference of the kind that can be performed by symbolic systems with schemata for various types of rooms. For example, the network can be told that some room contains a ceiling and an oven, and then be given the question: What else is likely to be in the room? The system settles down into a final state, and the inferences contained in that final state are that the room contains a coffee cup but no fireplace, a coffee pot but no computer.

The inference process in this system is simply one of greedily maximizing harmony. To describe the inferences of this system on a higher level, we can examine the global states of the system in terms of their harmony values. How internally consistent are the various states in the space? It is a 40-dimensional state space, but various 2-dimensional subspaces can be selected and the harmony values there can be graphically displayed. The harmony landscape has various peaks; looking at the features of the state corresponding to one of the peaks, we find that it corresponds to a prototypical bathroom; others correspond to a prototypical office, and so on, for all the kinds of rooms subjects were asked to describe. There are no *units* in this system for bathrooms or offices: there are just lower-level descriptors. The prototypical bathroom is a pattern of activation, and the system's recognition of its prototypicality is reflected in the harmony peak for that pattern. It is a consistent, "harmonious" combination of features: better than neighboring points like one representing a bathroom without a bathtub, which has distinctly lower harmony.

During inference, this system climbs directly uphill on the harmony landscape. When the system state is in the vicinity of the harmony peak representing the prototypical bathroom, the inferences it makes are governed by the shape of the harmony landscape there. This shape is like a "schema" that governs inferences about bathrooms. (In fact, harmony theory was created to give a connectionist formalization of the notion of schema; see Smolensky 1986a, 1986c.) Looking closely at the harmony landscape we can see that the terrain around the "bathroom" peak has many of the properties of a bathroom schema: variables and constants, default values, schemata embedded inside of schemata, and even cross-variable dependencies. The system behaves as though it had schemata for bathrooms, offices, and so on, even though they are not "really there" at the fundamental level. These schemata are strictly properties of a higher-level description. They are informal, approximate descriptions—one might even say they are merely metaphorical descriptions—of an inference process too subtle to admit such high-level descriptions with great precision. Even though these schemata may not be the sort of object on which to base a formal model, nonetheless they *are* useful descriptions—which may, in the end, be all that can really be said about schemata anyway.

4 Conclusion

The view of symbolic structures that emerges from viewing them as entities of high-level descriptions of dynamical systems is quite different from the view coming from the symbolic paradigm. "Rules" are not symbolic formulae, but the cooperative result of many smaller soft constraints. Macro-inference is not a process of firing a symbolic production; rather it is a process of qualitative state change in a dynamical system, such as a phase transition. Schemata are not large symbolic data structures but rather the potentially quite intricate shapes of harmony maxima. Similarly, categories turn out to be attractors in dynamical systems: states that "suck in" to a common place many nearby states, like peaks of harmony functions. Categorization is not the execution of a symbolic algorithm but the continuous evolution of the dynamical system—the evolution that drives states into the attractors, to maximal harmony. Learning is not the construction and editing of formulae, but the gradual adjustment of connection strengths with experience, with the effect of slowly shifting harmony landscapes, adapting old and creating new concepts, categories, schemata.

The heterogenous assortment of high-level mental structures that have been embraced in this paper suggests that the symbolic level lacks formal unity. This is just what one expects of approximate higher-level descriptions, which, capturing different aspects of global properties, can have quite different characters. The unity underlying cognition is to be found not at the symbolic level, but rather at the subsymbolic level, where a few principles in a single formal framework lead to a rich variety of global behaviors.

If connectionist models are interpreted within what I have defined as the subsymbolic paradigm, we can start to see how mental structures can emerge from neural structures. By seeing mental entities as higher-level structures implemented in connectionist systems, we get a new, more complex and subtle view of what these mental structures really are. Perhaps subsymbolic systems can achieve a truly rich mental life.

On the Nature of Theories: A Neurocomputational Perspective

Paul M. Churchland
1989

1 The classical view of theories

Not long ago, we all knew what a theory was: it was a set of sentences or propositions, expressible in the first-order predicate calculus. And we had what seemed to be excellent reasons for that view. Surely any theory had to be *statable*. And after it had been fully stated, as a set of sentences, what residue remained? Furthermore, the sentential view made systematic sense of how theories could perform the primary business of theories, namely, prediction, explanation, and intertheoretic reduction. It was basically a matter of first-order deduction from the sentences of the theory conjoined with relevant premises about the domain at hand.

Equally important, the sentential view promised an account of the nature of learning, and of rationality. Required was a set of formal rules to dictate appropriate changes or updates in the overall set of believed sentences as a function of new beliefs supplied by observation. Of course there was substantial disagreement about which rules were appropriate. Inductivists, falsificationists, hypothetico-deductivists, and Bayesian subjectivists each proposed a different account of them. But the general approach seemed clearly correct. Rationality would be captured as the proper set of formal rules emerged from logical investigation.

Finally, if theories are just sentences, then the ultimate virtue of a theory is truth. And it was widely expected that an adequate account of rational methodology would reveal why humans must tend, in the long run, toward theories that are true.

Hardly anyone will now deny that there are serious problems with every element of the preceding picture, difficulties we shall discuss below. Yet the majority of the profession is not yet willing to regard them as fatal. I profess myself among the minority that does so regard them. In urging the poverty of "sentential epistemologies" for over a decade now (Churchland 1975, 1979, 1981, 1986), I have been motivated primarily by the *pattern* of the failures displayed by that approach. Those failures suggest to me that what is defective in the classical approach is its fundamental assumption that language-like structures of some kind constitute the basic or most important form of representation in cognitive creatures, and the correlative assumption that cognition consists in the manipulation of those representations by means of structure-sensitive rules.

To be sure, not everyone saw the same pattern of failure, nor were they prepared to draw such a strong conclusion even if they did. For any research program has difficulties, and so long as we lack a comparably compelling *alternative* conception of representation and computation, it may be best to stick with the familiar research program of sentences and rules for their manipulation.

However, it is no longer true that we lack a comparably compelling alternative approach. Within the last five years, there have been some striking theoretical developments and experimental results within cognitive neurobiology and connectionist AI (artificial intelligence). These have provided us with a powerful and fertile framework with which to address problems of cognition, a framework that owes nothing to the sentential paradigm of the classical view. My main purpose in this essay is to make the rudiments of that framework available to a wider audience, and to explore its far-reaching consequences for traditional issues in the philosophy of science. Before turning to this task, let me prepare the stage by briefly summarizing the principal failures of the classical view, and the most prominent responses to them.

2 Problems and alternative approaches

The depiction of learning as the rule-governed updating of a system of sentences or propositional attitudes encountered a wide range of failures. For starters, even the best of the rules proposed failed to reproduce reliably our preanalytic judgments of credibility, even in the artificially restricted or toy situations in which they were asked to function. Paradoxes of confirmation plagued the hypothetico-deductive accounts (Hempel 1965, Scheffler 1963). The indeterminacy of falsification plagued the Popperian accounts (Lakatos 1970, Feyerabend 1970, Churchland 1975). Laws were assigned negligible credibility on Carnapian accounts (Salmon 1966). Bayesian accounts, like

Carnapian ones, presupposed a given probability space as the epistemic playground within which learning takes place, and they could not account for the rationality of major shifts from one probability space to another, which is what the most interesting and important cases of learning amount to. The rationality of large-scale *conceptual change*, accordingly, seemed beyond the reach of such approaches. Furthermore, simplicity emerged as a major determinant of theoretical credibility on most accounts, but none of them could provide an adequate definition of simplicity in syntactic terms, or give a convincing explanation of why it was relevant to truth or credibility in any case. One could begin to question whether the basic factors relevant to learning were to be found at the linguistic level at all.

Beyond these annoyances, the initial resources ascribed to a learning subject by the sentential approach plainly presupposed the successful completion of a good deal of sophisticated learning on the part of that subject already. For example, reliable observation judgments do not just appear out of nowhere. Living subjects have to *learn* to make the complex perceptual discriminations that make perceptual judgments possible. And they also have to *learn* the linguistic or propositional system within which their beliefs are to be constituted. Plainly, both cases of learning will have to involve some procedure quite distinct from that of the classical account. For that account presupposes antecedent possession of both a determinate propositional system and a capacity for determinate perceptual judgment, which is precisely what, prior to extensive learning, the human infant lacks. Accordingly, the classical story cannot possibly account for all cases of learning. There must exist a type of learning that is prior to and more basic than the process of sentence manipulation at issue.

Thus are we led rather swiftly to the idea that there is a level of representation *beneath* the level of the sentential or propositional attitudes, and to the correlative idea that there is a learning dynamic that operates primarily on sublinguistic factors. This idea is reinforced by reflection on the problem of cognition and learning in nonhuman animals, none of which appear to have the benefit of language, either the external speech or the internal structures, but all of which engage in sophisticated cognition. Perhaps their cognition proceeds entirely without benefit of any system for processing sentencelike representations.

Even in the human case, the depiction of one's knowledge as an immense set of individually stored sentences raises a severe problem concerning the relevant retrieval or application of those internal representations. How is it one is able to retrieve, from the millions of sentences stored, exactly the handful that is relevant to one's current predictive or explanatory problem, and how is it one is generally able to do this in a few tenths of a second? This is known as the "frame problem" in AI, and it arises because, from the point of view of fast and relevant retrieval, a long list of sentences is an appallingly inefficient way to store information. And the more information a creature has, the worse its application problem becomes.

A further problem with the classical view of learning is that it finds no essential connection whatever between the learning of *facts* and the learning of *skills*. This is a problem in itself, since one might have hoped for a unified account of learning, but it is doubly a problem when one realizes that so much of the business of understanding a theory and being a scientist is a matter of the skills one has acquired. Memorizing a set of sentences is not remotely sufficient: one must learn to *recognize* the often quite various instances of the terms they contain; one must learn to *manipulate* the peculiar formalism in which they may be embedded; one must learn to *apply* the formalism to novel situations; one must learn to *control* the instruments that typically produce or monitor the phenomena at issue. As T. S. Kuhn (1962/70) first made clear, these dimensions of a scientist's trade are only artificially separable from his understanding of its current theories. It begins to appear that even if we do harbor internal sentences, they capture only a small part of human knowledge.

These failures of the classical view over the full range of learning, both in humans and in nonhuman animals, are the more suspicious given the classical view's total disconnection from any theory concerning the structure of the biological *brain,* and the manner in which it might *implement* the kind of representations and computations proposed. Making acceptable contact with neurophysiological theory is a long-term constraint on any epistemology: a scheme of representation and computation that cannot be implemented in the machinery of the human brain cannot be an adequate account of human cognitive activities.

The situation on this score used to be much better than it now is: it was clear that the classical account of representation and learning could easily be realized in typical digital computers, and it was thought that the human brain would turn out to be relevantly like a digital computer. But quite aside from the fact that computer implementations of sentential learning chronically produced disappointing results, it has become increasingly clear that the brain is organized along computational lines radically different from those employed in conventional digital computers. The brain, as we shall see below, is a massively parallel processor, and it performs computational tasks of the classical kind at issue only very slowly and comparatively badly. It does not appear to be designed to perform the tasks the classical view assigns to it.

I conclude this survey by returning to specifically philosophical matters. A final problem with the classical approach has been the failure of all attempts to explain why the learning process must tend, at least in the long run, to lead us toward *true* theories. Surprisingly, and perhaps distressingly, this Panglossean hope has proved very resistant to vindication (Van Fraassen 1980, Laudan 1981). Although the history of human intellectual endeavor does support the view that, over the centuries, our theories have become dramatically *better* in many dimensions, it is quite problematic whether they are successively "closer" to "truth". Indeed, the notion of truth itself has recently come in for critical scrutiny (Putnam 1981, Churchland 1985, Stich 1988). It is no longer clear that there *is* any unique and unitary relation that virtuous belief systems must bear to the nonlinguistic world. Which leaves us free to reconsider the great many different dimensions of epistemic and pragmatic virtue that a cognitive system can display.

The problems of the preceding pages have not usually been presented in concert, and they are not usually regarded as conveying a unitary lesson. A few philosophers, however, have been moved by them, or by some subset of them, to suggest significant modifications in the classical framework. One approach that has captured some adherents is the "semantic view" of theories (Suppe 1974, Van Fraassen 1980, Giere 1988). This approach attempts to drive a wedge between a theory and its possibly quite various linguistic formulations by characterizing a theory as a *set of models,* those that will make a first-order linguistic statement of the theory come out *true* under the relevant assignments. The models in the set all share a common abstract structure, and that structure is what is important about any theory, according to the semantic view, not any of its idiosyncratic linguistic expressions. A theory is true, on this view, just in case it includes the actual world, or some part of it, as one of the models in the set.

This view buys us some advantages, perhaps, but I find it to be a relatively narrow response to the panoply of problems addressed above.

In particular, I think it strange that we should be asked, at this stage of the debate, to embrace an account of theories that has absolutely nothing to do with the question of how real physical systems might embody representations of the world, and how they might execute principled computations on those representations in such a fashion as to learn. Prima facie, at least, the semantic approach takes theories even farther into Plato's Heaven, and away from the buzzing brains that use them, than did the view that a theory is a set of sentences. This complaint does not do justice to the positive virtues of the semantic approach (see especially Giere), but it is clear that the semantic approach is a response to only a small subset of the extant difficulties.

A more celebrated response is embodied in Kuhn's *The Structure of Scientific Revolutions* (1962/70). Kuhn centers our attention not on sets of sentences, nor on sets of models, but on what he calls paradigms or exemplars, which are specific *applications* of our conceptual, mathematical, and instrumental resources. Mastering a theory, on this view, is more a matter of being able to perform in various ways, of being able to solve a certain class of problems, of being able to recognize diverse situations as relevantly similar to that of the original or paradigmatic application. Kuhn's view brings to the fore the historical, the sociological, and the psychological factors that structure our theoretical cognition. Of central importance is the manner in which one comes to perceive the world as one internalizes a theory. The perceptual world is redivided into new categories, and while the theory may be able to provide necessary and sufficient conditions for being an instance of any of its categories, the perceptual recognition of any instance of a category does not generally proceed by reference to those conditions, which often transcend perceptual experience. Rather, perceptual recognition proceeds by some inarticulable process that registers *similarity* to one or more perceptual *prototypes* of the category at issue. The recognition of new applications of the entire theory displays a similar dynamic. In all, a successful theory provides a prototypical beachhead which one attempts to expand by analogical extensions to new domains.

Reaction to this view has been deeply divided. Some applaud Kuhn's move toward naturalism, toward a performance conception of knowledge, and away from the notion of truth as the guiding compass of cognitive activity (Munevar 1981, Stich 1988). Others deplore his neglect of normative issues, his instrumentalism and relativism, and his alleged exaggeration of certain lessons from perceptual and developmental psychology (Fodor 1984). We shall address these issues later in the paper.

A third reaction to the classical difficulties has simply rejected the sentential or propositional attitudes as the most important form of representation used by cognitive creatures, and has insisted on the necessity of empirical and theoretical research into *brain* function in order to answer the question of what *are* the most important forms of representation and computation within cognitive creatures. (Early statements can be found in Churchland, P.M. 1975 and Hooker 1975; extended arguments appear in Churchland, P.M. 1979 and 1981; and further arguments appear in Churchland, P.S. 1980 and 1986, and in Hooker 1987.)

While the antisentential diagnosis could be given some considerable support, as the opening summary of this section illustrates, neuroscience as the recommended cure was always more difficult to sell, given the functional opacity of the biological brain. Recently, however, this has changed dramatically. We now have some provisional insight into the functional significance of the brain's microstructure, and some idea of how it represents and computes. What has been discovered so far appears to vindicate the claims of relevance and the expectations of fertility in this area, and it appears to vindicate some central elements in Kuhn's perspective as well. This neurofunctional framework promises to sustain wholly new directions of cognitive research. In the sections to follow I shall try to outline the elements of this framework and its applications to some familiar problems in the philosophy of science. I begin with the physical structure and the basic activities of the brainlike systems at issue.

3 Elementary brainlike networks

The functional atoms of the brain are cells called neurons (figure 10.1). These have a natural or default level of activity which can, however, be modulated up or down by external influences. From each neuron there extends a long, thin output fiber called an *axon,* which typically branches at the far end so as to make a large number of *synaptic connections* with either the central cell body or the bushy *dendrites* of other neurons. Each neuron thus receives inputs from a great many other neurons, which inputs tend to excite (or to inhibit, depending on the type of synaptic connection) its normal or default level of acti-

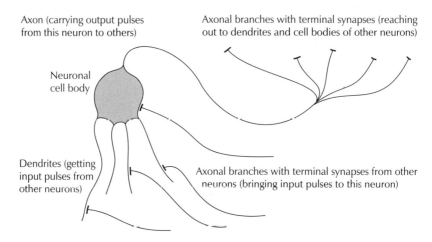

Axon (carrying output pulses from this neuron to others)

Axonal branches with terminal synapses (reaching out to dendrites and cell bodies of other neurons)

Neuronal cell body

Dendrites (getting input pulses from other neurons)

Axonal branches with terminal synapses from other neurons (bringing input pulses to this neuron)

Figure 10.1: Structure of a typical neuron (simplified in various ways).

vation. The level of activation induced is a function of the *number* of connections, of their size or *weight,* of their *polarity* (stimulatory or inhibitory), and of the *strength* of the incoming signals. Furthermore, each neuron is constantly emitting an output signal along its own axon, a signal whose strength is a direct function of the overall level of activation in the originating cell body. That signal is a train of pulses or *spikes,* as they are called, which are propagated swiftly along the axon. A typical cell can emit spikes along its axon at anything between zero and perhaps 200 hertz. Neurons, if you like, are humming to one another, in basso notes of varying frequency.

The networks to be explored attempt to simulate natural neurons with artificial units of the kind depicted in figure 10.2. These units admit of various levels of activation, which we shall assume to vary between 0 and 1. Each unit receives input signals from other units via "synaptic" connections of various weights and polarities. These are represented in the diagram as small end-plates of various sizes. For simplicity's sake, we dispense with dendritic trees: the "axonal" end branches from other units all make connections directly to the "cell body" of the receiving unit. The total modulating effect E impacting on that unit is just the sum of the contributions made by each of the connections. The contribution of a single connection is just the product of its weight w_i times the strength s_i of the signal arriving at that connection. Let me emphasize that if for some reason the connection weights were to change over time, then the unit would receive a quite

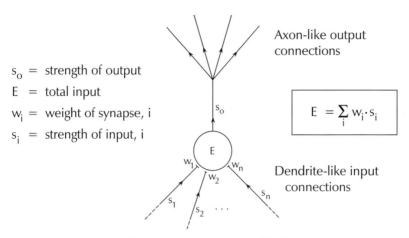

s_o = strength of output

E = total input

w_i = weight of synapse, i

s_i = strength of input, i

Axon-like output connections

$$E = \sum_i w_i \cdot s_i$$

Dendrite-like input connections

Figure 10.2: A neuronlike processing unit (simplified in various ways).

different level of overall excitation or inhibition in response to the very same configuration of input signals.

Turn now to the output side of things. As a function of the total input *E*, the unit modulates its activity level and emits an output signal of a certain strength s_o along its axonal output fiber. But s_o is not a direct or *linear* function of *E*. Rather, it is an S-shaped function as in figure 10.3. The reasons for this small wrinkle will emerge later. I mention it here because its inclusion completes the story of the elementary units. Of their intrinsic properties, there is nothing left to tell. They are very simple indeed.

It remains to arrange them into networks. In the brain, neurons frequently constitute a population all of which send their axons to the site of a second population of neurons, where each arriving axon divides into terminal end branches in order to make many different synaptic connections within the target population. Axons from this second

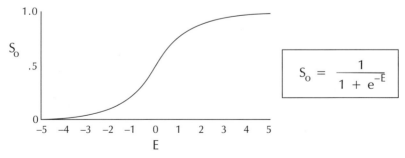

$$S_o = \frac{1}{1 + e^{-E}}$$

Figure 10.3: The sigmoid (S-shaped) axonal output function.

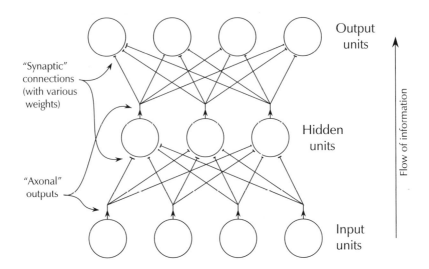

Figure 10.4: A simple network.

population can then project to a third, and so on. This is the inspiration for the arrangement of figure 10.4.

The units in the bottom or input layer of the network may be thought of as "sensory" units, since the level of activation in each is directly determined by aspects of the environment (or perhaps by the experimenter, in the process of simulating some environmental input). The activation level of a given input unit is designed to be a response to a specific aspect or dimension of the overall input stimulus that strikes the bottom layer. The assembled set of simultaneous activation levels in all of the input units is the network's *representation* of the input stimulus. We may refer to that configuration of stimulation levels as the *input vector,* since it is just an ordered set of numbers or magnitudes. For example, a given stimulus might produce the vector $\langle .5, .3, .9, .2 \rangle$.

These input activation levels are then propagated upwards, via the output signal in each unit's axon, to the middle layer of the network, to what are called the *hidden units.* As can be seen in figure 10.4, any unit in the input layer makes a synaptic connection of some weight or other with every unit at this intermediate layer. Each hidden unit is thus the target of several inputs, one for each cell at the input layer. The resulting activation level of a given hidden unit is essentially just the sum of all of the influences reaching it from the cells in the lower layer.

The result of this upwards propagation of the input vector is a set of activation levels across the three units in the hidden layer, called the *hidden unit activation vector*. The values of that three-element vector are strictly determined by

(1) the makeup of the *input vector* at the input layer, and

(2) the various values of the *connection weights* at the ends of the terminal branches from the input units.

What this bottom half of the network does, evidently, is convert or transform one activation vector into another.

The top half of the network does exactly the same thing, in exactly the same way. The activation vector at the hidden layer is propagated upwards to the output (topmost) layer of units, where an *output vector* is produced, whose character is determined by

(1) the makeup of the activation vector at the hidden layer, and

(2) the various values of the connection weights at the ends of the terminal branches projecting from the hidden units.

Looking now at the whole network, we can see that it is just a device for transforming any given input-level activation vector into a uniquely corresponding output-level activation vector. And what determines the character of the global transformation effected is the peculiar set of values possessed by the many connection weights. This much is easy to grasp. What is not so easy to grasp, prior to exploring examples, is just how very powerful and useful those transformations can be. So let us explore some real examples.

4 Representation and learning in brainlike networks

A great many of the environmental features to which humans respond are difficult to define or characterize in terms of their purely physical properties. Even something as mundane as being the vowel sound /ā/, as in 'rain', resists such characterization, for the range of acoustical variation among acceptable and recognizable /ā/s, is enormous. A female child at two years and a basso male at fifty will produce quite different sorts of atmospheric excitations in pronouncing this vowel, but each sound will be easily recognized as an /ā/, by other members of the same linguistic culture.

I do not mean to suggest that the matter is utterly intractable from a physical point of view, for an examination of the acoustical power spectrum of voiced vowels begins to reveal some of the similarities that unite all /ā/s. And yet the analysis continues to resist a simple list of necessary and sufficient physical conditions on being an /ā/. Instead, being an /ā/ seems to be a matter of being *close enough* to a *typical* /ā/ sound along a *sufficient* number of distinct *dimensions of relevance,* where each notion in italics remains difficult to characterize in a non-arbitrary way. Moreover, some of those dimensions are highly contextual. A sound type that would not normally be counted or recognized as an /ā/ when voiced in isolation may be unproblematically so counted if it regularly occurs, in someone's modestly accented speech, in all of the phonetic places that would normally be occupied by /ā/s. Evidently, what makes something an /ā/ is in part a matter of the entire linguistic surround. In this way do we very quickly ascend to the abstract and holistic level, for even the simplest of culturally embedded properties.

What holds for phonemes holds also for a great many other important features recognizable by us—colors, faces, flowers, trees, animals, voices, smells, feelings, songs, words, meanings, and even metaphorical meanings. At the outset, the categories and resources of physics, and even neuroscience, look puny and impotent in the face of such subtlety.

And yet it is purely physical systems that recognize such intricacies. Short of appealing to magic, or of simply refusing to confront the problem at all, we must assume that some configuration of purely physical elements is capable of grasping and manipulating these features, and by means of purely physical principles. Surprisingly, networks of the kind described in the preceding section have many of the properties needed to address precisely this problem. Let me explain

Suppose we are submarine engineers confronted with the problem of designing a sonar system that will distinguish between the sonar echoes returned from explosive mines, such as might lie on the bottom of sensitive waterways during wartime, and the sonar echoes returned from rocks of comparable sizes that dot the same underwater landscapes. The difficulty is twofold: echoes from both objects sound indistinguishable to the casual ear, and echoes from each type show wide variation in sonic character, since both rocks and mines come in various sizes, shapes, and orientations relative to the probing sonar pulse.

Enter the network of figure 10.5. This one has thirteen units at the input layer, since we need to code a fairly complex stimulus. A given

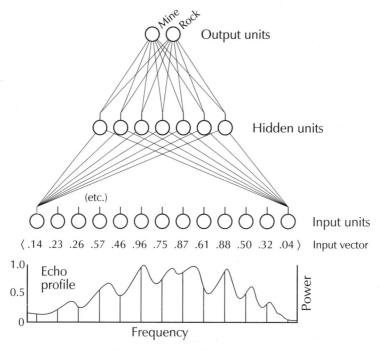

Figure 10.5: Perceptual recognition with a large network.

sonar echo is run through a frequency analyzer, and is sampled for its relative energy levels at thirteen frequencies. These thirteen values, expressed as fractions of 1, are then entered as activation levels in the respective units of the input layer, as indicated in figure 10.5. From here they are propagated through the network, being transformed as they go, as explained earlier. The result is a pair of activation levels in the two units at the output layer. We need only two units here, for we want the network eventually to produce an output activation vector at or near $\langle 1, 0 \rangle$ when a mine echo is entered as input, and an output activation vector at or near $\langle 0, 1 \rangle$ when a rock echo is entered as input. In a word, we want it to *distinguish* mines from rocks.

It would of course be a miracle if the network made the desired discrimination immediately, since the connection weights that determine its transformational activity are initially set at random values. At the beginning of this experiment then, the output vectors are sure to disappoint us. But we proceed to *teach* the network by means of the following procedure.

We procure a large set of recorded samples of various (genuine) mine echoes, from mines of various sizes and orientations, and a comparable set of genuine rock echoes, keeping careful track of which is which. We then feed these echoes into the network, one by one, and observe the output vector produced in each case. What interests us in each case is the amount by which the actual output vector *differs* from what would have been the "correct" vector, given the identity of the specific echo that produced it. The details of that error, for each element of the output vector, are then fed into a special rule that computes a set of small changes in the values of the various synaptic weights in the system. The idea is to identify those weights most responsible for the error, and then to nudge their values in a direction that would at least reduce the amount by which the output vector is in error. The slightly modified system is then fed another echo, and the entire procedure is repeated.

This provides the network with a "teacher". The process is called "training up the network" and it is standardly executed by an auxiliary computer programmed to feed samples from the training set into the network, monitor its responses, and adjust the weights according to the special rule after each trial. Under the pressure of such repeated corrections, the behavior of the network slowly converges on the behavior we desire. That is to say, after several thousands of presentations of recorded echoes and subsequent adjustments, the network starts to give the right answer close to 90 percent of the time. When fed a mine echo, it generally gives something close to a $\langle 1, 0 \rangle$ output. And when fed a rock echo, it generally gives something close to a $\langle 0, 1 \rangle$.

A useful way to think of this is captured in figure 10.6. Think of an abstract space of many dimensions, one for each weight in the network (105 in this case) plus one dimension for representing the overall error of the output vector on any given trial. Any point in that space represents a unique configuration of weights, plus the performance error that that configuration produces. What the learning rule does is steadily nudge that configuration away from erroneous positions and toward positions that are less erroneous. The system inches its way down an "error gradient" toward a global error minimum. Once there, it responds reliably to the relevant kinds of echoes. It even responds well to echoes that are "similar" to mine echoes, by giving output vectors that are closer to $\langle 1, 0 \rangle$ than to $\langle 0, 1 \rangle$.

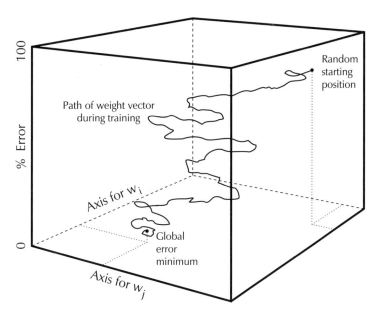

Figure 10.6: Learning by gradient descent in weight/error space. (Axes are shown for only two of the 105 synaptic weights.)

There was no guarantee the network would succeed in learning to discriminate the two kinds of echoes, because there was no guarantee that rock echoes and mine echoes would differ in any systematic or detectable way. But it turns out that mine echoes do indeed have some complex of relational or structural features that distinguishes them from rock echoes, and under the pressure of repeated error corrections, the network manages to lock onto, or become "tuned" to, that subtle but distinctive weave of features.

We can test whether it has truly succeeded in this by now feeding the network some mine and rock echoes not included in the training set, echoes it has never encountered before. In fact, the network does almost as well classifying the new echoes as it does with the samples in its training set. The "knowledge" it has acquired generalizes quite successfully to new cases. (This example is a highly simplified account of some striking results from Gorman and Sejnowski 1988.)

All of this is modestly amazing, because the problem is quite a difficult one, at least as difficult as learning to discriminate the phoneme /ā/. Human sonar operators, during a long tour of submarine duty, eventually learn to distinguish the two kinds of echoes with some uncertain but nontrivial regularity. But they never perform at the level of the artificial network. Spurred on by this success, work is currently underway to train up a network to distinguish the various phonemes characteristic of English speech (Zipser and Elman 1988). The idea is to produce a speech-recognition system that will not be troubled by the acoustic idiosyncracies of diverse speakers, as existing speech-recognition systems are.

The success of the mine/rock network is further intriguing because the "knowledge" the network has acquired, concerning the distinctive character of mine echoes, consists of nothing more than a carefully orchestrated set of connection weights. And it is finally intriguing because there exists a learning algorithm—the rule for adjusting the weights as a function of the error displayed in the output vector—that will eventually produce the required set of weights, given sufficient examples on which to train the network (Rumelhart et al. 1986).

How can a set of connection weights possibly embody knowledge of the desired distinction? Think of it in the following way. Each of the thirteen input units represents one aspect or dimension of the incoming stimulus. Collectively, they give a simultaneous profile of the input echo along thirteen distinct dimensions. Now perhaps there is only one profile that is roughly characteristic of mine echoes; or perhaps there are many different profiles, united by a common relational feature (for example, that the activation value of unit #6 is always three times the value of unit #12); or perhaps there is a disjunctive set of such relational features; and so forth. In each case, it is possible to rig the weights so that the system will respond in a typical fashion, at the output layer, to all and only the relevant profiles.

The units at the hidden layer are very important in this. If we consider the abstract space whose seven axes represent the possible activation levels of each of the seven hidden units, then what the system is searching for during the training period is a set of weights that *partitions* this space so that any mine input produces an activation vector across the hidden units that falls somewhere within one large subvolume of this abstract space, while any rock input produces a vector that falls somewhere into the complement of that subvolume (figure 10.7). The job of the top half of the network is then the relatively easy one of distinguishing these two subvolumes into which the abstract space has been divided.

Vectors near the center of (or along a certain path in) the mine-vector subvolume represent *prototypical* mine echoes, and these will produce an output vector very close to the desired ⟨1, 0⟩. Vectors nearer

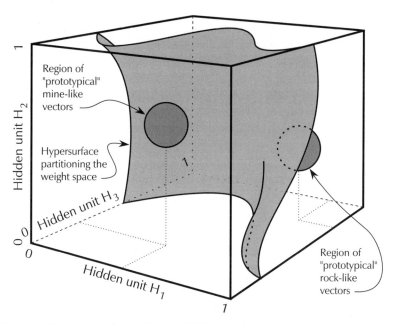

Figure 10.7: Learned partition on hidden-unit activation-vector space. Axes are shown for only three of the seven hidden-unit activation levels.

to the hypersurface that partitions the abstract space represent atypical or problematic mine echoes, and these produce more ambiguous output vectors such as $\langle .6, .4 \rangle$. The network's discriminative responses are thus graded responses: the system is sensitive to *similarities* along all of the relevant dimensions.

So we have a system that learns to discriminate hard-to-define perceptual features, and to be sensitive to similarities of a comparably diffuse but highly relevant character. And once the network is trained up, the recognitional task takes only a split second, since the system processes the input stimulus in parallel. It finally gives us a discriminatory system that performs something like a living creature, both in its speed and in its overall character.

I have explained this system in some detail, so that the reader will have a clear idea of how things work in at least one case. But the network described is only one instance of a general technique that works well in a large variety of cases. Networks can be constructed with a larger number of units at the output layer, so as to be able to express not just two, but a large number of distinct discriminations.

One network, aptly called NETtalk by its authors (Sejnowski and Rosenberg 1987), takes vector codings for seven-letter segments of printed words as inputs, and gives vector codings for phonemes as outputs. These output vectors can be fed directly into a sound synthesizer as they occur, to produce audible sounds. What this network learns to do is to transform printed words into audible speech. Though it involves no understanding of the words that it "reads", the network's feat is still very impressive, because it was given no rules whatever concerning the phonetic significance of standard English spelling. It began its training period by producing a stream of unintelligible babble in response to text entered as input. But in the course of many thousands of word presentations, and under the steady pressure of the weight-nudging algorithm, the set of weights slowly meanders its way to a configuration that reduces the measured error close to zero. After such training it will then produce as output, given arbitrary English text as input, perfectly intelligible speech with only rare and minor errors.

This case is significant for a number of reasons. The network makes a large number of discriminations, not just a binary one. It contains no explicit representation of any *rules,* however much it might seem to be following a set of rules. It has mastered a transformation that is notoriously irregular, and it must be sensitive to lexical context in order to do so. (Specifically, the phoneme it assigns to the center or focal letter of its seven-letter input is in large part a function of the identity of the three letters on either side.) And it portrays some aspects of a sensori-*motor* skill, rather than a purely sensory skill: it is producing highly complex behavior.

NETtalk has some limitations, of course. Pronunciations that depend on specifically semantic or grammatical distinctions will generally elude its grasp (unless they happen to be reflected in some way in the corpus of its training words, as occasionally they are), since NETtalk knows neither meanings nor syntax. But such dependencies affect only a very small percentage of the transformations appropriate to any text, and they are in any case to be expected. To overcome them completely would require a network that actually understands the text being read. And even then mistakes would occur, for even humans occasionally misread words as a result of grammatical or semantic confusion. What is arresting about NETtalk is just how very much of the complex and irregular business of text-based pronunciation can be mastered by a simple network with only a few hundred neuronlike units.

Another rather large network addresses problems in vision (Lehky and Sejnowski 1990). It takes codings for smoothly varying grey-scale pictures as input, and after training it yields as outputs surprisingly accurate codings for the curvatures and orientations of the physical objects portrayed in the pictures. It solves a form of the "shape from shading" problem long familiar to theorists in the field of vision. This network is of special interest because a subsequent examination of the "receptive fields" of the trained hidden units shows them to have acquired some of the same response properties as are displayed by cells in the visual cortex of mature animals. Specifically, they show a maximum sensitivity to spots, edges, and bars in specific orientations. This finding echoes the seminal work of Hubel and Wiesel (1962), in which cells in the visual cortex were discovered to have receptive fields of this same character. Results of this kind are very important, for if we are to take these artificial networks as models for how the brain works, then they must display realistic behavior not just at the macro level: they must also display realistic behavior at the micro level.

Enough examples. You have seen something of what networks of this kind can do, and of how they do it. In both respects they contrast sharply with the kinds of representational and processing strategies that philosophers of science, inductive logicians, cognitive psychologists, and AI workers have traditionally ascribed to us (namely, sentence-like representations manipulated by formal rules.) You can see also why this theoretical and experimental approach has captured the interest of those who seek to understand how the microarchitecture of the biological brain produces the phenomena displayed in human and animal cognition. Let us now explore the functional properties of these networks in more detail, and see how they bear on some of the traditional issues in epistemology and the philosophy of science.

5 Some functional properties of brainlike networks

The networks described above are descended from a device called the *Perceptron* (Rosenblatt 1962), which was essentially just a two-layer as opposed to a three-layer network. Devices of this configuration could and did learn to discriminate a considerable variety of input patterns. Unfortunately, having the input layer connected directly to the output layer imposes very severe limitations on the range of possible transformations a network can perform (Minsky and Papert 1969), and interest in Perceptron-like devices was soon eclipsed by the much faster-moving developments in standard "program-writing" AI, which exploited the high-speed general-purpose digital machines that were then starting to become widely available. Throughout the seventies, research in artificial "neural nets" was an underground vocation by comparison.

It has emerged from the shadows for a number of reasons. One important factor is just the troubled doldrums into which mainstream or program-writing AI has fallen. In many respects, these doldrums parallel the infertility of the classical approach to theories and learning within the philosophy of science. This is not surprising, since mainstream AI was proceeding on many of the same basic assumptions about cognition, and many of its attempts were just machine implementations of learning algorithms proposed earlier by philosophers of science and inductive logicians (Glymour 1987). The failures of mainstream AI—unrealistic learning, poor performance in complex perceptual and motor tasks, weak handling of analogies, and snail-like cognitive performance despite the use of very large and fast machines—teach us even more dramatically than do the failures of mainstream philosophy that we need to rethink the style of representation and computation we have been ascribing to cognitive creatures.

Other reasons for the resurgence of interest in networks are more positive. The introduction of additional layers of intervening or "hidden" units produced a dramatic increase in the range of possible transformations that the network could effect. As Sejnowski, Kienker, and Hinton (1986) describe it,

> only the first-order statistics of the input pattern can be captured by direct connections between input and output units. The role of the hidden units is to capture higher-order statistical relationships and this can be accomplished if significant underlying features can be found that have strong, regular relationships with the patterns on the visible units. The hard part of learning is to find the set of weights which turn the hidden units into useful feature detectors.
>
> (p. 264)

Equally important is the S-shaped, nonlinear response profile (figure 10.3) now assigned to every unit in the network. So long as this response profile remains linear, any network will be limited to computing purely linear transformations. (A transformation $f(x)$ is linear just in case $f(n \cdot x) = n \cdot f(x)$, and $f(x + y) = f(x) + f(y)$.) But a nonlinear response profile for each unit brings the entire range of possible nonlinear transformations within reach of three-layer networks, a dramatic expansion of their computational potential. Now there are *no* transformations that lie beyond the computational power of a large enough and suitably weighted network.

A third factor was the articulation, by Rumelhart, Hinton, and Williams (1986), of the *generalized delta rule* (a generalization, to three-layer networks, of Rosenblatt's original teaching rule for adjusting the weights of the Perceptron), and the empirical discovery that this new rule very rarely got permanently stuck in inefficient "local minima" on its way toward finding the best possible configuration of connection weights for a given network and a given problem. This was a major breakthrough, not so much because "learning by the back-propagation of error", as it has come to be called, was just like human learning, but because it provided us with an efficient technology for quickly training up various networks on various problems, so that we could study their properties and explore their potential.

The way the generalized delta rule works can be made fairly intuitive given the idea of an abstract synaptic-weight space as represented in figure 10.6. Consider any output vector produced by a network with a specific configuration of weights, a configuration represented by a specific position in weight space. Suppose that this output vector is in error by various degrees in various of its elements. Consider now a single synapse at the output layer, and consider the effect on the output vector that a small positive or negative change in its weight would have had. Since the output vector is a determinate function of the system's weights (assuming we hold the input vector fixed), we can calculate which of these two possible changes, if either, would have made the greater improvement in the output vector. The relevant change is made accordingly.

If a similar calculation is performed over every synapse in the network, and the change in its weight is then made accordingly, what the resulting shift in the position of the system's overall point in weight space amounts is a small slide *down* the steepest face of the local "error surface". There is no guarantee that this incremental shift moves the system directly toward the global position of zero error (that is why perfection cannot be achieved in a single jump). On the contrary, the descending path to a global error minimum may be highly circuitous. Nor is there any guarantee that the system must eventually reach such a global minimum. On the contrary, the downward path from a given starting point may well lead to a merely "local" minimum, from which only a large change in the system's weights will afford escape, a change beyond the reach of the delta rule. But in fact this happens relatively rarely, for it turns out that the more dimensions (synapses) a system has, the smaller the probability of there being an intersecting local minimum in *every one* of the available dimensions. The global point is usually able to slide down some narrow cleft in the local topography. Empirically then, the back-propagation algorithm is surprisingly effective at driving the system to the global error minimum, at least where we can identify that global minimum effectively.

The advantage this algorithm provides is easily appreciated. The possible combinations of weights in a network increases exponentially with the size of the network. Assuming conservatively that each weight admits of only ten possible values, the number of distinct positions in "weight space" (that is, the number of possible weight configurations) for the simple rock/mine network of figure 10.5 is already 10^{105}! This space is far too large to explore efficiently without something like the generalized delta rule and the back propagation of error to do it for us. But with the delta rule, administered by an auxiliary computer, researchers have shown that networks of the simple kind described are capable of learning some quite extraordinary skills, and of displaying some highly intriguing properties. Let me now return to an exploration of these.

An important exploratory technique in cognitive and behavioral neuroscience is to record, with an implanted microelectrode, the electrical activity of a single neuron during cognition or behavior in the intact animal. This is relatively easy to do, and it does give us tantalizing bits of information about the cognitive significance of neural activity (recall the results of Hubel and Weisel mentioned earlier). Single-cell recordings give us only isolated bits of information, however, and what we would really like to monitor are the *patterns* of simultaneous neural activation across large numbers of cells in the same subsystem. Unfortunately, effective techniques for simultaneous recording from large numbers of adjacent cells are still in their infancy. The task is extremely difficult.

By contrast, this task is extremely easy with the artificial networks we have been describing. If the network is real hardware, its units are far more accessible than the fragile and microscopic units of a living brain. And if the network is merely being simulated within a standard computer (as is usually the case), one can write the program so that the activation levels of any unit, or set of units, can be read out on command. Accordingly, once a network has been successfully trained up on some skill or other, one can then examine the collective behavior of its units during the exercise of that skill.

We have already seen the results of one such analysis in the rock/ mine network. Once the weights have reached their optimum configuration, the activation vectors (that is, the patterns of activation) at the hidden layer fall into two disjoint classes: the vector space is partitioned in two, as depicted in figure 10.7. But a mere binary discrimination is an atypically simple case. The reader NETtalk, for example, partitions its hidden-unit vector space into fully 79 subspaces. The reason is simple. For each of the 26 letters in the alphabet, there is at least one phoneme assigned to it, and for many letters there are several phonemes that might be signified, depending on the lexical context. As it happens, there are 79 distinct letter-to-phoneme associations to be learned if one is to master the pronunciation of English spelling, and in the successfully trained network a distinct hidden-unit activation vector occurs when each of these 79 possible transformations is effected.

In the case of the rock/mine network, we noted a similarity metric within each of its two hidden-unit subspaces. In the case of NETtalk, we also find a similarity metric, this time across the 79 functional hidden-unit vectors (by 'functional vector', I mean a vector that corresponds to one of the 79 desired letter-to-phoneme transformations). Sejnowski and Rosenberg (1987) did a cluster analysis of these vectors in the trained network. Roughly, their procedure was as follows. They asked, for every functional vector in that space, what other such vector is closest to it? The answers yielded about 30 vector pairs. They then constructed a secondary vector for each such pair, by averaging the two original vectors, and asked, for every such secondary vector, what other secondary vector (or so far unpaired primary vector) is closest to it? This produced a smaller set of secondary-vector pairs, on which the averaging procedure was repeated to produce a set of tertiary vectors. These were then paired in turn, and so forth. This procedure produces a hierarchy of groupings among the original transformations, and it comes to an end with a grand division of the 79 original vectors into two disjoint classes.

As it happens, that deepest and most fundamental division within the hidden-unit vector space corresponds to the division between the consonants and the vowels! Looking further into this hierarchy, into the consonant branch, for example, we find that there are subdivisions into the principal consonant types, and that within these branches there are further subdivisions into the most similar consonants. All of this is depicted in the tree diagram of figure 10.8. What the network has managed to recover, from its training set of several thousand English words, is the highly irregular phonological significance of standard English spelling, plus the hierarchical organization of the phonetic structure of English speech.

Here we have a clear illustration of two things at once. The first lesson is the capacity of an activation-vector space to embody a rich and well-structured hierarchy of categories, complete with a similarity metric embracing everything within it. And the second lesson is the capacity of such networks to embody representations of factors and patterns that are only partially or implicitly reflected in the corpus of inputs. Though I did not mention it earlier, the rock/mine network provides another example of this, in that the final partition made on its hidden-unit vector space corresponds in fact to the objective distinction between sonar targets made of *metal* and sonar targets made of *nonmetal.* That is the true uniformity that lies behind the apparently chaotic variety displayed in the inputs.

It is briefly tempting to suggest that NETtalk has the concept of a hard *c*, for example, and that the rock/mine network has the concept of metal. But this won't really do, since the vector-space representations at issue do not play a conceptual or computational role remotely rich enough to merit their assimilation to specifically human concepts. Nevertheless, it is plain that both networks have contrived a system of internal representations that truly corresponds to important distinctions and structures in the outside world, structures that are not explicitly represented in the corpus of their sensory inputs. The value of those representations is that they and only they allow the networks to "make sense" of their variegated and often noisy input corpus, in the sense that they and only they allow the network to respond to those inputs in a fashion that systematically reduces the error messages to a trickle. These, I need hardly remind, are the functions typically ascribed to *theories.*

What we are confronting here is a possible conception of knowledge or understanding that owes nothing to the sentential categories of current common sense. A global theory, we might venture, is a specific point in a creature's synaptic weight space. It is a configuration of connection weights, a configuration that partitions the system's activation-vector space(s) into useful divisions and subdivisions relative to the

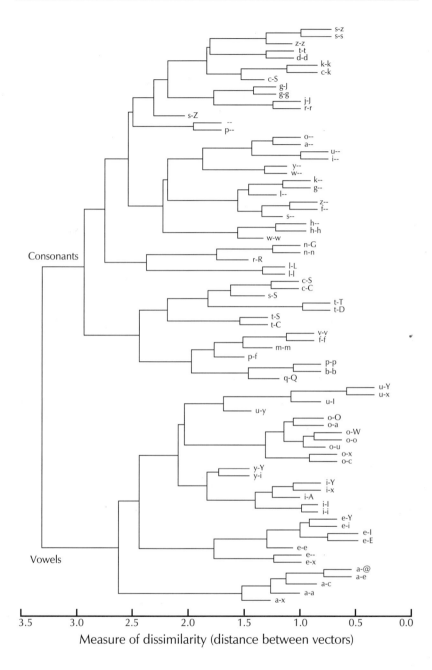

Figure 10.8: Hierarchy of partitions of hidden-unit vector space of NETtalk
(the space is partitioned into 79 recognizable vector types—
one for each desired letter-to-phoneme transformation).

inputs typically fed the system. 'Useful' here means: tends to minimize the error messages.

A possible objection here points to the fact that differently weighted systems can produce the same, or at least roughly the same, partitions on their activation-vector spaces. Accordingly, we might try to abstract from the idiosyncratic details of a system's connection weights, and identify its global theory directly with the set of partitions they produce within its activation-vector space. This would allow for differently weighted systems to have the same theory.

There is some virtue in this suggestion, but also some vice. While differently weighted systems can embody the same partitions and thus display the same output performance on any given input, they will still *learn* quite differently in the face of a protracted sequence of new and problematic inputs. This is because the learning algorithm that drives the system to new points in weight space does not care about the relatively global partitions that have been made in activation space. All it cares about are the individual *weights* and how they relate to apprehended error. The laws of cognitive evolution, therefore, do not operate primarily at the level of the partitions, at least on the view of things here being explored. Rather, they operate at the level of the weights. Accordingly, if we want our "unit of cognition" to figure in the *laws* of cognitive development, the point in weight space seems the wiser choice of unit. We need only concede that different global theories can occasionally produce identical short-term behavior.

The level of the partitions certainly corresponds more closely to the conceptual level, as understood in common sense and traditional theory, but the point is that this seems not to be the most important dynamical level, even when explicated in neurocomputational terms. Knowing a creature's vector-space partitions may suffice for the accurate short-term prediction of its behavior, but that knowledge is inadequate to predict or explain the evolution of those partitions over the course of time and cruel experience. This gives substance to the conviction, voiced back in section 2, that to explain the phenomenon of *conceptual change*, we need to unearth a level of sub-conceptual combinatorial elements within which different concepts can be articulated, evaluated, and then modified according to their performance. The connection weights provide a level that meets all of these conditions.

This general view of how knowledge is embodied and accessed in the brain has some further appealing features. If we assume that the brains of the higher animals work in something like the fashion outlined, but with much more in the way of physical resources, then we can explain a number of puzzling features of human cognition. For one thing, the speed-of-relevant-access problem simply disappears. A network the size of a human brain—with 10^{11} neurons, 10^3 connections on each, 10^{14} total connections, and at least 10 distinct layers of hidden units—can be expected, in the course of growing up, to partition its internal vector spaces into many billions of functionally relevant subdivisions, each responsive to a broad but proprietary range of highly complex stimuli. When the network receives a stimulus that falls into one of these classes, the network produces the appropriate activation vector in a matter of only tens or hundreds of milliseconds, because that is all the time it takes for the parallel-coded stimulus to make its way through only two or three or ten layers of the massively parallel network to the functionally relevant layer that drives the appropriate behavioral response. Since information is not stored in a long list that must somehow be searched, but rather in the myriad connection weights that configure the network, relevant aspects of the creature's total information are automatically accessed by the coded stimuli themselves.

A third advantage of this model is its explanation of the functional persistence of brains in the face of minor damage, disease, and the normal but steady loss of its cells with age. Human cognition degrades fairly gracefully as the physical plant deteriorates, in sharp contrast to the behavior of typical computers, which have a very low fault tolerance. The explanation of this persistence lies in the massively parallel character of the computations the brain performs, and in the very tiny contribution that each synapse or each cell makes to the overall computation. In a large network of 100,000 units, the loss or misbehavior of a single cell will not even be detectable. And in the more dramatic case of widespread cell loss, so long as the losses are more or less randomly distributed throughout the network, the gross character of the network's activity will remain unchanged: what happens is that the *quality* of its computations will be progressively degraded.

Turning now toward more specifically philosophical concerns, we may note an unexpected virtue of this approach concerning the matter of *simplicity*. This important notion has two problems. It is robustly resistant to attempts to define or measure it, and it is not clear why it should be counted an epistemic virtue in any case. There seems no obvious reason, either a priori or a posteriori, why the world should be simple rather than complex, and epistemic decisions based on the contrary assumption thus appear arbitrary and unjustified. Simplicity, conclude some (Van Fraassen 1980), is a merely pragmatic or aesthetic virtue, as opposed to a genuinely epistemic virtue. But consider the following story.

The rock/mine network of figure 10.5 displayed a strong capacity for generalizing beyond the sample echoes in its training set: it can accurately discriminate entirely new samples of both kinds. But trained networks do not always generalize so well, and it is interesting what determines their success in this regard. How well the training generalizes is in part a function of *how many* hidden units the system possesses, or uses to solve the problem. There is, it turns out, an optimal number of units for any given problem. If the network to be trained is given more than the optimal number of hidden units, it will learn to respond appropriately to all of the various samples in its training set, but it will generalize to new samples only very poorly. On the other hand, with less than the optimal number, it never really learns to respond appropriately to all of the samples in its training set.

The reason is as follows. During the training period, the network gradually generates a set of internal representations at the level of the hidden units. One class of hidden-unit activation vectors is characteristic of rock-like input vectors; another class is characteristic of mine-like input vectors. During this period, the system is *theorizing* at the level of the hidden units, exploring the space of possible activation vectors, in hopes of finding some partition or set of partitions on it that the output layer can then exploit in turn, so as to draw the needed distinctions and thus bring the process of error-induced synaptic adjustments to an end.

If there are far too many hidden units, then the learning process can be partially subverted in the following way. The lazy system cheats: it learns a set of *unrelated* representations at the level of the hidden units. It learns a distinct representation for each sample input (or for a small group of such inputs) drawn from the very finite training set, a representation that does indeed prompt the correct response at the output level. But since there is nothing common to all of the hidden-unit rock representations, or to all of the hidden-unit mine representations, an input vector from outside the training set produces a hidden-unit representation that bears no relation to the representations already formed. The system has not learned to see *what is common* within each of the two stimulus classes, which would allow it to generalize effortlessly to new cases that shared that common feature. It has just knocked together an *ad hoc* "look-up table" that allows it to deal successfully with the limited samples in the training set, at which point the error messages cease, the weights stop evolving, and the system stops learning. (I am grateful to Terry Sejnowski for mentioning to me this wrinkle in the learning behavior of typical networks.)

There are two ways to avoid this ad hoc, unprojectable learning. One is to enlarge dramatically the size of the training set. This will overload the system's ability to just "memorize" an adequate response for each of the training samples. But a more effective way is just to reduce the number of hidden units in the network, so that it lacks the resources to cobble together such wasteful and ungeneralizable internal representations. We must reduce them to the point where it has to find a *single* partition on the hidden-unit vector space, a partition that puts all of the sample rock representations on one side, and all of the sample mine representations on the other. A system constrained in this way will generalize far better, for the global partition it has been forced to find corresponds to something *common* to each member of the relevant stimulus class, even if it is only a unifying dimension of variation (or set of such dimensions) that unites them all by a similarity relation. It is the generation of that similarity relation that allows the system to respond appropriately to novel examples. They may be new to the system, but they fall on a spectrum for which the system now has an adequate representation.

Networks with only a few hidden units in excess of the optimal number will sometimes spontaneously achieve the maximally simple "hypothesis" despite the excess units. The few unneeded units are slowly shut down by the learning algorithm during the course of training. They become zero-valued elements in all of the successful vectors. Networks will not always do this, however. The needed simplicity must generally be forced from the outside, by a progressive reduction in the available hidden units.

On the other hand, if the network has too few hidden units, then it lacks the resources even to express an activation vector that is adequate to characterize the underlying uniformity, and it will never master completely even the smallish corpus of samples in the training set. In other words, simplicity may be a virtue, but the system must command sufficient complexity at least to meet the task at hand.

We have just seen how forcing a neural network to generate a smaller number of distinct partitions on a hidden-unit vector space of fewer dimensions can produce a system whose learning achievements generalize more effectively to novel cases. Ceteris paribus, the simpler hypotheses generalize better. Getting by with fewer resources is of course a virtue in itself, though a pragmatic one, to be sure. But this is not the principal virtue here displayed. Superior generalization is a genuinely epistemic virtue, and it is regularly displayed by networks constrained, in the fashion described, to find the simplest hypothesis concerning whatever structures might be hidden in or behind their input vectors.

Of course, nothing guarantees successful generalization: a network is always hostage to the quality of its training set relative to the total population. And there may be equally simple alternative hypotheses that generalize differentially well. But from the perspective of the relevant microdynamics, we can see at least one clear reason why simplicity is more than a merely pragmatic virtue. It is an epistemic virtue, not principally because simple hypotheses avoid the vice of being complex, but because they avoid the vice of being ad hoc.

6 How faithfully do these networks depict the brain?

The functional properties so far observed in these model networks are an encouraging reward for the structural assumptions that went into them. But just how accurate are these models, as depictions of the brain's microstructure? A wholly appropriate answer here is uncertain, for we continue to be uncertain about what features of the brain's microstructure are and are not functionally relevant, and we are therefore uncertain about what is and is not a legitimate simplifying assumption in the models we make. Even so, it is plain that the models are *in*accurate in a variety of respects, and it is the point of the present section to summarize and evaluate these failings. Let me begin by underscoring the basic respects in which the models appear to be correct.

It is true that real nervous systems display, as their principal organizing feature, layers or populations of neurons that project their axons *en masse* to some distinct layer or population of neurons, where each arriving axon divides into multiple branches whose end bulbs make synaptic connections of various weights onto many cells at the target location. This description captures all of the sensory modalities and their primary relations to the brain; it captures the character of various areas of the central brain stem; and it captures the structure of the cerebral cortex, which in humans contains at least six distinct layers of neurons, where each layer is the source and/or the target of an orderly projection of axons to and/or from elsewhere.

But the details present all manner of difficulties. To begin with small ones, note that in real brains an arriving axon makes synaptic contact with only a relatively small percentage of the thousands or millions of cells in its target population, not with every last one of them as in the models. This is not a serious difficulty, since model networks with comparably pared connections still manage to learn the required transformations quite well, though perhaps not so well as a fully connected network.

More seriously, so far as is known, real axons have terminal end bulbs that are uniformly inhibitory, or uniformly excitatory, depending on the type of neuron. We seem not to find a mixture of both kinds of connections radiating from the same neuron, nor do we find connections changing their sign during learning, as is the case in the models. Moreover, that mixture of positive and negative influences is essential to successful function in the models: the same input cell must be capable of inhibiting some cells down the line at the same time that it is busy exciting others. Further, cell populations in the brain typically show extensive "horizontal" cell-to-cell connections *within* a given layer. In the models there are none at all. Their connections join cells only to cells in distinct layers.

These last two difficulties might conceivably serve to cancel each other. One way in which an excitatory end bulb might serve to *inhibit* a cell in its target population is first to make an excitatory connection onto one of the many small *interneurons* typically scattered throughout the target population of main neurons, which interneuron has made an inhibitory synaptic connection onto the target main neuron. Exciting the inhibitory interneuron would then have the effect of inhibiting the main neuron, as desired. And such a system would display a large number of short horizontal intra-layer connections, as is observed. This is just a suggestion, however, since it is far from clear that the elements mentioned are predominantly connected in the manner required.

More seriously still, there are several major problems with the idea that networks in the brain learn by means of the learning algorithm so effective in the models: the procedure of back-propagating apprehended errors according to the generalized delta rule. That procedure requires two things: (1) a computation of the partial correction needed for each synapse at the output layer, and via these a computation of a partial correction for each synapse at the earlier layers, and (2) a method of causally conveying these correction messages back through the network to the sites of the relevant synaptic connections in such a fashion that each weight gets nudged up or down accordingly. In a computer simulation of the networks at issue (which is currently the standard technique for exploring their properties), both the computation and the subsequent weight adjustments are easily done: the computation is done *outside* the network by the host computer, which has direct access to and control over every element of the network being simulated. But in the self-contained biological brain, we have to find some real source of adjustment signals, and some real pathways to convey them back to the relevant units. Unfortunately, the empirical brain displays little that answers to exactly these requirements.

On the hardware side, therefore, the situation does not support the idea that the specific back-propagation procedure of Rumelhart et al. is the brain's central mechanism for learning. (Neither, it should be mentioned, did they claim that it is.) And it is implausible on some functional grounds as well. First, in the process of learning a recognition task, living brains typically show a progressive reduction in the reaction time required for the recognitional output response. With the delta rule however, learning involves a progressive reduction in error, but reaction times are constant throughout. A second difficulty with the delta rule is as follows. A necessary element in its calculated apportionment of error is a representation of what would have been the *correct* vector in the output layer. That is why back propagation is said to involve a global *teacher,* an information source that always knows the correct answers and can therefore provide a perfect measure of output error. Real creatures generally lack any such perfect information. They must struggle along in the absence of any sure compass toward the truth, and their synaptic adjustments must be based on much poorer information.

And yet their brains learn. Which means that somehow the configuration of their synaptic weights must undergo change, change steered in some way by error or related dissatisfaction, change that carves a path toward a regime of decreased error. Knowing this much, and knowing something about the microstructure and microdynamics of the brain, we can explore the space of possible learning procedures with some idea of what features to look for. If the generalized delta rule is not the brain's procedure, as it seems not to be, there remain other possible strategies for back-propagating sundry error measures, strategies which may find more detailed reflection in the brain. If these prove unrealizable, there are other procedures that do not require the organized distribution of any global error measures at all; they depend primarily on local constraints (Hinton and Sejnowski 1986, Hopfield and Tank 1985, Barto 1985, Bear et al. 1987).

While the matter of how real neural networks generate the right configurations of weights remains obscure, the matter of how they perform their various cognitive tasks once configured is a good deal clearer. If even small artificial networks can perform the sophisticated cognitive tasks illustrated earlier in this paper, there is no mystery that real networks should do the same or better. What the brain displays in the way of hardware is not radically different from what the models contain, and the differences invite exploration rather than disappointment. The brain is of course very much larger and denser than the models so far constructed. It has many layers rather than just two or three. It boasts perhaps a hundred distinct and highly specialized cell types, rather than just one. It is not a single n-layer network, but rather a large committee of distinct but parallel networks, interacting in sundry ways. It plainly commands many spaces of stunning complexity, and many skills in consequence. It stands as a glowing invitation to make our humble models yet more and more realistic, in hopes of unlocking the many secrets remaining.

7 Computational neuroscience: the naturalization of epistemology

One test of a new framework is its ability to throw a new and unifying light on a variety of old phenomena. I will close this essay with an exploration of several classic issues in the philosophy of science. The aim is to reconstruct them within the framework of the computational neuroscience outlined above. In section 5 we saw how this could be done for the case of theoretical simplicity. We there saw a new way of conceiving of this feature, and found a new perspective on why it is a genuine epistemic virtue. The hope in what follows is that we may do the same for other problematic notions and issues.

A good place to begin is with the issue of foundationalism. Here the central bone of contention is whether our observation judgments must always be theory laden. The traditional discussion endures largely for the good reason that a great deal hangs on the outcome, but also for the less momentous reason that there is ambiguity in what one might wish to count as an "observation judgment"—an explicitly uttered sentence? a covert assertion? a propositional attitude? a conscious experience? a sensation?—and a slightly different issue emerges depending on where the debate is located.

But from the perspective of this essay, it makes no difference at what level the issue might be located. If our cognitive activities arise from a weave of networks of the kind discussed above, and if we construe a global theory as a global configuration of synaptic weights, as outlined in section 5, then it is clear that no cognitive activity whatever takes place in the absence of vectors being processed by some specific configuration of weights. That is, no cognitive activity whatever takes place in the absence of some theory or other.

This perspective bids us see even the simplest of animals and the youngest of infants as possessing theories, since they too process their activation vectors with some configuration of weights or other. The difference between us and them is not that they lack theories. Rather, their theories are just a good deal simpler than ours, in the case of animals; and their theories are much less coherent and organized and informed than ours, in the case of human infants. Which is to say, they have yet to achieve points in overall weight space that partition their activation-vector spaces into useful and well-structured subdivisions. But insofar as there is cognitive activity at all, it exploits whatever theory the creature embodies, however useless or incoherent it might be.

The only place in the network where the weights need play no role is at the absolute sensory periphery of the system, where the external stimulus is transduced into a coded input vector, for subsequent delivery to the transforming layers of weights. However, at the first occasion on which these preconceptual states have any effect at all on the downstream cognitive system, it is through a changeable configuration of synaptic weights, a configuration that produces one set of partitions on the activation vector space of the relevant layer of neurons, one set out of millions of alternative possible sets. In other words, the very first thing that happens to the input signal is that it gets conceptualized in one of many different possible ways. At subsequent layers of processing, the same process is repeated, and the message that finally arrives at the linguistic centers, for example, has been shaped at least as much by the partitional constraints of the embedded conceptual system(s) through which it has passed, as by the distant sensory input that started things off.

From the perspective of computational neuroscience, therefore, cognition is constitutionally theory-laden. Presumptive processing is not a blight on what would otherwise be an unblemished activity; it is just the natural signature of a cognitive system doing what it is supposed to be doing. It is just possible that some theories are endogenously specified, of course, but this will change the present issue not at all. Innateness promises no escape from theory-ladenness, for an endogenous theory is still a *theory*.

In any case, the idea is not in general a plausible one. The visual system, for example, consists of something in the neighborhood of 10^{10} neurons, each of which enjoys better than 10^3 synaptic connections, for a total of at least 10^{13} weights each wanting specific genetic determination. That is an implausibly heavy load to place on the coding capacity of our DNA molecules. (The entire human genome contains only about 10^9 nucleotides.) It would be much more efficient to specify endogenously only the general structural principles of a type of learning network that is then likely to learn in certain standard directions, given the standard sorts of inputs and error messages that a typical human upbringing provides. This places the burden of steering our conceptual development where it belongs—on the external world, an information source far larger and more reliable than the genes.

It is a commonplace that we can construct endlessly different theories with which to explain the familiar facts of the observable world. But it is an immediate consequence of the perspective here adopted that we can also apprehend the "observable world" itself in a similarly endless variety of ways. For there is no preferred set of partitions into which our sensory spaces must inevitably fall. It all depends on how the relevant networks are *taught*. If we systematically change the pattern of the error messages delivered to the developing network, then even the very same history of sensory stimulations will produce a quite differently weighted network, one that partitions the world into classes that cross-classify those of current common sense, one that finds perceptual similarities along dimensions quite alien to the ones we currently recognize, one that feeds its outputs into a very differently configured network at the higher cognitive levels as well.

In relatively small ways, this phenomenon is already familiar to us. Specialists in various fields, people required to spend years mastering the intricacies of some domain of perception and manipulation, regularly end up being able to perceive facts and to anticipate behaviors that are wholly opaque to the rest of us. But there is no reason why such variation should be confined to isolated skills and specialized understanding. In principle, the human cognitive system should be capable of sustaining any one of an enormous variety of decidedly global theories concerning the character of its common-sense *Lebenswelt* as a whole. (This possibility, defended in Feyerabend 1965/81, is explored at some length via examples in Churchland 1979. For extended criticism of this general suggestion see Fodor 1984. For a rebuttal see Churchland 1988, and a counter-rebuttal, Fodor 1988.)

To appreciate just how great is the conceptual variety that awaits us, consider the following numbers. With a total of perhaps 10^{11} neurons with an average of at least 10^3 connections each, the human brain has something like 10^{14} weights to play with. Supposing, conservatively, that each weight admits of only ten possible values, the total number of distinct possible configurations of synaptic weights (= distinct possible positions in weight space) is 10 for the first weight, times 10 for the second weight, times 10 for the third weight, and so on, for a total of $10^{10^{14}}$, or $10^{100,000,000,000,000}$! This is the total number of (just barely) distinguishable theories embraceable by humans, given the cognitive resources we currently command. To put this number into some remotely adequate perspective, recall that the total number of elementary particles in the entire universe is only about 10^{87}.

In this way, a neurocomputational approach to perception allows us to reconstruct an old issue, and to provide novel reasons for the view that our perceptual knowledge is both theory-laden and highly plastic. And it will do more. Notice that the activation-vector spaces that a matured brain has generated, and the prototypes they embody, can encompass far more than the simple sensory types such as phonemes, colors, smells, tastes, faces, and so forth. Given high-dimensional spaces, which the brain has in abundance, those spaces and the prototypes they embody can encompass categories of great complexity, generality, and abstraction, including those with a temporal dimension, such as harmonic oscillator, projectile, travelling wave, Samba, twelve-bar blues, democratic election, six-course dinner, courtship, elephant hunt, civil disobedience, and stellar collapse. It may be that the input dimensions that feed into such abstract spaces will themselves often have to be the expression of some earlier level of processing, but that is no problem. The networks under discussion are hierarchically arranged to do precisely this as a matter of course. In principle then, it is no harder for such a system to represent types of *processes, procedures,* and *techniques* than to represent the "simple" sensory qualities. From the point of view of the brain, these are just more high-dimensional vectors.

This offers us a possible means for explicating the notion of a *paradigm*, as used by T. S. Kuhn (1962/70) in his arresting characterization of the nature of scientific understanding and development. A paradigm, for Kuhn, is a prototypical *application* of some set of mathematical, conceptual, or instrumental resources, an application expected to have distinct but similar instances which it is the job of normal science to discover or construct. Becoming a scientist is less a matter of learning a set of laws than it is a matter of mastering the details of the prototypical applications of the relevant resources in such a way that one can recognize and generate further applications of a relevantly similar kind.

Kuhn was criticized for the vagueness of the notion of a paradigm, and for the unexplicated criterion of similarity that clustered further applications around it. But from the perspective of the neurocomputational approach at issue, he can be vindicated on both counts. For a brain to command a paradigm is for it to have settled into a weight configuration that produces some well-structured similarity space whose central hypervolume locates the prototypical application(s). And it is only to be expected that even the most reflective subject will be incompletely articulate on what dimensions constitute this highly complex and abstract space, and even less articulate on what metric distributes examples along each dimension. A complete answer to these questions would require a microscopic examination of the subject's brain. That is one reason why exposure to a wealth of examples is so much more effective in teaching the techniques of any science than is exposure to any attempt at listing all the relevant factors. We are seldom able to articulate them all, and even if we were able, listing them is not the best way to help a brain construct the relevant internal similarity space.

Kuhn makes much of the resistance typically shown by scientific communities to change or displacement of the current paradigm. This stubbornness here emerges as a natural expression of the way in which networks learn, or occasionally fail to learn. The process of learning by gradient descent is always threatened by the prospect of a purely *local* minimum in the global error gradient. This is a position where the error messages are not yet zero, but where every *small* change in the system produces even larger errors than those currently encountered. With a very high-dimensional space the probability of there being a simultaneous local minimum in every dimension of the weight space is small: there is usually some narrow cleft in the canyon out which the configuration point can eventually trickle, thence to continue its wandering slide down the error gradient and toward some truly global minimum. But genuine local minima do occur, and the only way to escape them, once caught, is to introduce some sort of random noise into the system in hopes of bouncing the system's configuration point out of such tempting cul-de-sacs. Furthermore, even if a local quasi-minimum does have an escape path along one or more dimensions, the error gradient along them may there be quite shallow, and the system may take a very long time to find its way out of the local impasse.

Finally, and just as importantly, the system can be victimized by a highly biased training set. Suppose the system has reached a weight configuration that allows it to respond successfully to all of the examples in the (narrow and biased) set it has so far encountered. Subsequent exposure to the larger domain of more diverse examples will not necessarily result in the system's moving any significant distance away from its earlier configuration, unless the relative frequency with which it encounters those new and anomalous examples is quite high. For if the encounter frequency is low, the impact of those examples will be insufficient to overcome the gravity of the false minimum that captured the initial training set. The system may require blitzing by new examples if their collective lesson is ever to sink in.

Even if we do present an abundance of the new and diverse examples, it is quite likely that the delta rule discussed earlier will force the system through a sequence of new configurations that perform very poorly indeed when re-fed examples from the original training set. This temporary loss of performance on certain previously understood cases is the price the system pays for the chance at achieving a broader payoff later, when the system finds a new and deeper error minimum. In the case of an artificial system chugging coolly away at the behest of the delta rule, such temporary losses need not impede the learning process, at least if their frequency is sufficiently high. But with humans the impact of such a loss is often more keenly felt. The new examples that confound the old configuration may simply be ignored or rejected in some fashion, or they may be quarantined and made the target of a distinct and disconnected learning process in some adjacent network. Recall the example of sublunary and superlunary physics.

This raises the issue of explanatory unity. A creature thrown unprepared into a complex and unforgiving world must take its understanding wherever it can find it, even if this means generating a disconnected set of distinct similarity spaces each providing the creature with a roughly appropriate response to some of the more pressing types of situation it typically encounters. But far better if it then manages to generate a single similarity space that unifies and replaces the variation that used to reside in two entirely distinct and smaller spaces. This provides the creature with an effective grasp on the phenomena that lay *between* the two classes already dealt with, but which were successfully comprehended by neither of the two old spaces. These are phenomena that the creature had to ignore, or avoid, or simply endure. With a new and more comprehensive similarity space now generating systematic responses to a wider range of phenomena, the creature has succeeded in a small piece of conceptual unification.

The payoff here recalls the virtue earlier discovered for simplicity. Indeed, it is the same virtue, namely, superior generalization to cases beyond those already encountered. This result was achieved, in the case described in section 5, by reducing the number of hidden units, thus forcing the system to make more efficient use of the representational resources remaining. This more efficient use is realized when the system partitions its activation-vector space into the minimal number of distinct similarity subspaces consistent with reducing the error messages to a minimum. When completed, this process also produces the maximal *organization* within and among those subspaces, for the system has found those enduring dimensions of variation that successfully unite the diversity confronting it.

Tradition speaks of developing a single "theory" to explain everything. Kuhn speaks of extending and articulating a "paradigm" into novel domains. Kitcher (1981, 1988) speaks of expanding the range of application of a given "pattern of argument". It seems to me that we might unify and illuminate all of these notions by thinking in terms of the evolving structure of a hidden-unit activation-vector space, and its development in the direction of representing all input vectors somewhere within a single similarity space.

This might seem to offer some hope for a convergent realist position within the philosophy of science, but I fear that exactly the opposite is the case. For one thing, nothing guarantees that we humans will avoid getting permanently stuck in some very deep but relatively local error minimum. For another, nothing guarantees that there exists a possible configuration of weights that would reduce the error messages to *zero*. A unique global error minimum relative to the human neural

network there may be, but for us and for any other finite system interacting with the real world, it may always be non-zero. And for a third
thing, nothing guarantees that there is only *one* global minimum. Perhaps there will in general be many quite different minima, all of them
equally low in error, all of them carving up the world in quite different
ways. Which one a given thinker reaches may be a function of the
idiosyncratic details of its learning history. These considerations seem
to remove the goal itself—a unique truth—as well as any sure means of
getting there. Which suggests that the proper course to pursue in epistemology lies in the direction of a highly naturalistic and pluralistic
form of pragmatism. (For a running start on precisely these themes, see
Munevar 1981 and Stich 1988.)

8 Concluding remarks

This essay opened with a survey of the problems plaguing the classical
or "sentential" approach to epistemology and the philosophy of science. I have tried to sketch an alternative approach that is free of all or
most of those problems, and has some novel virtues of its own. The
following points are worth noting. Simple and relatively small networks of the sort described above have already demonstrated the
capacity to learn a wide range of quite remarkable cognitive skills and
capacities, some of which lie beyond the reach of the older approach to
the nature of cognition (for instance, instantaneous discrimination of
subtle perceptual qualities, effective recognition of similarities, and
real-time administration of complex motor activity). While the specific
learning algorithm currently used to achieve these results is unlikely to
be the brain's algorithm, it does provide an existence proof: by procedures of this general sort, networks can indeed learn with fierce efficiency. And there are many other procedures awaiting our exploration.

The picture of learning and cognitive activity here painted encompasses the entire animal kingdom: cognition in human brains is fundamentally the same as cognition in brains generally. We are all of us
processing activation vectors through artfully weighted networks. This
broad conception of cognition puts cognitive theory firmly in contact
with neurobiology, which adds a very strong set of empirical constraints on the former, to its substantial long-term advantage.

Conceptual change is no longer a problem: it happens continuously
in the normal course of all cognitive development. It is sustained by
many small changes in the underlying hardware of synaptic weights,

which changes gradually repartition the activation-vector spaces of the affected population of cells. Conceptual *simplicity* is also rather clearer when viewed from a neurocomputational perspective, both in its nature and in its epistemological significance.

The old problem of how to retrieve relevant information is transformed by the realization that it does not need to be retrieved. Information is stored in brain-like networks in the global pattern of their synaptic weights. An incoming vector activates the relevant portions, dimensions, and subspaces of the trained network by virtue of its own vectorial makeup. Even an incomplete version of a given vector (that is, one with several elements missing) will often provoke essentially the same response as the complete vector by reason of its relevant similarity. For example, the badly-whistled first few bars of a familiar tune will generally evoke both its name and the rest of the entire piece. And it can do this in a matter of milliseconds, because even if the subject knows thousands of tunes, there are still no lists to be searched.

It remains for this approach to comprehend the highly discursive and linguistic dimensions of human cognition, those that motivated the classical view of cognition. We need not pretend that this will be easy, but we can see how to start. We can start by exploring the capacity of networks to manipulate the structure of existing language, its syntax, its semantics, its pragmatics, and so forth. But we might also try some novel approaches, such as allowing each of two distinct networks, whose principal concerns and activities are nonlinguistic, to try to learn from scratch some systematic means of manipulating, through a proprietary dimension of input, the cognitive activities of the other network. What system of mutual manipulation—what *language*—might they develop?

The preceding pages illustrate some of the systematic insights that await us if we adopt a more naturalistic approach to traditional issues in epistemology, an approach that is grounded in computational neuroscience. However, a recurring theme in contemporary philosophy is that normative epistemology *cannot* be "naturalized" or reconstructed within the framework of any purely descriptive scientific theory. Notions such as justified belief and rationality, it is said, cannot be adequately defined in terms of the non-normative categories to which any natural science is restricted, since 'ought's cannot be derived from 'is's. Conclusions are then drawn from this to the principled autonomy of epistemology from any natural science.

While it may be true that normative discourse cannot be replaced without remainder by descriptive discourse, it would be a distortion to represent this as the aim of those who would naturalize epistemology. The aim is rather to enlighten our normative endeavors by reconstructing them within a more adequate conception of what cognitive activity consists in, and thus to free ourselves from the burden of factual misconceptions and tunnel vision. It is only the *autonomy* of epistemology that must be denied.

Autonomy must be denied because normative issues are never independent of factual matters. This is easily seen for our judgments of instrumental value, as these always depend on factual premises about causal sufficiencies and dependencies. But it is also true of our most basic normative concepts and our judgments of intrinsic value, for these have factual presuppositions as well. We speak of *justification,* but we think of it as a feature of *belief,* and whether or not there are any beliefs and what properties they have is a robustly factual matter. We speak of *rationality,* but we think of it as a feature of *thinkers,* and it is a substantive factual matter what thinkers are and what cognitive kinematics they harbor. Normative concepts and normative convictions are thus always hostage to some background factual presuppositions, and these can always prove to be superficial, confused, or just plain wrong. If they are, then we may have to rethink whatever normative framework has been erected upon them. The lesson of the preceding pages is that the time for this has already come.

Connectionism and Cognition

Jay F. Rosenberg
1990

I propose to preach a modest sermon against the mediaeval sin of *Enthusiasm.* There's a bright and powerful new paradigm abroad in the philosophy and psychology of mind—the *connectionist* paradigm of brainlike neural networks, distributed representations, and learning by the back propagation of error—and I fear that it is well on the way to becoming a new gospel as well. It has its array of saints and prophets—McClelland and Rumelhart, Hinton and Sejnowski, Churchland and Churchland—and it has its ritual observances—spirited meetings of the San Diego Traveling Connectionist Extravaganza, complete with tape recordings, video cassettes, and multicolored overhead transparencies. It is a very impressive business indeed.

There can be no doubt that the connectionist paradigm has equipped us with potent new tools for understanding *something,* even *many* things. It is less clear, however, just *what* the connectionist paradigm equips us to understand. The San Diego Enthusiasts tend to say "everything mental"—that's what makes them capital-E Enthusiasts—but especially they tend to say "cognition", and at least one of them has begun to talk of the connectionist paradigm as the opening wedge of a global challenge to "sentential epistemologies" in general. Here, however, I do have my doubts, and these doubts are what I want primarily to talk about. But first, even the devil must be given his due—and connectionism is certainly no devil.

What *can* brain-like connectionist networks (of the sorts that I trust I can assume are familiar) help us to understand? I think there are at least three impressive accomplishments, each well worthy of being welcomed with some (small-e) enthusiasm.

First, connectionist networks give us considerable insight into the specific mechanisms by means of which the brain might function as a *transducer.* This role has a variety of aspects. NETtalk (Sejnowski and Rosenberg 1987), for example, neatly illustrates one of them, the *transposition of sensory modalities*, in this instance from visual inputs into acoustic outputs, printed words into audible speech. More broadly, as Paul Churchland (1986) has elegantly argued, connectionist networks allow us to begin to address the problem of *motor control*, for instance, eye-hand coordination. The cerebellum, in particular, appears to be structured in layers whose intra- and interconnectivities echo those of a multilayered connectionist network. The partitionings of the corresponding hidden-unit activation-vector phase spaces can then be understood as "maps" of the organism's visual and tactile environments whose interconnections (forming a "phase-space sandwich") constitute, from the formal point of view, a "matrix multiplier" that can directly instantiate the sophisticated mathematical transformations requisite for smooth sensory-motor coupling.

Second, the connectionist paradigm equips us with the valuable notion of a *distributed representation*. It exhibits a method of *globally* encoding a family of discriminations—in a configuration of connection weights that induces a family of partitions on a connectionist system's hidden-unit vector-activation phase space interpretable, in turn, as a structure of prototypes and associated similarity metrics—which allows us to address problems classically formulated under the rubrics of *pattern recognition* and *information retrieval* (without positing exponential searches), and to understand the *graceful degradation* of information-carrying systems (without positing massive reduplications).

Third, supplemented by the mechanism of back propagation of error, the connectionist paradigm gives us a handle on certain traditional problems of *learning*, and the possibility of a system's acquiring discrimination capacities ab initio. Such examples as the training-up of a connectionist network to respond differentially to sonar echoes from rocks and from mines (Gorman and Sejnowski 1988) shows us vividly how an initially unstructured back-propagation system can function as a *pattern-extractor* given only a suitably rich set of inputs.

Those are significant accomplishments indeed, and they take us a good distance toward understanding how some of the achievements traditionally characterized as "mental" might be operationally realized in organs structured in much the way the human brain is evidently structured. It is not surprising, on that account, to find more than one Enthusiast arriving promptly at the conclusion that what we need to understand the residue of human "mentality" is, in essence, more of the same.

> If even small artificial networks can perform [such] sophisticated cognitive tasks …, there is no mystery that real networks should do the same or better. What the brain displays in the way of hardware is not radically different from what the models contain, and the differences invite exploration rather than disappointment. The brain is of course very much larger and denser than the models so far constructed. … It plainly commands many spaces of stunning complexity, and many skills in consequence. It stands as a glowing invitation to make our humble models yet more and more realistic, in hopes of unlocking the many secrets remaining.   (p. 187 [283])

Thus says Paul Churchland, in his essay "On the Nature of Theories: A Neurocomputational Perspective" (1990/89 [chapter 10 in this volume]), which will be my chief stalking horse here. Setting aside for the moment the question of whether these accomplishments are properly described as "sophisticated cognitive tasks", the first thing that needs to be said about such remarks is that, even *if* they are properly so described, the only sense in which small artificial connectionist networks *perform* them is the sense in which my portable computer regularly performs even *more* "sophisticated cognitive tasks": computing amortization tables, correcting misspellings in my documents, and roundly defeating me at games of Reversi.

The habit of thus nonchalantly importing the personal vocabulary appropriate to what Dennett calls "intentional systems" (1971/78, 1981/87 [chapter 3 in this volume])—prototypically human beings—into descriptions of the operations and functions of *subpersonal* systems (brains, for example) is one of the sure signs of Enthusiasm, and Churchland is one of the worst offenders in this regard. Here he is discussing the rock/mine network:

> [During the training period,] the system is *theorizing* at the level of the hidden units, *exploring* the space of possible activation vectors, *in hopes of finding* some partition or set of partitions on it that the output layer can then *exploit* in turn, so as to *draw the needed distinctions* and thus bring the process of error-induced synaptic adjustments to an end.
> (pp. 179f [278]; all but the first emphasis mine.)

This transposition of a characteristically personal vocabulary to subpersonal systems is, I think, an essential element of Churchland's strategy in proposing that the new connectionist paradigm finally supplies a "comparably compelling *alternative* conception of representation and computation" to the "sentential epistemologies" whose poverty he has been urging for more than a decade. Such "sentential epistemologies", he says (p. 154 [252]), are characterized by two fundamental assumptions:

(1) that language-like structures of some kind constitute the basic or most important form of representation in cognitive creatures, and

(2) that cognition consists in the manipulation of those representations by means of structure-sensitive rules.

It is not entirely clear, however, what either of these claims amounts to. To begin with, in the case of (1), there are surely *many* senses in which a structure might properly be described as "language-like" and in which language-like structures might constitute the "basic" or "most important" form of representation in cognitive creatures. In particular, a structure, or, better, a family of structures, could be "language-like" in the strong sense of being usefully characterized as having *logical form*, and thereby as instantiating a *compositional syntax* strongly analogous to the linear, concatenative, recursive syntax of a formal system or a spoken or written natural language. In a much less restrictive sense, however, a family of structures might be "language-like" only functionally, in being usefully characterized as having *propositional form*, that is, as representing states of affairs by both *referring* to objects and *characterizing* them as being such-and-such. In the latter sense, graphs and pictographs, hieroglyphics, ideographs, portraits, photographs, and maps could all, in different ways, qualify as "language-like structures"—and so too, perhaps, even the distributed representations encoded in some trained connectionist networks.[1]

Again, to sound an Aristotelian note, language-like structures (of some determinate sort) might well turn out to be "basic" or "most important" in one respect, say in the order of knowing, without being "basic" or "most important" in another, such as the order of being. Something like this would be the case, for example, if, as has been proposed (Bechtel 1988a, 1988b), connectionist networks stand to some traditional "rule-following" information processing systems as microstructure to macrostructure, an underlying framework in terms of which those traditional systems are *implemented*. Again, the difference between the connectionist and traditional models of a single information-processing system might turn out to be a function primarily of the level of analytical regard. A fully-trained NETtalk system, for example, can be viewed "syntactically", simply as an interconnected system of activation-weighted nodes, but *also* "semantically", as encoding both the 79 fundamental letter-to-phoneme correlations requisite for transposing written into spoken English (in its partitioning of its hidden-unit activation-vector phase space) and the hierarchical organization of the phonetic structure of English speech (straightforwardly recoverable by a cluster analysis of that partitioning).

Similarly, the assumption, formulated in (2), that cognition consists in the "manipulation" of such language-like representations "by means of structure-sensitive rules" admits of various understandings. These range from the strong, but wildly implausible, view that cognitive activity is a species of (deliberate, self-conscious) *rule-obeying* conduct—a game in which explicitly formulated (meta-level) representations of rules function as reasons, authorizing transformational "moves" from one representation to another—to the much less striking, but almost inescapable, view that cognitive activity is (at least) a species of *rule-conforming conduct*—a family of practices that (at least) accord with permissible "moves" of some explicitly formulable representation-transformation game.

The word 'cognition' is, of course, nobody's personal property, but unless the intent is to weaken the term's commitments beyond all recognition, one thing that should be clear, at least since the publication of Sellars's "Empiricism and the Philosophy of Mind" (1956/63), is that the mere exercise of a discrimination capacity, however complex, is not yet an example of *cognition*. A magnet quite efficiently discriminates between ferrous and nonferrous materials, but that does not put it in the running for the title of "cognitive system". Just as one can "train up" a modest connectionist network regularly to respond differentially to sonar echoes from mines and those from rocks—or, more precisely, as it turns out, to sonar targets made of metal and those made of nonmetal—I can (by stroking it with a strong magnet) "train up" a screwdriver regularly to respond differentially to brass and steel screws. There is no more reason to regard the trained network's acquired response to a (metal) mine as its possession of an ur-concept of metal (or ur-*awareness* of the mine as made of metal) than there is to ascribe an ur-*concept* of steel or (ur-awareness of certain screws as made of steel) to the "trained" (magnetized) screwdriver simply on the basis of its acquired propensity to respond differently to steel and brass screws.

Churchland apparently would not quarrel with these last remarks. Indeed, he himself writes that:

It is briefly tempting to suggest that NETtalk has the concept of 'hard *c*', for example, and that the rock/mine network has the concept of 'metal'. But this won't really do, since the vector-space representations at issue do not play a conceptual or computational role remotely rich enough to merit their assimilation to specifically human concepts.   (pp. 175f [274])

But if this is right, as it surely is, then Churchland's later sanguine characterizations of the accomplishments of such connectionist systems as NETtalk and the rock/mine network as the performance of "sophisticated cognitive tasks" is just so much Enthusiastic hyperbole. Whatever else performing a "sophisticated cognitive task" requires, it at least requires some sort of utilization of concepts. It follows that, if a connectionist system's arriving at a determinate stable partitioning of its hidden-unit activation-vector phase space does not count as its possessing or having mastered a concept, then neither will its ensuing successful discriminations count as *cognitive* performances, sophisticated or unsophisticated.

At this point, Churchland might well object that he has not rejected the identification of connectionist vector-space representations with concepts in general, but only the assimilation of such representations to "specifically human" concepts. Thus, while it would not be correct to say that the trained rock/mine network has the concept of 'metal' *as opposed to*, for example, the concept 'mine' (or some other concept extensionally equivalent over the training class of inputs), the fact that the partitioning of its vector-space is not only stable but also *generalizable*, in that the network successfully classifies *new* sonar echoes from both rocks and mines, warrants our ascribing to it primitive or rudimentary concepts at least of two *kinds* of sonar targets. *We*, given further experimentation and our more sophisticated representational resources, can then subsequently come to recognize and identify these as primitive concepts of metal and nonmetal as opposed to (the locally extensionally equivalent distinction between) rocks and mines.

Now I do not know whether Churchland would in fact adopt the conciliatory strategy I have just been outlining, but in any event, I want to resist the particular sort of blurring of useful distinctions I am convinced it represents. Although I have already granted that no one *owns* the term 'concept', in contrast to Quine's (1948/53) cheerful generosity to McX vis-à-vis the word 'exists', I am reluctant just to give Churchland the word 'concept' and go off in search of an alternative idiom for my own use. Instead, I would like to hold fast to the Kantian

insight that the notion of a judgment is *prior* to that of a concept—
"the only use that the understanding can make of ... concepts is to
judge by means of them" (1787/1929, A68=B93)—and that, consequently, since whatever else a *judgment* may be, it is something fitted
to play the role of a premiss or conclusion in *reasoning*, there is an
essential connection between the notion of a concept and that of *inference*. Sellars (1981) analogously argues that we must be careful not to
conclude straightaway that a rat which has acquired a propensity to
leap at panels with varieties of triangles painted on them has, simply by
virtue of its training, acquired an ur-concept of a triangle:

> To suppose that it *has* reflects the common conviction that the con-
> nection between representational states and objects is a direct one-
> one correlation. Obviously, the representational state ("symbol") is
> correlated with what it represents—but this correlation may *essen-
> tially* involve other correlations—thus between it and other repre-
> sentational states and between representational states and action.
>   (p. 335)

What differentiates the exercise of a mere discriminative capacity, a
systematic propensity to respond differentially to systematically different stimuli, from a conceptual representing properly so called, is that
the latter has a place and a role in a system of *inferential* transformations, a web of consequences and contrarieties in terms of which the
representational state admits of being (more or less determinately)
located in a "logical space" with respect to *other* representations.[2]

> [A particular state of a rat, for example] wouldn't be a state of
> representing something as a triangle, unless [the rat] had the pro-
> pensity to move from [that state] to another state which counts as a
> primitive form of representing it as three-sided or as having, say,
> pointed edges.   (p. 336)

Churchland, we recall, grants that the vector-space representations
generated by NETtalk or the rock/mine network "do not play a conceptual or computational role remotely rich enough to merit their
assimilation to specifically human concepts" (p. 177 [274]), but neither does he pause to tell us what sort of "conceptual or computational
role" would be "rich enough". One might suppose, then, that he could
and would accept with equanimity our most recent remarks connecting the notion of specifically *conceptual* content of representations to
their inferential roles. This, however, would be to misread him. For
consider how the passage from which I have just quoted continues:

Nevertheless, it is plain that both networks have contrived a system of internal representations that truly corresponds to important distinctions and structures in the outside world, structures that are not explicitly represented in the corpus of their sensory inputs. The value of those representations is that they and only they allow the networks to "make sense" of their variegated and often noisy input corpus in the sense that they and only they allow the network to respond to those inputs in a fashion that systematically reduces the error messages to a trickle. These, I need hardly remind, are the functions typically ascribed to *theories.*

What we are confronting here is a possible conception of knowledge or understanding that owes nothing to the sentential categories of current common sense. A global theory, we might venture, is a specific point in a creature's synaptic weight space. It is a configuration of connection weights, a configuration that partitions the system's activation-vector space(s) into useful divisions and subdivisions relative to the inputs typically fed the system. 'Useful' here means: tends to minimize the error messages.

The problem is that an account of a "rich enough conceptual or computational role" for a connectionist network's representations which takes as its model *inferential relations among propositions* could hardly be said to "owe nothing to the sentential categories of current common sense". On the contrary, such an account would retain precisely what is *essential* to traditional "sentential epistemologies"—namely, items that have propositional form and stand in logical relations, while sloughing off as *adventitious* only the fact that, in natural languages, the referring and characterizing *functions* requisite for propositional form are characteristically performed with the aid of distinct notational devices (utterance tokens or sign-designs).[3]

Two further aspects of the passage we have just been examining deserve some comment. Of course the application of such personal psychological predicates as "contrives" and "make sense" (with only the latter in cautionary quotes) to these small and distinctly subpersonal networks is once again best understood as an outcropping of Enthusiastic excess. But so too, and more significantly, I want to suggest, is the not-so-innocent definite article in Churchland's phrase "*the* functions typically ascribed to theories". For while classifying or redescribing the elements of a corpus of sensory inputs in terms positing distinctions and structures in the world that are not explicitly (phenomenally) represented in those inputs is certainly *a* function of theories, only someone intent on constructing an extraordinarily impoverished view of natural science could possibly speak of it as *the* function of theories.

Now Churchland is notoriously not an advocate of an impoverished view of natural science. He is a scientific realist, who has no patience with fictionalist or instrumentalist views that assign any special *epistemically* privileged status to the observational concepts of common sense. But, for all that, I do not think that we can write off the definite article here as a mere *lapsus linguae*. As Churchland very well knows, a theoretical redescription of some family of observable phenomena is essentially a prolegomenon to the theoretical *explanation* of those phenomena as phenomena. It is the explanatory subsumption of the redescribed phenomenon under *laws*, belonging to a system of *inferentially interrelated* principles, that gives the redescription its point. But that, of course, just is "sentential epistemology" all over again. The problem, however, is that the *only* thing a connectionist network ever learns to do is to partition its input. Since Churchland (like everyone else) has no idea how to pry the notion of an explanatory understanding of phenomena as phenomena loose from traditional sentential epistemics, his only choice, in order to characterize such networks as *theorizers*, is subtly to scale down the notion of a *theory* until it fits their limited competences.

The second aspect of the quoted passage worth attending to is that it highlights again the role of the notion of *error* in the connectionist paradigm. Now, in the course of examining the question of how faithfully connectionist networks depict the organic brain, Churchland does raise some questions about the *de facto applicability* of the connectionist model of learning by the back propagation of apprehended errors to real biological systems. What he does not do, however, is to raise any questions regarding the *sense* of the notion of "learning by back propagation of apprehended errors" in its envisioned application to natural creatures. Specifically, he does not pause to inquire in virtue of *what* some particular output from a connectionist network could be apprehended *by that network* as an *error*.

What makes this question worth asking is that it is precisely at this point in the connectionist story that its paradigm acquires whatever *normative epistemological* import it has. Churchland claims that we now possess "a powerful and fertile framework with which to address problems of cognition ... that owes nothing to the sentential paradigm of the classical view" (154 [252]), and he professes to be deeply skeptical about even the very notion of truth:

It is no longer clear that there is any unique and unitary relation that virtuous belief systems must bear to the nonlinguistic world. Which leaves us free to reconsider the great many different dimensions of epistemic and pragmatic virtue that a cognitive system can display.   (p. 157 [255])

But when the chips are down, what drives the connectionist picture of learning is an *assumed* bipolarity of "correct" versus "erroneous" responses—and since distributed connectionist representations *can* be functionally understood as "language-like"—that is, as having propositional form—this bipolarity is close enough to "true" versus "false" beliefs as to make no difference.

Churchland is not, of course, insensitive to these points, and, indeed, remarks on them in the course of (pessimistically) assessing the plausibility of the idea that the back propagation of apprehended error is in fact the central mechanism for learning in organic brains.

> A necessary element in [the delta rule's] calculated apportionment of error is a representation of what would have been the *correct* vector in the output layer. This is why back propagation is said to involve a global *teacher*, an information source that always knows the correct answers and can therefore provide a perfect measure of output error. Real creatures generally lack any such perfect information. They must struggle along in the absence of any sure compass toward the truth, and their synaptic weights must undergo change, change steered in some way by error or related dissatisfaction, change that carves a path toward a regime of decreased error.
> (p. 186 [282])

Now the brains, of course, do *not* learn; the creatures do. But to the extent (evidently considerable) that a creature's brain is or resembles a system of networks of the connectionist sort, the configurations of its synaptic weights surely must undergo changes as the creature learns. One can sensibly say that such changes are "steered in some way by error" and "carve a path toward a regime of decreased error", however, only if one is *either* equipped with an *antecedent* notion of "correct representation" or prepared to say that a "correct representation" just *is* whatever configuration of weights *in fact* stabilizes the system over the actual inputs to it.

Churchland makes it unmistakably clear that he would be loathe to adopt the latter course, along with its "convergent realist" implication that we cannot but arrive at correct representations of the world.

For one thing, nothing guarantees that we humans will avoid getting permanently stuck in some very deep but relatively local error minimum. For another, nothing guarantees that there exists a possible configuration of weights that would reduce the error messages to *zero*.   (p. 194 [289])

Such remarks make sense, however, only if the notion of an "error"—or equivalently, that of a "correct representation"—admits of characterization independently of the *de facto* achievements of connectionist representers. One would expect, then, to find Churchland offering us an account of the *antecedent* notion of "correct representation" required for speaking sensibly of "error" in this connection in the first place. But one does not. What one finds instead is another subtle Enthusiastic blur.

That a connectionist system learns by the back propagation of *error* requires that its hidden-layer activation weights be adjusted in the direction of decreasing the difference between what its outputs *are* and what those outputs *ought to be*. It is only this implicit appeal to a *norm-driven* model of learning, I suggest, that makes it appropriate to describe the activities and accomplishments of such systems in *epistemic* terms at all. At the crucial juncture, however, Churchland speaks, not simply of "error", but more cagily of "error or related dissatisfaction". Now we can certainly imagine highly plastic "self-teaching" organic connectionist systems which are hard-wired to "learn" by adjusting their activation weights so as to minimize *something*—perhaps, indeed, something describable as a "dissatisfaction", such as pain, hunger, thirst, fatigue, or what have you. But to characterize the resultant accomplishments (for instance, acquired discrimination capacities, and inter-sensory or sensory-motor coordinations) in *epistemic* terms is an Enthusiastic vice of the sort against which Sellars cautioned us over thirty years ago.

[The] idea that epistemic facts can be analyzed without remainder—even "in principle"—into non-epistemic facts, whether phenomenal or behavioral, public or private, with no matter how lavish a sprinkling of subjunctives and hypotheticals is ... a radical mistake—a mistake of a piece with the so-called "naturalistic fallacy" in ethics.   (1956/63, p. 257/131)

The essential point is that characterizing a state or transaction or condition or episode in epistemic terms is not providing an empirical, mater-of-factual description of it, but rather locating it within a "logical space" of *reasons* and *justification*. A creature properly in this logical space of justification is one capable of recognizing or acknowledging the superior (epistemic) authority of some representings vis-à-vis others. Such a creature responds to epistemic authority, for example, by adopting or endorsing some (implied) representations *because* they are consequences of others and by abandoning or modifying some (contrary) representations *because* they conflict with others to which it is committed. This, not surprisingly, brings us around again, although at a deeper level, to the notion of inference that I have already argued is essential to distinguishing the exercise of mere discriminative capacities, however sophisticated, from authentically cognitive performances, however primitive.

What needs to be stressed is that, for a creature properly to be said to move in the logical space of reasons and justification, it is not enough that it be usefully characterizable as "rational", in the sense, for example, of behaving in ways fruitfully described, understood, and predicted from Dennett's intentional stance. Such a creature, we may say, is "logic-*conforming*"; but a creature capable of acting for reasons *acknowledged as* (epistemically) authoritative and of responding to errors apprehended *as* errors must do more than merely behave in ways that conform to logic. It must *use* logic.

The distinction between merely logic-conforming or rational creatures and logic-using or *ratiocinative* creatures, although clear enough in the abstract, is one that remains unmarked by the intentional stance as such. From the intentional stance, the behavior of a deer who flees when it scents smoke can perhaps fruitfully be explained by ascribing to the deer a belief that there is a fire nearby and a desire to avoid perishing in it. The deer, we may say in a Humean tone of voice, has learned to "associate" smoke with fire, and it is this "association" that, when smoke is present, gives rise to its representation of a belief. Furthermore, since the presence of smoke is indeed evidence that a fire is nearby, we may go on to say that the deer then "has a good reason" for believing that a fire is nearby. Its belief is "well grounded".

The Enthusiastic mistake which needs to be avoided here does *not* lie in this move from "the deer represents the presence of smoke, and the presence of smoke is a good reason for believing that a fire is nearby" to "the deer has a good reason for believing that a fire is nearby", but in the misinterpretation of this line of thought as licensing the further conclusion that the deer acknowledges and responds to the reason that it "has" *as* a reason—in other words, to the available evidence *as evidence*. This stronger claim requires that the deer be capable of *representing* its evidence *as* evidence. That is, not only must the deer have the propensity to represent that a fire is nearby whenever it represents that smoke is present (a propensity it shares with the smoke detector in my apartment), but it must also be equipped, so to speak, in *some* way, to form a judgment to the effect that the presence of smoke is evidence that a fire is nearby.

This is not yet to demand that the deer be in possession of generic epistemic concepts as such—that is, *concepts* of evidence, good or poor reasons, correct or erroneous representations, and so on—although, obviously, any such *epistemic* creature would satisfy the condition in question. There is an intermediate sense in which even a creature rather like our deer could be said to respond to the reason it "has" *as* a reason, or to its evidence *as* evidence. What is needed is that its representation of the "conclusion" that there is a fire nearby be mediated by a representation of the *material counterpart* of the specific epistemic relation of "good evidence" in question, namely, by a representation of a *generalization* to the effect that whenever smoke is present anywhere, there is likely to be a fire nearby there. But this would imply, in turn, that the creature in question must be not only a rational or logic-conforming creature, in the sense we have recently been exploring, but also something that no actual deer is, a ratiocinative or logic-using creature as well.

As Leibniz put it, in passing from a representation of smoke as present to a representation of fire as nearby *simply* in accordance with an acquired propensity to do so, the deer does not reason but manifests only "a sort of *consecutiveness* which imitates reason".[4] The crucial point for our present purposes is that genuinely ratiocinative creatures must be capable of a range of representations that extends significantly beyond those that the connectionist paradigm admittedly helps us to understand. Ratiocinative creatures, that is, must be capable not only of representings that have propositional form and thereby stand in logical relations of consequence and contrariety, but also of representings of representings *as* thus logically related, and consequently of those logical relations themselves. In Sellars's words:

> [We] carve nature at the joint by distinguishing between those
> [representational systems] which contain representational items
> which function as do logical connectives and quantifiers, that is,
> which have logical expressions "in their vocabularies", and those
> which do not.   (1981, p. 341)

What these considerations help us recover is a second, more robust, sense of 'rational' in which a "rational creature" is one not only fruit-fully understood as manifesting the sort of "practical rationality" defin-itive of the intentional stance but also meaningfully characterizable as possessing "theoretical rationality" as well.[5] This comes about as follows.

A ratiocinative creature is capable not only of generalizable repre-sentations, but also of representations of generalities. Again, while a system at the level of complexity of, say, the rock/mine network might, with some license, be said *not to* "believe" of a given input that it is the echo of a mine, only a genuinely ratiocinative system, possessing resources adequate for representing negation, could sensibly be said to "believe" of a given input *that it is not* the echo of a mine. Such resources, however, enable a ratiocinative system to do what a connec-tionist system of the sort we have been examining cannot do, namely, to "internalize" a test for erroneous representation in the form of a glo-bal constraint of logical consistency. It shows us, that is, how a repre-sentation could in principle come to be apprehended as an error *by the system itself.*

Two representations having the *logical* forms "All A's are B's" and "This is an A, but not a B" cannot both be correct; and while such an inconsistency by itself is, of course, insufficient to determine which of the representations is in error, in a ratiocinative system operating under a global consistency constraint, it can certainly suffice to set into motion precisely the sort of homeostatic "web of belief" interadjust-ments of representational and inferential commitments that are the stock in trade of *sentential* epistemologies. There is a clear sense, there-fore, in which a ratiocinative system not only responds to reasons *as* reasons, but, even without the aid of a "teacher", can respond to errors *as* errors as well. (The role of global consistency constraints of this sort is provocatively discussed in Millikan 1984.)

The moral to be carried away from this discussion is not that a rati-ocinative system cannot in principle be thought of as assembled from connectionist-style resources. Although we do not have the slightest idea how representations having the logical forms of conditionals and negations might be encoded in the "distributed" way appropriate to connectionist networks, none of the considerations we have adduced implies that they *cannot* be so encoded. And, *if* they can, then there is also no reason to reject out of hand the suggestion that the homeo-static "web of belief" interadjustments among such representational and inferential commitments take the de facto operational form of adjustments of the activation weights of the hidden units of some complex multi-layered system of the connectionist sort.

The point, however, is that *this* connectionist story is *essentially* the story, not of an alternative to a sentential epistemology, but of the *implementation* of a sentential epistemology. The "language-like" character of the logically articulated representations thus encoded is not adventitious, but necessary for us to be able to understand the operation of such a system in *epistemic* terms at all. Absent even the minimalist interpretations of "responding to reasons as reasons" and "responding to errors as errors" that first become possible in the case of a system understood as ratiocinative—given, for example, a system exhibiting only the "dissatisfaction minimizing" learning envisioned in passing by Churchland—the specifically epistemic vocabulary finds no point of purchase.

The sin of Connectionist Enthusiasm, we have seen, takes many forms. It expresses itself in sanguine applications of the personal epistemic vocabulary to subpersonal systems. It expresses itself in the subtle paring down of rich epistemic notions—in neglecting the inferential embeddings that minimally distinguish *concepts* from mere discrimination capacities and the explanatory applications that minimally distinguish *theories* from mere taxonomies. And it expresses itself in the blurring of distinctions among the diverse ways, structural and functional, in which a representational system can be "language-like".

Most significantly, however, Connectionist Enthusiasm manifests itself in its willingness to take *normative* epistemic force for granted. For the connectionist paradigm locates this normative epistemic force *outside* the network itself, in its "teacher's" infallible knowledge of which of its outputs are erroneous and of how they differ from the correct outputs—that is, from what they *ought* to be.

The resulting problem can be solved. Normative epistemic force can be "internalized" by a representational system which can respond to reasons *as* reasons and errors *as* errors. But it can be solved only by "splitting" the intentional stance, by distinguishing the ratiocinative from the *merely* rational, and so only by acknowledging representational systems whose representations are "language-like" in the strong sense of possessing not merely propositional form but logical form as well. Sentential epistemology, in short, is the only *epistemology* we've got, and connectionism is at best its implementationist underlaborer.

To say this is not to disparage the brilliance of the connectionist achievement. For what it shows us is nothing less than how we might begin to put sentential epistemology together with the organic brain, and that is well worth celebrating. As is so often the case on such occasions, however, some of the revelers have a tendency to celebrate to excess. They claim that what connectionism shows us is an epistemology, that is not sentential, and that the organic brain might use instead. But that, I have argued, is just Enthusiasm—and in philosophy, too, Enthusiasm is still a sin.

Notes

1. See, in this connection, Sellars 1981, to which the present discussion is, and will continue to be, deeply indebted.

2. The priority of the notion of a judgment to that of a concept is also, of course, a central principle of Frege's philosophy. Frege's strategy, recall, is precisely to replace a "bottom up" account of judgments in terms of the composition of concepts by a "top down" analysis of the notion of "conceptual content" in terms of intersubstitutivity of and in judgments *salva* correct inferences.

3. This fact, in turn, is explained by the (temporal) *linearity* of speech (and the spatial linearity of script). As Wittgenstein was the first to see—in the *Tractatus* (1922/74)—the predicate expressions of such a linear representational system are, from the *functional* point of view, auxiliary signs, serving only to guarantee a stock of characteristics of and relations among referring expressions [*names*] (that is, "being concatenated with a 'red'", "standing respectively to the left and right of a 'taller than'") adequate for representing possible characteristics of and relations among the objects to which those expressions refer.

4. *Monadology*, #26 (Leibniz 1714/1977), cited in Sellars 1981, p. 342.

5. It is this sense of 'rational', I think, that Jonathan Bennett proposes to isolate and examine in his delightful and insightful little book, *Rationality* (1964).

Connectionism and Cognitive Architecture: A Critical Analysis

12

Jerry A. Fodor
Zenon W. Pylyshyn
1988

1 Introduction

Connectionist or *PDP* models are catching on. There are conferences and new books nearly every day, and the popular science press hails this new wave of theorizing as a breakthrough in understanding the mind. There are also, inevitably, descriptions of the emergence of connectionism as a Kuhnian "paradigm shift". (See Schneider 1987, for an example of this and for further evidence of the tendency to view connectionism as the "new wave" of cognitive science.) The fan club includes the most unlikely collection of people. Almost everyone who is discontent with contemporary cognitive psychology and current "information processing" models of the mind has rushed to embrace "the connectionist alternative".

When taken as a way of modeling *cognitive architecture*, connectionism really does represent an approach that is quite different from that of the classical cognitive science that it seeks to replace. Classical models of the mind were derived from the structure of Turing and Von Neumann machines. They are not, of course, committed to the details of these machines as exemplified in Turing's original formulation or in typical commercial computers—only to the basic idea that the kind of computing that is relevant to understanding cognition involves operations on symbols (see Newell 1980, 1982; Fodor 1976, 1987; and Pylyshyn 1980, 1984). In contrast, connectionists propose to design systems that can exhibit intelligent behavior without storing, retrieving, or otherwise operating on structured symbolic expressions. The style of processing carried out in such models is thus strikingly unlike what goes on when conventional machines are computing some function.

Connectionist systems are networks consisting of very large numbers of simple but highly interconnected "units". Certain assumptions are generally made both about the units and the connections. Each unit is assumed to receive real-valued activity (either excitatory or inhibitory or both) along its input lines. Typically the units do little more than sum this activity and change their state as a function (usually a threshold function) of this sum. Each connection is allowed to modulate the activity it transmits as a function of an intrinsic (but modifiable) property called its "weight". Hence the activity on an input line is typically some non-linear function of the state of activity of its sources. The behavior of the network as a whole is a function of the initial state of activation of the units and of the weights on its connections, which serve as its only form of memory.

Numerous elaborations of this basic connectionist architecture are possible. For example, connectionist models often have stochastic mechanisms for determining the level of activity or the state of a unit. Moreover, units may be connected to outside environments. In this case the units are sometimes assumed to respond to a narrow range of combinations of parameter values and are said to have a certain "receptive field" in parameter-space. These are called "value units" (Ballard 1986). In some versions of connectionist architecture, environmental properties are encoded by the pattern of states of entire populations of units. Such "coarse coding" techniques are among the ways of achieving what connectionists call "distributed representation".[1] The term 'connectionist model' (like 'Turing Machine' or 'Von Neumann machine') is thus applied to a family of mechanisms that differ in details but share a galaxy of architectural commitments. We shall return to the characterization of these commitments below.

Connectionist networks have been analyzed extensively—in some cases using advanced mathematical techniques. They have also been simulated on computers and shown to exhibit interesting aggregate properties. For example, they can be "wired" to recognize patterns, to exhibit rule-like behavioral regularities, and to realize virtually any mapping from patterns of (input) parameters to patterns of (output) parameters—though in most cases multi-parameter, multi-valued mappings require very large numbers of units. Of even greater interest is the fact that such networks can be made to learn; this is achieved by modifying the weights on the connections as a function of certain kinds of feedback (the exact way in which this is done constitutes a preoccupation of connectionist research and has lead to the development of such important techniques as "back propagation").

In short, the study of connectionist machines has led to a number of striking and unanticipated findings; it's surprising how much computing can be done with a uniform network of simple interconnected elements. Moreover, these models have an appearance of neural plausibility that classical architectures are sometimes said to lack. Perhaps, then, a new cognitive science based on connectionist networks should replace the old cognitive science based on classical computers. Surely this is a proposal that ought to be taken seriously; if it is warranted, it implies a major redirection of research.

Unfortunately, however, discussions of the relative merits of the two architectures have thus far been marked by a variety of confusions and irrelevances. It's our view that when you clear away these misconceptions, what's left is a real disagreement about the nature of mental processes and mental representations. But it seems to us that it is a matter that was substantially put to rest about thirty years ago; and the arguments that then appeared to militate decisively in favor of the classical view appear to us to do so still.

In the present paper we will proceed as follows. First, we discuss some methodological questions about levels of explanation that have become enmeshed in the substantive controversy over connectionism. Second, we try to say what it is that makes connectionist and classical theories of mental structure incompatible. Third, we review and extend some of the traditional arguments for the classical architecture. Though these arguments have been somewhat recast, very little that we'll have to say here is entirely new. But we hope to make it clear how various aspects of the classical doctrine cohere and why rejecting the classical picture of reasoning leads connectionists to say the very implausible things they do about logic and semantics. In section 4, we return to the question what makes the connectionist approach appear attractive to so many people. In doing so we'll consider some arguments that have been offered in favor of connectionist networks as general models of cognitive processing.

1.1 Levels of explanation

There are two major traditions in modern theorizing about the mind, one that we'll call 'representationalist' and one that we'll call 'eliminativist'. Representationalists hold that postulating representational (or 'intentional' or 'semantic') states is essential to a theory of cognition;

according to representationalists, there are states of the mind which function to encode states of the world. Eliminativists, by contrast, think that psychological theories can dispense with such semantic notions as representation. According to eliminativists the appropriate vocabulary for psychological theorizing is neurological or, perhaps behavioral, or perhaps syntactic; in any event, not a vocabulary that characterizes mental states in terms of what they represent. (For a neurological version of eliminativism, see Patricia Churchland 1986; for a behavioral version, see Watson 1930; for a syntactic version, see Stich 1983).

Connectionists are on the representationalist side of this issue. As Rumelhart and McClelland say, PDPs "are explicitly concerned with the problem of internal representation" (1986, p. 121). Correspondingly, the specification of what the states of a network *represent* is an essential part of a connectionist model. Consider, for example, the well-known connectionist account of the bi-stability of the Necker cube (Feldman and Ballard 1982). "Simple units representing the visual features of the two alternatives are arranged in competing coalitions, with inhibitory … links between rival features and positive links within each coalition… The result is a network that has two dominant stable states" (see figure 12.1). Notice that, in this as in all other such

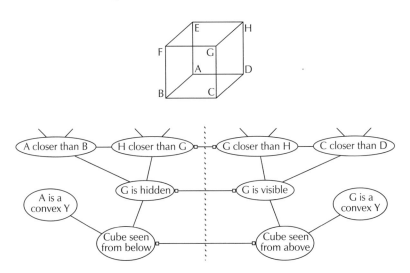

Figure 12.1: A connectionist network illustrating the two stable states of the Necker cube. Plain links are mutually supportive; links with circles are inhibitive. The dashed line separates the two stable states. (Adapted from Feldman and Ballard 1982.)

connectionist models, the commitment to mental representation is explicit: the label of a node is taken to express the representational content of the state that the device is in when the node is excited, and there are nodes corresponding to monadic and to relational properties of the reversible cube when it is seen in one way or the other.

There are, to be sure, times when connectionists appear to vacillate between representationalism and the claim that the "cognitive level" is dispensable in favor of a more precise and biologically-motivated level of theory. In particular, there is a lot of talk in the connectionist literature about processes that are "subsymbolic"—and therefore presumably *not* representational. But this is misleading: connectionist modeling is consistently representationalist in practice, and representationalism is generally endorsed by the very theorists who also like the idea of cognition "emerging from the subsymbolic". Thus, Rumelhart and McClelland (1986, p. 121) insist that PDP models are "strongly committed to the study of representation and process". Similarly, though Smolensky (1988, p. 2) takes connectionism to articulate regularities at the "subsymbolic level" of analysis, it turns out that subsymbolic states do have a semantics—though it's not the semantics of representations at the "conceptual level". According to Smolensky, the semantical distinction between symbolic and subsymbolic theories is just that "entities that are typically represented in the symbolic paradigm by [single] symbols are typically represented in the subsymbolic paradigm by a large number of subsymbols". Both the conceptual and the subsymbolic levels thus postulate representational states, but subsymbolic theories slice them thinner.

We are stressing the representationalist character of connectionist theorizing because much connectionist methodological writing has been preoccupied with the question: What level of explanation is appropriate for theories of cognitive architecture? (See, for example, the exchange between Broadbent 1985 and Rumelhart and McClelland 1985.) And, as we're about to see, what one says about the levels question depends a lot on what stand one takes about whether there are representational states.

It seems certain that the world has causal structure at very many different levels of analysis, with the individuals recognized at the lowest levels being, in general, very small and the individuals recognized at the highest levels being, in general, very large. Thus there is a scientific story to be told about quarks; and a scientific story to be told about atoms; and a scientific story to be told about molecules, ... ditto rocks and stones and rivers, … ditto galaxies. And the story that scientists tell about the causal structure that the world has at any one of these levels may be quite different from the story that they tell about its causal structure at the next level up or down. The methodological implication for psychology is this: if you want to have an argument about *cognitive* architecture, you have to specify the level of analysis that's supposed to be at issue.

If you're *not* a representationalist, this is quite tricky since it is then not obvious what makes a phenomenon cognitive. But specifying the level of analysis relevant for theories of cognitive architecture is no problem for either classicists or connectionists. Since classicists and connectionists are both representationalists, for them any level at which states of the system are taken to encode properties of the world counts as a *cognitive* level; and no other levels do. (Representations of "the world" include of course, representations of symbols; for example, the concept WORD is a construct at the cognitive level because it represents something, namely words.) Correspondingly, it's the architecture of representational states and processes that discussions of *cognitive architecture* are about. Put differently, the architecture of the cognitive system consists of the set of basic operations, resources, functions, principles, and so on, (generally the sorts of properties that would be described in a "user's manual" for that architecture if it were available on a computer) whose domain and range are the *representational states* of the organism.

It follows that, if you want to make good the connectionist theory *as a theory of cognitive architecture*, you have to show that the processes which operate on *the representational states* of an organism are those which are specified by a connectionist architecture. It is, for example, *no use at all*, from the cognitive psychologist's point of view, to show that the *non*representational (for instance, neurological, or molecular, or quantum mechanical) states of an organism constitute a connectionist network, because that would *leave open* the question whether the mind is a such a network *at the psychological level*. It is, in particular, perfectly possible that nonrepresentational neurological states are interconnected in the ways described by connectionist models *but that the representational states themselves are not*. This is because, just as it is possible to implement a *connectionist* cognitive architecture in a network of causally interacting nonrepresentational elements, so too it is perfectly possible to implement a *classical* cognitive architecture in such a network. In fact, the question whether connectionist networks should be treated as models at the implementation level is moot, and will be discussed at some length in section 4.

It is important to be clear about this matter of levels on pain of simply trivializing the issues about cognitive architecture. Consider, for example, the following remark of Rumelhart's (1984, p. 60).

> It has seemed to me for some years now that there must be a unified account in which the so-called rule-governed and [the] exceptional cases were dealt with by a unified underlying process—a process which produces rule-like and rule-exception behavior through the application of a single process ... [In this process] both the rule-like and non-rule-like behavior is a product of the interaction of a very large number of "subsymbolic" processes.

It's clear from the context that Rumelhart takes this idea to be very tendentious; one of the connectionist claims that classical theories are required to deny.

But in fact it's not. For, *of course* there are "subsymbolic" interactions that implement both rule-like and rule-violating behavior; for example, quantum mechanical processes do. *That's* not what classical theorists deny; indeed, it's not denied by anybody who is even vaguely a materialist. Nor does a classical theorist deny that rule-following and rule-violating behaviors are both implemented by the very same neurological machinery. For a classical theorist, neurons implement *all* cognitive processes in precisely the same way: namely, by supporting the basic operations that are required for symbol processing.

What *would* be an interesting and tendentious claim is that there's no distinction between rule-following and rule-violating mentation *at the cognitive or representational or symbolic level*; specifically, that it is not the case that the etiology of rule-following behavior is mediated by the representation of explicit rules. We will consider this idea in section 4, where we will argue that it too is *not* what divides classical from connectionist architecture; classical models *permit* a principled distinction between the etiologies of mental processes that are explicitly rule governed and mental processes that aren't; but they don't demand one.

In short, the issue between classical and connectionist architecture is not about the explicitness of rules; as we'll presently see, classical architecture is not, per se, committed to the idea that explicit rules mediate the etiology of behavior. And it is not about the reality of representational states; classicists and connectionists are all representational realists. And it is not about nonrepresentational architecture; a connectionist neural network can perfectly well implement a classical architecture at the cognitive level.

So, then, what *is* the disagreement between classical and connectionist architecture about?

2 The nature of the dispute

Classicists and connectionists all assign semantic content to *something*. Roughly, connectionists assign semantic content to 'nodes' (that is, to units or aggregates of units; see footnote 1)—to the sorts of things that are typically labeled in connectionist diagrams; whereas classicists assign semantic content to *expressions*—to the sorts of things that get written on the tapes of Turing machines and stored at addresses in Von Neumann machines. But classical theories disagree with connectionist theories about what primitive relations hold among these content-bearing entities. Connectionist theories acknowledge *only causal connectedness* as a primitive relation among nodes; when you know how activation and inhibition flow among them, you know everything there is to know about how the nodes in a network are related. By contrast, classical theories acknowledge not only causal relations among the semantically evaluable objects that they posit, but also a range of structural relations, of which constituency is paradigmatic.

This difference has far reaching consequences for the ways that the two kinds of theories treat a variety of cognitive phenomena, some of which we will presently examine at length. But, underlying the disagreements about details are two architectural differences between the theories.

(1) COMBINATORIAL SYNTAX AND SEMANTICS FORM MENTAL REPRESENTATIONS. Classical theories—but not connectionist theories—postulate a "language of thought" (see, for example, Fodor 1975); they take mental representations to have *a combinatorial syntax and semantics*, in which (a) there is a distinction between structurally-atomic and structurally-molecular representations; (b) structurally-molecular representations have syntactic constituents that are themselves either structurally-molecular or are structurally-atomic; and (c) the semantic content of a (molecular) representation is a function of the semantic contents of its syntactic parts, together with its constituent structure. For purposes of convenience, we'll sometime abbreviate (a)–(c) by speaking of classical theories as committed to "complex" mental representations or to "symbol structures".

(2) STRUCTURE SENSITIVITY OF PROCESSES. In classical models, the principles by which mental states are transformed, or by which an input selects the corresponding output, are defined over structural properties of mental representations. Because classical mental *representations* have combinatorial structure, it is possible for classical mental *operations* to apply to them by reference to their *form*. The result is that a paradigmatic classical mental process operates upon any mental representation that satisfies a given structural description, and transforms it into a mental representation that satisfies another structural description. (So, for example, in a model of inference, one might recognize an operation that applies to any representation of the form $P \& Q$ and transforms it into a representation of the form P.) Notice that, since formal properties can be defined at a variety of levels of abstraction, such an operation can apply equally to representations that differ widely in their structural complexity. The operation that applies to representations of the form $P \& Q$ to produce P is satisfied by, for example, an expression like '$(A \vee B \vee C) \& (D \vee E \vee F)$', from which it derives the expression '$(A \vee B \vee C)$'.

We take (1) and (2) as the claims that define classical models, and we take these claims quite literally; they constrain the physical realizations of symbol structures. In particular, the symbol structures in a classical model are assumed to correspond to real physical structures in the brain and the *combinatorial structure* of a representation is supposed to have a counterpart in structural relations among physical properties of the brain. For example, the relation *part-of*, which holds between a relatively simple symbol and a more complex one, is assumed to correspond to some physical relation among brain states. This is why Newell (1980) speaks of computational systems such as brains and classical computers as "*physical* symbols systems".

This bears emphasis because the classical theory is committed not only to there being a system of physically instantiated symbols, but also to the claim that the physical properties onto which the structure of the symbols is mapped *are the very properties that cause the system to behave as it does*. In other words, the physical counterparts of the symbols, and their structural properties, *cause* the system's behavior. A system which has symbolic expressions, but whose operation does not depend upon the structure of these expressions, does not qualify as a classical machine since it fails to satisfy condition (2). In this respect, a classical model is very different from one in which behavior is caused by mechanisms, such as energy minimization, that are not responsive to the physical encoding of the structure of representations.

From now on, when we speak of "classical" models, we will have in mind *any* model that has complex mental representations, as characterized in (1) and structure-sensitive mental processes, as characterized in (2). Our account of classical architecture is therefore neutral with respect to such issues as whether or not there is a separate executive. For example, classical machines can have an "object-oriented" architecture, like that of the computer language *Smalltalk*, or a "message-passing" architecture, like that of Hewett's (1977) *Actors*—so long as the objects or the messages have a combinatorial structure which is causally implicated in the processing. Classical architecture is also neutral on the question whether the operations on the symbols are constrained to occur one at a time or whether many operations can occur at the same time.

Here, then, is the plan for what follows. In the rest of this section, we will sketch the connectionist proposal for a computational architecture that does away with complex mental representations and structure-sensitive operations. (Although our purpose here is merely expository, it turns out that describing exactly what connectionists are committed to requires substantial reconstruction of their remarks and practices. Since there is a great variety of points of view within the connectionist community, we are prepared to find that some connectionists in good standing may not fully endorse the program when it is laid out in what we take to be its bare essentials.) Following this general expository (or reconstructive) discussion, section 3 provides a series of arguments favoring the classical story. Then the remainder of the paper considers some of the reasons why connectionism appears attractive to many people and offers further general comments on the relation between the classical and the connectionist enterprise.

2.1 Complex mental representations

To begin with, consider a case of the most trivial sort; two machines, one classical in spirit and one connectionist. Here is how the connectionist machine might reason. There is a network of labelled nodes as in figure 12.2. Paths between the nodes indicate the routes along which activation can spread (that is, they indicate the consequences that exciting one of the nodes has for determining the level of excitation of the others). Drawing an inference from **A & B** to **A** thus corresponds to an excitation of node 2 being caused by an excitation of

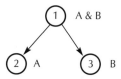

Figure 12.2: A possible connectionist network for drawing inferences
from A & B to A or to B.

node 1 (alternatively, if the system is in a state in which node 1 is
excited, it eventually settles into a state in which node 2 is excited).

Now consider a classical machine. This machine has a tape on
which it writes expressions. Among the expressions that can appear on
this tape are: 'A', 'B', 'A & B', 'C', 'D', 'C & D', 'A & C & D', and so
on. The machine's causal constitution is as follows: whenever a token
of the form $P \& Q$ appears on the tape, the machine writes a token of
the form P. An inference from **A & B** to **A** thus corresponds to a
tokening of type 'A & B' on the tape causing a tokening of type 'A'.

So then, what does the architectural difference between the
machines consist in? In the classical machine, the objects to which the
content **A & B** is ascribed (namely, tokens of the expression 'A & B')
literally contain, as proper parts, objects to which the content **A** is
ascribed (namely, tokens of the expression 'A'.) Moreover, the semantics (the satisfaction condition, say) of the expression 'A & B' is determined in a uniform way by the semantics of its constituents. By
contrast, in the connectionist machine none of this true; the object to
which the content **A & B** is ascribed (node 1) is *causally* connected to
the object to which the content **A** is ascribed (node 2); but there is no
structural (for instance, no part/whole) relation that holds between
them. In short, it is characteristic of classical systems, but not of connectionist systems, to exploit arrays of symbols, some of which are
atomic (such as 'A'), but indefinitely many of which have other symbols as syntactic and semantic parts (as does 'A & B').

2.1.4* Representations as "distributed" over microfeatures

Many connectionists hold that the mental representations that correspond to common-sense concepts (CHAIR, JOHN, CUP, and so on)
are "distributed" over galaxies of lower-level units which themselves

---

* *Editor's note:* Section numbers have been retained from the original, and
hence are not always sequential in this abridged edition.

have representational content. To use common connectionist terminology (see Smolensky 1988), the higher or "conceptual-level" units correspond to vectors in a "subconceptual" space of microfeatures. The model here is something like the relation between a defined expression and its defining feature analysis; thus, the concept BACHELOR might be thought to correspond to a vector in a space of features that includes ADULT, HUMAN, MALE, and MARRIED—in particular, as an assignment of the value + to the first three features, and of − to the last. Notice that distribution over microfeatures (unlike distribution over neural units) is a relation among representations, hence a relation at the cognitive level.

On the most frequent connectionist accounts, theories articulated in terms of microfeature vectors are supposed to show how concepts are *actually* encoded, hence the feature vectors are intended to *replace* "less precise" specifications of macrolevel concepts. For example, where a classical theorist might recognize a psychological state of entertaining the concept CUP, a connectionist may acknowledge only a *roughly analogous* state of tokening the corresponding feature vector. (One reason that the analogy is only rough is that which feature vector "corresponds" to a given concept may be viewed as heavily context dependent.) The generalizations that "concept-level" theories frame are thus taken to be only approximately true, the exact truth being stateable only in the vocabulary of the microfeatures. Smolensky, for example, is explicit in endorsing this picture: "Precise, formal descriptions of the intuitive processor are generally tractable not at the conceptual level, but only at the subconceptual level."[2] This treatment of the relation between common-sense concepts and microfeatures is exactly analogous to the standard connectionist treatment of rules; in both cases, macrolevel theory is said to provide a vocabulary adequate for formulating generalizations that roughly approximate the facts about behavioral regularities. But the constructs of the macrotheory do *not* correspond to the causal mechanisms that generate these regularities. If you want a theory of these mechanisms, you need to replace talk about rules and concepts with talk about nodes, connections, microfeatures, vectors, and the like.

Now, it is among the major misfortunes of the connectionist literature that the issue about whether common-sense concepts should be represented by sets of microfeatures has gotten thoroughly mixed up with the issue about combinatorial structure in mental representations. The crux of the mixup is the fact that sets of microfeatures can overlap, so that, for example, if a microfeature corresponding to '+has-a-han-dle' is part of the array of nodes over which the common-sense concept CUP is distributed, then you might think of the theory as representing '+has-a-handle' as a *constituent* of the concept CUP; from which you might conclude that connectionists have a notion of constituency after all—contrary to the claim that connectionism is not a language-of-thought architecture. (See Smolensky 1988).

A moment's consideration will make it clear, however, that even on the assumption that concepts are distributed over microfeatures, '+has-a-handle' is not a constituent of CUP in anything like the sense that 'Mary' (the word) is a constituent of (the sentence) 'John loves Mary'. In the former case, "constituency" is being (mis)used to refer to a semantic relation between predicates; roughly, the idea is that mac-rolevel predicates like CUP are defined by sets of microfeatures like 'has-a-handle', so that it's some sort of semantic truth that CUP applies to a subset of what 'has-a-handle' applies to. Notice that while the extensions of these predicates are in a set/subset relation, the predi-cates themselves are not in any sort of part-to-whole relation. The expression 'has-a-handle' isn't *part of* the expression CUP any more than the English phrase 'is an unmarried man' is part of the English phrase 'is a bachelor'.

So far as we know, there are no worked-out attempts in the connec-tionist literature to deal with the syntactic and semantical issues raised by relations of real constituency. There is, however, a proposal that comes up from time to time: namely, that what are traditionally treated as complex symbols should actually be viewed as just sets of units, with the role relations that traditionally get coded by constituent structure represented by units belonging to these sets. So, for example, the mental representation corresponding to the belief that John loves Mary might be the feature vector ⟨+*John-subject;* +*loves;* +*Mary-object*⟩. Here 'John-subject' 'Mary-object' and the like, are the labels of units; that is, they are primitive (or: micro-) features, whose status is analo-gous to 'has-a-handle'. In particular, they have no internal syntactic or semantic structure, and there is no relation (except the orthographic one) between the feature 'Mary-object' that occurs in the set ⟨John-subject; loves; Mary-object'⟩ and the feature 'Mary-subject' that occurs in the set ⟨Mary-subject; loves; John-object⟩.

As we understand it, the proposal really has two parts. On the one hand, it is suggested that, although connectionist representations cannot exhibit real constituency, nevertheless the classical distinction between complex symbols and their constituents can be replaced by the distinction between feature sets and their subsets; and, on the other hand, it is suggested that role relations can be captured by features. We'll consider these ideas in turn.

(1) Instead of having sentences like "John loves Mary" in the representational system, you have feature sets like ⟨+*John-subject;* +*loves;* +*Mary-object*⟩. Since this set has ⟨+*John-subject*⟩, ⟨+*loves;* +*Mary-object*⟩, and so forth, as subsets, it may be supposed that the force of the constituency relation has been captured by employing the subset relation.

However, it's clear that this idea won't work since not all subsets of features correspond to genuine constituents. For example, among the subsets of ⟨+*John-subject;* +*loves;* +*Mary-object*⟩ are the sets ⟨+*John-subject;* +*Mary-object*⟩ and the set ⟨+*John-subject;* +*loves*⟩ which do not, of course, correspond to constituents of the complex symbol "John loves Mary".

(2) Instead of defining roles in terms of relations among constituents, as one does in classical architecture, introduce them as primitive features.

Consider a system in which the mental representation that is entertained when one believes that John loves Mary is the feature set ⟨+*John-subject;* +*loves;* +*Mary-object*⟩. What representation corresponds to the belief that John loves Mary and Bill hates Sally? Suppose, pursuant to the present proposal, that it's the set ⟨+*John-subject;* +*loves;* +*Mary-object;* +*Bill-subject;* +*hates;* +*Sally-object*⟩. We now have the problem of distinguishing that belief from the belief that John loves Sally and Bill hates Mary, and from the belief that John hates Mary and Bill loves Sally, and from the belief John hates Mary and Sally and Bill loves Mary, and so on, since these other beliefs will all correspond to precisely the same set of features. The problem is, of course, that nothing in the representation of Mary as +*Mary-object* specifies whether it's the loving or the hating that she is the object of; similarly, mutatis mutandis, with the representation of John as +*John-subject.*

It's important to see that this problem arises precisely because the theory is trying to use sets of atomic representations to do a job that you really need complex representations for. Thus, the question we're wanting to answer is: Given the total set of nodes active at a time, what distinguishes the subvectors that correspond to propositions from the subvectors that don't? This question has a straightforward answer if, contrary to the present proposal, complex representations are assumed. When representations express concepts that belong to the same proposition, they are not merely simultaneously active, but also *in construction with each other.* By contrast, representations that express concepts that don't belong to the same proposition may be simultaneously active; but they are ipso facto *not* in construction with each other. In short, you need *two* degrees of freedom to specify the thoughts that an intentional system is entertaining at a time: one parameter (active versus inactive) picks out the nodes that express concepts that the system has in mind; the other (in construction versus not) determines how the concepts that the system has in mind are distributed in the propositions that it entertains. For symbols to be "in construction" in this sense is just for them to be constituents of a single complex symbol. Representations that are in construction form parts of a geometrical whole, *where the geometrical relations are themselves semantically significant.* The representation that corresponds to the thought that John loves Fido is not a *set* of concepts but something like a *tree* of concepts, and it's the geometrical relations in this tree that mark (for example) the difference between the thought that John loves Fido and the thought that Fido loves John.

We've occasionally heard it suggested that you could solve the present problem consonant with the restriction against complex representations if you allow networks like this:

The intended interpretation is that the thought that Fido bites corresponds to the simultaneous activation of these nodes; that is, to the vector ⟨+FIDO, +SUBJECT-OF, +BITES⟩—with similar though longer vectors for more complex role relations.

But, on second thought, this proposal merely begs the question that it set out to solve. For, if there's a problem about what justifies assigning the proposition *John loves Fido* as the content of the set ⟨JOHN, LOVES, FIDO⟩, there is surely the same problem about what justifies assigning the proposition *Fido is the subject of bites* to the set ⟨FIDO, SUBJECT-OF, BITES⟩. If this is not immediately clear, consider the case where the simultaneously active nodes are ⟨FIDO,

SUBJECT-OF, BITES, JOHN⟩. Is it the propositional content that Fido bites or that John does?

There are, to reiterate, two questions that you need to answer to specify the content of a mental state: "Which concepts are 'active'?" and "Which of the active concepts are in construction with which others?" Identifying mental states with sets of active nodes provides resources to answer the first of these questions but not the second. That's why the version of network theory that acknowledges sets of atomic representations but no complex representations fails, in indefinitely many cases, to distinguish mental states that are in fact distinct.

But we are *not* claiming that you *can't* reconcile a connectionist architecture with a combinatorial syntax and semantics for mental representations. On the contrary, of course you can. All that's required is that you use your network to implement a Turing machine, and specify a combinatorial structure for its computational language. What it appears that you can't do, however, is have both a combinatorial representational system and a connectionist architecture *at the cognitive level.*

2.2 Structure-sensitive operations

Classicists and connectionists both offer accounts of mental processes, but their theories differ sharply. In particular, the classical theory relies heavily on the notion of the logico/syntactic form of mental representations to define the ranges and domains of mental operations. This notion is, however, unavailable to orthodox connectionists since it presupposes that there are nonatomic mental representations.

The classical treatment of mental processes rests on *two ideas,* each of which corresponds to an aspect of the classical theory of computation. Together they explain why the classical view postulates at least three distinct levels of organization in computational systems: not just a physical level and a semantic (or "knowledge") level, but a syntactic level as well.

The first idea is that it is possible to construct languages in which certain features of the syntactic structures of formulas correspond systematically to certain of their semantic features. Intuitively, the idea is that in such languages the syntax of a formula encodes its meaning—most especially, those aspects of its meaning that determine its role in inference. All the artificial languages that are used for logic have this property, and English has it more or less. Classicists believe that it is a crucial property of the language of thought.

A simple example of how a language can use syntactic structure to encode inferential roles and relations among meanings may help to illustrate this point. Thus, consider the relation between the following two sentences:

(1) John went to the store and Mary went to the store.

(2) Mary went to the store.

On the one hand, from the semantic point of view, (1) entails (2) (so, of course, inferences from (1) to (2) are truth-preserving). On the other hand, from the syntactic point of view, (2) is a constituent of (1). These two facts can be brought into phase by exploiting the principle that sentences with the *syntactic* structure '(S1 and S2)$_S$' entail their sentential constituents. Notice that this principle connects the syntax of these sentences with their inferential roles. Notice too that the trick relies on facts about the grammar of English; it wouldn't work in a language where the formula that expresses the conjunctive content *John went to the store and Mary went to the store* is *syntactically* atomic.

The second main idea underlying the classical treatment of mental processes is that it is possible to devise machines whose function is the transformation of symbols, and whose operations are sensitive to the syntactical structure of the symbols they operate on. This is the classical conception of a computer; it's what the various architectures that derive from Turing and Von Neumann machines all have in common.

Perhaps it's obvious how the two "main ideas" fit together. If, in principle, syntactic relations can be made to parallel semantic relations, and if, in principle, you can have a mechanism whose operations on formulas are sensitive to their syntax, then it may be possible to construct a *syntactically* driven machine whose state transitions satisfy *semantical* criteria of coherence. Such a machine would be just what's required for a mechanical model of the semantical coherence of thought; correspondingly, the idea that the brain *is* such a machine is the foundational hypothesis of classical cognitive science.

So much for the classical story about mental processes. The connectionist story must, of course, be quite different. Since connectionists eschew postulating mental representations with combinatorial syntactic/semantic structure, they are precluded from postulating mental processes that operate on mental representations in a way that is sensitive to their structure. The sorts of operations that connectionist models do have are of two sorts, depending on whether the process under examination is learning or reasoning.

2.2.1 Learning

If a connectionist model is intended to learn, there will be processes that determine the weights of the connections among its units as a function of the character of its training. Typically in a connectionist machine (such as a Boltzmann Machine) the weights among connections are adjusted until the system's behavior comes to model the statistical properties of its inputs. In the limit, the stochastic relations among machine states recapitulate the stochastic relations among the environmental events that they represent.

This should bring to mind the old associationist principle that the strength of association between "ideas" is a function of the frequency with which they are paired "in experience" and the learning-theoretic idea that the strength of a stimulus-response connection is a function of the frequency with which the response is rewarded in the presence of the stimulus. But though connectionists, like other associationists, are committed to learning processes that model statistical properties of inputs and outputs, the simple mechanisms based on co-occurrence statistics that were the hallmarks of old-fashioned associationism have been augmented in connectionist models by a number of technical devices. (Hence the 'new' in 'new connectionism'). For example, some of the earlier limitations of associative mechanisms are overcome by allowing the network to contain "hidden" units (or aggregates) that are not directly connected to the environment, and whose purpose is, in effect, to detect statistical patterns in the activity of the "visible" units including, perhaps, patterns that are more abstract or more "global" than the ones that could be detected by old-fashioned perceptrons.

In short, sophisticated versions of the associative principles for weight setting are on offer in the connectionist literature. The point of present concern, however, is what all versions of these principles have in common with one another and with older kinds of associationism: namely, that these processes are all *frequency*-sensitive. To return to the example discussed above: if a connectionist learning machine converges on a state where it is prepared to infer **A** from **A & B** (that is, to a state in which, when the 'A & B' node is excited, it tends to settle into a state in which the 'A' node is excited), the convergence will typically be caused by statistical properties of the machine's training experience (for instance, by correlations between firings of the 'A & B' node and firings of the 'A' node, or by correlations of the firings of both with some feedback signal). Like traditional associationism, connectionism treats learning as basically a sort of statistical modeling.

2.2.2 Reasoning

Association operates to alter the structure of a network *diachronically* as a function of its training. Connectionist models also contain a variety of types of 'relaxation' processes which determine the *synchronic* behavior of a network; specifically, they determine what output the device provides for a given pattern of inputs. In this respect, one can think of a connectionist model as a species of analog machine constructed to realize a certain function. The inputs to the function are (i) a specification of the connectedness of the machine (of which nodes are connected to which); (ii) a specification of the weights along the connections; (iii) a specification of the values of a variety of idiosyncratic parameters of the nodes (such as intrinsic thresholds, time since last firing, and the like); (iv) a specification of a pattern of excitation over the input nodes. The output of the function is a specification of a pattern of excitation over the output nodes; intuitively, the machine chooses the output pattern that is most highly associated to its input.

Much of the mathematical sophistication of connectionist theorizing has been devoted to devising analog solutions to this problem of finding a "most highly associated" output corresponding to an arbitrary input; but, once again, the details needn't concern us. What is important, for our purposes, is another property that connectionist theories share with other forms of associationism. In traditional associationism, the probability that one idea will elicit another is sensitive to the strength of the association between them (including "mediating" associations, if any). And the strength of this association is in turn sensitive to the extent to which the ideas have previously been correlated. Associative strength was not, however, presumed to be sensitive to features of the content or the structure of representations per se. Similarly, in connectionist models, the selection of an output corresponding to a given input is a function of properties of the paths that connect them (including the weights, the states of intermediate units, and so on). And the weights, in turn, are a function of the statistical properties of events in the environment (or, perhaps, of relations between patterns of events in the environment and implicit "predictions" made by the network). But the syntactic/semantic structure of the representation of an input is *not* presumed to be a factor in determining the selection of a corresponding output since, as we have seen, syntactic/semantic structure is not defined for the sorts of representations that connectionist models acknowledge.

To summarize: classical and connectionist theories disagree about the nature of mental representation; for the former, but not for the latter, mental representations characteristically exhibit a combinatorial constituent structure and a combinatorial semantics. Classical and connectionist theories also disagree about the nature of mental processes; for the former, but not for the latter, mental processes are characteristically sensitive to the combinatorial structure of the representations on which they operate.

We take it that these two issues define the present dispute about the nature of cognitive architecture. We now propose to argue that the connectionists are on the wrong side of both.

3 The need for symbol systems: productivity, systematicity, and inferential coherence

Classical psychological theories appeal to the constituent structure of mental representations to explain three closely related features of cognition: its productivity, its systematicity, and its inferential coherence. The traditional argument has been that these features of cognition are, on the one hand, pervasive and, on the other hand, explicable only on the assumption that mental representations have internal structure. This argument—familiar in more or less explicit versions for the last thirty years or so—is still intact, so far as we can tell. It appears to offer something close to a demonstration that an empirically adequate cognitive theory must recognize not just causal relations among representational states but also relations of syntactic and semantic constituency; hence that the mind cannot be, in its general structure, a connectionist network.

3.1 Productivity of thought

There is a classical productivity argument for the existence of combinatorial structure in any rich representational system (including natural languages and the language of thought). The representational capacities of such a system are, by assumption, unbounded under appropriate idealization; in particular, there are indefinitely many propositions which the system can encode. However, this unbounded expressive power must presumably be achieved by finite means. The way to do this is to treat the system of representations as consisting of expressions belonging to a generated set. More precisely, the correspondence between a representation and the proposition it expresses is, in arbitrarily many cases, built up recursively out of correspondences between parts of the expression and parts of the proposition. But, of course, this strategy can operate only when an unbounded number of the expressions are nonatomic. So linguistic (and mental) representations must constitute *symbol systems*. So the mind cannot be a PDP.

Very often, when people reject this sort of reasoning, it is because they doubt that human cognitive capacities are correctly viewed as productive. In the long run, there can be no a priori arguments for (or against) idealizing to productive capacities; whether you accept the idealization depends on whether you believe that the inference from finite performance to finite capacity is justified, or whether you think that finite performance is typically a result of the interaction of an unbounded competence with resource constraints.

In the meantime, however, we propose to view the status of productivity arguments for classical architectures as moot; we're about to present a different sort of argument for the claim that mental representations need an articulated internal structure. It is closely related to the productivity argument, but it doesn't require the idealization to unbounded competence. Its assumptions should thus be acceptable even to theorists who—like connectionists—hold that the finitistic character of cognitive capacities is intrinsic to their architecture.

3.2 Systematicity of cognitive representation

The form of the argument is this. Whether or not cognitive capacities are really *productive*, it seems indubitable that they are what we shall call *systematic*. And we'll see that the systematicity of cognition provides as good a reason for postulating combinatorial structure in mental representation as the productivity of cognition does. You get, in effect, the same conclusion, but from a weaker premise.

The easiest way to understand what the systematicity of cognitive capacities amounts to is to focus on the systematicity of language comprehension and production. In fact, the systematicity argument for combinatorial structure in *thought* exactly recapitulates the traditional structuralist argument for constituent structure in *sentences*. But we pause to remark upon a point that we'll reemphasize later: linguistic capacity is a paradigm of systematic cognition, but it's wildly unlikely that it's the only example. On the contrary, there's every reason to believe that systematicity is a thoroughly pervasive feature of human and infrahuman mentation.

What we mean when we say that linguistic capacities are *systematic* is that the ability to produce/understand some sentences is *intrinsically* connected to the ability to produce/understand certain others. You can see the force of this if you compare learning languages the way we really do learn them, with learning a language by memorizing an enormous phrase book. The point isn't that phrase books are finite and can therefore exhaustively specify only *non*productive languages; that's true, but we've agreed not to rely on productivity arguments for our present purposes. Our point is rather that you can learn *any part of a phrase book without learning the rest.* Hence, on the phrase book model, it would be perfectly possible to learn that uttering the form of words "Granny's cat is on Uncle Arthur's mat" is the way to say (in English) that Granny's cat is on Uncle Arthur's mat, and yet have no idea at all how to say that it's raining (or, for that matter, how to say that Uncle Arthur's cat is on Granny's mat.) Perhaps it's self-evident that the phrase-book story must be wrong about language acquisition because a speaker's knowledge of his native language is never like that. You don't, for example, find native speakers who know how to say in English that John loves the girl but don't know how to say in English that the girl loves John.

Notice, in passing, that systematicity is a property of the mastery of the syntax of a language, not of its lexicon. The phrase-book model really does fit what it's like to learn the *vocabulary* of English, since when you learn English vocabulary you acquire a lot of basically *independent* capacities. So you might perfectly well learn that using the expression 'cat' is the way to refer to cats and yet have no idea that using the expression 'deciduous conifer' is the way to refer to deciduous conifers. Systematicity, like productivity, is the sort of property of cognitive capacities that you're likely to miss if you concentrate on the psychology of learning and searching lists.

There is, as we remarked, a straightforward (and quite traditional) argument from the systematicity of language capacity to the conclusion that sentences must have syntactic and semantic structure. If you assume that sentences are constructed out of words and phrases, and that many different sequences of words can be phrases of the same type, the very fact that one formula is a sentence of the language will often imply that other formulas must be too. In effect, systematicity follows from the postulation of constituent structure.

Suppose, for example, that it's a fact about English that formulas with the constituent analysis 'NP Vt NP' are well formed; and suppose that 'John' and 'the girl' are NPs and 'loves' is a Vt. It follows from these assumptions that 'John loves the girl', 'John loves John', 'the girl loves the girl', and 'the girl loves John' must *all* be sentences. It follows too that anybody who has mastered the grammar of English must have linguistic capacities that are systematic in respect of these sentences; he *can't but* assume that all of them are sentences if he assumes that any of them are. Compare the situation on the view that the sentences of English are all atomic. There is, then, no structural analogy between 'John loves the girl' and 'the girl loves John' and hence no reason why understanding one sentence should imply understanding the other—no more than understanding 'rabbit' implies understanding 'tree'.

On the view that the sentences are atomic, the systematicity of linguistic capacities is a mystery; on the view that they have constituent structure, the systematicity of linguistic capacities is what you would predict. So we should prefer the latter view to the former.

We can now, finally, come to the point. The argument from the systematicity of linguistic capacities to constituent structure in *sentences* is quite clear. *But thought is systematic too,* so there is a precisely parallel argument from the systematicity of thought to syntactic and semantic structure in *mental* representations.

What does it mean to say that thought is systematic? Well, just as you don't find people who can understand the sentence 'John loves the girl' but not the sentence 'the girl loves John', so too you don't find people who can *think the thought* that John loves the girl but can't think the thought that the girl loves John. Indeed, in the case of verbal organisms the systematicity of thought *follows from* the systematicity of language if you assume—as most psychologists do—that understanding a sentence involves entertaining the thought that it expresses; on that assumption, nobody *could* understand both of the sentences about John and the girl unless he were able to think both of the thoughts about John and the girl.

But now, if the ability to think that John loves the girl is intrinsically connected to the ability to think that the girl loves John, that fact will somehow have to be explained. For a representationalist (which, as we have seen, connectionists are), the explanation is obvious. Entertaining thoughts requires being in representational states (that is, it requires tokening mental representations). And, just as the systematicity of language shows that there must be structural relations between the sentence 'John loves the girl' and the sentence 'the girl loves John,' so the systematicity of thought shows that there must be structural relations between the mental representation that corresponds to the thought that John loves the girl and the mental representation that corresponds to the thought that the girl loves John;[3] namely, the two mental representations, like the two sentences, *must be made of the same parts.* But if this explanation is right (and there don't seem to be any others on offer), then mental representations have internal structure and there is a language of thought. So the architecture of the mind is not a connectionist network.

To summarize the discussion so far: productivity arguments infer the internal structure of mental representations from the presumed fact that nobody has a *finite* intellectual competence. By contrast, systematicity arguments infer the internal structure of mental representations from the patent fact that nobody has a *punctate* intellectual competence. Just as you don't find linguistic capacities that consist of the ability to understand sixty-seven unrelated sentences, so too you don't find cognitive capacities that consist of the ability to think seventy-four unrelated thoughts. Our claim is that this isn't, in either case, an accident. A linguistic theory that allowed for the possibility of punctate languages would have gone not *just* wrong, but *very profoundly* wrong. And similarly for a cognitive theory that allowed for the possibility of punctate minds.

3.4 The systematicity of inference

In section 2, we saw that, according to classical theories, the syntax of mental representations mediates between their semantic properties and their causal roles in mental processes. Take a simple case: it's a "logical" principle that conjunctions entail their constituents (so the argument from $P \& Q$ to P and to Q is valid). Correspondingly, it's a psychological law that thoughts that $P \& Q$ tend to cause thoughts that P and thoughts that Q, all else being equal. Classical theory exploits the constituent structure of mental representations to account for both these facts, the first by assuming that the combinatorial semantics of mental representations is sensitive to their syntax and the second by assuming that mental processes apply to mental representations in virtue of their constituent structure.

A consequence of these assumptions is that classical theories are committed to the following striking prediction: inferences that are of similar logical type ought, pretty generally,[4] to elicit correspondingly similar cognitive capacities. You shouldn't, for example, find a kind of mental life in which you get inferences from $P \& Q \& R$ to P but you

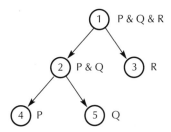

Figure 12.3 A possible connectionist network which draws inferences
        from *P* & *Q* & *R* to *P* and also draws inferences from *P* & *Q* to *P*.

don't get inferences from *P* & *Q* to *P*. This is because, according to the classical account, this logically homogeneous class of inferences is carried out by a correspondingly homogeneous class of psychological mechanisms. The premises of both inferences are expressed by mental representations that satisfy the same syntactic analysis (namely: S_1 & S_2 & S_3 & ... S_n); and the process of drawing the inference corresponds, in both cases, to the same formal operation of detaching the constituent that expresses the conclusion.

A connectionist can certainly model a mental life in which, if you can reason from *P* & *Q* & *R* to *P*, then you can also reason from *P* & *Q* to *P*. For example, the network in figure 12.3 would do. But notice that *a connectionist can equally-well model a mental life in which you get one of these inferences and not the other.* In the present case, since there is no structural relation between the *P* & *Q* & *R* node and the *P* & *Q* node (remember, all nodes are atomic—don't be misled by the node *labels*) there's no reason why a mind that contains the first should also contain the second, or vice versa. [Thus, figure 12.3 does not contain a *Q* & *R* node. (*Ed.*)] So, the connectionist architecture tolerates gaps in cognitive capacities; it has no mechanism to enforce the requirement that logically homogeneous inferences should be executed by correspondingly homogeneous computational processes.

But, we claim, you don't find cognitive capacities that have these sorts of gaps. You don't, for example, get minds that are prepared to infer *John went to the store* from *John and Mary and Susan and Sally went to the store* and from *John and Mary went to the store* but not from *John and Mary and Susan went to the store*. Given a notion of logical syntax—the very notion that the classical theory of mentation requires to get its account of mental processes off the ground—it is a *truism* that you don't get such minds. Lacking a notion of logical syntax, it is a *mystery* that you don't.

3.5 Summary

What's deeply wrong with connectionist architecture is this. Because it acknowledges neither syntactic nor semantic structure in mental representations, it perforce treats them not as a generated set but as a list. But lists, qua lists, have no structure; any collection of items is a possible list. And, correspondingly, on connectionist principles, any collection of (causally connected) representational states is a possible mind. So, as far as connectionist architecture is concerned, there is nothing to prevent minds that are arbitrarily unsystematic. But that result is *preposterous*. Cognitive capacities come in structurally related clusters; their systematicity is pervasive. All the evidence suggests that *punctate minds can't happen*. This argument seemed conclusive against the connectionism of Hebb, Osgood and Hull twenty or thirty years ago. So far as we can tell, nothing of any importance has happened to change the situation in the meantime.[5]

A final comment to round off this part of the discussion. It's possible to imagine a connectionist being prepared to admit that, while systematicity doesn't *follow from*—and hence is not explained by—connectionist architecture, it is nonetheless *compatible* with that architecture. It is, after all, perfectly possible to follow a policy of building networks that have $a\mathbf{R}b$ nodes only if they have $b\mathbf{R}a$ nodes, and so on. There is therefore nothing to stop a connectionist from stipulating—as an independent postulate of his theory of mind—that all biologically instantiated networks are, de facto, systematic.

But this misses a crucial point. It's not enough just to stipulate systematicity; one is also required to specify a mechanism that is able to enforce the stipulation. To put it another way, it's not enough for a connectionist to agree that all minds are systematic; he must also explain *how nature contrives to produce only systematic minds*. Presumably there would have to be some sort of mechanism, over and above the ones that connectionism per se posits, the functioning of which insures the systematicity of biologically instantiated networks; a mechanism such that, in virtue of its operation, every network that has an $a\mathbf{R}b$ node also has a $b\mathbf{R}a$ node, and so forth. There are, however, no proposals for such a mechanism. Or, rather, there is just one. The only mechanism that is known to be able to produce pervasive systematicity is classical architecture. And, as we have seen, classical architecture is not compatible with connectionism since it requires internally structured representations.

4 The allure of connectionism

The current popularity of the connectionist approach among psychologists and philosophers is puzzling in view of the sorts of problems raised above—problems which were largely responsible for the development of a syntax-based (proof-theoretic) notion of computation and a Turing-style, symbol-processing notion of cognitive architecture in the first place. There are, however, a number of apparently plausible arguments, repeatedly encountered in the literature, that stress certain limitations of conventional computers as models of brains. These may be seen as favoring the connectionist alternative. Below we will sketch a number of these before discussing the general problems which they appear to raise.

- RAPIDITY OF COGNITIVE PROCESSES RELATIVE TO NEURAL SPEEDS: THE "HUNDRED-STEP" CONSTRAINT. It has been observed (Feldman and Ballard 1982) that neurons take tens of milliseconds to fire. Consequently, in the time it takes people to carry out many of the tasks at which they are fluent (like recognizing a word or a picture, either of which may require considerably less than a second) a *serial* neurally-instantiated program would only be able to carry out about 100 instructions. Yet such tasks might typically require many thousands—or even millions—of instructions in present-day computers (if they can be done at all). Thus, it is argued, the brain must operate quite differently from computers. In fact, the argument goes, the brain must be organized in a highly parallel manner ("massively parallel" is the preferred term of art).

- DIFFICULTY OF ACHIEVING LARGE-CAPACITY PATTERN RECOGNITION AND CONTENT-BASED RETRIEVAL IN CONVENTIONAL ARCHITECTURES. Closely related to the issues about time constraints is the fact that humans can store and make use of an enormous amount of information—apparently without effort (Fahlman and Hinton 1987). One particularly dramatic skill that people exhibit is the ability to recognize patterns from among tens or even hundreds of thousands of alternatives (for instance, word or face recognition). In fact, there is reason to believe that many expert skills may be based on large, fast recognition memories (see Simon and Chase 1973). If one had to search through one's memory serially, the way conventional computers do, the complexity would overwhelm any machine. Thus, the knowledge that people have must be stored and retrieved differently from the way conventional computers do it.

- LACK OF PROGRESS IN DEALING WITH PROCESSES THAT ARE NONVER-
  BAL OR INTUITIVE. Most of our fluent cognitive skills do not consist in
  accessing verbal knowledge or carrying out deliberate conscious reasoning (Fahlman and Hinton 1987; Smolensky 1988). We appear to
  know many things that we would have great difficulty in describing
  verbally, such as how to ride a bicycle, what our close friends look like,
  and how to recall the name of the President. Such knowledge, it is
  argued, must not be stored in linguistic form, but in some other
  "implicit" form. The fact that conventional computers typically operate in a "linguistic mode", inasmuch as they process information by
  operating on syntactically structured expressions, may explain why
  there has been relatively little success in modeling implicit knowledge.

- ACUTE SENSITIVITY OF CONVENTIONAL ARCHITECTURES TO DAMAGE
  AND NOISE. Unlike digital circuits, brain circuits must tolerate noise
  arising from spontaneous neural activity. Moreover, they must tolerate
  a moderate degree of damage without failing completely. With a few
  notable exceptions, if a part of the brain is damaged, the degradation
  in performance is usually not catastrophic but varies more or less gradually with the extent of the damage. This is especially true of memory.
  Damage to the temporal cortex (usually thought to house memory
  traces) does not result in selective loss of particular facts and memories. This and similar facts about brain damaged patients suggest that
  human memory representations, and perhaps many other cognitive
  skills as well, are *distributed* spatially, rather than being neurally localized. This appears to contrast with conventional computers, where
  hierarchical-style control keeps the crucial decisions highly localized
  and where memory storage consists of an array of location-addressable
  registers.

- CONVENTIONAL RULE-BASED SYSTEMS DEPICT COGNITION AS "ALL-
  OR-NONE". But cognitive skills appear to be characterized by various
  kinds of continuities. For example:

  - CONTINUOUS VARIATION IN DEGREE OF APPLICABILITY OF DIF-
    FERENT PRINCIPLES, OR IN THE DEGREE OF RELEVANCE OF
    DIFFERENT CONSTRAINTS, "RULES", OR PROCEDURES. There
    are frequent cases (especially in perception and memory
    retrieval), in which it appears that a variety of different con-
    straints are brought to bear on a problem simultaneously and
    the outcome is a combined effect of all the different factors (see,
    for example, the informal discussion by McClelland, Rumel-
    hart and Hinton 1986, pp. 3-9). That's why "constraint propa-
    gation" techniques are receiving a great deal of attention in
    artificial intelligence (see Mackworth 1987).

- **NONDETERMINISM OF HUMAN BEHAVIOR.** Cognitive processes are never rigidly determined or precisely replicable. Rather, they appear to have a significant random or stochastic component. Perhaps that's because there is randomness at a microscopic level, caused by irrelevant biochemical or electrical activity, or perhaps even by quantum mechanical events. To model this activity by rigid deterministic rules can only lead to poor predictions because it ignores the fundamentally stochastic nature of the underlying mechanisms. Moreover, deterministic, all-or-none models will be unable to account for the gradual aspect of learning and skill acquisition.

- **FAILURE TO DISPLAY GRACEFUL DEGRADATION.** When humans are unable to do a task perfectly, they nonetheless do something reasonable. If the particular task does not fit exactly into some known pattern, or if it is only partly understood, a person will not give up or produce nonsensical behavior. By contrast, if a classical rule-based computer program fails to recognize the task, or fails to match a pattern to its stored representations or rules, it usually will be unable to do anything at all. This suggests that, in order to display graceful degradation, we must be able to represent prototypes, match patterns, recognize problems, and so on, in various *degrees*.

- **CONVENTIONAL MODELS ARE DICTATED BY CURRENT TECHNICAL FEATURES OF COMPUTERS AND TAKE LITTLE OR NO ACCOUNT OF THE FACTS OF NEUROSCIENCE.** Classical symbol processing systems provide no indication of how the kinds of processes that they postulate could be realized by a brain. The fact that this gap between high-level systems and brain architecture is so large might be an indication that these models are on the wrong track. Whereas the architecture of the mind has evolved under the pressures of natural selection, some of the classical assumptions about the mind may derive from features that computers have only because they are explicitly designed for the convenience of programmers. Perhaps this includes even the assumption that the description of mental processes at the cognitive level can be divorced from the description of their physical realization. At a minimum, by building our models to take account of what is known about neural structures we may reduce the risk of being misled by metaphors based on contemporary computer architectures.

4.1 Replies: why the usual reasons given for preferring a connectionist architecture are invalid

It seems to us that, as arguments against classical cognitive architecture, all these points suffer from one or other of the following two defects.

(1) The objections depend on properties that are not in fact intrinsic to classical architectures, since there can be perfectly natural classical models that don't exhibit the objectionable features. (We believe this to be true, for example, of the arguments that classical rules are explicit and classical operations are "all or none".)

(2) The objections are true of classical architectures insofar as they are implemented on current computers, but need not be true of such architectures when differently (for instance, neurally) implemented. They are, in other words, directed at the implementation level rather than the cognitive level, as these were distinguished in our earlier discussion. (We believe that this is true, for example, of the arguments about speed and resistance to damage and noise.)

In the remainder of this section we will expand on these two points and relate them to some of the arguments presented above. Following this analysis, we will present what we believe may be the most tenable view of connectionism—namely that it is a theory of how (classical) cognitive systems might be implemented, either in real brains or in some "abstract neurology".

4.1.1 Parallel computation and the issue of speed

Consider the argument that cognitive processes must involve large-scale parallel computation. In the form that it takes in typical connectionist discussions, this issue is irrelevant to the adequacy of classical *cognitive* architecture. The "hundred-step constraint", for example, is clearly directed at the implementation level. All it rules out is the (absurd) hypothesis that cognitive architectures are implemented in the brain in the same way as they are implemented on electronic computers.

The absolute speed of a process is a property *par excellence* of its implementation. (By contrast, the *relative* speed with which a system responds to different inputs is diagnostic of distinct processes; but this has always been a prime empirical basis for deciding among alternative algorithms in information-processing psychology.) Thus, the fact that individual neurons require tens of milliseconds to fire can have no bearing on the predicted speed at which an algorithm will run *unless there is at least a partial, independently motivated, theory of how the operations of the functional architecture are implemented in neurons.* Since, in the case of the brain, it is not even certain that the firing of neurons is invariably the relevant implementation property (at least for higher-level cognitive processes like learning and memory) the hundred-step "constraint" excludes nothing.

Finally, absolute constraints on the number of serial steps that a mental process can require, or on the time that can be required to execute them, provide weak arguments against classical architecture because classical architecture in no way excludes parallel execution of multiple symbolic processes. Indeed, it seems extremely likely that many classical symbolic processes are going on in parallel in cognition, and that these processes interact with one another (for instance, they may be involved in some sort of symbolic constraint propagation). Operating on symbols can even involve "massively parallel" organizations; that might indeed imply new architectures, but they are all *classical* in our sense, since they all share the classical conception of computation as symbol processing. (For examples of serious and interesting proposals on organizing classical processors into large parallel networks, see Hewett's (1977) "Actor" system, Hillis's (1985) "Connection Machine", as well as various recent commercial multi-processor machines.) The point here is that an argument for a network of parallel computers is not in and of itself either an argument against a classical architecture or an argument for a connectionist architecture.

4.1.2 Resistance to noise and physical damage (and the argument for distributed representation)

Some of the other advantages claimed for connectionist architectures over classical ones are just as clearly aimed at the implementation level. For example, the "resistance to physical damage" criterion is so obviously a matter of implementation that it should hardly arise in discussions of cognitive-level theories.

It is true that a certain kind of damage resistance appears to be incompatible with localization, and it is also true that representations in PDPs are distributed over groups of units (at least when "coarse coding" is used). But distribution over units achieves damage resistance only if it entails that representations are also *neurally* distributed.

However, neural distribution of representations is just as compatible with classical architectures as it is with connectionist networks. In the classical case, all you need are memory registers that distribute their contents over physical space. You can get that with fancy storage systems like optical ones, or chemical ones, or even with registers made of connectionist nets.

The physical requirements of a classical symbol-processing system are easily misunderstood. For example, conventional architecture requires that there be distinct symbolic expressions for each state of affairs that it can represent. Since such expressions often have a structure consisting of concatenated parts, the adjacency relation must be instantiated by *some* physical relation when the architecture is implemented. However, since the relation to be physically realized is *functional* adjacency, there is no necessity that physical instantiations of adjacent symbols be *spatially* adjacent. Similarly, although complex expressions are made out of atomic elements, and the distinction between atomic and complex symbols must somehow be physically instantiated, there is no necessity that a token of an atomic symbol be assigned a smaller region in space than a token of a complex symbol— even a token of a complex symbol of which it is a constituent. In classical architectures, as in connectionist networks, functional elements can be physically distributed or localized to any extent whatever.

4.1.3 "Soft" constraints, continuous magnitudes, and stochastic mechanisms

The notion that "soft" constraints, which can vary continuously (as degree of activation does), are incompatible with classical rule-based symbolic systems is another example of the failure to keep the psychological (or symbol-processing) and the implementation levels separate. One can have a classical rule system in which the decision concerning which rule will fire resides in the functional architecture and depends on continuously varying magnitudes. Indeed, this is typically how it is done in practical "expert systems" which, for example, use a Bayesian mechanism in their production-system rule interpreter. The soft or stochastic nature of rule-based processes arises from the interaction of deterministic rules with real-valued properties of the implementation, or with noisy inputs or noisy information transmission.

It should also be noted that rule applications need not issue in "all-or-none" behaviors, since several rules may be activated at once and can have interactive effects on the outcome. Or, alternatively, each of the activated rules can generate independent parallel effects, which might get sorted out later—depending, say, on which of the parallel streams reaches a goal first. An important, though sometimes neglected, point about such aggregate properties of overt behavior as continuity, "fuzziness", randomness, and the like, is that they need not arise from underlying mechanisms that are themselves fuzzy, continuous or random. It is not only possible in principle, but often quite reasonable in practice, to assume that apparently variable or nondeterministic behavior arises from the interaction of multiple deterministic sources.

A similar point can be made about the issue of "graceful degradation". Classical architecture does not require that when the conditions for applying the available rules aren't precisely met, the process should simply fail to do anything at all. As noted above, rules could be activated in some measure depending upon how close their conditions are to holding. Exactly what happens in these cases may depend on how the rule-system is implemented. On the other hand, it could be that the failure to display "graceful degradation" really is an intrinsic limit of the current class of models or even of current approaches to designing intelligent systems. It seems clear that the psychological models now available are inadequate over a broad spectrum of measures, so their problems with graceful degradation may be a special case of their general unintelligence. They may simply not be smart enough to know what to do when a limited stock of methods fails to apply. But this needn't be a principled limitation of classical architectures.

4.1.4 Explicitness of rules

According to McClelland, Feldman, Adelson, Bower and McDermott (1986, p. 6),

> connectionist models are leading to a reconceptualization of key psychological issues, such as the nature of the representation of knowledge ... One traditional approach to such issues treats knowledge as a body of rules that are consulted by processing mechanisms in the course of processing; in connectionist models, such knowledge is represented, often in widely distributed form, in the connections among the processing units.

As we remarked in the Introduction, we think that the claim that most psychological processes are rule-implicit, and the corresponding claim that divergent and compliant behaviors result from the same cognitive mechanisms, are both interesting and tendentious. We regard these matters as entirely empirical and, in many cases, open. In any case, however, one should not confuse the rule-implicit/rule-explicit distinction with the distinction between classical and connectionist architecture.

This confusion is just ubiquitous in the connectionist literature. It is universally assumed by connectionists that classical models are committed to claiming that regular behaviors must arise from explicitly encoded rules. But this is simply untrue. Not only is there no reason why classical models are required to be rule-explicit but—as a matter of fact—arguments over which, *if any*, rules are explicitly mentally represented have raged for decades *within* the classicist camp. (See, for relatively recent examples, the discussion of the explicitness of grammatical rules in Stabler 1985, and replies; for a philosophical discussion, see Cummins 1983). The one thing that classical theorists do agree about is that it *can't* be that *all* behavioral regularities are determined by explicit rules; at least some of the causal determinants of compliant behavior *must* be *im*plicit. (The arguments for this parallel Lewis Carroll's observations in "What the Tortoise Said to Achilles"; see Carroll 1956). All other questions of the explicitness of rules are viewed by classicists as moot; and every shade of opinion on the issue can be found in the classicist camp.

The basic point is this: not all the functions of a classical computer can be encoded in the form of an explicit program—some of them must be wired in. In fact, the entire program can be hard-wired in cases where it does not need to modify or otherwise examine itself. In such cases, classical machines can be *rule implicit* with respect to their programs, and the mechanism of their state transitions is entirely subcomputational (that is, subsymbolic).

What *does* need to be explicit in a classical machine is not its program but the symbols that it writes on its tapes (or stores in its registers). These, however, correspond not to the machine's rules of state transition but to its data structures. Data structures are *the objects that the machine transforms, not the rules of transformation*. In the case of programs that parse natural language, for example, classical architecture requires the explicit representation of the structural descriptions of sentences, but is entirely neutral on the explicitness of grammars, contrary to what many connectionists believe.

So, then, you can't attack classical theories of cognitive architecture by showing that a cognitive process is rule-implicit; classical architecture *permits* rule-explicit processes but does *not* require them. However, you *can* attack connectionist architectures by showing that a cognitive process is rule-*ex*plicit since, by definition, connectionist architecture precludes the sorts of logico-syntactic capacities that are required to encode rules and the sorts of executive mechanisms that are required to apply them.

4.1.5 On "brain-style" modeling

The relation of connectionist models to neuroscience is open to many interpretations. On the one hand, people like Ballard (1986), and Sejnowski (1981), are explicitly attempting to build models based on properties of neurons and neural organizations, even though the neuronal units in question are idealized (some would say more than a little idealized; see, for example the commentaries following Ballard 1986). On the other hand, Smolensky (1988) views connectionist units as mathematical objects which can be given an interpretation in either neural or psychological terms. Most connectionists find themselves somewhere in between, frequently referring to their approach as "brain-style" theorizing.[6]

Understanding both psychological principles *and* the way that they are neurophysiologically implemented is much better (and, indeed, more empirically secure) than only understanding one or the other. That is not at issue. The question is whether there is anything to be gained by designing "brain-style" models that are uncommitted about how the models map onto brains.

Presumably the point of "brain style" modeling is that theories of cognitive processing should be influenced by the facts of biology (especially neuroscience). The biological facts that influence connectionist models appear to include the following: neuronal connections are important to the patterns of brain activity; the memory "engram" does not appear to be spatially local; to a first approximation, neurons appear to be threshold elements which sum the activity arriving at their dendrites; many of the neurons in the cortex have multidimensional "receptive fields" that are sensitive to a narrow range of values of a number of parameters; the tendency for activity at a synapse to cause a neuron to "fire" is modulated by the frequency and recency of past firings.

Let us suppose that these and similar claims are both true and relevant to the way the brain functions—an assumption that is by no means unproblematic. The question we might then ask is: What follows from such facts that is relevant to inferring the nature of the cognitive architecture? The unavoidable answer appears to be: very little. That's not an a priori claim. The degree of relationship between facts at different levels of organization of a system is an empirical matter. However, there is reason to be skeptical about whether the sorts of properties listed above are reflected in any more-or-less direct way in the structure of the system that carries out reasoning.

The point is that the structure of "higher levels" of a system are rarely isomorphic, or even similar, to the structure of "lower levels" of a system. No one expects the theory of protons to look very much like the theory of rocks and rivers, even though, to be sure, it is protons and the like that rocks and rivers are "implemented in". Lucretius got into trouble precisely by assuming that there must be a simple correspondence between the structure of macrolevel and microlevel theories. He thought, for example, that hooks and eyes hold the atoms together. He was wrong, as it turns out.

The moral seems to be that one should be deeply suspicious of the heroic sort of brain modeling that purports to address the problems of cognition. We sympathize with the craving for biologically respectable theories that many psychologists seem to feel. But, given a choice, truth is more important than respectability.

4.2 Concluding comments: connectionism as a theory of implementation

A recurring theme in the previous discussion is that many of the arguments for connectionism are best construed as claiming that cognitive architecture is *implemented* in a certain kind of network (of abstract "units"). Understood this way, these arguments are neutral on the question of what the cognitive architecture is. In these concluding remarks we'll briefly consider connectionism from this point of view.

Almost every student who enters a course on computational or information-processing models of cognition must be disabused of a very general misunderstanding concerning the role of the physical computer in such models. Students are almost always skeptical about "the computer as a model of cognition" on such grounds as that "computers don't forget or make mistakes", "computers function by exhaustive search", "computers are too logical and unmotivated", "computers can't learn by themselves, they can only do what they're told", or "computers are too fast (or too slow)", or "computers never get tired or bored", and so on. If we add to this list such relatively more

sophisticated complaints as that "computers don't exhibit graceful degradation" or "computers are too sensitive to physical damage" this list
will begin to look much like the arguments put forward by connectionists.

The answer to all these complaints has always been that the *implementation*, and all properties associated with the particular realization
of the algorithm that the theorist happens to use in a particular case, is
irrelevant to the psychological theory; only the algorithm and the representations on which it operates are intended as a psychological
hypothesis. Students are taught the notion of a "virtual machine" and
shown that *some* virtual machines *can* learn, forget, get bored, make
mistakes, and whatever else one likes, providing one has a theory of the
origins of each of the empirical phenomena in question.

Given this principled distinction between a model and its implementation, a theorist who is impressed by the virtues of connectionism
has the option of proposing PDPs as theories of implementation. But
then, far from providing a revolutionary new basis for cognitive science, these models are in principle neutral about the nature of cognitive processes. In fact, they might be viewed as advancing the goals of
classical information-processing psychology by attempting to explain
how the brain (or perhaps some idealized brain-like network) might
realize the types of processes that conventional cognitive science has
hypothesized.

Connectionists do sometimes explicitly take their models to be theories of implementation. Ballard (1986) even refers to connectionism
as "the implementational approach". Touretzky (1986) clearly views
his BoltzCONS model this way; he uses connectionist techniques to
implement conventional symbol processing mechanisms such as push-
down stacks and other LISP facilities. Rumelhart and McClelland
(1986, p. 117), who are convinced that connectionism signals a radical
departure from the conventional symbol processing approach, nonetheless refer to "PDP implementations" of various mechanisms such as
attention. Later in the same essay, Rumelhart and McClelland make
their position explicit: unlike "reductionists", they believe "that new
and useful concepts emerge at different levels of organization".
Although they then defend the claim that one should understand the
higher levels "… through the study of the interactions among lower
level units", the basic idea that there *are* autonomous levels seems
implicit everywhere in the essay.

But once one admits that there really are cognitive-level principles distinct from the (putative) architectural principles that connectionism articulates, there seems to be little left to argue about. Clearly it is pointless to ask whether one should or shouldn't do cognitive science by studying "the interaction of lower levels" as opposed to studying processes at the cognitive level, since we surely have to do *both*. Some scientists study geological principles, others study "the interaction of lower level units" like molecules. But since the fact that there are genuine, autonomously-stateable principles of geology is never in dispute, people who build molecular-level models do not claim to have invented a "new theory of geology" that will dispense with all that old fashioned "folk-geological" talk about rocks, rivers, and mountains!

We have, in short, no objection at all to networks as potential implementation models, nor do we suppose that any of the arguments we've given are incompatible with this proposal. The trouble is, however, that if connectionists do want their models to be construed this way, then they will have to radically alter their practice. For, it seems utterly clear that most of the connectionist models that have actually been proposed must be construed as theories of cognition, not as theories of implementation. This follows from the fact that it is intrinsic to these theories to ascribe representational content to the units (and/or aggregates) that they postulate. And, as we remarked at the beginning, a theory of the relations among representational states is ipso facto a theory at the level of cognition, not at the level of implementation. It has been the burden of our argument that, when construed as a cognitive theory, rather than as an implementation theory, connectionism appears to have fatal limitations. The problem with connectionist models is that all the reasons for thinking that they might be true are reasons for thinking that they couldn't be *psychology*.

5 Conclusion

What, in light of all of this, are the options for the further development of connectionist theories? As far as we can see, there are four routes that they could follow:

(1) Hold out for unstructured mental representations as against the classical view that mental representations have a combinatorial syntax and semantics. Productivity and systematicity arguments make this option appear not attractive.

(2) Abandon network architecture to the extent of opting for structured mental *representations* but continue to insist upon an asso-
ciationistic account of the nature of mental *processes*. This is, in
effect, a retreat to Hume's picture of the mind (see footnote 5),
and it has a problem that we don't believe can be solved;
although mental representations are, on the present assumption, structured objects, *association is not a structure sensitive
relation*. The problem is thus how to reconstruct the semantical
coherence of thought without postulating psychological processes that are sensitive to the structure of mental representations. (Equivalently, in more modern terms, it's how to get the
causal relations among mental representations to mirror their
semantical relations without assuming a proof-theoretic treatment of inference and—more generally—a treatment of semantic coherence that is syntactically expressed, in the spirit of
proof theory). This is the problem on which traditional associationism foundered, and the prospects for solving it now strike
us as not appreciably better then they were a couple of hundred
years ago. To put it a little differently: if you need structure in
mental representations anyway to account for the productivity
and systematicity of minds, why not postulate mental processes
that are structure sensitive to account for the coherence of mental processes? Why not be a classicist, in short.

In any event, notice that the present option gives the classical picture a lot of what it wants: namely, the identification of
semantic states with relations to structured arrays of symbols
and the identification of mental processes with transformations
of such arrays. Notice too that, as things now stand, this proposal is Utopian, since there are no serious proposals for incorporating constituent structure in connectionist architectures.

(3) Treat connectionism as an implementation theory. We have no
principled objection to this view (though there are, as connectionists are discovering, technical reasons why networks are
often an awkward way to implement classical machines). This
option would entail rewriting quite a lot of the polemical material in the connectionist literature, as well as redescribing what
the networks are doing as operating on symbol structures,
rather than spreading of activation among semantically interpreted nodes.

Moreover, this revision of policy is sure to lose the movement a lot of fans. As we have pointed out, many people have
been attracted to the connectionist approach because of its
promise to (a) do away with the symbol level of analysis, and

(b) elevate neuroscience to the position of providing evidence that bears directly on issues of cognition. If connectionism is considered simply as a theory of how cognition is neurally implemented, it may constrain cognitive models no more than theories in biophysics, biochemistry, or, for that matter, quantum mechanics do. All of these theories are also concerned with processes that *implement* cognition, and all of them are likely to postulate structures that are quite different from cognitive architecture. The point is that 'implements' is transitive, and it goes all the way down.

(4) Give up on the idea that networks offer (to quote Rumelhart and McClelland 1986, p. 110) "a reasonable basis for modeling cognitive processes in general". It could still be held that they sustain *some* cognitive processes. A good bet might be that they sustain such processes as can be analyzed as the drawing of statistical inferences; as far as we can tell, what network models really are is just analog machines for computing such inferences. Since we doubt that much of cognitive processing does consist of analyzing statistical relations, this would be quite a modest estimate of the prospects for network theory compared to what the connectionists themselves have been offering.

There is an alternative to the empiricist idea that all learning consists of a kind of statistical inference, realized by adjusting parameters; it's the rationalist idea that some learning is a kind of theory construction, effected by framing hypotheses and evaluating them against evidence. We seem to remember having been through this argument before. We find ourselves with a gnawing sense of *deja vu*.

Notes

1. The difference between connectionist networks in which the state of a single unit encodes properties of the world (the so-called "localist" networks) and ones in which the pattern of states of an entire population of units does the encoding (the so-called "distributed-representation" networks) is considered to be important by many people working on connectionist models. Although connectionists debate the relative merits of localist (or "compact") versus distributed representations (for instance, Feldman 1986), the distinction will usually be of little consequence for our purposes, for reasons that we give later. For simplicity, when we wish to refer indifferently to either single-unit codes or aggregate distributed codes, we shall refer to the

nodes in a network. When the distinction is relevant to our discussion, however, we shall explicitly mark the difference by referring either to units or to aggregates of units.

2. Smolensky (1988, p. 14) remarks that "unlike symbolic tokens, these vectors lie in a topological space, in which some are close together and others are far apart". However, this seems to radically conflate claims about the connectionist model and claims about its implementation (a conflation that is not unusual in the connectionist literature, as we'll see in section 4). If the space at issue is *physical*, then Smolensky is committed to extremely strong claims about adjacency relations in the brain—claims which there is, in fact, no reason at all to believe. But if, as seems more plausible, the space at issue is *semantical*, then what Smolensky says isn't true. Practically any cognitive theory will imply distance measures between mental representations. In classical theories, for example, the distance between two representations is plausibly related to the number of computational steps it takes to derive one representation from the other. In connectionist theories, it is plausibly related to the number of intervening nodes (or to the degree of overlap between vectors, depending on the version of connectionism one has in mind). The interesting claim is not that an architecture offers *a* distance measure but that it offers the *right* distance measure—one that is empirically certifiable.

3. It may be worth emphasizing that the structural complexity of a mental representation is not the same thing as, and does *not* follow from, the structural complexity of its content (that is, of what we're calling "the thought that one has"). Thus, connectionists and classicists can agree to agree that *the thought that P & Q* is complex (and has the thought that *P* among its parts) while agreeing to disagree about whether mental representations have internal syntactic structure.

4. The hedge is meant to exclude cases where inferences of the same logical type nevertheless differ in complexity in virtue of, for example, the length of their premises. The inference from $(A \lor B \lor C \lor D \lor E)$ and $(\neg B \& \neg C \& \neg D \& \neg E)$ to A is of the same logical type as the inference from $A \lor B$ and $\neg B$ to A. But it wouldn't be very surprising, or very interesting, if there were minds that could handle the second inference but not the first.

5. Historical footnote: connectionists are associationists, but not every associationist holds that mental representations must be unstructured. Hume didn't, for example. Hume thought that mental repre-

sentations are rather like pictures, and pictures typically have a compositional semantics. The parts of a picture of a horse are generally pictures of horse parts.

On the other hand, allowing a compositional semantics for mental representations doesn't do an associationist much good, so long as he is true to this spirit of his associationism. The virtue of having mental representations with structure is that it allows for structure-sensitive operations to be defined over them; specifically, it allows for the sort of operations that eventuate in productivity and systematicity. Association is not, however, such an operation; all *it* can do is build an internal model of redundancies in experience by altering the probabilities of transitions among mental states. So far as the problems of productivity and systematicity are concerned, an associationist who acknowledges structured representations is in the position of having the can but not the opener.

Hume, in fact, cheated. He allowed himself not just association but also "imagination", which he takes to be an "active" faculty that can produce new concepts out of old parts by a process of analysis and recombination. (The idea of a unicorn is pieced together out of the idea of a horse and the idea of a horn, for example.) Qua associationist, Hume had, of course, no right to active mental faculties. But allowing imagination in gave Hume precisely what modern connectionists don't have: an answer to the question how mental processes can be productive. The moral is that, if you've got structured representations, the temptation to postulate structure-sensitive operations and an executive to apply them is practically irresistible.

6. The PDP Research Group views its goal as being "to replace the 'computer metaphor' as a model of the mind with the 'brain metaphor'" (Rumelhart, Hinton, and McClelland 1986, p. 75). But the issue is not at all which *metaphor* we should adopt; metaphors (whether "computer" or "brain") tend to be a license to take one's claims as something less than serious hypotheses. As Pylyshyn (1984) points out, the claim that the mind has the architecture of a classical computer is *not* a metaphor but a *literal* empirical hypothesis.

Connectionism, Eliminativism, and the Future of Folk Psychology

William Ramsey
Stephen Stich
Joseph Garon
1990

1 Introduction

In the years since the publication of Thomas Kuhn's *Structure of Scientific Revolutions*, the term 'scientific revolution' has been used with increasing frequency in discussions of scientific change, and the magnitude required of an innovation before someone or other is tempted to call it a revolution has diminished alarmingly. Our thesis in this paper is that, if a certain family of connectionist hypotheses turn out to be right, they will surely count as revolutionary, even on stringent pre-Kuhnian standards. There is no question that connectionism has already brought about major changes in the way many cognitive scientists conceive of cognition. However, as we see it, what makes certain kinds of connectionist models genuinely revolutionary is the support they lend to a thorough-going eliminativism about some of the central posits of common-sense (or "folk") psychology. Our focus in this paper will be on beliefs or propositional memories, though the argument generalizes straightforwardly to all the other propositional attitudes. If we are right, the consequences of this kind of connectionism extend well beyond the confines of cognitive science, since these models, if successful, will require a radical reorientation in the way we think about ourselves.

Here is a quick preview of what is to come. Section 2 gives a brief account of what eliminativism claims, and sketches a pair of premises that eliminativist arguments typically require. Section 3 says a bit about how we conceive of common-sense psychology, and the propositional attitudes that it posits. It also illustrates one sort of psychological model that exploits and builds upon the posits of folk psychology. Section 4 is devoted to connectionism. Models that have been called "connectionist" form a fuzzy and heterogeneous set whose members often share little more than a vague family resemblance. However, our argument linking connectionism to eliminativism will work only for a restricted domain of connectionist models, interpreted in a particular way; the main job of section 4 is to say what that domain is and how the models in the domain are to be interpreted. In section 5 we will illustrate what a connectionist model of belief that comports with our strictures might look like, and go on to argue that, if models of this sort are correct, then things look bad for common-sense psychology. Section 6 assembles some objections and replies. The final section is a brief conclusion.

Before plunging in, we should emphasize that the thesis we propose to defend is a *conditional* claim: *If* connectionist hypotheses of the sort we will sketch turn out to be right, so too will eliminativism about propositional attitudes. Since our goal is only to show how connectionism and eliminativism are related, we will make no effort to argue for the truth or falsity of either doctrine. In particular, we will offer no argument in favor of the version of connectionism required in the antecedent of our conditional. Indeed our view is that it is early days yet—too early to tell with any assurance how well this family of connectionist hypotheses will fare. Those who are more confident of connectionism may, of course, invoke our conditional as part of a larger argument for doing away with the propositional attitudes.[1] But, as John Haugeland once remarked, one man's modus ponens is another man's modus tollens.* And those who take eliminativism about propositional attitudes to be preposterous or unthinkable may well view our arguments as part of a larger case against connectionism. Thus, we'd not be at all surprised if trenchant critics of connectionism, like Fodor and Pylyshyn (1988 [chapter 11 of this volume]), found both our conditional and the argument for it to be quite congenial.

2 Eliminativism and folk psychology

'Eliminativism', as we shall use the term, is a fancy name for a simple thesis. It is the claim that some category of entities, processes, or properties exploited in a common sense or scientific account of the world do not exist. So construed, we are all eliminativists about many sorts of

---

* *Editor's note:* I heard this quip from Nuel Belnap, who attributes it to Wes Salmon, who acknowledges it as his own.

things. In the domain of folk theory, witches are the standard example. Once upon a time witches were widely believed to be responsible for various local calamities. But people gradually became convinced that there are better explanations for most of the events in which witches had been implicated. There being no explanatory work for witches to do, sensible people concluded that there were no such things. In the scientific domain, phlogiston, caloric fluid, and the luminiferous ether are the parade cases for eliminativism. Each was invoked by serious scientists pursuing sophisticated research programs. But in each case the program ran aground in a major way, and the theories in which the entities were invoked were replaced by successor theories in which the entities played no role. The scientific community gradually came to recognize that phlogiston and the rest do not exist.

As these examples suggest, a central step in an eliminativist argument will typically be the demonstration that the theory in which certain putative entities or processes are invoked should be rejected and replaced by a better theory. And that raises the question of how we go about showing that one theory is better than another. Notoriously, this question is easier to ask than to answer. However, it would be pretty widely agreed that if a new theory provides more accurate predictions and better explanations than an old one, and does so over a broader range of phenomena, and if the new theory comports as well or better with well established theories in neighboring domains, then there is good reason to think that the old theory is inferior, and that the new one is to be preferred. This is hardly a complete account of the conditions under which one theory is to be preferred to another, though for our purposes it will suffice.

But merely showing that a theory in which a class of entities plays a role is inferior to a successor theory plainly is not sufficient to show that the entities do not exist. Often a more appropriate conclusion is that the rejected theory was wrong, perhaps seriously wrong, about some of the properties of the entities in its domain, or about the laws governing those entities, and that the new theory gives us a more accurate account *of those very same entities.* Thus, for example, pre-Copernican astronomy was very wrong about the nature of the planets and the laws governing their movement. But it would be something of a joke to suggest that Copernicus and Galileo showed that the planets Ptolemy spoke of do not exist.[2]

In other cases the right thing to conclude is that the posits of the old theory are reducible to those of the new. Standard examples here include the reduction of temperature to mean molecular kinetic energy, the reduction of sound to wave motion in the medium, and the reduction of genes to sequences of polynucleotide bases.[3] Given our current concerns, the lesson to be learned from these cases is that, even if the common sense theory in which propositional attitudes find their home is replaced by a better theory, that would not be enough to show that the posits of the common sense theory do not exist.

What more would be needed? What is it that distinguishes cases like phlogiston and caloric, on the one hand, from cases like genes or the planets on the other? Or, to ask the question in a rather different way, what made phlogiston and caloric candidates for elimination? Why wasn't it concluded that phlogiston is oxygen, that caloric is kinetic energy, and that the earlier theories had just been rather badly mistaken about some of the properties of phlogiston and caloric?

Let us introduce a bit of terminology. We will call theory changes in which the entities and processes of the old theory are retained or reduced to those of the new one *ontologically conservative* theory changes. Theory changes that are not ontologically conservative we will call *ontologically radical*. Given this terminology, the question we are asking is how to distinguish ontologically conservative theory changes from ontologically radical ones.

Once again, this is a question that is easier to ask than to answer. There is, in the philosophy of science literature, nothing that even comes close to a plausible and fully general account of when theory change sustains an eliminativist conclusion and when it does not. In the absence of a principled way of deciding when ontological elimination is in order, the best we can do is to look at the posits of the old theory—the ones that are at risk of elimination—and ask whether there is anything in the new theory that they might be identified with or reduced to. If the posits of the new theory strike us as deeply and fundamentally different from those of the old theory, in the way that molecular motion seems deeply and fundamentally different from the "exquisitely elastic" fluid posited by caloric theory, then it will be plausible to conclude that the theory change has been a radical one, and that an eliminativist conclusion is in order. But since there is no easy measure of how "deeply and fundamentally different" a pair of posits are, the conclusion we reach is bound to be a judgment call.[4]

To argue that certain sorts of connectionist models support eliminativism about the propositional attitudes, we must make it plausible that these models are not ontologically conservative. Our strategy will be to contrast these connectionist models, models like those set out in section 5, with ontologically conservative models like the one sketched at the end of section 3, in an effort to underscore just how ontologically radical the connectionist models are. But here we are getting ahead of ourselves. Before trying to persuade you that connectionist models are ontologically radical, we need to take a look at the folk psychological theory that the connectionist models threaten to replace.

3 Propositional attitudes and common-sense psychology

For present purposes we will assume that common-sense psychology can plausibly be regarded as a theory, and that beliefs, desires and the rest of the propositional attitudes are plausibly viewed as posits of that theory. Though this is not an uncontroversial assumption, the case for it has been well argued by others.[5] Once it is granted that common sense psychology is indeed a theory, we expect it will be conceded by almost everyone that the theory is a likely candidate for replacement. In saying this, we do not intend to disparage folk psychology, or to beg any questions about the status of the entities it posits. Our point is simply that folk wisdom on matters psychological is not likely to tell us all there is to know. Common-sense psychology, like other folk theories, is bound to be incomplete in many ways, and very likely to be inaccurate in more than a few. If this were not the case, there would be no need for a careful, quantitative, experimental science of psychology. With the possible exception of a few die-hard Wittgensteinians, just about everyone is prepared to grant that there are many psychological facts and principles beyond those embedded in common sense. If this is right, then we have the first premise needed in an eliminativist argument aimed at beliefs, propositional memories, and the rest of the propositional attitudes. The theory that posits the attitudes is indeed a prime candidate for replacement.

Though common-sense psychology contains a wealth of lore about beliefs, memories, desires, hopes, fears, and the other propositional attitudes, the crucial folk psychological tenets in forging the link between connectionism and eliminativism are the claims that propositional attitudes are *functionally discrete, semantically interpretable* states that play a *causal role* in the production of other propositional attitudes, and ultimately in the production of behavior. Following a suggestion of Stich (1983, pp. 237ff.), we'll call this cluster of claims *propositional modularity*. (The reader is cautioned not to confuse this notion of propositional modularity with the very different notion of modularity defended in Fodor 1983.)

The fact that common sense psychology takes beliefs and other propositional attitudes to have semantic properties deserves special emphasis. According to common sense:

(1) when people see a dog nearby they typically come to believe *that there is a dog nearby*;

(2) when people believe *that the train will be late if there is snow in the mountains*, and come to believe *that there is snow in the mountains*, they will typically come to believe *that the train will be late*;

(3) when people who speak English say "There is a cat in the yard", they typically believe *that there is a cat in the yard.*

And so on, for indefinitely many further examples. Note that these generalizations of common-sense psychology are couched in terms of the *semantic* properties of the attitudes. It is in virtue of being the belief *that p* that a given belief has a given effect or cause. Thus common-sense psychology treats the predicates expressing these semantic properties, predicates like 'believes *that the train is late*', as *projectable* predicates—the sort of predicates that are appropriately used in nomological or law-like generalizations.

There is a great deal of evidence that might be cited in support of the thesis that folk psychology is committed to the tenets of propositional modularity. Perhaps the most obvious way to bring out folk psychology's commitment to the thesis that propositional attitudes are *functionally discrete* states is to note that it typically makes perfectly good sense to claim that a person has acquired (or lost) a single memory or belief. Thus, for example, on a given occasion it might plausibly be claimed that when Henry awoke from his nap he had completely forgotten that the car keys were hidden in the refrigerator, though he had forgotten nothing else. In saying that folk psychology views beliefs as the sorts of things that can be acquired or lost one at a time, we do not mean to be denying that having any particular belief may presuppose a substantial network of related beliefs. The belief that the car keys are in the refrigerator is not one that could be acquired by a primitive tribesman who knew nothing about cars, keys, or refrigerators. But once the relevant background is in place, as we may suppose it is for us and for Henry, it seems that folk psychology is entirely comfortable with the possibility that a person may acquire (or lose) the belief that the car keys are in the refrigerator, while the remainder of his beliefs remain unchanged. Propositional modularity does not, of course, deny that acquiring one belief often leads to the acquisition of a cluster of related beliefs. When Henry is told that the keys are in the refrigerator, he may come to believe that they haven't been left in the ignition, or in his jacket pocket. But then again he may not. Indeed, on the folk psychological conception of belief it is perfectly possible for a person to have a long standing belief that the keys are in the refrigerator, and to continue searching for them in the bedroom.[6]

To illustrate the way in which folk psychology takes propositional attitudes to be functionally discrete, *causally active* states let us sketch a pair of more elaborate examples.

1. In common-sense psychology, behavior is often explained by appeal to certain of the agent's beliefs and desires. Thus, to explain why Alice went to her office, we might note that she wanted to send some e-mail messages (and, of course, she believed she could do so from her office). However, in some cases an agent will have several sets of beliefs and desires, each of which *might* lead to the same behavior. Thus we may suppose that Alice also wanted to talk to her research assistant, and that she believed he would be at the office. In such cases, common-sense psychology assumes that Alice's going to her office might have been caused by either one of the belief/desire pairs, or by both, and that determining which of these options obtains is an empirical matter. So it is entirely possible that on *this* occasion Alice's desire to send some e-mail played no role in producing her behavior; it was the desire to talk with her research assistant that actually caused her to go to the office. However, had she not wanted to talk with her research assistant, she might have gone to the office anyhow, because the desire to send some e-mail, which was causally inert in her actual decision making, might then have become actively involved. Note that in this case common sense psychology is prepared to recognize a pair of quite distinct semantically characterized states, one of which may be causally active while the other is not.

2. Our second illustration is parallel to the first, but focuses on beliefs and inference, rather than desires and action. On the common sense view, it may sometimes happen that a person has a number of belief clusters, any one of which might lead him to infer some further belief. When he actually does draw the inference, folk psychology assumes that it is an empirical question what he inferred it from, and that this question typically has a determinate answer. Suppose, for example,

that Inspector Clouseau believes that the butler said he spent the evening at the village hotel, and that he said he arrived back on the morning train. Suppose Clouseau also believes that the village hotel is closed for the season, and that the morning train has been taken out of service. Given these beliefs, along with some widely shared background beliefs, Clouseau might well infer that the butler is lying. If he does, folk psychology presumes that the inference might be based either on his beliefs about the hotel, or on his beliefs about the train, or both. It is entirely possible, from the perspective of common-sense psychology, that, although Clouseau has long known that the hotel is closed for the season, this belief played no role in his inference on this particular occasion. Once again we see common-sense psychology invoking a pair of distinct propositional attitudes, one of which is causally active on a particular occasion while the other is causally inert.

In the psychological literature there is no shortage of models for human belief or memory which follow the lead of common-sense psychology in supposing that propositional modularity is true. Indeed, prior to the emergence of connectionism, just about all psychological models of propositional memory, save for those urged by behaviorists, were comfortably compatible with propositional modularity. Typically, these models view a subject's store of beliefs or memories as an interconnected collection of functionally discrete, semantically interpretable states which interact in systematic ways. Some of these models represent individual beliefs as sentence-like structures—strings of symbols which can be individually activated by transferring them from long-term memory to the more limited memory of a central processing unit. Other models represent beliefs as a network of labeled nodes and labeled links through which patterns of activation may spread. Still other models represent beliefs as sets of production rules.[7] In all three sorts of model, it is generally the case that for any given cognitive episode, like performing a particular inference or answering a question, some of the memory states will be actively involved, and others will be dormant.

In figure 13.1 we have displayed a fragment of a "semantic network" representation of memory, in the style of Collins and Quillian (1972). In this model, each distinct proposition in memory is represented by an oval node along with its labeled links to various concepts. By adding assumptions about the way in which questions or other sorts of memory probes lead to activation spreading through the network, the model enables us to make predictions about speed and

Propositions:

1. Dogs have fur.
2. Dogs have paws.
3. Cats have fur.
4. Cats have paws.

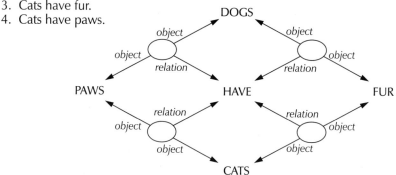

Figure 13.1: A fragment of a typical *semantic* network.

accuracy in various experimental studies of memory. For our purposes there are three facts about this model that are of particular importance. First, since each proposition is encoded in a functionally discrete way, it is a straightforward matter to add or subtract a *single* proposition from memory, while leaving the rest of the network unchanged. Thus, for example, figure 13.2 depicts the result of removing one proposition from the network in figure 13.1. Second, the model treats predicates expressing the semantic properties of beliefs or memories as *project-able*.[8] They are treated as the sorts of predicates that pick out scientifi-

Propositions:

1. Dogs have fur.
2. Dogs have paws.
3. Cats have fur.

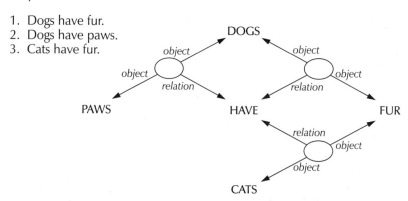

Figure 13.2: Same network, but with one proposition removed.

cally genuine *kinds*, rather than mere accidental conglomerates, and thus are suitable for inclusion in the statement of lawlike regularities. To see this, we need only consider the way in which such models are tested against empirical data about memory acquisition and forgetting. Typically, it will be assumed that if a subject is told (for example) that the policeman arrested the hippie, then the subject will (with a certain probability) remember *that the policeman arrested the hippie*.[9] And this assumption is taken to express a nomological generalization—it captures something lawlike about the way in which the cognitive system works. So, while the class of people who *remember that the policeman arrested the hippie* may differ psychologically in all sorts of ways, the theory treats them as a psychologically natural kind. Third, in any given memory search or inference task exploiting a semantic network model, it makes sense to ask which propositions were activated and which were not. Thus, a search in the network of figure 13.1 might terminate without ever activating the proposition that cats have paws.

4 A family of connectionist hypotheses

Our theme, in the previous section, was that common sense psychology is committed to propositional modularity, and that many models of memory proposed in the cognitive psychology literature are comfortably compatible with this assumption. In the present section we want to describe a class of connectionist models which, we will argue, are *not* readily compatible with propositional modularity. The connectionist models we have in mind share three properties:

(1) their encoding of information in the connection weights and in the biases on units is *widely distributed*, rather than *localist*;

(2) individual hidden units in the network have no comfortable symbolic interpretation—they are *subsymbolic*, to use a term suggested by Paul Smolensky; and

(3) the models are intended *as cognitive models*, not merely as *implementations of* cognitive models.

A bit later in this section we will elaborate further on each of these three features, and in the next section we will describe a simple example of a connectionist model that meets our three criteria. However, we are under no illusion that what we say will be sufficient to give a sharp-edged characterization of the class of connectionist models we have in mind. Nor is such a sharp-edged characterization essential for our

argument. It will suffice if we can convince you that there is a significant class of connectionist models which are incompatible with the
propositional modularity of folk psychology.

Before saying more about the three features on our list, we would
do well to give a more general characterization of the sort of model we
are calling "connectionist," and introduce some of the jargon that
comes with the territory. To this end, let us quote at some length from
Paul Smolensky's lucid overview.

> Connectionist models are large networks of simple, parallel computing
> elements, each of which carries a numerical *activation value* which it
> computes from neighboring elements in the network, using some sim-
> ple numerical formula. The network elements or *units* influence each
> other's values through connections that carry a numerical strength or
> *weight* ...
>
> In a typical ... model, input to the system is provided by imposing
> activation values on the *input units* of the network; these numerical
> values represent some encoding or *representation* of the input. The
> activation on the input units propagates along the connections until
> some set of activation values emerges on the *output units*; these activa-
> tion values encode the output the system has computed from the
> input. In between the input and output units there may be other
> units, often called *hidden units*, that participate in representing neither
> the input nor the output.
>
> The computation performed by the network in transforming the
> input pattern of activity to the output pattern depends on the set of
> connection strengths; *these weights are usually regarded as encoding the
> system's knowledge.* In this sense, the connection strengths play the role
> of the program in a conventional computer. Much of the allure of the
> connectionist approach is that many connectionist networks *program
> themselves,* that is, they have autonomous procedures for tuning their
> weights to eventually perform some specific computation. Such *learn-
> ing procedures* often depend on training in which the network is pre-
> sented with sample input/output pairs from the function it is
> supposed to compute. In learning networks with hidden units, the
> network itself "decides" what computations the hidden units will per-
> form; because these units represent neither inputs nor outputs, they
> are never "told" what their values should be, even during training ...[10]

One point must be added to Smolensky's portrait. In many connectionist models, the hidden units and the output units are assigned a
numerical "bias" which is added into the calculation determining the
unit's activation level. The learning procedures for such networks

typically set both the connection strengths and the biases. Thus in these networks the system's knowledge is usually regarded as encoded in *both* the connection strengths and the biases.

So much for a general overview. Let us now try to explain the three features that characterize those connectionist models we take to be incompatible with propositional modularity.

1. In many nonconnectionist cognitive models, like the one illustrated at the end of section 3, it is an easy matter to locate a functionally distinct part of the model encoding each proposition or state of affairs represented in the system. Indeed, according to Fodor and Pylyshyn, "conventional [computational] architecture requires that there be distinct symbolic expressions for each state of affairs that it can represent" (1988 [chapter 12 in this volume], p. 57 [340]). In some connectionist models an analogous sort of functional localization is possible, not only for the input and output units but for the hidden units as well. Thus, for example, in certain connectionist models, various individual units or small clusters of units are themselves intended to represent specific properties or features of the environment. When the connection strength from one such unit to another is strongly positive, this might be construed as the system's representation of the proposition that if the first feature is present, so too is the second. However, in many connectionist networks it is not possible to localize propositional representation beyond the input layer. That is, there are no particular features or states of the system which lend themselves to a straightforward semantic evaluation. This can sometimes be a real inconvenience to the connectionist model builder when the system as a whole fails to achieve its goal because it has not represented the world the way it should. When this happens, as Smolensky notes,

> it is not possible to localize a failure of veridical representation. Any particular state is part of a large causal system of states, and failures of the system to meet goal conditions cannot in general be localized to any particular state or state component.
>
> (1988, p. 15)

   It is connectionist networks of this sort—in which it is not possible to isolate the representation of particular propositions or states of affairs within the nodes, connection strengths, and biases—that we have in mind when we talk about the encoding of information in the biases, weights and hidden nodes being *widely distributed* rather than *localist*.

2. As we've just noted, there are some connectionist models in which some or all of the units are intended to represent specific properties or features of the system's environment. These units may be viewed as the

model's symbols for the properties or features in question. However, in models where the weights and biases have been tuned by learning algorithms it is often not the case that any single unit or any small collection of units will end up representing a specific feature of the environment in any straightforward way. As we shall see in the next section, it is often plausible to view such networks as collectively or holistically encoding a set of propositions, although none of the hidden units, weights or biases are comfortably viewed as *symbols*. When this is the case we will call the strategy of representation invoked in the model *subsymbolic*. Typically (perhaps always?) networks exploiting subsymbolic strategies of representation will encode information in a widely distributed way.

3. The third item on our list is not a feature of connectionist models themselves, but rather a point about how the models are to be interpreted. In making this point we must presuppose a notion of theoretical or explanatory level which, despite much discussion in the recent literature,[11] is far from being a paradigm of clarity. Perhaps the clearest way to introduce the notion of explanatory level is against the background of the familiar functionalist thesis that psychological theories are analogous to programs which can be implemented on a variety of very different sorts of computers.[12] If one accepts this analogy, then it makes sense to ask whether a particular connectionist model is intended as a model at the psychological level or at the level of underlying neural implementation. Because of their obvious, though in many ways very partial, similarity to real neural architectures, it is tempting to view connectionist models as models of the implementation of psychological processes. And some connectionist model builders endorse this view quite explicitly. So viewed, however, connectionist models are not *psychological* or *cognitive* models at all, any more than a story of how cognitive processes are implemented at the quantum-mechanical level is a psychological story.

A very different view that connectionist model builders can and often do take is that their models are at the psychological level, not at the level of implementation. So construed, the models are in competition with other psychological models of the same phenomena. Thus a connectionist model of word recognition would be an alternative to— and not simply a possible implementation of—a nonconnectionist model of word recognition; a connectionist theory of memory would be a competitor to a semantic network theory, and so on. Connectionists who hold this view of their theories often illustrate the point by drawing analogies with other sciences. Smolensky, for example, suggests that connectionist models stand to traditional cognitive models (such as semantic networks) in much the same way that quantum mechanics stands to classical mechanics. In each case the newer theory is deeper, more general and more accurate over a broader range of phenomena. But in each case the new theory and the old are competing at the same explanatory level. If one is right, the other must be wrong.

In light of our concerns in this paper, there is one respect in which the analogy between connectionist models and quantum mechanics may be thought to beg an important question. For while quantum mechanics is conceded to be a *better* theory than classical mechanics, a plausible case could be made that the shift from classical to quantum mechanics was an ontologically *conservative* theory change. In any event, it is not clear that the change was ontologically *radical.* If our central thesis in this paper is correct, then the relation between connectionist models and more traditional cognitive models is more like the relation between the caloric theory of heat and the kinetic theory. The caloric and kinetic theories are at the same explanatory level, though the shift from one to the other was pretty clearly ontologically radical. In order to make the case that the caloric analogy is the more appropriate one, it will be useful to describe a concrete, though very simple, connectionist model of memory that meets the three criteria we have been trying to explicate.

5 A connectionist model of memory

Our goal in constructing the model was to produce a connectionist network that would do at least some of the tasks done by more traditional cognitive models of memory, and that would perspicuously exhibit the sort of distributed, subsymbolic encoding described in the previous section. We began by constructing a network, we'll call it network A, that would judge the truth or falsehood of the sixteen propositions displayed above the double line in table 13.1. The network was a typical three-tiered feed-forward network consisting of 16 input units, four hidden units, and one output unit, as shown in figure 13.3. The input coding of each proposition is shown in the center column in table 13.1. Outputs close to 1 were interpreted as 'true' and outputs close to zero were interpreted as 'false'. Back propagation, a familiar connectionist learning algorithm, was used to "train up" the network, thereby setting the connection weights and biases. Training was terminated when the network consistently gave an output higher than .9 for each true proposition and lower than .1 for each false proposition. Figure 13.4 shows the connection weights between the input units and

	Propositions	Input activations	Outputs
1	Dogs have fur.	11000011 00001111	1 (true)
2	Dogs have paws.	11000011 00110011	1 (true)
3	Dogs have fleas.	11000011 00111111	1 (true)
4	Dogs have legs.	11000011 00111100	1 (true)
5	Cats have fur.	11001100 00001111	1 (true)
6	Cats have paws.	11001100 00110011	1 (true)
7	Cats have fleas.	11001100 00111111	1 (true)
8	Fish have scales.	11110000 00110000	1 (true)
9	Fish have fins.	11110000 00001100	1 (true)
10	Fish have gills.	11110000 00000011	1 (true)
11	Cats have gills.	11001100 00000011	0 (false)
12	Fish have legs.	11110000 00111100	0 (false)
13	Fish have fleas.	11110000 00111111	0 (false)
14	Dogs have scales.	11000011 00110000	0 (false)
15	Dogs have fins.	11000011 00001100	0 (false)
16	Cats have fins.	11001100 00001100	0 (false)
	Additional proposition		
17	Fish have eggs.	11110000 11001000	1 (true)

Table 13.1: Training sets for connectionist network examples.

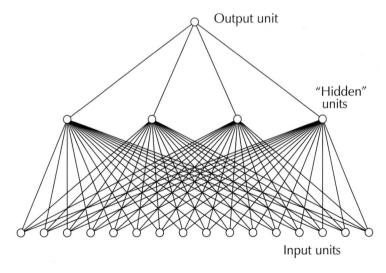

Figure 13.3: Network A—a typical connectionist network (of the feed-forward type).

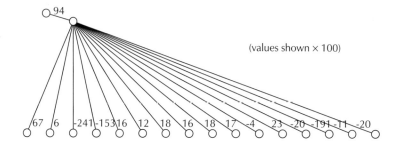

Figure 13.4: Network A, after learning 16 propositions—just a part of it, showing connection weights and bias to first hidden unit.

the leftmost hidden unit in the trained-up network, along with the bias on that unit. Figure 13.5 indicates the connection weights and biases further upstream. Figure 13.6 shows the way in which the network computes its response to the proposition *'Dogs have fur'* when that proposition is encoded in the input units.

There is a clear sense in which the trained-up network A may be said to have stored information about the truth or falsity of propositions (1)–(16), since when any one of these propositions is presented to the network it correctly judges whether the proposition is true or false. In this respect it is similar to various semantic network models which can be constructed to perform much the same task. However,

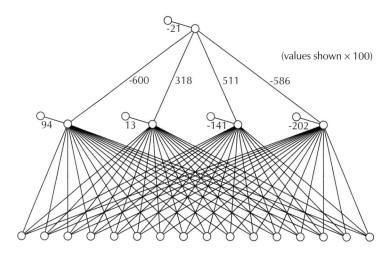

Figure 13.5: Network A again—now complete, but showing connection weights and biases only for hidden and output units.

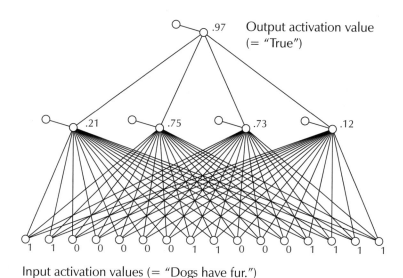

Input activation values (= "Dogs have fur.")

Figure 13.6: Network A again—here showing input, hidden, and output
             unit activation values (for a particular input proposition).

there is a striking difference between network A and a semantic network model like the one depicted in figure 13.1. For, as we noted earlier, in the semantic network there is a functionally distinct subpart associated with each proposition, and thus it makes perfectly good sense to ask, for any probe of the network, whether or not the representation of a specific proposition played a causal role. In the connectionist network, by contrast, there is no distinct state or part of the network that serves to represent any particular proposition. The information encoded in network A is stored holistically and distributed throughout the network. Whenever information is extracted from network A, by giving it an input string and seeing whether it computes a high or a low value for the output unit, *many* connection strengths, *many* biases and *many* hidden units play a role in the computation. And any particular weight or unit or bias will help to encode information about *many* different propositions. It simply makes no sense to ask whether or not the representation of a particular proposition plays a causal role in the network's computation. It is in just this respect that our connectionist model of memory seems radically incongruent with the propositional modularity of common sense psychology. For, as we saw in section 3, common-sense psychology seems to presuppose that

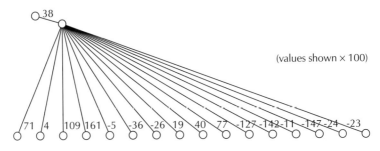

Figure 13.7: Network B (same as network A, but after learning 17 propositions)—just weights and bias to first hidden unit.

there is generally some answer to the question of whether a particular belief or memory played a causal role in a specific cognitive episode. But if belief and memory are subserved by a connectionist network like ours, such questions seem to have no clear meaning.

The incompatibility between propositional modularity and connectionist models like ours can be made even more vivid by contrasting network A with a second network, we'll call it network B, depicted in figures 13.7 and 13.8. Network B was trained up just as the first one was, except that one additional proposition was added to the training set (coded as indicated below the double line in table 13.1). Thus network B encodes all the same propositions as network A plus one more. In semantic-network models, and other traditional cognitive models, it

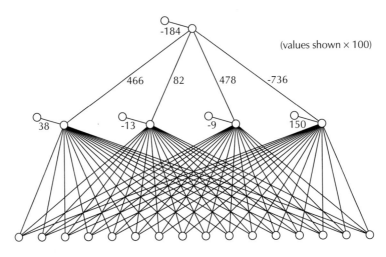

Figure 13.8: Network B, complete—showing weights and biases for hidden and output units.

would be an easy matter to say which states or features of the system encode the added proposition, and it would a simple task to determine whether or not the representation of the added proposition played a role in a particular episode modeled by the system. But plainly in the connectionist network those questions are quite senseless. The point is not that there are no differences between the two networks. Quite the opposite is the case; the differences are many and widespread. But these differences do not correlate in any systematic way with the functionally discrete, semantically interpretable states posited by folk psychology and by more traditional cognitive models. Since information is encoded in a highly distributed manner, with each connection weight and bias embodying information salient to many propositions, and information regarding any given proposition scattered throughout the network, the system lacks functionally distinct, identifiable substructures that are semantically interpretable as representations of individual propositions.

The contrast between network A and network B enables us to make our point about the incompatibility between common-sense psychology and these sorts of connectionist models in a rather different way. We noted in section 3 that common-sense psychology treats predicates expressing the semantic properties of propositional attitudes as projectable. Thus 'believes-that-dogs-have-fur' or 'remembers-that-dogs-have-fur' will be projectable predicates in common-sense psychology. Now both network A and network B might serve as models for a cognitive agent who believes that dogs have fur; both networks store or represent the information that dogs have fur. Nor are these the only two. If we were to train up a network on the 17 propositions in figure 3 plus a few (or minus a few) we would get yet another system which is as different from networks A and B as these two are from each other. The moral here is that, though there are *indefinitely* many connectionist networks that represent the information that dogs have fur just as well as network A does, these networks have no projectable features in common that are describable in the language of connectionist theory. From the point of view of the connectionist model builder, the class of networks that might model a cognitive agent who believes that dogs have fur is not a genuine kind at all, but simply a chaotically disjunctive set. Common-sense psychology treats the class of people who believe that dogs have fur as a psychologically natural kind; connectionist psychology does not.[13]

6 Objections and replies

The argument we've set out in the previous five sections has encountered no shortage of objections. In this section we will try to reconstruct the most interesting of these, and indicate how we would reply.

> **OBJECTION 1:** Models like A and B are not serious models for human belief or propositional memory.

Of course, the models we've constructed are tiny toys that were built to illustrate the features set out in section 4 in a perspicuous way. They were never intended to model any substantial part of human propositional memory. But various reasons have been offered for doubting that *anything like* these models could ever be taken seriously as psychological models of propositional memory. Some critics have claimed that the models simply will not scale up—that, while teaching a network to recognize fifteen or twenty propositions may be easy enough, it is just not going to be possible to train up a network that can recognize a few thousand propositions, still less a few hundred thousand.[14] Others have objected that while more traditional models of memory—including those based on sentence-like storage, those using semantic networks, and those based on production systems—all provide some strategy for *inference* or *generalization* which enables the system to answer questions about propositions it was not explicitly taught, models like those we have constructed are incapable of inference and generalization. It has also been urged that these models fail as accounts of human memory because they provide no obvious way to account for the fact that suitably prepared humans can easily acquire propositional information one proposition at a time. Under ordinary circumstances, we can just *tell* Henry that the car keys are in the refrigerator, and he can readily record this fact in memory. He doesn't need anything like the sort of massive retraining that would be required to teach one of our connectionist networks a new proposition.

> **REPLY 1:** If this were a paper aimed at defending connectionist models of propositional memory, we would have to take on each of these putative shortcomings in some detail. And in each instance there is at least something to be said on the connectionist side. Thus, for example, it just is not true that networks like A and B don't generalize beyond the propositions on which they've been trained. In network A, for example, the training set included:

Dogs have fur	Cats have fur
Dogs have paws	Cats have paws
Dogs have fleas	Cats have fleas.

It also included

Dogs have legs

but not

Cats have legs.

When the network was given an encoding of this last proposition, however, it generalized correctly and responded affirmatively. Similarly, the network responded negatively to an encoding of

Cats have scales

though it had not previously been exposed to this proposition.

However, it is important to see that this sort of point by point response to the charge that networks like ours are inadequate models for propositional memory is not really required, given the thesis we are defending in this paper. For what we are trying to establish is a *conditional* thesis: *if* connectionist models of memory of the sort we describe in section 4 are right, *then* propositional attitude psychology is in serious trouble. Since conditionals with false antecedents are true, we win by default if it turns out that the antecedent of our conditional is false.

> **OBJECTION 2:** Our models do not really violate the principle of propositional modularity, since the propositions the system has learned are coded in functionally discrete ways, though this may not be obvious.

We've heard this objection elaborated along three quite different lines. The first line—let's call it **OBJECTION 2A**—notes that functionally discrete coding may often be *very* hard to notice, and can not be expected to be visible on casual inspection. Consider, for example, the way in which sentences are stored in the memory of a typical von Neuman architecture computer—for concreteness we might suppose that the sentences are part of an English text and are being stored while the computer is running a word processing program. Parts of sentences may be stored at physically scattered memory addresses linked together in complex ways; and, given an account of the contents of all relevant memory addresses, one would be hard put to say where a particular sentence is stored. But nonetheless each sentence is stored in a *functionally discrete* way. Thus, if one knew enough about the system, it would be possible to erase any particular sentence it is storing by tampering with the contents of the appropriate memory addresses, while leaving the rest of the sentences the system is storing untouched. Similarly, it has been urged, connectionist networks may in fact encode propositions in functionally discrete ways, even though this may not be evident from a casual inspection of the trained up network's biases and connection strengths.

REPLY 2A: It is a bit difficult to come to grips with this objection, since what the critic is proposing is that in models like those we have constructed there *might* be some covert functionally discrete system of propositional encoding that has yet to be discovered. In response to this we must concede that indeed there might. We certainly have no argument that even comes close to demonstrating that the discovery of such a covert functionally discrete encoding is impossible. Moreover, we concede that if such a covert system were discovered, then our argument would be seriously undermined. However, we're inclined to think that the burden of argument is on the critic to show that such a system is not merely possible but *likely*; in the absence of any serious reason to think that networks like ours do encode propositions in functionally discrete ways, the mere logical possibility that they might is hardly a serious threat.

The second version of objection 2—we'll call it OBJECTION 2B—makes a specific proposal about the way in which networks like A and B might be discretely, though covertly, encoding propositions. The encoding, it is urged, is to be found in the pattern of activation of the hidden nodes, when a given proposition is presented to the network. Since there are four hidden nodes in our networks, the activation pattern on presentation of any given input may be represented as an ordered 4-tuple. Thus, for example, when network A is presented with the encoded proposition '*Dogs have fur*', the relevant 4-tuple would be $\langle .21, .75, .73, .12 \rangle$, as shown in figure 13.6. Equivalently, we may think of each activation pattern as a point in a four-dimensional hyperspace. Since each proposition corresponds to a unique point in the hyperspace, that point may be viewed as the encoding of the proposition. Moreover, that point represents a functionally discrete state of the system.[15]

REPLY 2B: What is being proposed is that the pattern of activation of the system on presentation of an encoding of the proposition p be identified with the belief that p. But this proposal is singularly implausible. Perhaps the best way to see this is to note that, in common-sense psychology, beliefs and propositional memories are typically of substantial duration; and they are the sorts of things that cognitive agents generally have lots of even when they are not using them. Consider an example. Are kangaroos marsupials? Surely you've believed for years that they are, though in all likelihood this is the first time today that your belief has been activated or used.[16] An activation pattern, however, is not an enduring state of a network; indeed, it is not a state of the network at all except when the network has had the relevant proposition as input. Moreover, there is an enormous number of other beliefs that you've had for years. But it makes no sense to suppose that a network could have many activation patterns simultaneously over a period of time. At any given time a network exhibits at most one pattern of activation. So activation patterns are just not the sort of thing that can plausibly be identified with beliefs or their representations.

Objection 2C: At this juncture, a number of critics have suggested that long standing beliefs might be identified not with activation patterns, which are transient states of networks, but rather with *dispositions to produce activation patterns*. Thus, in network A, the belief that dogs have fur would not be identified with a location in activation hyperspace but with the network's *disposition* to end up at that location when the proposition is presented. This *dispositional state* is an enduring state of the system; it is a state the network can be in no matter what its current state of activation may be, just as a sugar cube may have a disposition to dissolve in water even when there is no water nearby.[17] Some have gone on to suggest that the familiar philosophical distinction between dispositional and occurrent beliefs might be captured, in connectionist models, as the distinction between dispositions to produce activation patterns and activation patterns themselves.

Reply 2C: Our reply to this suggestion is that while dispositions to produce activation patterns are indeed *enduring* states of the system, they are not the right sort of enduring states—they are not the discrete, independently causally active states that folk psychology requires. Recall that on the folk-psychological conception of belief and inference, there will often be a variety of quite different underlying causal patterns that may lead to the acquisition and avowal of a given belief. When Clouseau says that the butler did it, he may have just inferred this with the help of his long-standing belief that the train is out of service. Or he may have inferred it by using his belief that the hotel is closed. Or both long-standing beliefs may have played a role in the inference. Moreover, it is also possible that Clouseau drew this inference some time ago, and is now reporting a relatively long-standing belief. But it is hard to see how anything like these distinctions can be captured by the dispositional account in question. In reacting to a given input, say p, a network takes on a specific activation value. It may also have dispositions to take on other activation values on other inputs, say q and r. But there is no obvious way to interpret the claim that these further dispositions play a causal role in the network's reaction to p—or, for that matter, that they do not play a role. Nor can we make any sense of the idea that on one occasion the encoding of q (say, the proposition that the train is out of service) played a role while the encoding of r (say, the proposition that the hotel is closed) did not, and on another occasion, things went the other way around. The propositional modularity presupposed by common-sense psychology requires that belief tokens be functionally discrete states capable of causally interacting with one another in some cognitive episodes and of remaining causally inert in other cognitive episodes. However, in a distributed connectionist system like network A, the dispositional state which produces one activation pattern is functionally inseparable from the dispositional state which produces another. Thus it is impossible to isolate some propositions as causally active in certain cognitive episodes, while others are not. We conclude that reaction-pattern dispositions won't do as belief tokens. Nor, so far as we can see, are there any other states of networks like A and B that will fill the bill.

7 Conclusion

The thesis we have been defending in this paper is that connectionist models of a certain sort are incompatible with the propositional modularity embedded in common sense psychology. The connectionist models in question are those that are offered as models at the *cognitive* level, and in which the encoding of information is widely distributed and subsymbolic. In such models, we have argued, there are no *discrete, semantically interpretable* states that play a *causal role* in some cognitive episodes but not others. Thus there is, in these models, nothing with which the propositional attitudes of common-sense psychology can plausibly be identified. If these models turn out to offer the best accounts of human belief and memory, we will be confronting an *ontologically radical* theory change—the sort of theory change that will sustain the conclusion that propositional attitudes, like caloric and phlogiston, do not exist.

Notes

1. See, for example, Churchland (1981, 1986), where explicitly eliminativist conclusions are drawn on the basis of speculations about the success of cognitive models similar to those we shall discuss.

2. We are aware that certain philosophers and historians of science have actually entertained ideas similar to the suggestion that the planets spoken of by pre-Copernican astronomers do not exist. See, for example, Kuhn (1970), chapter 10, and Feyerabend (1981), chapter 4. However, we take this suggestion to be singularly implausible. Eliminativist arguments can't be that easy. Just what has gone wrong with the accounts of meaning and reference that lead to such claims is less clear. For further discussion on these matters see Kuhn (1983), and Kitcher (1978, 1983).

3. For some detailed discussion of scientific reduction, see Nagel (1961), Schaffner (1967), Hooker (1981), and Kitcher (1984). The genetics case is not without controversy; see Kitcher (1982, 1984).

4. It's worth noting that judgments on this matter can differ quite substantially. At one end of the spectrum are writers like Feyerabend (1981), and perhaps Kuhn (1962/70), for whom relatively small differences in theory are enough to justify the suspicion that there has been an ontologically radical change. Toward the other end are writers like Lycan (1988), who writes:

> I am at pains to advocate a very liberal view... I am entirely willing to give up fairly large chunks of our commonsensical or platitudinous theory of belief or of desire (or of almost anything else) and decide that we were just wrong about a lot of things, without drawing the inference that we are no longer talking about belief or desire .... I think the ordinary word 'belief' (qua theoretical term of folk psychology) points dimly toward a natural kind that we have not fully grasped and that only mature psychology will reveal. I expect that 'belief' will turn out to refer to some kind of information-bearing inner state of a sentient being ..., but the kind of state it refers to may have only a few of the properties usually attributed to beliefs by common sense.   (pp. 31–2)

On our view, both extreme positions are implausible. As we noted earlier, the Copernican revolution did not show that the planets studied by Ptolemy do not exist. But Lavosier's chemical revolution did show that phlogiston does not exist. Yet on Lycan's "very liberal view" it is hard to see why we should not conclude that phlogiston really does exist after all—it's really oxygen, and prior to Lavosier "we were just very wrong about a lot of things".

5. For an early and influential statement of the view that common sense psychology is a theory, see Sellars (1956/63). More recently the view has been defended by Churchland (1970; 1979, chapters 1 and 4); and by Fodor (1987, chapter 1). For the opposite view, see Wilkes (1978), Madell (1986), and Sharpe (1987).

6. Cherniak (1986), chapter 3, notes that this sort of absent mindedness is common in literature and in daily life, and is sometimes disastrous.

7. For sentential models, see McCarthy (1968, 1980, 1986); and Kintsch (1974). For semantic networks, see Quillian (1969), Collins and Quillian (1972), Rumelhart, Lindsay and Norman (1972), Anderson and Bower (1973), and Anderson (1976; 1980, chapter 4). For production systems, see Newell and Simon (1972), Newell (1973), Anderson (1983), and Holland et al. (1986).

8. For the classic discussion of the distinction between projectable and non-projectable predicates, see Goodman (1965).

9. See, for example, Anderson and Bower (1973).

10. Smolensky (1988), p. 1; first emphasis in third paragraph added.

11. Broadbent (1985), Rumelhart and McClelland (1985; 1986, chapter 4), Smolensky (1988), Fodor and Pylyshyn (1988).

12. The notion of program being invoked here is itself open to two quite different interpretations. For the right reading, see Ramsey (1989).

13. This way of making the point about the incompatibility between connectionist models and common sense psychology was suggested to us by Jerry Fodor.

14. This point has been urged by Daniel Dennett, among others.

15. Quite a number of people have suggested this move, including Gary Cottrell and Adrian Cussins.

16. As Lycan notes (1988, p. 57) regarding the common-sense notion of belief, people have lots of them "even when they are asleep".

17. Something like this objection was suggested to us by Ned Block and by Frank Jackson.

The Presence
of a Symbol

Andy Clark
1992

1 A slippery LOT

The received philosophical understanding of a language of thought (Fodor 1975, 1987) and of a symbol system (Fodor and Pylyshyn 1988 [chapter 12 of this volume]) embodies a confused reliance on the idea of a symbol's *physical presence*. Arguments in favor of classicism (Fodor and Pylyshyn 1988) and arguments from connectionism to eliminativism (Ramsey, Stich, and Garon 1991 [chapter 13 of this volume]) trade on this confusion. Their proponents are victims of a pathology which we may label "code-fixation"—that is, they believe they have a clear conception of the conditions under which a semantic item is physically present as a symbol in an inner code. It is a false clarity, encouraged by an uncritical reliance on our intuitions about the information carrying properties of written sentences. Such intuitions are tacitly driven by characteristics of the processor (the human being!) of the sentences. The presence of a symbol is always processor relative. Once this is understood, the basis for some common intuitions concerning connectionism, classicism and the language of thought (LOT) is removed,

The strategy of the paper is as follows. Section 2 begins by reviewing some features of the language of thought hypothesis, in particular, its commitment to *explicit representations* in an inner code. Then section 3 discusses a trenchant critique of the code-oriented explicit/implicit distinction, developed by David Kirsh. Once the code/process gestalt switch has been achieved, I try, in section 4, to shed new light on the old chestnut "Do connectionist systems use explicit representations?" and, in section 5, to address some pressing arguments concerning compositionality and systematicity. Finally, section 6 plots an interesting consequence of the process-oriented view, namely that the question of whether a system explicitly represents a given content can only be answered relative to an environment in which it is situated.

2 The pocket Fodor

There are three ingredients to the proprietary Fodorian language-of-thought theory mix. First, propositional attitudes are computational relations to *mental representations.* Second, the mental representations form a *symbol system.* Third, mental processes are *causal* processes involving the explicit tokening of symbols from the symbol system. Expansion on these points is certainly in order.

The idea that propositional attitudes are computational relations to mental representations goes back a long way (Fodor 1975). A currently fashionable way of expressing the claim is to introduce the idea of a *belief box, hope box, desire box,* and so on. The "box" talk just indicates a kind of role in a complex functional economy. To be in a particular propositional attitude state is then to have a representation of the content of the proposition tokened in a functional role appropriate to that attitude. Thus:

> to believe that such and such is to have a mental symbol that means that such and such tokened in your head in a certain way; it's to have such a token "in your belief box" as I'll sometimes say.
> (Fodor 1987, p. 17)

To hope that P is thus to token, in a suitable functional role, a mental symbol that means that P. The same symbol, tokened in a different functional role, might cause effects appropriate to the fear that P, or the longing that P, and so on.

So far, then, we have a requirement that there should be mental symbols (that is, items which can be nonsemantically individuated but which are consistently the vehicles of a certain kind of content) and that the recurrence of such symbols in different functional roles should explain the content commonalities between various attitudes to a single proposition. As it stands, however, these mental symbols could be unique and unstructured. That is, there might be one symbol for each and every proposition. This has seemed empirically unattractive since we seem capable of an infinite or, at least, very large number of distinct thoughts. Hence the second feature, that such representations form a symbol system.

A *symbol system* is a collection of symbols (nonsemantically individuable items that are consistently the vehicles of a particular content) that are provided with a syntax allowing for *semantic compositionality*. In such a system, we will find atomic symbols and molecular representations. A molecular representation is just a string of symbols such that the content of the string is a direct function of the meanings of its atomic parts and the (syntactic) rules of combination. Thus a very simple symbol system might consist of the atomic symbols 'A', 'B' and 'C', and a rule of concatenation such that the content 'A and B' is tokened as 'AB', the content 'A and B and C' as 'ABC', the content 'C and B' as 'CB', and so on. Such symbol structures are supposed to "correspond to real physical structures in the brain" and their syntactic (combinatorial) properties to correspond to real "structural relations". For example, just as the *symbol* 'A' is literally part of the complex molecule 'AB', so the brain state which means that A could be literally part of the brain state which means that AB (see Fodor and Pylyshyn 1988, p. 13 [317]).

The advantages of deploying a symbol system include the ease with which we can specify that certain operations can be applied to *any* string of a given syntactic form. Thus, for any string in the above example, you may derive any member from the string: AB implies A, ABC implies A, CAB implies A, and so on. Another advantage is the ease with which such systems yield a *systematic mental life*. Any being deploying the simple symbol system described above, who can think (that is, token) AB, can ipso facto think (token) BA. This systematicity is echoed, so Fodor and Pylyshyn claim, in a distinctive feature of human mental life—that, for example, humans who can think that Mary loves John can *also* think that John loves Mary. This a posteriori argument for a language of thought is the mainstay of Fodor and Pylyshyn (1988). It is worth noticing that, for the argument to have any force, the symbols which feature in the public language ascriptions of thoughts must have recombinable correlates in the internal code. They need not constitute atomic items in such a code, but the code must support recombinable content-bearing structures whose syntactic combinatorics match the semantic combinatorics highlighted by Fodor and Pylyshyn.

Finally, and before the wood vanishes beneath the foliage, we should touch base with the mental causation issue. The content-faithful causal powers of our mental states, according to Fodor, are nothing but the causal powers of the physical tokens in the inner symbol system. Thus, consider the two characteristic kinds of effect (according to folk psychology) of a mental state of believing that P. One kind of effect consists in the belief's bringing about an action. The other, in its bringing about some further mental state. In both cases, Fodor's motto is: "No intentional causation without explicit representation" (1987, p. 25). The idea is that a particular propositional attitude that P can act as a cause only when there occurs a token of the syntactic kind that means that P and when that token causes either an appropriate action or a further thought content Q (or both). By understanding the way a symbol's syntactic properties (in the context of a particular functional economy and symbol system) determine its causal powers, we can see one way in which content and the physical world can march in step. The Fodorian vision is thus sold as

> a vindication of intuitive belief/desire psychology [insofar as it] shows how intentional states could have causal powers; precisely the aspect of common-sense intentional realism that seemed most perplexing from a metaphysical point of view.   (1987, p. 26)

Fodor rounds off the account with a few subtleties meant to take the sting out of familiar objections. Thus consider the case of emergent rule following. A classic case of emergent rule following is Dennett's example of a chess-playing program which is described as "wanting to get its queen out early" even though

> for all the many levels of explicit representation to be found in that program, nowhere is anything roughly synonymous with "I should get my queen out early" explicitly tokened … I see no reason to believe that the relation between belief talk and psychological-process talk will be any more direct.   (1977/78, p. 107)

Fodor's response to this worry is to introduce an idea of *core cases*. The vindication of common sense psychology by cognitive science requires, he suggests, only that

> tokenings of attitudes must correspond to tokenings of mental representations when they—the attitude tokenings—are episodes in mental processes.   (p. 25)

The core cases, then, are cases in which a given content (the belief *that it is raining*, say) is supposed to figure in a mental process or to consti-tute an "episode in a mental life". In such cases (and only in such cases) there must, according to Fodor, be an explicit representation of the content which is at once a syntactic item (hence a bearer of causal powers) and an item which gets a recognizably folk-psychological interpretation (as in the belief about rain). The chess program "counter example" is thus said to be defused since (Fodor insists) "entertaining the thought 'Better get the queen out early' never constitutes an episode in the mental life of the machine" (p. 25). By contrast:

> The representations of the board—of actual or possible states of play—over which the machine's computations are defined *must* be explicit, *precisely* because the machine's computations are defined over them. These computations constitute the machine's "mental processes", so either they are causal sequences of explicit representations or the representational theory of chess playing is simply false of the machine.   (p. 25)

The claim then is that the *contents* of our thoughts must be tokened in an explicit inner code. However, the "laws of thought"—the rules which determine how one content yields another or yields an action—need not be explicitly represented. In the familiar form of words, "programs … may be explicitly represented but 'data structures' … *have to be*" (p. 25, original emphasis).

This may seem a little confusing, since, twelve years earlier, Fodor wrote that:

> What distinguishes what organisms do … is that a representation of the rules they follow constitutes one of the causal determinants of their behavior.   (1975, p. 74, note 15)

Despite appearances, this is consistent with the current claim. The idea must be that in any case where the *consideration of a rule* is meant causally to explain a judgement or action, then the rule must be explicitly tokened. Otherwise not.[1] Thus a novice chess player whose action involved a train of thought in which the rule figured would have had (according to Fodor) to token the rule in an inner code (distinct from her public language).

The trouble with all this, I shall now suggest, is that it depends on a fundamentally unclear notion of *explicit representation*. Once we see this, the whole project of vindicating common-sense psychology via a syntax/semantics parallel in some simple internal code is called into question.

3 On being more explicit

The idea of an explicit representation has been seen to bear considerable weight. The language of thought is, precisely, the syntactic vehicle of explicit representation and it is explicitness which is (for Fodor) essential to the vindication of the folk's use of propositional attitude talk. Propositional attitudes pick out causally efficacious items in mental processes just in case their contents are explicitly tokened. However, David Kirsh (1991) offers some persuasive reasons for caution. He argues that a good account of explicit representation should not focus on the form of an inner code but on the combination of information bearing states *and processors*. The quality of explicitness, on that model, is always relative to the *usability* of information rather than (directly) to its form. What misleads us, according to Kirsh, is the "bewitching image of a word printed on a page" (p. 350).

Kirsh argues that our intuitions about explicitness are inconsistent, insofar as we are inclined to postulate two sets of criteria which may come into conflict.

The first set of criteria is structural. In this sense, a representation is seen as explicit if it is "on the surface" of a data structure. Thus the word 'cat' is explicit in the list {cat, dog, fly}. However, what exactly is the intuition here? Is 'cat' equally explicit if the word is "hidden in a tangle of other words"? Furthermore, we think that if a word is encrypted in a hard to decipher code, it is not explicitly represented. However, what is the difference between the encryption case and the tangle-of-words case? It very quickly begins to look as if the structural notion of explicitness is trading on a *processing* notion which ties explicitness to the ease with which information is recovered and put to use. Being the kind of processor we are (as human readers of text) we find it easier to extract the 'cat' information from a typed list than from a jumbled-up tangle of words. However, if we were a different kind of processing tool, we might have no difficulty with the tangle— hence the 'cat' information ought (relative to such a tool) to count as explicit. We are thus drawn toward a second set of criteria, according to which information is explicit if it is ready for immediate use by an embedding system.

If we now consider some standard ideas about explicit representation, we shall see that they rely too heavily on the superficial *structural* notion of explicitness—a notion which is illegitimately building in the idea of visibility to inspection by a human agent as the mark of immediate usability. Thus we find ourselves reflecting on the idea of a word on a page as a paradigm of explicitness. But that case, if we are not aware of the processing dimension, will mislead. Thus consider the following properties, drawn from Kirsh (1991, pp. 350–358).

(1) Words are *localized* in space. This is a great aid to a human visual system. However, all that is required if meaning is to be easily extracted is that the overall system have the power to spot the relevant information without extensive computational effort. Thus spatially superposed information may be visible, with minimal computational effort, given the right "reading tool". Examples of such tools include parallel distributed processing (PDP) systems, telephone message decoders (where several conversations run on a single line), and color filters (which separate out spatially superposed wavelengths of light).

(2) Words are *movable*. 'Cat' means the same in the sentence "The cat sat on the mat" and in the sentence "The cat ate the budgerigar". Why should this matter? It matters because the extent to which meaning depends on context determines (in part) the amount of effort involved in recovery of meaning. Thus the numeral '5' carries meaning in a context-dependent way—the '5' in '501 means 500 whereas the '5' in '51' means 50. To extract the significance of the '5' we need to survey the context; that takes effort (and hence is a move away from total explicitness, in the sense of easy visibility). However, once we foreground the *processing* measure, we can see that the *extent* to which context dependence defeats explicitness is relative to the ease with which context is taken into account by the processor. And some kinds of processor (such as connectionist ones) are very well adapted to the fluent processing of contextual data. Thus the requirement of total movability as a constraint on explicitness is revealed as an artifact of lack of attention to the processing roots of the requirement and the richness of the space of possible processors.

Kirsh goes on to develop a precise computational account of ease of processing which allows us to say that information is explicit if it can be retrieved and made available for use in constant time.[2] The moral is: it is really the processing requirements that drive our intuitions, and the structural vision is a distorted vision of these requirements, warped by the image of words on a page. On the Kirsh model:

Explicitness really concerns how quickly information can be accessed, retrieved, or in some other manner put to use.   (p. 361)

The view has its price. As Kirsh notes, we shall need to accept that, relative to a processor like me, the structure 'add (1,1)' explicitly encodes the information '2'. It also implies that one and the same static structure may explicitly carry different information relative to different processing environments.

What is perhaps even more problematic is Kirsh's account of *implicit* information. Kirsh is tempted to regard as implicit just that information that "is not explicit in a system but which could be made so" (p. 347). The system, if it is to encode implicitly the information that P, must be able to recover that information and explicitly encode it. However, what exactly can this amount to once we adopt a processing perspective on explicitness? It seems to imply that whatever is truly implicit (visible only with a high degree of computational effort) must be translatable into something which is explicit (usable with a low degree of effort). But this is either trivial (since to use it *at all,* we must somehow get it into directly usable shape, albeit after some effort) or overly restrictive. Why can we not allow that a system which can only *ever* access certain types of information by a complex deciphering procedure nonetheless *implicitly* encodes that information? It seems more natural (to me at least) to take a processing perspective as arguing for a continuum of cases such that information is implicit relative to the amount of effort needed to bring it to bear.

Finally, I believe Kirsh's account leaves out a fundamental extra dimension—namely, that truly explicit items of information should be usable in a wide variety of ways, that is, not restricted to use in a single task. The implicit/explicit continuum is, I suggest, better viewed as a two-dimensional space whose dimensions are, first, ease of usability of information and, second, variety of *modes of use.* Information which is easily deployed but only in a rigidly circumscribed way is not, *pace* the basic account offered by Kirsh, fully explicit. Our view thus adds to Kirsh's basic account the idea (found in, for instance, Dretske 1988) that representations which are usable only in a specific context should be regarded (ceteris paribus) as more implicit than those whose content is available for many purposes.

To give a simple example which Dretske himself uses (pp. 33–34), consider the case of a rat which has learned to discriminate safe and poisoned food. Does it rely on an explicit representation of the content "that food is poisoned" to do so? It is certainly relying on an inner state which provides for the easy use of the "poisoned" information to guide avoidance behavior. However, the fact that the rat can *only* use the information in that way works *against* the intuition that the information is explicitly represented. Likewise, developmental psychologists such as Karmiloff-Smith (1986) depict human cognition as involving a progression from the context-bound use of stored information to much more context-flexible uses, and wish to characterize this as a progression from an implicit to an explicit representational form. It does not seem unreasonable, then, to extend Kirsh's basic proposal (that ease of use in the context of a given processor is the key to explicitness) so that information is increasingly explicitly tokened according to *both* (i) ease of use and (ii) variety of modes of use (relative to an overall system). This maintains the stress on the use of information, but expands our conception of the dimensions of the implicit/explicit continuum.

4 Connectionism and explicit representation

Having (I hope) begun to switch the structure/process gestalt, it is time to return to our old chestnut: do connectionist systems support explicit representations? Now a funny thing happens. Relative to a more process-oriented notion of explicitness, connectionist systems begin to look very capable of supporting explicit representations! There is, however, a catch.

The encouraging news is that, within a standard distributed Smolensky-style network, a good deal of stored knowledge is extremely easy to access and use. Thus consider a network which encodes items of information such as "dogs have fur". It is simplicity itself to access and use this information to answer "yes" to the input question "Do dogs have fur?" More generally, connectionist systems are capable of the swift retrieval of any one of the multiple such patterns stored in superpositional distributed style. According to the Kirsh criterion, then, that information must be counted as explicitly represented in the array of weights (in the context of a connectionist input and retrieval system). Indeed, the very distinction between the information store and the retrieval tool is blurred in these cases. The retrieval tool is built into the knowledge representation itself. Thus we read that

> [in connectionist systems] the representation of the knowledge is set up in such a way that the knowledge necessarily influences the course of processing. Using knowledge in processing is no longer a matter of finding the relevant information in memory and bringing it to bear; it is part and parcel of the processing itself.
>
> (McClelland et al. 1986, p. 32.)

However, at this point our intuitions become tangled once again. For it may seem as if a key feature of (old fashioned, structural) explicitness has now been missed. It is a feature which I shall (somewhat opaquely) label *reflectivity*. The idea is simple. It is that one task of the idea of explicit representation was to distinguish reflection and considered action from "mere animal reflexes". As Fodor once said, what distinguishes me from a paramecium is that when I act there is an intervening stage of representation. In the paramecium, there is (let us assume) no such buffer. It is now obvious how the various intuitions might tangle. For the criterion of process explicitness is ease of use. The limiting case here is a fast direct input/output link. However, such a link begins to look a lot like a reflex response. If you have the intuition that explicit representation should mark the difference between reflex responses and the rest, you have tied yourself into a knot!

The key to successful unraveling is, I believe, the notion of a second dimension of usability assessment, as mentioned briefly in section 3. For the relative explicitness of information should not be assessed without reference to the *variety* of uses to which the information can be put. The idea of a genuine difference between reflex and considered action is, I suggest, a distorted vision of two genuine considerations. First, some creatures are *consciously aware* of their reasons. Let us bracket this issue. Second, some creatures can use stored information in more flexible ways than others. A neural network which is *only* capable of using the stored information "dogs have fur" to answer "yes" to the input "do dogs have fur?" is not breathtakingly flexible. A human being who knows that dogs have fur can use the information to plan ways of making fur coats, to irritate allergenic neighbors, to predict musty smells in the rain, and all the rest.

On our account, a full-blooded process-oriented account of explicit representation will demand *both* ease of retrieval and flexibility of use. That, of course, is the catch for standard connectionist proposals. For despite the advertising, the information thus stored is often very limited in its range of usability. Particular limitations (see Clark and Karmiloff-Smith 1993) involve the systematic adaptation of the stored knowledge to new tasks, the systematic debugging of the stored information and the integration of new information. In short, the reflex/ nonreflex distinction may often really be a distinction between flexible and less flexible uses of information. A more process-oriented account of explicitness, *as long as* it includes the dimension of *variety* of use, will be well able to accommodate it. The fate of connectionism as a locus of fully explicit representations must therefore remain undecided until the flexibility issue (more on which below) is resolved.

5 Code-fixation: its symptoms and cure

The cash value of a process-oriented conception of representation is its power to treat a common pathology which we may label *code-fixation*. Sufferers from code-fixation expect explanations of cognitive phenomena to fall naturally out of considerations about the form of an inspectable internal code. A particularly striking example is Fodor and Pylyshyn's (1988) argument against connectionist models of mind.

The argument, briefly rehearsed in section 2 above, is that humans have a systematic mental life. Those who can think that Margaret and John love Mary can think that Mary loves John, and that Mary and John love Margaret, and that Margaret loves John, and so on. This fact, Fodor and Pylyshyn argue, lends strong support to the idea of a language of thought in which internal tokens carry the meanings 'John', 'loves', and so on, and are recombinable according to syntactic rules. More generally, Fodor and Pylyshyn insist that:

> In classical models, the principles by which mental states are transformed, or by which an input selects the corresponding output, are defined over structural properties of mental representations. Because classical mental *representations* have combinatorial structure, it is possible for classical mental *operations* to apply to them by reference to their form.   (1988, p. 13 [317])

However, what does it really mean for a representation to have such combinatorial structure? Fodor and Pylyshyn are certain that distributed connectionist cognitive models cannot provide it. Yet a variety of recent proposals show that it is possible to *process* connectionist distributed representations in ways which yield the very abilities (to perform structure-sensitive operations) that Fodor and Pylyshyn foreground.

Thus Smolensky (1991), Pollack (1990), and Elman (1992) all offer treatments in which distributed representations sustain various kinds of compositional, iterative, and recursive operations. Elman, for example, used a simple recurrent network to learn some grammatical structures, including multiple levels and types of embedding.

To get more of the flavor of such proposals, consider Chalmers (1990) model of active-to-passive transformations. The model uses a RAAM (Recursive Auto Associative Memory) architecture due to Pollack (1988). This consists of a three-layer feed-forward network with a small number of hidden units, and a larger (and equal) number of input and output units (for example: 39 input, 13 hidden, and 39 output). The net is taught to develop compressed distributed representations of linguistic tree structures. Thus it may be fed inputs coding for the contents of three terminal nodes on a tree by dividing the input units into groups and using one group per terminal node. The network is required to *reproduce* the input tree at the output layer. To do so, it uses the back-propagation learning rule to learn a compressed distributed representation of the tree structure at the hidden unit layer (13 units). These hidden-unit patterns are also fed to the network as inputs, thus forcing it to "auto associate on higher order structures" (Chalmers 1990, p. 55). The upshot is a network which *can decode* compressed representations of trees of arbitrary depth. To perform the decoding, you give the compressed representation direct to the hidden-unit layer and read an expanded version at the output layer. If the expanded version contains only terminal tree structures, the decoding is complete. If it does not, any nonterminal structure must again be fed in to the hidden-unit layer until they are discharged.

Chalmers trained a RAAM architecture to encode tree structures representing sentences of active form (such as "John love Michael") and passive form ("Michael is love by John"). Forty sentences of each type were used. As expected, the network learned to decode the compressed representations of the sentences which it formed at the hidden unit layer. Chalmers then went on to train a further network to take as input the compressed representation of an active form, and yield as output the compressed representation of its passive correlate. The point of this exercise was to show that a standard network could transform the RAAM representations from active to passive form *without* first decomposing the RAAM representation into its constituent structures. The experiment was a success. The new network learned the transformation of the training cases and was then able to perform quite well even on new sentences. Thus new active sentences, once compressed by the RAAM network, were transformed into appropriate passives with *at least* 65% accuracy (Chalmers, 1990, p. 59).

It is worth quoting Chalmers own discussion of his results at some length. He claims that the experiment shows that:

> Not only is compositional structure *encoded* implicitly in a pattern of activation, but this implicit structure can be utilized by the familiar connectionist devices of feed-forward/back-propagation in a meaningful way. Such a conclusion is by no means obvious a priori—it might well have turned out that the structure was "buried too deeply" to be directly used, and that all useful processing would have had to proceed first through the step of extraction.   (p. 60)

He goes on to suggest that the model constitutes a disproof of the idea (see Fodor and McLaughlin 1990) that the only way to support genuinely structure sensitive operations is to deploy representations that concatenate explicit tokens of the constituent parts of the structure. To quote Chalmers once more:

> [According to Fodor and McLaughlin] If a representation of "John loves Michael" is not a concatenation of tokens of 'John' 'loves' and 'Michael' ... then later processing cannot be sensitive to the compositional structure that is represented. The results presented here show that this conclusion is false. In the distributed representations formed by RAAM there is no such explicit tokening of the original words ... Nevertheless the representations still support systematic processing. Explicit constituent structure is not needed for systematicity; implicit structure is enough.   (p. 61)

According to our analysis of explicit representation, this characterization of the situation is nonetheless slightly misleading. For Chalmers is still relying on what we (following Kirsh) have called the structural notion of explicitness, in which a constituent part is explicitly represented if it is easily visible, to a human theorist, in an informational structure. However, rather than rest content with this ill-motivated notion, we might do better to expand our idea of explicit representation of structure. If we do this along the lines sketched in section 3, then the ease of use of the structured information (the constant time active/passive transformations) gives us some cause to regard the RAAM representations (in the context of the transformation net) as *explicit representations* of constituent structure. The fact that such structure is not directly visible to the human theorist is neither here nor there.

It would be tempting to stop here and conclude that the sense in which a suitably advanced connectionist system must fail to account for structure sensitive processing and systematicity is in failing to do so *transparently,* by means of an inner code in which the semantic constituents of complex representations are *easily visible.* The kind of *concatenative* (see van Gelder 1990) compositionality which Fodor and Pylyshyn seem to seek is, indeed, one which is often nicely transparent to us. However, it is not the only kind available. The functional compositionality exhibited by the new wave of connectionist models is proof that at least some degree of compositional structure can be preserved in distributed representations *and readily exploited.*

Such a conclusion, would, however, be premature. For the second functional dimension of explicitness—variety of use—has still to be addressed.

Thus suppose we ask what it is about, for example, the representation of information as a string of LISP atoms, which (relative to the processing tool provided by a standard CPU) inclines us to view such a string as an explicit and highly structured representation? According to the Kirsh-style account developed above, the answer lies in the fact that information thus encoded is (relative to the usual embedding processing environment) nicely available for use. We saw, however, that the same could be said of the structural information contained in the RAAM encoded sentence representation. Relative to the embedding environment of the transformation network, the structural information is nicely teed-up and ready for use. Now notice, however, what I believe is a revealing difference. Call the LISP string environment provided by the CPU a *CPU environment* and call the RAAM representation environment provided by the transformation network a *TN environment.* The difference, then, is this: relative to the TN environment, the target information is easily usable but *only* in one specific way—namely, to mediate an active/passive transformation. But relative to the CPU environment, the target information is easily usable for an open-ended variety of purposes. Thus, given the LISP representation, it is a simple matter to write additional programs that recursively refer to the elements of the target data structure, that treat particular elements as variables, or that reorganize the elements in new ways for other purposes. This is in stark contrast to the one-track usability of the RAAM representation relative to the TN environment.

It might reasonably be objected that we are not comparing like with like—that is, that the proper comparison is, for example, between a LISP representation relative to the environment provided by a *specific program* (say, to take active into passive voice) and the RAAM representation relative to the TN environment. However, that is to miss the essential point. We may *agree* that relative to a specific program environment the LISP string is no more explicit than the RAAM representation. Nonetheless, the usual CPU environment still provides a tool capable of cheaply exploiting the LISP string information in a very flexible set of ways. Perhaps it will one day be possible to create an environment in which the structural information encoded in the RAAM representation is just as easily and variously exploitable. As things stand, however, this does not seem to be the case. To exploit the

RAAM representation for a different purpose (for instance, to take present into past tense) would at the moment require the extensive training of a wholly separate transformation network. In short, the structural information in the RAAM encoding is indeed easily usable (relative to the TN environment), but in a very *domain-specific* manner. Until such domain specificity is overcome, connectionist representations will fail to live up to even our functionally-oriented criterion of explicitness.

In sum, the move toward a functional or process-based vision of explicitness and structure, combined with recent demonstrations like Chalmers (1990), goes some way toward defusing the force of Fodor and Pylyshyn's worries. However, until the deeper issue of the multi-track usability of the information encoded by a network is fully resolved, we must bring back an open verdict.

6 All the world's a processor

Sections 2 through 5 argued for a processing-device-relative account of explicitness. A representation is explicit if it is both cheaply and multiply deployable by the system in which it is embedded.

Once we have embraced such a processing-device-relative view of explicitness, however, it becomes necessary to ask *what counts* as a processing device. Kirsh raises, but does not pursue, the claim that

> information can be implicit in a system because that system is embedded in a particular environment.   (1991, p. 12)

The case which he has in mind, it seems, is one in which, in a certain sense:

> A system well adapted to its environment contains information about that environment and about its momentary relations to that environment even though the information is built into the design of the system and so is in principle inaccessible.   (p. 12)

Thus (I suppose) someone might say that in a certain sense a fish's shape embodies information concerning the hydrodynamics of sea water, or that the visual system, since its processing uses heuristics which rely on certain properties of the distal environment, implicitly carries information about these properties.

Consider, however, a somewhat different range of cases—cases in which a system can (unlike the fish and visual system) in fact *access* certain information (generate an internal representation of it), but *only* in virtue of some wider processing environment than that constituted by its on-board processing and storage apparatus. Thus, I may be able to exploit the distinct informational elements represented in some inner code *only* if, for example, I am augmented by some external memory (like paper and pencil). I may also be able to *computationally cheaply* retrieve and deploy some specific item of information only in a particular external setting (such as one in which it is cued by a written reminder). It seems to me that in those cases we have to allow that, relative to the broader processing tool of me plus my environment, information which would *otherwise* count as unstructured and/or inexplicit should count as structured and/or explicit! It is unclear why the skin should constitute the boundary of the processing environment relative to which such questions are to be decided.

To see this, consider the case where my brain is augmented with an add-on mechanical processing device which increases my short-term memory span. There seems little doubt that in such a case the processing tool, relative to which the internal representational states are to be judged as structured, explicit, and so on, has been altered. But why is this different from taking the original processor (of brain and body) and setting it in front of an external environmental device (the pad and pencil) which likewise allows the augmentation of my short-term memory? I conclude that: to take *seriously* our picture of structure and explicitness as processing-environment-relative properties of inner states is *necessarily* to allow that both the nature and ultimately the content (a structured content is different from an unstructured one, after all) of our inner states is always a joint function of their intrinsic nature and the broader environment in which they exist. In short, there is just *no answer* to the questions "What is the content of that state?", "Is it explicit?", and so on, independent of considerations involving the processing capacities of the local system as currently embedded in some wider environment.

7 Conclusions: from code to process

A familiar image depicts mental processes as the logico-manipulative transformation of static symbols in a concatenative and recombinative inner code. Commensurate with such an image is a model of intentional causation as involving the explicit tokening of content-bearing symbol strings as an intervening layer between input and action. Connectionist approaches do not lend themselves easily to interpretation in these terms. As a result we find ourselves pushed toward a more liberal (process oriented) understanding of the key notion of explicit representation. Such a revised understanding should, I have argued, build in two dimensions of functional assessment. The first (ably canvassed by Kirsh) highlights ease of usability of information. The second (neglected by Kirsh, but vital to our intuitions concerning the difference between considered action and reflex) highlights the multitrack usability of stored information. The second dimension reveals a problem with current connectionist representations of structured information. Despite some demonstrations of single-track fluency in the exploitation of such information, the issue of its wider deployability remains unresolved. The explicit representation of structure thus remains a key research target, even once the text-based image of the inner code is abandoned.

Notes

1. Indeed, as Fodor concedes (1987 p. 23), not all the rules can be merely explicitly represented or else the machine could not actually do anything!

2. Constant time is a complexity measure according to which the number of steps needed to solve a kind of problem is a constant—for example, if all instances of that problem type can be solved in three steps. This is a very strong requirement which he is forced to water down a little. The details of this proposal are, however, not important for our argument.

Intelligence without Representation

15

Rodney A. Brooks
1991

1 Introduction

Artificial intelligence started as a field whose goal was to replicate human-level intelligence in a machine. Early hopes diminished as the magnitude and difficulty of that goal was appreciated. Slow progress was made over the next 25 years in demonstrating isolated aspects of intelligence. Some recent work has tended to concentrate on commercializable aspects of "intelligent assistants" for human workers.

No one talks about replicating the full gamut of human intelligence anymore. Instead we see a retreat into specialized subproblems, such as knowledge representation, natural language understanding, vision, or even more specialized areas such as truth maintenance or plan verification. All the work in these subareas is benchmarked against the sorts of tasks humans do within those areas. Amongst the dreamers still in the field of AI (those not dreaming about dollars, that is) there is a feeling that one day all these pieces will fall into place and we will see "truly" intelligent systems emerge.

However, I and others believe that human-level intelligence is too complex and too little understood to be correctly decomposed into the right subpieces at the moment, and that even if we knew the subpieces we still wouldn't know the right interfaces between them. Furthermore we will never understand how to decompose human-level intelligence until we've had a lot of practice with simpler intelligences.

In this paper I therefore argue for a different approach to creating artificial intelligence.

- We must incrementally build up the capabilities of intelligent systems, having *complete* systems at each step, thus automatically ensuring that the pieces and their interfaces are valid.

- At each step, we should build complete intelligent systems that we let loose in the real world with real sensing and real action.

Anything less provides a candidate with which we can delude ourselves.

We have been following this approach and have built a series of autonomous mobile robots. We have reached an unexpected conclusion (**C**) and have a rather radical hypothesis (**H**).

(**C**) When we examine very simple level intelligence we find that explicit representations and models of the world simply get in the way. It turns out to be better to let the world itself serve as its own model.

(**H**) Representation is the wrong unit of abstraction in building the bulkiest parts of intelligent systems.

Representation has been the central issue in artificial intelligence work over the last 15 years only because it has provided an interface between otherwise isolated modules and conference papers.

2 The evolution of intelligence

We already have an existence proof of the possibility of intelligent entities: human beings. Additionally, many animals are intelligent to some degree. (This is a subject of intense debate, much of which really centers around a definition of intelligence.) They have evolved over the 4.6 billion year history of the earth.

It is instructive to reflect on the way in which earth-based biological evolution spent its time. Single-cell entities arose out of the primordial soup roughly 3.5 billion years ago. A billion years passed before photosynthetic plants appeared. After almost another billion and a half years, around 550 million years ago, the first fish and vertebrates arrived, and then insects 450 million years ago. Then things started moving fast. Reptiles arrived 370 million years ago, followed by dinosaurs at 330 and mammals at 250 million years ago. The first primates appeared 120 million years ago and the immediate predecessors to the great apes a mere 18 million years ago. Man arrived in roughly his present form 2.5 million years ago. He invented agriculture a scant 19,000 years ago, writing less than 5000 years ago and "expert" knowledge only over the last few hundred years.

This suggests that problem-solving behavior, language, expert knowledge and application, and reason are all pretty simple once the essence of acting and reacting are available. That essence is the ability to move around in a dynamic environment, sensing the surroundings to a degree sufficient to achieve the necessary maintenance of life and reproduction. This part of intelligence is where evolution has concentrated its time—it is much harder.

I believe that mobility, acute vision and the ability to carry out survival related tasks in a dynamic environment provide a necessary basis for the development of true intelligence. Moravec (1984) argues this same case rather eloquently.

Human level intelligence has provided us with an existence proof, but we must be careful about what lessons are to be gained from it.

A story

Suppose it is the 1890's. Artificial flight is the glamor subject in science, engineering, and venture capital circles. A bunch of AF researchers are miraculously transported by a time machine to the 1990's for a few hours. They spend the whole time in the passenger cabin of a commercial passenger Boeing 747 on a medium duration flight.

Returned to the 1890's they feel invigorated, knowing that AF is possible on a grand scale. They immediately set to work duplicating what they have seen. They make great progress in designing pitched seats, double pane windows, and know that if only they can figure out those weird 'plastics' they will have the grail within their grasp. (A few connectionists amongst them caught a glimpse of an engine with its cover off and they are preoccupied with inspirations from that experience.)

3 Abstraction as a dangerous weapon

Artificial intelligence researchers are fond of pointing out that AI is often denied its rightful successes. The popular story goes that when nobody has any good idea of how to solve a particular sort of problem (for example, playing chess) it is known as an AI problem. When an algorithm developed by AI researchers successfully tackles such a problem, however, AI detractors claim that since the problem was solvable by an algorithm, it wasn't really an AI problem after all. Thus AI never has any successes.

But have you ever heard of an AI failure?

I claim that AI researchers are guilty of the same (self-)deception. They partition the problems they work on into two components. The AI component, which they solve, and the non-AI component which they don't solve. Typically, AI "succeeds" by defining the parts of the problem that are unsolved as not AI. The principal mechanism for this partitioning is abstraction. Its application is usually considered part of good science, and not (as it is in fact used in AI) as a mechanism for self-delusion. In AI, abstraction is usually used to factor out all aspects of perception and motor skills. I argue below that these are the hard problems solved by intelligent systems, and further that the shape of solutions to these problems constrains greatly the correct solutions of the small pieces of intelligence which remain.

Early work in AI concentrated on games, geometrical problems, symbolic algebra, theorem proving, and other formal systems (see the classic papers in Feigenbaum and Feldman 1963 and Minsky 1968). In each case, the semantics of the domains were fairly simple.

In the late sixties and early seventies, the "blocks world" became a popular domain for AI research. It had a uniform and simple semantics. The key to success was to represent the state of the world completely and explicitly. Search techniques could then be used for planning within this well-understood world. Learning could also be done within the blocks world; there were only a few simple concepts worth learning, and they could be captured by enumerating the set of subexpressions which must be contained in any formal description of a world containing an instance of the concept. The blocks world was even used for vision research and mobile robotics, as it provided strong constraints on the perceptual processing necessary (see, for instance, Nilsson 1984).

Eventually, criticism surfaced that the blocks world was a "toy world" and that within it there were simple special purpose solutions to what should be considered more general problems. At the same time there was a funding crisis within AI (both in the US and the UK, the two most active places for AI research at the time). AI researchers found themselves forced to become relevant. They moved into more complex domains, such as trip planning, going to a restaurant, medical diagnosis, and such like.

Soon there was a new slogan: "Good representation is the key to AI" (as in: *conceptually efficient programs*, Bobrow and Brown 1975). The idea was that by representing only the *pertinent* facts explicitly, the semantics of a world (which on the surface was quite complex) were reduced to a simple closed system once again. Abstraction to only the relevant details thus simplified the problems.

Consider chairs, for example. While these two characterizations are true,

```
(CAN (SIT-ON PERSON CHAIR)), and
(CAN (STAND-ON PERSON CHAIR)),
```

there is really much more to the concept of a chair. Chairs have some flat (maybe) sitting place, with perhaps a back support. They have a range of possible sizes, requirements on strength, and a range of possibilities in shape. They often have some sort of covering material—unless they are made of wood, metal or plastic. They sometimes are soft in particular places. They can come from a range of possible styles. In sum, the concept of what is a chair is hard to characterize simply. There is certainly no AI vision program that can find arbitrary chairs in arbitrary images; they can at best find one particular type of chair in carefully selected images.

This characterization, however, is perhaps the correct AI representation for solving certain problems—for instance, one in which a hungry person sitting on a chair in a room can see a banana hanging from the ceiling just out of reach. Such problems are never posed to AI systems by showing them a photo of the scene. A person (even a young child) can make the right interpretation of the photo and suggest a plan of action. For AI planning systems, however, the experimenter is required to abstract away most of the details to form a simple description in terms of atomic concepts such as PERSON, CHAIR and BANANA.

But this abstraction process is the essence of intelligence and the hard part of the problems being solved. Under the current scheme, the abstraction is done by the researchers, leaving little for the AI programs to do but search. A truly intelligent program would study the photograph, perform the abstraction itself, and solve the problem.

The only input to most AI programs is a restricted set of simple assertions deduced from the real data by humans. The problems of recognition, spatial understanding, dealing with sensor noise, partial models, and the like, are all ignored. These problems are relegated to the realm of input black boxes. Psychophysical evidence suggests they are all intimately tied up with the representation of the world used by an intelligent system.

There is no clean division between perception (abstraction) and reasoning in the real world. The brittleness of current AI systems attests to this fact. For example, MYCIN (Shortliffe 1976) is an expert at diagnosing human bacterial infections; but it really has no model of what a human (or any living creature) is or how they work, or what are

plausible things to happen to a human. If told that the aorta is rup-
tured and the patient is losing blood at the rate of a pint every minute,
MYCIN will try to find a bacterial cause of the problem.

Thus, because we still perform all the abstractions for our programs, most AI work is still done in the equivalent of the blocks world.
Now the blocks are slightly different shapes and colors, but their
underlying semantics have not changed greatly.

It could be argued that performing this abstraction (perception) for
AI programs is merely the normal reductionist use of abstraction common in all good science. The abstraction reduces the input data so that
the program experiences the same "perceptual world" (what von
Uexküll 1921 called a *Merkwelt*) as humans. Other (vision) researchers
will independently fill in the details at some other time and place. I
object to this on two grounds. First, as von Uexküll and others have
pointed out, each animal species, and clearly each robot species with
its own distinctly nonhuman sensor suites, will have its own different
Merkwelt. Second, the *Merkwelt* we humans provide our programs is
based on our own introspection. It is by no means clear that such a
Merkwelt is anything like what we actually use internally—it could just
as easily be an output coding for communication purposes (thus, most
humans go through life never realizing they have a large blind spot
almost in the center of their visual fields).

The first objection warns of the danger that reasoning strategies
developed for the human-assumed *Merkwelt* may not be valid when
real sensors and perceptual processing are used. The second objection
says that, even with human sensors and perception, the *Merkwelt* may
not be anything like that used by humans. In fact, it may be the case
that our introspective descriptions of our internal representations are
completely misleading and quite different from what we really use.

A continuing story

Meanwhile our friends in the 1890's are busy at work on their AF
machine. They have come to agree that the project is too big to be
worked on as a single entity and that they will need to become
specialists in different areas. After all, they had asked questions of
fellow passengers on their flight and discovered that the Boeing Co.
employed over 6000 people to build such an airplane.

Everyone is busy, but there is not a lot of communication
between the groups. The people making the passenger seats used
the finest solid steel available as the framework. There was some

muttering that perhaps they should use tubular steel to save weight, but the general consensus was that if such an obviously big and heavy airplane could fly then clearly there was no problem with weight.

On their observation flight, none of the original group managed a glimpse of the driver's seat, but they have done some hard thinking and believe they have established the major constraints on what should be there and how it should work. The pilot, as he will be called, sits in a seat above a glass floor so that he can see the ground below so he will know where to land. There are some side mirrors so he can watch behind for other approaching airplanes. His controls consist of a foot pedal to control speed (just as in these new fangled automobiles that are starting to appear), and a steering wheel to turn left and right. In addition the wheel stem can be pushed forward and back to make the airplane go up and down. A clever arrangement of pipes measures airspeed of the airplane and displays it on a dial. What more could one want? Oh yes. There's a rather nice setup of louvers in the windows so that the driver can get fresh air without getting the full blast of the wind in his face.

An interesting sidelight is that all the researchers have by now abandoned the study of aerodynamics. Some of them had intensely questioned their fellow passengers on this subject and not one of the modern flyers had known a thing about it. Clearly the AF researchers had previously been wasting their time in its pursuit.

4 Incremental intelligence

I wish to build completely autonomous mobile agents that co-exist in the world with humans, and are seen by those humans as intelligent beings in their own right. I will call such agents *Creatures*. This is my intellectual motivation. I have no particular interest in demonstrating how human beings work—although humans, like other animals, are interesting objects of study in this endeavor, inasmuch as they are successful autonomous agents. I have no particular interest in applications; it seems clear to me that, if my goals can be met, then the range of applications for such Creatures will be limited only by our (or their) imagination. I have no particular interest in the philosophical implications of Creatures, although clearly there will be significant implications.

Given the caveats of the previous two sections, and considering the parable of the AF researchers, I am convinced that I must tread carefully in this endeavor to avoid some nasty pitfalls.

For the moment then, consider the problem of building Creatures as an engineering problem. We will develop an *engineering methodology* for building Creatures.

First, let us consider some of the requirements for our Creatures.

- A Creature must cope appropriately and in a timely fashion with changes in its dynamic environment.

- A Creature should be robust with respect to its environment. Minor changes in the properties of the world should not lead to total collapse of the Creature's behavior; rather one should expect only a gradual change in capabilities of the Creature as the environment changes more and more.

- A Creature should be able to maintain multiple goals and, depending on the circumstances it finds itself in, change which particular goals it is actively pursuing; thus it can both adapt to surroundings and capitalize on fortuitous circumstances.

- A Creature should do *something* in the world; it should have some purpose in being.

Now, let us consider some of the valid engineering approaches to achieving these requirements. As in all engineering endeavors, it is necessary to decompose a complex system into parts, build the parts, and then interface them into a complete system.

4.1 Decomposition by function

Perhaps the strongest traditional notion of intelligent systems (at least implicitly among AI workers) has been of a central system, with perceptual modules as inputs and action modules as outputs. The perceptual modules deliver a symbolic description of the world and the action modules take a symbolic description of desired actions and make sure they happen in the world. The central system then is a symbolic information processor.

Traditionally, work in perception (and vision is the most commonly studied form of perception) and work in central systems has been done by different researchers and even totally different research laboratories. Vision workers are not immune to earlier criticisms of AI workers. Most vision research is presented as a transformation from one image representation (such as a raw grey-scale image) to another registered image (such as an edge image). Each group, AI and vision, makes assumptions about the shape of the symbolic interfaces. Hardly anyone has ever connected a vision system to an intelligent central system.

Thus the assumptions independent researchers make are not forced to be realistic. There is a real danger from pressures to neatly circumscribe the particular piece of research being done.

The central system must also be decomposed into smaller pieces. We see subfields of artificial intelligence such as "knowledge representation", "learning", "planning", "qualitative reasoning", etc. The interfaces between these modules are also subject to intellectual abuse.

When researchers working on a particular module get to choose both the inputs and the outputs that specify the module requirements, I believe there is little chance the work they do will fit into a complete intelligent system.

This bug in the functional decomposition approach is hard to fix. One needs a long chain of modules to connect perception to action. In order to test any of them, they all must first be built. But until realistic modules are built, it is highly unlikely that we can predict exactly what modules will be needed or what interfaces they will need.

4.2 Decomposition by activity

An alternative decomposition makes no distinction between peripheral systems, such as vision, and central systems. Rather, the fundamental slicing up of an intelligent system is in the orthogonal direction, dividing it into *activity* producing subsystems. Each activity, or behavior-producing system, individually connects sensing to action. We refer to an activity producing system as a *layer*. An activity is a pattern of interactions with the world. Another name for our activities might well be *skills*—since each activity can, at least post facto, be rationalized as pursuing some purpose. We have chosen the word 'activity', however, because our layers must decide when to act for themselves—not be some subroutine to be invoked at the beck and call of some other layer. We call Creatures that are decomposable into activities or behavior-producing layers in this way *behavior-based systems*.

The advantage of this approach is that it gives an incremental path from very simple systems to complex autonomous intelligent systems. At each step of the way, it is only necessary to build one small piece, and interface it to an existing, working, complete intelligence.

The idea is to build first a very simple complete autonomous system, and *test it in the real world*. Our favorite example of such a system is a Creature, actually a mobile robot, which avoids hitting things. It senses objects in its immediate vicinity and moves away from them, halting if it senses something in its path. It is still necessary to build this system by decomposing it into parts, but there need be no clear distinction between a "perception system", a "central system" and an "action system". In fact, there may well be two independent channels connecting sensing to action—one for initiating motion, and one for emergency halts—so there is no single place where "perception" delivers a representation of the world in the traditional sense.

Next we build an incremental layer of intelligence which operates in parallel to the first system. It is pasted onto the existing debugged system and tested again in the real world. This new layer might directly access the sensors and run a different algorithm on the delivered data. The first-level autonomous system continues to run in parallel, and unaware of the existence of the second level. For example, in Brooks (1986) we reported on building a first layer of control which let the Creature avoid objects, and then adding a layer which instilled an activity of trying to visit distant visible places. The second layer injected commands to the motor control part of the first layer, directing the robot towards the goal; but, independently, the first layer would cause the robot to veer away from previously unseen obstacles. The second layer monitored the progress of the Creature and sent updated motor commands, thus achieving its goal without being explicitly aware of obstacles, which had been handled by the lower level of control.

5 Who has the representations?

With multiple layers, the notion of perception delivering a description of the world gets blurred even more, as the part of the system doing perception is spread out over many pieces which are not particularly connected by data paths or related by function. Certainly there is no identifiable place where the "output" of perception can be found. Furthermore, totally different sorts of processing of the sensor data proceed independently and in parallel, each affecting the overall system activity through quite different channels of control.

In fact, not by design but rather by observation, we note that a common theme in the ways in which our layered and distributed approach helps our Creatures meet our goals is that there is no central representation.

- Low-level simple activities can instill the Creature with reactions to dangerous or important changes in its environment. Without complex representations and the need to maintain those representations and reason about them, these reactions can easily be made quick enough to serve their purpose. The key idea is to sense the environment often, and so have an up-to-date idea of what is happening in the world.

- By having multiple parallel activities, and by removing the idea of a central representation, there is less chance that any given change in the class of properties enjoyed by the world can cause total collapse of the system. Rather, one might expect that a given change will at most incapacitate some but not all of the levels of control. Gradually, as a more alien world is entered (alien in the sense that the properties it holds are different from the properties of the world in which the individual layers were debugged) the performance of the Creature might continue to degrade. By not trying to have an analogous model of the world, centrally located in the system, we are less likely to have built in a dependence on that model being completely accurate. Rather, individual layers extract only those *aspects* (Agre and Chapman 1987) of the world which they find relevant—projections of a representation into a simple subspace, if you like. Changes in the fundamental structure of the world have less chance of being reflected in every one of those projections than they would have of showing up as a difficulty in matching some query to a single central world model.

- Each layer of control can be thought of as having its own implicit purpose (or goal, if you insist). Since they are *active* layers, running in parallel and with access to sensors, they can monitor the environment and decide on the appropriateness of their goals. Sometimes goals can be abandoned when circumstances seem unpromising, and other times fortuitous circumstances can be taken advantage of. The key idea here is to use *the world itself as its own best model*, and to match the preconditions of each goal continuously against the real world. Because there is separate hardware for each layer, we can match as many goals as can exist in parallel; we do not pay any price for higher numbers of goals, as we would if we tried to add more and more sophistication to a single processor, or even some multi-processor with a capacity-bounded network.

- The purpose of the Creature is implicit in its higher level purposes, goals, or layers. There need be no explicit representation of goals that some central (or distributed) process selects from, to decide what is most appropriate for the Creature to do next.

5.1 No representation versus no central representation

Just as there is no central representation, there is not even a central system. Each activity-producing layer connects perception to action directly. It is only the observer of the Creature who imputes a central representation or central control. The Creature itself has none; it is a collection of competing behaviors. Out of the local chaos of their interactions, there emerges, in the eye of an observer, a coherent pattern of behavior. There's no central, purposeful locus of control. (Minsky 1986 gives a similar account of how human behavior is generated.)

Note carefully that we are not claiming that chaos is a necessary ingredient of intelligent behavior. Indeed, we advocate careful engineering of all the interactions within the system (evolution had the luxury of incredibly long time scales and enormous numbers of individual experiments, and thus perhaps was able to do without this careful engineering).

We do claim, however, that there need be no explicit representation of either the world or the intentions of the system to generate intelligent behaviors for a Creature. Without such explicit representations, and when viewed locally, the interactions may indeed seem chaotic and without purpose.

I claim there is more than this, however. Even at a local level, we do not have traditional AI representations. We never use tokens which have any semantics that can be attached to them. The best that can be said in our implementations is that a number is passed from one process to another. But it is only by looking at the state of both the first and second processes that that number can be given any interpretation at all. An extremist might say that we really do have representations, but they are just implicit. With an appropriate mapping of the complete system and its state to another domain, we could define representations that these numbers and topological connections between processes somehow encode.

However we are not happy with calling such things representations. They differ from standard representations in too many ways.

There are no variables that need instantiation in reasoning processes. (See Agre and Chapman 1987 for a more thorough treatment of this.) There are no rules that need to be selected through pattern matching. There are no choices to be made. To a large extent, the state of the world determines the action of the Creature. Simon (1969/81) noted that the complexity of behavior of a system was not necessarily inherent in the complexity of the Creature, but perhaps in the complexity of the environment. He made this analysis in his description of an ant wandering the beach, but ignored its implications in the next paragraph when he talked about humans. We hypothesize (following

Agre and Chapman) that much of even human-level activity is similarly a reflection of the world through very simple mechanisms without detailed representations.

6 The methodology in practice

In order to build systems based on an activity decomposition so that they are truly robust, we must rigorously follow a careful methodology.

6.1 Methodological maxims

First, it is vitally important to test the Creatures we build *in the real world*—the same world that we humans inhabit. It is disastrous to fall into the temptation of testing them in a simplified world first, even with the best intentions of later transferring activity to an unsimplified world. With a simplified world (matte painted walls, rectangular vertices everywhere, colored blocks as the only obstacles) it is very easy to build a submodule of the system that happens accidentally to rely on some of those simplified properties. This reliance can then easily be reflected in the requirements on the interfaces between that submodule and others. The disease spreads and the complete system depends in a subtle way on the simplified world. When it comes time to move to the unsimplified world, we gradually and painfully realize that every piece of the system must be rebuilt. Worse than that, we may need to rethink the total design, as the issues may change completely. We are not so concerned that it might be dangerous to test simplified Creatures first, and later add more sophisticated layers of control, because evolution has been successful using this approach.

Second, as *each* layer is built, it must be tested *extensively* in the real world. The system must interact with the real world over extended periods. Its behavior must be observed and be carefully and thoroughly debugged. When a second layer is added to an existing layer, there are three potential sources of bugs: the first layer, the second layer, and the interaction of the two layers. Eliminating the first of these sources of bugs as a possibility makes finding bugs much easier. Furthermore, there remains only one thing that it is possible to vary in order to fix the bugs—the second layer.

6.2 An instantiation of the methodology: Allen

We have now built a series of robots based on the methodology of task decomposition. They all operate in an unconstrained dynamic world

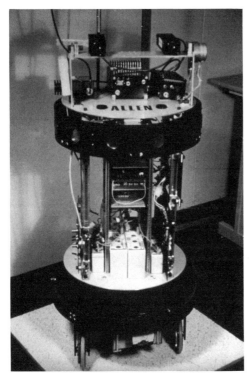

Figure 15.1: This is the first robot we built, called Allen.

(laboratory and office areas in the MIT Artificial Intelligence Laboratory). They successfully operate with people walking by, people deliberately trying to confuse them, and people just standing around
watching them. All these robots are Creatures in the sense that, on
power-up, they exist in the world and interact with it, pursuing multiple goals determined by their control layers implementing different
activities. This is in contrast to other mobile robots that are given programs or plans to follow for a specific mission.

Our first robot, named *Allen*, is shown in figure 15.1. Allen uses an
offboard Lisp machine for most of its computations. Allen implements
the abstract architecture that we call the *subsumption architecture*,
embodying the fundamental ideas of decomposition into layers of
task-achieving behaviors, and incremental composition through
debugging in the real world. (Details of this and other implementations can be found in Brooks 1987.)

Each layer in the subsumption architecture is composed of a fixed-topology network of simple finite state machines. Each finite state machine has a handful of states, one or two internal registers, one or two internal timers, and access to simple computational machines which can compute things such as vector sums. The finite state machines run asynchronously, sending and receiving fixed-length (in this case, 24-bit) messages over *wires*. For Allen, these were virtual wires; on our later robots we have used physical wires to connect computational components.

There is no central locus of control. Rather, the finite state machines are data-driven by the messages they receive. The arrival of messages or the expiration of designated time periods cause the finite state machines to change state. The finite state machines have access to the contents of the messages and might output them, test them with a predicate and conditionally branch to a different state, or pass them to simple computation elements. There is no possibility of access to global data, nor of dynamically established communications links. There is thus no possibility of global control. All finite state machines are equal, yet at the same time they are prisoners of their fixed-topology connections.

Layers are combined through mechanisms we call *suppression* (whence the name 'subsumption architecture') and *inhibition*. In both cases, as a new layer is added, one of the new wires is side-tapped into an existing wire. A predefined time constant is associated with each side-tap. In the case of suppression, the side-tapping occurs on the input side of a finite state machine. If a message arrives on the new wire, it is directed to the input port of the finite state machine as though it had arrived on the existing wire. Additionally any new messages on the existing wire are suppressed (that is, rejected) for the specified time period. For inhibition, the side-tapping occurs on the output side of a finite state machine. A message on the new wire simply inhibits messages being emitted on the existing wire for the specified time period. Unlike suppression, the new message is not delivered in their place.

As an example, consider the three layers of figure 15.2. These are three layers of control that we have run on Allen for well over a year. The robot has a ring of 12 ultrasonic sonars as its primary sensors. Every second, these sonars are run to give twelve radial depth measurements. Sonar is extremely noisy due to many objects being mirrors to sonar. There are thus problems with specular reflection and return

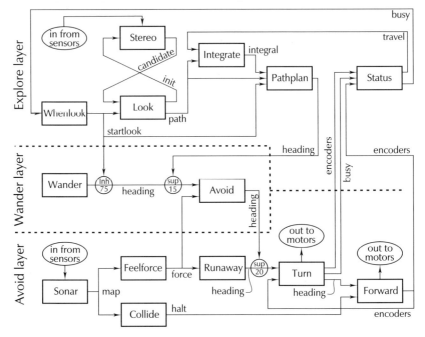

Figure 15.2: We wire finite state machines together into layers of control. Each layer is built on top of existing layers. Lower layers never rely on the existence of higher-level layers. (This is Allen.)

paths following multiple reflections due to surface skimming with low angles of incidence (less than thirty degrees).

In more detail the three layers work as follows.

1. The lowest-level layer implements a behavior which makes the robot (the physical embodiment of the Creature) avoid hitting objects. It avoids both static objects and moving objects—even those that are actively attacking it. The finite state machine labelled *sonar* simply runs the sonar devices and every second emits an instantaneous map with the readings converted to polar coordinates. This map is passed on to the *collide* and *feelforce* finite state machines. The first of these simply watches to see of there is anything dead ahead, and if so sends a *halt* message to the finite state machine in charge of running the robot forwards. (If that finite state machine is not in the correct state the message may well be ignored.) Simultaneously, the other finite state machine computes a repulsive force on the robot, based on an inverse-square law, where each sonar return is considered to indicate the presence of a repulsive object. The contributions from all the sonars are

vector-added to produce an overall force acting on the robot. The output is passed to the *runaway* machine, which thresholds it and passes it on to the *turn* machine, which orients the robot directly away from the summed repulsive force. Finally the *forward* machine drives the robot forward. Whenever this machine receives a halt message while the robot is driving forward, it commands the robot to halt.

This network of finite state machines generates behaviors which let the robot avoid objects. If it starts in the middle of an empty room it simply sits there. If someone walks up to it, the robot moves away. If it moves in the direction of other obstacles it halts. Overall, it manages to exist in a dynamic environment without hitting or being hit by objects.

2. The next layer makes the robot wander about, when not busy avoiding objects. The *wander* finite state machine generates a random heading for the robot every ten seconds or so. The *avoid* machine treats that heading as an attractive force and sums it with the repulsive force computed from the sonars. It uses the result to suppress the lower-level behavior, forcing the robot to move in a direction close to what *wander* decided but at the same time avoiding any obstacles. Note that if the *turn* and *forward* finite state machines are busy running the robot, the new impulse to wander will be ignored.

3. The third layer makes the robot try to explore. It looks for distant places, then tries to reach them. This layer suppresses the wander layer, and observes how the bottom layer diverts the robot due to obstacles (perhaps dynamic). It corrects for any divergences, and the robot achieves the goal.

The *whenlook* finite state machine notices when the robot is not busy moving, and starts up the free space finder (labelled *stereo* in the diagram) finite state machine. At the same time it inhibits wandering behavior so that the observation will remain valid. When a path is observed it is sent to the *pathplan* finite state machine, which injects a commanded direction to the *avoid* finite state machine. In this way lower-level obstacle avoidance continues to function. This may cause the robot to go in a direction different from that desired by *pathplan*. For that reason, the actual path of the robot is monitored by the *integrate* finite state machine, which sends updated estimates to the *pathplan* machine. This machine then acts as a difference engine, forcing the robot in the desired direction and compensating for the actual path of the robot as it avoids obstacles.

These are just the particular layers that were first implemented on Allen. (See Brooks 1986 for more details; Brooks and Connell 1986 report on another three layers implemented on that particular robot.)

Figure 15.3: This is Herbert, a more ambitious robot than Allen.

6.3 A second example: Herbert

Allen's lowest layer was entirely reactive: it merely avoided collisions. But its next two layers, *wander* and *explore*, were not entirely reactive. Our second Creature, a mobile robot named *Herbert* (Connell 1989), was a much more ambitious project, and pushed the idea of reactivity—as in Allen's lowest layer—much further.

Herbert (shown in figure 15.3) used thirty infrared proximity sensors to navigate along walls and through doorways, a magnetic compass to maintain a global sense of direction, a laser scanner to find soda-can-like objects visually, and a host of sensors on an arm with a set of fifteen behaviors which, together, were sufficient to locate and pick up soda cans reliably. Herbert's task was to wander around people's offices looking for soda cans, pick one up, and bring it back to where the robot had started from. Herbert did succeed at this task (although mechanical failures in the seating of its onboard chips limited reliable operation to about fifteen minutes at a time).

In programming Herbert, it was decided that it should maintain no internal state longer than three seconds, and that there would be no internal communication between behavior generating modules. Each one was connected to sensors on the input side, and a fixed-priority arbitration network on the output side. The arbitration network drove the actuators.

Since Herbert maintained hardly any internal state—hardly any memory—it often had to rely on the world itself as its only available "model" of the world. Further, the world itself was the only effective medium of communication between Herbert's separate modules. The laser-based soda-can finder, for example, drove the robot so that its arm was lined up in front of the soda can. But it did not tell the arm controller that there was now a soda can ready to be picked up. Rather, the arm behaviors monitored the shaft encoders on the wheels, and, when they noticed that there was no body motion, initiated motions of the arm—which, in turn, triggered other behaviors such that, eventually, the robot would pick up the soda can.

The advantage of this approach was that there was no need to set up internal expectations for what was going to happen next. That meant that the control system could both (1) be naturally opportunistic if fortuitous circumstances presented themselves, and (2) easily respond to changed circumstances—such as some other object approaching on a collision course.

As one example of how the arm behaviors cascaded upon one another, consider actually grasping a soda can. The hand had a grasp reflex that operated whenever something broke an infrared beam between the fingers. When the arm located a soda can with its local sensors, it simply drove the hand so that the two fingers lined up on either side of the can. The hand then independently grasped the can. Given this arrangement, it was possible for a human to hand a soda can to the robot. As soon as it was grasped, the arm retracted—it did not matter whether it was a soda can that was intentionally grasped, or one that magically appeared. The same opportunism among behaviors let the arm adapt automatically to a wide variety of cluttered desktops, and still successfully find the soda can.

The point of Herbert is two-fold:

- It demonstrates complex, apparently goal-directed and intentional behavior in a system which has no long-term internal state and no internal communication; and

- It is very easy for an observer of such a system to attribute more complex internal structure than really exists—Herbert, for instance, appeared to be doing things like path planning and map building, even though it was not.

7 What this is not

The subsumption architecture with its network of simple machines is reminiscent, at the surface level at least, of a number of mechanistic approaches to intelligence, such as connectionism and neural networks. But it is different in many respects from these endeavors, and also quite different from many other post-Dartmouth* traditions in artificial intelligence. We very briefly explain those differences in the following paragraphs.

7.1 It isn't connectionism

Connectionists try to make networks of simple processors. In that regard, the things they build (in simulation only—no connectionist system has ever driven a real robot in a real environment, no matter how simple) are similar to the subsumption networks we build. However, their processing nodes tend to be uniform, and they seek insights (as their name suggests) from learning how best to interconnect them (which is usually assumed to mean richly, at least). Our nodes, by contrast, are all unique finite state machines, the density of connections among them is much lower, is not at all uniform, and is especially low between layers. Additionally, connectionists seem to be looking for explicit distributed representations to arise spontaneously from their networks. We harbor no such hopes because we believe representations are not necessary and appear only in the eye or mind of the observer.

7.2 It isn't neural networks

Neural-network research is the parent discipline, of which connectionism is a recent incarnation. Workers in neural networks claim that there is some biological significance to their network nodes, as models of neurons. Most of the models seem wildly implausible given the paucity of modeled connections relative to the thousands found in real neurons. We claim no biological significance in our choice of finite state machines as network nodes.

---

* *Editor's note:* Newell and Simon presented the first working AI program, *The Logic Theorist*, at a famous workshop organized by John McCarthy at Dartmouth College in the summer of 1956.

7.3 It isn't production rules

Each individual activity-producing layer of our architecture could be viewed as in implementation of a production rule. When the right conditions are met in the environment, a certain action will be performed. We feel that analogy is a little like saying that any FORTRAN program with IF statements is implementing a production-rule system. But a production system really is more than that—it has a rule base, from which a particular rule is selected by matching the preconditions for some or all of the rules to a given database; and these preconditions may include variables which must be bound to individuals in that database. Our layers, on the other hand, run in parallel and have no variables or need for matching. Instead, aspects of the world are extracted and directly trigger or modify certain behaviors of the layer.

7.4 It isn't a blackboard

If one really wanted, one could make an analogy of our networks to a blackboard control architecture. Some of the finite state machines would be localized knowledge sources. Others would be processes acting on these knowledge sources by finding them on the blackboard. There is a simplifying point in our architecture however: all the processes know exactly where to look on the "blackboard", since they are hardwired to the correct place. I think this forced analogy indicates its own weakness. There is no flexibility at all in where a process can gather appropriate knowledge. Most advanced blackboard architectures make heavy use of the general sharing and availability of almost all knowledge. Furthermore, in spirit at least, blackboard systems tend to hide from a consumer of knowledge who the particular producer was. This is the primary means of abstraction in blackboard systems. In our system we make such connections explicit and permanent.

7.5 It isn't German philosophy

In some circles, much credence is given to Heidegger as one who understood the dynamics of existence. Our approach has certain similarities to work inspired by this German philosopher (for instance, Agre and Chapman 1987) but our work was not so inspired. It is based purely on engineering considerations. That does not preclude it from being used in philosophical debate as an example on any side of any fence, however.

8 Key ideas

Situatedness, embodiment, intelligence, and emergence can be identified as key ideas that have led to the new style of artificial intelligence research that we are calling "behavior-based robots".

8.1 Situatedness

Traditional artificial intelligence has adopted a style of research where the agents that are built to test theories about intelligence are essentially problem solvers that work in a symbolic abstracted domain. The symbols may have referents in the minds of the builders of the systems, but there is nothing to ground those referents in any real world. Furthermore, the agents are not situated in a world at all. Rather, they are simply given a problem, and they solve it. Then they are given another problem, and they solve that one. They are not participating in a *world* at all, as do agents in the usual sense.

In these systems, there is no external world per se, with continuity, surprises, or history. The programs deal only with a model world, with its own built-in physics. There is a blurring between the knowledge of the agent and the world it is supposed to be operating in. Indeed, in many artificial intelligence systems, there is no distinction between the two: the agent is capable of direct and perfect perception as well as direct and perfect action. When consideration is given to porting such agents or systems to operate in the world, the question arises of what sort of representation they need of the real world. Over the years within traditional artificial intelligence, it has become accepted that they will need an objective model of the world with individuated entities, tracked and identified over time. The models of knowledge representation that have been developed expect and require such a one-to-one correspondence between the world and the agent's representation of it.

Early AI robots, such as Shakey and the Cart, certainly followed this approach. They built models of the world, planned paths around obstacles, and updated their estimates of where the objects were relative to themselves as they moved. We have developed a different approach (Brooks 1986) in which a mobile robot uses the world itself as its own model—continuously referring to its sensors rather than to an internal world model. The problems of object class and identity disappear. The perceptual processing becomes much simpler. And the performance of this robot (Allen) is better in comparable tasks than the Cart. (The tasks carried out by Allen, not to mention Herbert, are in a different class from those attempted by Shakey—Shakey could certainly not have done what Allen does.)

A situated agent must respond in a timely fashion to its inputs. Modelling the world completely under these conditions can be computationally challenging. But a world in which it is situated also provides some continuity to the agent. That continuity can be relied upon, so that the agent can use its perception of the world instead of an objective world model. The representational primitives that are useful then change quite dramatically from those in traditional artificial intelligence.

The key idea from situatedness is: *The world is its own best model.*

8.2 Embodiment

There are two reasons that embodiment of intelligent systems is critical. First, only an embodied intelligent agent is fully validated as one that can deal with the real world. Second, only through a physical grounding can any internal symbolic or other system find a place to bottom out, and give "meaning" to the processing going on within the system.

The physical grounding of a robot within the world forces its designer to deal with all the issues. If the intelligent agent has a body, has sensors, and has actuators, then all the details and issues of being in the world must be faced. It is no longer possible to argue in conference papers that the simulated perceptual system is realistic, or that problems of uncertainty in action will not be significant. Instead, physical experiments can be done simply and repeatedly. There is no room for "cheating" (in the sense of self-delusion). When this is done, it is usual to find that many of the problems that used to seem significant are not so in the physical system. Typically, "puzzle-like" situations, where symbolic reasoning had seemed necessary, tend not to arise in embodied systems. At the same time, many issues that had seemed like non-problems become major hurdles. Typically, these concern aspects of perception and action. (In fact, there is some room for cheating even here: for instance, the physical environment can be specially simplified for the robot—and it can be very hard in some cases to identify such self-delusions.)

Without an ongoing participation in and perception of the world, there is no meaning for an agent—everything is empty symbols referring only to other symbols. Arguments might be made that, at some level of abstraction, even the human mind operates in this solipsist position. However, biological evidence suggests that the human mind's connection to the world is so strong, and so many-faceted, that these philosophical abstractions may not be correct.

The key idea from embodiment is: *The world grounds the regress of meaning-giving.*

8.3 Intelligence

Earlier, I argued that the sorts of activities we usually think of as demonstrating intelligence in humans have been taking place for only a very small fraction of our evolutionary lineage. I argued further that the "simple" things concerning perception and mobility in a dynamic environment took evolution much longer to perfect, and that all those capabilities are a necessary basis for "higher-level" intellect.

Therefore, I proposed looking at simpler animals as a bottom-up model for building intelligence. It is soon apparent, when "reasoning" is stripped away as the prime component of a robot's intellect, that the dynamics of the interaction of the robot and its environment are primary determinants of the structure of its intelligence.

Simon's (1969) discussion of the ant walking along a beach started off in a similar vein. He pointed out that the complexity of the behavior of the ant is more a reflection of the complexity of its environment than of its own internal complexity. He speculated that the same might be true of humans—but then, within two pages of text, reduced the study of human behavior to the domain of crypt-arithmetic problems.

It is hard to draw a line between what is intelligence and what is environmental interaction. In a sense, it doesn't really matter which is which, inasmuch as all intelligent systems must be situated in some world or other if they are to be successful or useful entities.

The key idea from intelligence is: *Intelligence is determined by the dynamics of interaction with the world.*

8.4 Emergence

In discussing where intelligence resides in an artificial intelligence program, Minsky (1961) points out that "there is never any 'heart' in a program", but rather that, if we look, "we find senseless loops and sequences of trivial operations". It is hard to point at a single component as the seat of intelligence. There is no homunculus. Rather, intelligence emerges from the interaction of the components of the system.

The way in which it emerges, however, is quite different for traditional and for behavior-based artificial intelligence systems.

In traditional artificial intelligence, the modules that are defined are information-processing or functional modules. Typically, these might include a perception module, a planner, a world modeler, a learner, and the like. Such components directly participate in the functions of perceiving, planning, modeling, learning, and so on. Intelligent behavior of the system as a whole—such as avoiding obstacles, standing up, controlling gaze, et cetera—emerges from the interaction of the components.

In behavior-based artificial intelligence, by contrast, the modules that are defined are behavior-producing. Typically, these might include modules for obstacle avoidance, standing up, gaze control, and the like. Such components directly participate in producing the behaviors of avoiding obstacles, standing up, controlling gaze, and so on. Intelligent functionality of the system as a whole—such as perception, planning, modeling, learning, et cetera—emerges from the interaction of the components.

Although this dualism between traditional and behavior-based systems looks pretty, it is not entirely accurate. Traditional systems have hardly ever been really connected to the world, and so the emergence of intelligent behavior is, in most cases, more of an expectation than an established phenomenon. Conversely, because of the many behaviors present in a behavior-based system, and their individual dynamics of interaction with the world, it is often hard to say that a particular series of actions was produced by a particular behavior-module. Sometimes many behaviors are occurring simultaneously, or are switching rapidly.

It is not feasible to identify the seat of intelligence within any system, since intelligence is produced by the interactions of many components. Intelligence can only be determined by the total behavior of the system and how that behavior appears in relation to the environment.

The key idea from emergence is: *Intelligence is in the eye of the observer.*

9 Limits to growth

Since our approach is performance based, it is the performance of the systems we build which must be used to measure its usefulness and to point to its limitations.

We claim that our behavior-based robots, using the subsumption architecture to implement complete Creatures, are by now the most reactive real-time mobile robots in existence. Most other mobile robots are still at the stage of individual "experimental runs" in static environments, or at best in completely mapped static environments. Ours, on the other hand, operate completely autonomously in complex dynamic environments at the flick of their on-switches, and continue until their batteries are drained. We believe they operate at a level closer to simple insect-level intelligence than to bacteria-level intelligence. Evolution took 3 billion years to get from single cells to insects, and only another 500 million years from there to humans. This statement is not intended as a prediction of our future performance, but rather to indicate the nontrivial nature of insect-level intelligence.

Despite this good performance to date, there are a number of serious questions about our approach. We have beliefs and hopes about how these questions will be resolved, but under our criteria only performance truly counts. Experiments and building more complex systems take time. So, in the interim, the best we can do is indicate where the main questions lie, with the hope that there is at least a plausible path forward to more intelligent machines from our current situation.

Our belief is that the sorts of activity-producing layers of control we are developing (mobility, vision, and survival related tasks) are necessary prerequisites for higher-level intelligence in the style we attribute to human beings. The most natural and serious questions concerning limits of our approach are:

- How many behavior-based layers can be built in the subsumption architecture before the interactions between layers become too complex to continue?

- How complex can the behaviors be that are developed without the aid of central representations?

- Can higher-level functions such as learning occur in these fixed topology networks of simple finite state machines?

Only experiments with real Creatures in real worlds can answer the natural doubts about our approach. Time will tell.

Dynamics and Cognition

Timothy van Gelder

1996

What is cognition? Contemporary orthodoxy maintains that it is computation: the mind is a special kind of computer, and cognitive processes are internal manipulations of symbolic representations. This broad idea has dominated the philosophy and the rhetoric of cognitive science—and even, to a large extent, its practice—ever since the field emerged from the post-war cybernetic melee. It has provided the general framework for much of the most well-developed and insightful research into the nature of mental operation. Yet, over the last decade or more, the computational vision has lost much of its lustre. Although work within it continues, a variety of difficulties and limitations have become increasingly apparent, and researchers throughout cognitive science have been casting about for other ways to understand cognition. As a result, under the broad umbrella of cognitive science, there are now many research programs which, one way or another, stand opposed to the traditional computational approach; these include connectionism, neurocomputational approaches, ecological psychology, situated robotics, and artificial life.

Is any alternative conception of the nature of cognition emerging from these programs? More generally, is there any real alternative to understanding cognition as computation? One of the most persuasive considerations favoring the computational conception has been the so-called *What-else-could-it-be?* argument. As Allen Newell put it,

> although a small chance exists that we will see a new paradigm emerge for mind, it seems unlikely to me. Basically, there do not seem to be any viable alternatives. This position is not surprising. In lots of sciences we end up where there are no major alternatives around to the particular theories we have. Then, all the interesting kinds of scientific action occur inside the major view. It seems to me that we are getting rather close to that situation with respect to the computational theory of mind. (1990, p. 5)

The central claim of this paper is that there is indeed a viable alternative. Rather than computers, cognitive systems may be *dynamical* systems; rather than computation, cognitive processes may be state-space evolution within these very different kinds of systems. If correct, this effectively disarms the *What-else-could-it-be?* argument, and advances the broader project of evaluating competing hypotheses concerning the nature of cognition. Note that these aims do not require establishing that the dynamical hypothesis is *true*. All they require is describing and motivating it sufficiently to show that it does in fact amount to a genuine alternative conception of cognition—one that is viable as a serious and fruitful avenue of research, as far as we can now tell.

A helpful way to introduce the dynamical conception is via a somewhat unusual detour through the early industrial revolution in England, circa 1788.

1 The governing problem

A central engineering challenge for the industrial revolution was to find a source of power that was reliable, smooth and uniform. In the latter half of the eighteenth century, this had become the problem of translating the oscillating action of a steam piston into the rotating motion of a flywheel. In one of history's most significant technological achievements, Scottish engineer James Watt designed and patented a gearing system for a rotary steam engine. Steam power was no longer limited to pumping; it could be applied to any machinery that could be driven by a flywheel. The cotton industry was particularly eager to replace its horses and water wheels with the new engines. However, high-quality spinning and weaving required that the source of power be highly uniform—that is, there should be little or no variation in the speed of rotation of the main driving flywheel. This is a problem, since the speed of the flywheel is affected both by the pressure of the steam from the boilers, and by the total workload being placed on the engine, and these are constantly fluctuating.

It was clear enough how the speed of the flywheel had to be regulated. In the pipe carrying steam from the boiler to the piston there was a throttle valve. The pressure in the piston chamber, and so the speed of the wheel, could be adjusted by turning this valve. To keep engine speed uniform the throttle valve would have to be turned, at just the right time and by just the right amount, to cope with changes in boiler pressure and workload. How was this to be done? The most

obvious solution was to employ a human mechanic to turn the valve as
necessary. However, this had several drawbacks: mechanics required
wages, and were often unable to react sufficiently swiftly and accurately. The industrial revolution thus confronted a second engineering
challenge: to design a device that could *automatically* adjust the throttle valve so as to maintain uniform flywheel speed despite changes in
steam pressure or workload. Such a device is known as a *governor.*

Difficult engineering problems are often best approached by breaking the overall task down into simpler subtasks, continuing the process
of decomposition until one can see how to construct devices that can
directly implement the various component tasks. In the case of the
governing problem, the relevant decomposition seems clear. A change
need only be made to the throttle valve if the flywheel is not currently
running at the correct speed. Therefore, the first subtask must be to
measure the speed of the wheel, and the second must be to calculate
whether there is any discrepancy between the desired speed and the
actual speed. If there is no discrepancy, no change is needed, for the
moment at least. If there *is* a discrepancy, then the governor must
determine by how much the throttle valve should be adjusted to bring
the speed of the wheel to the desired level. This will depend, of course,
on the current steam pressure, and so the governor must measure the
current steam pressure and then on that basis calculate how much to
adjust the valve. Finally, the valve must actually be adjusted. This overall sequence of subtasks must be carried out often enough to keep the
speed of the wheel sufficiently close to the desired speed.

A device able to solve the governing problem would have to carry
out these various subtasks repeatedly in the correct order. So we could
think of it as obeying the following algorithm:

(1) Begin:

    (i) Measure the speed of the flywheel;

    (ii) Compare the actual speed against the desired speed.

(2) If there is no discrepancy, return to step 1; otherwise:

    (i) Measure the current steam pressure;

    (ii) Calculate the desired alteration in steam pressure;

    (iii) Calculate the necessary throttle-valve adjustment;

    (iv) Make the throttle-valve adjustment.

(3) Return to step 1.

There must be some physical device capable of actually carrying out each of these subtasks. So we can think of the governor as incorporating a tachometer (for measuring the speed of the wheel), a device for calculating the speed discrepancy, a steam-pressure meter, a device for calculating the throttle-valve adjustment, a throttle-valve adjuster, and some kind of central executive to handle sequencing of operations. This conceptual breakdown of the governing task may even correspond to the governor's actual composition; that is, each subtask may be implemented by a distinct physical component. The engineering problem would then reduce to the (presumably much simpler) one of constructing the various components and hooking them together so that the whole system functions in a coherent fashion.

Now, as obvious as this approach now seems, it was not the way the governing problem was actually solved. For one thing, it presupposes devices that can swiftly perform some fairly complex calculations; and, for another, it presupposes transducers that can transform physical conditions into symbolic arguments for these calculations, and then transform the results back into physical adjustments. Both are well beyond the capabilities of anything available in the eighteenth century.

The real solution, adapted by Watt from existing windmill technology, was much more direct and elegant. It consisted of a vertical spindle geared into the main flywheel so that it rotated at a speed directly dependent upon that of the flywheel itself (see figure 16.1). Attached to the spindle by hinges were two arms, and on the end of each arm was a metal ball. As the spindle turned, centrifugal force drove the balls outwards and hence upwards. By a clever arrangement, this arm motion was linked directly to the throttle valve. The result was that, as the speed of the main wheel increased, the arms rose, closing the valve and restricting the flow of steam; as the speed decreased, the arms fell, opening the valve and allowing more steam to flow. The engine adopted a constant speed, maintained with extraordinary swiftness and smoothness in the presence of large fluctuations in pressure and load.

It is worth emphasizing how remarkably well the centrifugal governor actually performed its task. This device was not just an engineering hack employed because computer technology was unavailable. In 1858, *Scientific American* claimed that an American variant of the basic centrifugal governor, "if not absolutely perfect in its action, is so nearly so, as to leave in our opinion nothing further to be desired".

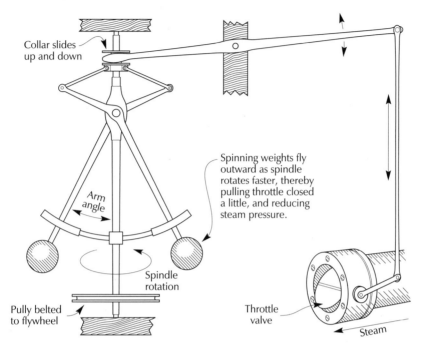

Collar slides
up and down

Spinning weights fly
outward as spindle
rotates faster, thereby
pulling throttle closed
a little, and reducing
steam pressure.

Arm angle

Spindle
rotation

Pully belted
to flywheel

Throttle
valve

Steam

Figure 16.1: The Watt centrifugal governor for controlling the speed of a steam engine. (Drawing adapted from Farey 1827.)

But why should any of this be of any interest in the philosophy of cognitive science? The answer may become apparent as we examine a little more closely some of the differences between the two governors.

2 Two kinds of governor

The two governors described in the previous section are patently different in construction, yet they both solve the same control problem, and we can assume (for purposes of discussion) that they both solve it sufficiently well. Does it follow that, deep down, they are really the same kind of device, despite superficial differences in construction? Or are they deeply different, despite their similarity in overt performance?

It is natural to think of the first governor as a *computational* device; one which, as part of its operation *computes* some result—namely, the desired change in throttle-valve angle. Closer attention reveals that there is in fact a complex group of properties working together here, a group whose elements are worth teasing apart.

Perhaps the most central of the computational governor's distinctive properties is its dependence on *representation*. Every aspect of its operation, as outlined above, deals with representations in some manner or other. The very first thing it does is measure its environment (the engine) to obtain a symbolic representation of current engine speed. It then performs a series of operations on this and other representations, resulting in an output representation, a symbolic specification of the alteration to be made in the throttle valve. This final representation then causes the valve-adjusting mechanism to make the corresponding change.

This is why it is appropriately described as *computational* (now in a somewhat narrower sense): it literally computes the desired change in the throttle valve by manipulating symbols according to a schedule of rules. Those symbols, in the context of the device and its situation, have meaning; and the success of the governor in its task is owed to its symbol manipulations being in systematic accord with those meanings. The manipulations are discrete operations which necessarily occur in a determinate *sequence*; for example, the appropriate change in the throttle valve can only be calculated after the discrepancy, if any, between the current and desired speeds has been calculated. At the highest level, the whole device operates in a *cyclic* fashion: it first measures (or "perceives") its environment; it then internally computes an appropriate change in the throttle valve; and then it effects this change ("acts" on its environment). After the change has been made and given time to affect engine speed, the governor runs through whole the cycle again and again, repeatedly.

Finally, notice that the governor is *homuncular* in construction. Homuncularity is a special kind of breakdown of a system into parts or components, each of which is responsible for a particular subtask. Homuncular components are ones that, like departments or committees within bureaucracies, interact by communicating (that is, by passing meaningful messages). Obviously, the representational and computational nature of the governor is essential to its homuncular construction: if the system as a whole did not operate by manipulating representations, it would not be possible for its components to interact by communicating.

These properties—representation, computation, sequential and cyclic operation, and homuncularity—form a mutually interdependent cluster; a device with any of them will typically possess the others. Now, the Watt centrifugal governor does not exhibit this cluster of properties as a whole, nor any of them individually. As obvious as this may seem, it deserves some discussion and argument, since it often meets resistance, and a few useful insights can be gained along the way.

There is a common intuition to the effect that the angle at which the arms are swinging represents the current speed of the engine, and that it is because the quantities are related in this way that the governor is able to control that speed. This intuition is misleading, however: the concept of representation gets no real explanatory grip in this situation. Serious explanations of how governors work—ranging from a mid-nineteenth-century mechanic's manual for constructing them, through Maxwell's original dynamical analysis (see below), to contemporary mathematical treatments—never in fact traffic in representational talk. Why not?

The heart of the matter is this. At all times, the speed of the engine influences the angle of the arms. Yet the arms are directly connected to the throttle valve, which controls the flow of steam to the engine. Thus, at all times, the angle of the arms is also influencing the speed of the engine. The quantities are thus simultaneously determining the shapes of each other's changes. There is nothing mysterious about this relationship; it is quite amenable to mathematical description. However, it is much more subtle and complex than the standard concept of representation—very roughly, one thing "standing in" for another— can handle. In order to describe the relationship between arm angle and engine speed, we need a framework that is *more powerful,* with respect to this kind of situation, than talk of representations. That framework is the mathematical language of dynamics; and, in that language, the two quantities are said to be *coupled.* The real problem with describing the governor as a representational device, then, is that the relation of representing—something standing in for something else— is just too *simple* to capture the actual interaction between the centrifugal governor and the engine.

If the centrifugal governor is not representational, then it cannot be computational, at least in the specific sense that its processing cannot be a matter of the rule-governed manipulation of symbolic representations. Its noncomputational nature can also be established in another way. Not only are there no representations to be manipulated, there are also no distinct manipulations that might count as computational operations—no discrete, identifiable steps in which one representation could get transformed into another. Rather, the system's entire operation is smooth and continuous; there is no possibility of nonarbitrarily dividing its changes over time into distinct manipulations, and no point in trying to do so. From this, it follows that the centrifugal governor is not *sequential* and not *cyclic* in its operation in anything like the manner of the computational governor. Since there are no distinct processing steps, there can be no sequence in which those steps occur. There is never any one operation that must occur before another one can take place. Consequently, there is nothing cyclical about its operation. The device has, to be sure, an "input" end (where the spindle is driven by the engine) and an "output" end (the connection to the throttle valve). But the centrifugal governor does not follow a repetitive sequence in which it first takes a measurement, then computes a throttle-valve change, then makes that adjustment, and then starts over with another measurement, and so on. Rather, input, internal activity, and output are all happening continuously and at the very same time, much as a radio is producing music at the same time as its antenna is receiving signals.

The fact that the centrifugal governor is not sequential or cyclic in any respect points to yet another deep difference between the two kinds of governor. There is an important sense in which *time does not matter* in the operation of the computational governor. Of course, inasmuch as the device must control the engine speed adequately, its internal operations must be fast *enough*; moreover, they must happen in the right order. Beyond these minimal adequacy constraints, however, there is nothing that dictates *when* each internal operation should take place, *how long* each should take to carry out, or *how long* should elapse between them. There are only pragmatic implementation considerations: which algorithms to use, what kind of hardware to use to run the algorithms, and so forth. The timing of the internal operations is thus essentially *arbitrary* relative to that of any wider course of events. It is as if the wheel said to the governing system: "go away and figure out how much to change the valve to keep me spinning at 100 rpm. I don't care how you do it, how many steps you take, or how long you take over each step, as long as you report back within (say) 10 ms."

In the centrifugal governor, by contrast, there is simply nothing that is temporally unconstrained in this way. There are no occurrences whose timing or velocity or acceleration is arbitrary relative to the operation of the engine. All behavior in the centrifugal governor happens in the very same real time frame as both the speed and changes in speed of the flywheel. We can sum up the point this way: the two kinds of governor differ fundamentally in their *temporality*, and the temporality of the centrifugal governor is essentially that of the engine itself.

Finally, it need hardly be labored that the centrifugal governor is not a homuncular system. It has parts, to be sure, and its overall behavior is the direct result of the organized interaction of those parts. The difference is that those parts are not modules interacting by communicating; they are not like little bureaucratic agents passing representations among themselves as the system achieves the overall task.

3 Conceptual frameworks

In the previous section I argued that the differences in nature between the two governors run much deeper than the obvious differences in mechanical construction. Not surprisingly, these differences in nature are reflected in the kinds of conceptual tools that we must bring to bear if we wish to understand their operation. That is, the two different governors require very different conceptual frameworks in order to understand how they function *as governors*—that is, how they manage to control their environments.

In the case of the computational governor, the behavior is captured in all relevant detail by an algorithm, and the general conceptual framework we bring to bear is that of mainstream computer science. Computer scientists are typically concerned with what can be achieved by stringing together, in an appropriate order, some set of basic operations: either how best to string them together to achieve some particular goal (programming, theory of algorithms), or what is achievable in principle in this manner (computation theory). So we understand the computational governor as a device capable of carrying out some set of basic operations (measurings, subtractings, and so on), and whose sophisticated overall behavior results from nothing more than the complex sequencing of these basic operations. Note that there is a direct correspondence between elements of the governor (the basic processing steps it goes through) and elements of the algorithm that describes its operation (the basic instructions).

The Watt centrifugal governor, by contrast, cannot be understood in this way at all. There is nothing in it for any algorithm to latch onto. Very different conceptual tools have always been used instead. The terms in which it was described above, and indeed by Watt and his peers, are straightforwardly mechanical: rotations, spindles, levers, displacements, forces. Last century, more precise and powerful descriptions became available, but these also have nothing to do with computer science. In 1868, the physicist James Clerk Maxwell made a pioneering extension of the mathematical tools of *dynamics* to regulating and governing devices (Maxwell 1868). The general approach he established has been standard ever since. Though familiar to physicists and control engineers, it is less so to most cognitive scientists and philosophers of mind, and hence is worth describing in a little detail.

The key feature of the governor's behavior is the angle at which the arms are hanging, for this angle determines how much the throttle valve is opened or closed. Therefore, in order to understand the behavior of the governor we need to understand the basic principles governing how arm angle changes over time. Obviously, the arm angle depends on the speed of the engine; hence we need to understand change in arm angle as a function of engine speed. If we suppose for the moment that the link between the governor and the throttle valve is disconnected, then this change is given by the differential equation

$$\frac{d^2\theta}{dt^2} = (n\omega)^2 \cos\theta \sin\theta - \frac{g}{l}\sin\theta - r\frac{d\theta}{dt}$$

where θ is the angle of the arms, n is a gearing constant, ω is the speed of the engine, g is a constant for gravity, l is the length of the arms, and r is a constant of friction at the hinges (Beltrami 1987, p. 163). This nonlinear, second-order differential equation tells us the instantaneous *acceleration* in arm angle, as a function of what the current arm angle happens to be (designated by the *state variable* θ), how fast the arm angle is currently changing (the derivative of θ with respect to time, $d\theta/dt$), and the current engine speed (ω). In other words, the equation tells us how change in arm angle is changing, depending on the current arm angle, the way it is changing already, and the engine speed. Note that in the system defined by this equation, change over time occurs only in arm angle, θ (and its derivatives). The other quantities (ω, n, g, l, and r) are assumed to stay fixed, and are called *parameters*. The particular values at which the parameters are fixed determine the precise shape of the change in θ. For this reason, the parameter settings are said to fix the *dynamics* of the system.

This differential equation is perfectly general and highly succinct: it is a way of describing how the governor behaves for any arm angle and engine speed. That generality and succinctness come at a price, however. If we happen to know what the current arm angle is, how fast it is changing, and what the engine speed is, then from this equation all we can figure out is the current instantaneous acceleration. If we want to know at what angle the arms will be in a half-second, for example, we need to find a *solution* to the general equation—that is, an equation which tells us what values θ takes as a function of time. There are of course any number of such solutions, corresponding to all the different behavioral trajectories that the governor might exhibit; but these solutions often have important general properties in common. Thus, as long as the parameters stay within certain bounds, the arms will always eventually settle into a particular angle of equilibrium for that engine speed; that angle is known as a *point attractor.*

Thus far I have been discussing the governor without taking into account its effect on the engine, and thereby indirectly on itself. Here, the situation gets a little more complicated, but the same mathematical tools apply. Suppose we think of the steam engine itself as a dynamical system governed by a set of differential equations, one of which gives us some derivative of engine speed as a function of current engine speed and a number of other variables and parameters:

$$\frac{d^n \omega}{dt^n} = F(\omega, \dots, \tau, \dots)$$

One of these parameters is the current setting of the throttle valve, τ, which depends directly on the governor arm angle, θ. We can thus think of θ as a parameter of the engine system, just as engine speed ω is a parameter of the governor system. (Alternatively, we can think of the governor and steam engine as comprising a single dynamical system in which both arm angle and engine speed are state variables.) This *coupling* relationship is particularly interesting and subtle. Changing a parameter of a dynamical system changes its total dynamics (that is, the way its state variables change their values depending on their current values, across the full range of values they may take). Thus, any change in engine speed, no matter how small, changes not the state of the governor directly, but rather the way the state of the governor *changes,* and any change in arm angle changes not the speed of the engine directly, but the way the speed of the engine changes. Again, however, the overall system (engine and governor coupled together) settles quickly into a point attractor; that is, engine speed and arm angle remain constant—which is exactly the desired situation. Indeed, the remarkable thing about this coupled system is that under a wide variety of conditions it always settles swiftly into states at which the engine is running at a particular speed.

In this discussion, two very broad, closely related sets of conceptual resources have (in a very modest way) been brought into play. The first is *dynamical modeling*, that branch of applied mathematics which attempts to describe change in real-world systems by describing the states of the system numerically and then writing equations which capture how these numerical states change over time. The second set of resources is *dynamical systems theory*, the general study of dynamical systems considered as abstract mathematical structures. Roughly speaking, dynamical modeling attempts to understand natural phenomena as the behavior of real-world realizations of abstract dynamical systems, whereas dynamical systems theory studies the abstract systems themselves. There is no sharp distinction between these two sets of resources, and for our purposes they can be lumped together under the general heading of *dynamics*.

4 Morals

This discussion of the governing task suggests a number of closely related lessons for cognitive science. First, various different kinds of systems, fundamentally different in nature and requiring very different conceptual tools for their understanding, can subserve sophisticated tasks—including interacting with a changing environment—which may initially appear to demand that the system have knowledge of, and reason about, its environment. Second, in any given case, our sense that a specific cognitive task *must* be subserved by a (generically) computational system *may* be due to deceptively compelling preconceptions about how systems solving complex tasks must work. It may be that the basically computational shape of most mainstream models of cognition results not so much from the nature of cognition itself as it does from the shape of the conceptual equipment that cognitive scientists typically bring to the study of cognition. Third, cognitive systems may in fact be *dynamical* systems, and cognition the behavior of some (noncomputational) dynamical system. Perhaps, that is, cognitive systems are more relevantly similar to the centrifugal governor than they are either to the computational governor, or to that more famous exemplar of the broad category of computational systems, the Turing machine.

In what follows, this third suggestion will be developed into a specifically dynamical conception of cognition via an explication of the key concept of *dynamical system*. An example will then illustrate how even "high level" cognitive performances may be intelligible in thoroughly dynamical terms. The final section will briefly defend the viability of the dynamical conception as a research program in contemporary cognitive science.

5 Three kinds of system

What are dynamical systems? How do they differ not only from computers, but also from connectionist networks—hitherto the main competition for computational models in cognitive science?

Begin with the concept of a *system.* The term 'system' is often used very loosely, designating pretty much any complex thing we wish to talk about (for example, a roulette betting system). For current purposes, however, systems are best defined more tightly as sets of *variables* (things, aspects, features, and the like) which change over time, such that the way any one variable *changes* at a given time depends on the *states* of other variables in the system at that time. Taken together, the states of all the variables make up the state of the system as a whole. Systems can be affected by external factors as well; these are commonly known as *parameters* when they are relatively fixed and influence only the way the variables interact, and as *inputs* when they are occasional and set the actual states of some variables directly.

Systems can be classified in many different ways. The most useful classifications are those that are neither too wide nor too narrow. For example, sometimes computers are taken very broadly as systems that *compute,* dynamical systems as systems that *change,* and connectionist networks as just a species of dynamical system. However, such wide definitions wash out the very contrasts that are most important for understanding what is going on in cognitive science. In what follows, informal, but more restrictive, specifications will be adopted as guides: computers are *symbol manipulators,* dynamical systems are *sets of coupled magnitudes,* and connectionist systems are *networks of neural units.* The differences among these ideas can be articulated by focusing on four points of contrast: the kinds of variables involved, the ways states change, the tools for describing the changes, and more general features that lend each kind of system its distinctive character (see table 16.1).

Thus, computers (in the relevant sense) always have digital variables.[1] For a variable to be digital, there must be some set of discrete values, such that at any relevant time the variable has unambiguously taken on one or another of those values. Thus a memory location (bit)

	Computational systems	Dynamical systems	Connectionist systems
Informal description	Symbol manipulators	Sets of coupled magnitudes	Networks of neural units
Classic exemplars	Turing machine; LISP machine	Solar system; Watt governor	Perceptron; Hopfield net
Kinds of variable	Digital—often syntactical	Quantitative— states and rates	Quantitative— activation levels
Changes in states	Discrete steps (sequential)	Interdependent in "real" time	Propagated interaction
Tools for description	Transition rules ("programs")	Differential equations	Weighted-sum equations
General character	Interpretable as representations	Coupled—with environment too	Homogenous & high-dimensional

Table 16.1: Differences among kinds of systems.

in an ordinary electronic computer is on or off; an abacus rod has a definite number of beads on each end; a Turing-tape square is either empty or occupied by a '1'; and so on. Variables in a dynamical system, by contrast, are not essentially digital (or not); rather, the important thing is that they be *quantities*—that is, variables for which it makes sense to talk about *amounts* or about *distances*[2] between values. Amounts and distances are subject to measurement: the use of some standard "yardstick" for systematically assigning numbers to values and differences. Thus the height of a falling object can be measured in meters, and the distance between any two heights determined by subtraction to yield a distance fallen. This contrasts with computers, in which there is a critical *difference* but no relevant *distance* between values of a variable (such as being empty as opposed to being occupied by a '1'). Since the variables of dynamical systems are quantities, a little mathematics allows us to talk of distances between total states. Hence the state *set* of a dynamical system is, in an interesting sense, a *space*, within which any state is a *position*, and any behavior a *trajectory*. These in turn clear the way for other important and powerful dynamical notions, such as *attractor, bifurcation, stability, and equilibrium.*

Connectionist networks have quantities as variables, so they also differ in this respect from computers. How do they differ from dynamical systems? An essential feature of connectionist networks is that their variables are modeled, in a very generic way, on biological neurons; consequently, they exhibit a distinctively "neural" form of interactive change. Each variable has a certain *activity level* (its value), and can be influenced by a certain subset of other variables. This influence, thought of as flowing or propagating along a "connection", is modulated by a parameter, known as a *weight*. The way in which units in connectionist networks change their activity values is specified by a simple function (usually just summation) of the modulated activities of all the units by which they are influenced.[3]

Now, dynamical systems *can* change state in this neural fashion, but they need not (consider the centrifugal governor, which has no connections or weights). Rather, what really makes change *dynamical*, in a strong sense, is an orthogonal requirement: it happens *in "real" time*. What does this mean?

Obviously, any system that changes at all, changes "in" time in *some* sense. But consider an abstract Turing machine, a mathematical entity standing outside the actual time of everyday events. This machine has states, and it "changes" from one state to the next; but there is no sense in which it *spends* time in any state, or *takes* time to change state. "Time" here is nothing more than an ordered series of discrete points $(t_1, t_2, \ldots)$. These points have no *duration*; nothing *elapses*. The integers are a convenient way to index these time points, since they have a familiar order. But this use can be misleading, since it falsely suggests that there are *amounts* of time involved. Practical considerations aside, one might just as well use proper names, ordered alphabetically, as labels for points of time.

Now, *real* (actual, everyday, worldly) time has two obvious properties that mere orders lack. First, real time is at least dense (between any two points of time there is another one); and second, real time is a *quantity* (there are *amounts* of time and *distances* between times). These give rise to a distinctive sense in which a process can happen *in* time (real or otherwise). The system must be in some state or other at every point of time; and so, if time is dense, the system's states and state changes must themselves be densely ordered in time. A system that is in time in this sense is potentially always changing. Further, if time is a quantity, we can relate happenings in the system in terms amounts of time; we can talk for example of how long they take, and (if the variables are quantities) of the *rate* of change. This latter fact is particularly important. For, if both time and system variables are continuous, we can talk of instantaneous rates of change, accelerations, and so on, and thus of systems in which rates of change depend on the current states, and even *current rates of change,* of the system variables (for example, the solar system and the centrifugal governor). In order to describe such systems, we need mathematical tools that can relate rates of change in variables to those variables themselves; that is, we need *differential equations.*

But doesn't change in *any* actual system—including computers—happen in real time, and thus *in* time in the relevant sense? Yes and no. Consider classical computation and complexity theory—the study of what computers as such can do. This theory is founded on the idea that details of *timing* don't matter; time is measured simply in steps or operations. But the theory carries over in its entirety to concrete, physical computers such as my Macintosh. This is to say that, in understanding the behavior of ordinary computers *as computers,* we can abstract away from the dense and quantitative nature of real time. From this point of view, they are only incidentally in time; changing the timing details would not affect what they are computing in any way. By contrast, one could never understand the behavior of the solar system while ignoring its timing. This is one of the most important differences between computers and systems that are genuinely *dynamical* in the current sense.[4]

What can be said more positively about state changes in a computer? Well, the variables are digital, and so any state change must be from one digital configuration to another. This means that transitions are *essentially* discrete: there is no theoretically relevant time between any time and the next, and no theoretically relevant state between any state and the next. These properties are reflected in the nature of the rules which describe the behavior of computers. These rules ("programs") always specify what the *next* state is, usually by specifying a discrete *operation* which transforms the current state into the next state. Further, the rules are always expressed in terms of digital properties of variables: for example, change a square from *empty* to *occupied by a '1'.*

So far, computers have been characterized in terms of the nature of their variables, their state changes, and how these state changes are specified—effectively, as *automatic formal systems* (Haugeland 1985). Yet nothing could count as a computer, in the full sense, without computing. In the most general terms, computing requires a computer, an external domain, and a systematic correspondence between the two such that states and transitions of the former *make sense* in relation to the latter. In other words, computers are those automatic formal systems whose structure supports a systematic and sensible correspondence with some domain (such as arithmetic, baseball, or whatever). Note that the digital nature of computers characteristically supports computing of a more particular kind: namely, that in which the domain itself has a clear, well-ordered structure. Relevant states of the system are structured configurations of tokens interpretable as *symbolic representations* of the domain; and state changes amount to *inferences* from one symbolic representation to another.

Now, it is clearly not essential to dynamical systems that they be systematically and sensibly interpretable with respect to some external domain. Despite the best efforts of astrologers, there is no good way to interpret the motions of the planets with regard to any other concerns. But this is not to say that dynamical systems *cannot* be interpreted; sometimes they can, and this may enable them to be understood as exhibiting cognitive functions. But any interpretation, if there is one, is always after the fact; it is no part of the dynamical system as such. A system is dynamical in virtue of *other* properties. The nature of their variables and state-changes have already been discussed, but—as in the case of computers—there is more to the story. Much of the unique flavor of dynamical systems is captured by the idea of *coupling*. As explained above, two variables are coupled when the way each *changes* at any given time depends directly on the way the other *is* at that time. In other words, coupled variables simultaneously, interdependently co-evolve, just like arm angle and engine speed in the centrifugal governor. Genuinely dynamical systems exhibit high degrees of coupling; every variable is changing all the time, and all pairs of variables are, either directly or indirectly, mutually determining the shapes of each other's changes. For example, in the solar system, the position and momentum of every massive body is constantly changing, and every variable influences every other one.

In a computer, by contrast, at each step most variables remain unchanged; and the changes that do occur are influenced by at most a few other values. Interestingly, this is also a point of contrast between connectionist networks and dynamical systems. Some networks (for example, fully recurrent networks) are dynamical in our sense; but others—such as archetypal three-layer feed-forward networks (generalized perceptrons)—exhibit no coupling at all.[5] What distinguishes connectionist networks, apart from their basically neural interaction, is that they are typically *high-dimensional* and *homogeneous*. The former property is nothing more than having a relatively[6] large number of variables; the latter is having all variables change in basically the same way. Standard mathematical specifications of connectionist networks involve just a single equation schema with indexes for variables and parameters; this form of description is made possible by homogeneity, and necessary by high-dimensionality.

This completes our brief tour of computers, dynamical systems, and connectionist networks as categories of systems. Two points are worth noting before moving on. First, the aim has been to capture the core idea in each case, rather than to provide sets of conditions which provide precise, rigid and mutually exclusive boundaries. Second, there are many different notions of computer, dynamical system, and so on, that are useful for different purposes. Those offered here are not intended to be better or more correct in general, but, at best, more useful for the philosophy of cognitive science.

6 Three conceptions of cognition

The essence of the dynamical conception of cognition is the idea that cognitive systems are dynamical systems, and cognition the behavior of such systems. The distinctions drawn in the preceding section now combine with the earlier discussion of governors to yield a more precise elaboration of this idea. Both the dynamical and the computational conceptions of cognition turn out to comprise clusters of mutually compatible and constraining commitments with three layers. The core in each case is a specific empirical hypothesis concerning the kind of system that natural cognitive systems are. Wrapped around this core are two further commitments, one concerning the "cognitive level" properties of cognitive systems, and the other concerning the kinds of conceptual tools that are most appropriate for the study of cognition. Thus, the dynamical and computational conceptions both constitute richly textured visions of the nature of cognition.

Thus, in the computational vision, cognitive systems are computers (digital, rule-governed, interpretable systems) with a modular internal structure; they interact with their environments in a cyclic process that begins with input transducers producing symbolic representations in response to the environment, continues with sequential internal computations over symbolic structures, and ends with output transducers affecting the environment in response to symbolic specifications. Each internal operation is algorithmically specified and takes place in the system's own arbitrary time frame; the whole process can be considered independently of the body and the environment except insofar as they deliver occasional inputs and receive outputs. Since the cognitive system is a computer that works by sequential transformations of symbolic representations, its most revealing descriptions are those using the conceptual apparatus of mainstream computer science. In short, the computational vision sees people as computational governors writ large.

This contrasts at every level with the dynamical vision, in which people bear deeper similarities to the *centrifugal* governor. Cognitive systems are taken to consist of sets of coupled quantities evolving in real time. These quantities may be abstract "cognitive" features (see the example below) or they may be aspects of the body or even of the environment. At a higher level, cognitive systems are understood to be complexes of continuous, ongoing, mutually constraining *changes*. The fundamental mode of interaction with the environment is not to represent it, or even to exchange inputs and outputs with it; rather, the relation is better understood via the technical notion of coupling. To be sure, cognition can, in sophisticated cases, involve representation and sequential processing; but such phenomena are best understood as emerging from a dynamical substrate, rather than as constituting the basic level of cognitive performance. As complexes of continuous, ongoing change, cognitive systems are best understood using the very same tools that have proven so effective for such processes elsewhere in science: dynamical modeling and dynamical systems theory.

Where does connectionism fit into all of this? Somewhere awkwardly in the middle. Some connectionist networks are thoroughly dynamical; but others, such as layered feed-forward networks, are configured to behave more in the cyclic and sequential fashion of computational systems. Not surprisingly, when trying to understand their systems, connectionists sometimes borrow from computer science, sometimes from dynamics, and sometimes from other fields such as statistics. Connectionist networks sometimes transform static input representations into static output representations; other times, they settle dynamically into attractors, bifurcate, and so on. In short, connectionism may be kind of half-way house between two conceptions of cognition each of which has a greater theoretical integrity on its own. Of course, it might turn out that understanding cognition really does require an eclectic mix of ingredients from several conceptual frameworks. Alternatively, it may be that connectionism is an unstable mongrel, little more than a temporary phase in the transition from generically computational to generically dynamical approaches to the study of cognition.

7 An example of dynamical research

At this stage, an example may help convey an intuitive sense of how the dynamical approach, just specified in very abstract terms, can yield real insights into the nature of cognition. Consider the process of coming to make a decision among a variety of options, each of which has attractions and drawbacks. This is surely a high-level cognitive task, if anything is. Psychologists have done countless experimental studies of how people choose, and have produced almost as many mathematical models to describe and explain that behavior. The dominant approach in modeling stems from the classic expected-utility theory and statistical decision theory, as originally developed by von Neumann and Morgenstern (1944/80). The basic idea is that an agent makes a decision by selecting the option that has the highest expected utility, which is calculated in turn by combining some formal measure of the utility of each possible outcome with the probability that it will eventuate if that option is chosen. Much of the work within this framework is mathematically elegant and provides a useful account of optimal reasoning strategies. As an account of the *actual* decisions people reach, however, classical utility theory is seriously flawed; human subjects typically deviate from its recommendations in a variety of ways. As a result, many theories proposing variations on the classical core have been developed—typically relaxing certain of its standard assumptions, with varying degrees of success in matching actual human choice behavior. Nevertheless, virtually all such theories remain subject to some further drawbacks:

- They do not incorporate any account of the underlying *motivations* which give rise to the utility that an object or outcome holds at a given time.

- They conceive of the utilities themselves as static values, and can offer no good account of how and why they might change over time, or why actual preferences are often inconsistent and inconstant.

- They offer no serious account of the deliberation *process*, with its attendant vacillations, inconsistencies and distress; and they have nothing to say about the relationships that have been uncovered between time spent deliberating and the choices eventually made.

Curiously, these drawbacks appear to have a common theme; they all concern, one way or another, *temporal* aspects of decision making. It is worth asking whether they arise because of some deep structural feature inherent in the whole framework which conceptualizes decision-making behavior in terms of calculating expected utilities.

Notice that utility-theory based accounts of human decision making ("utility theories") are deeply akin to the computational solution to the governing task. That is, if we take such accounts as not just describing the *outcome* of decision making behavior, but also as a guide to the structures and processes that *generate* the behavior, then there are basic structural similarities to the computational governor. Thus, utility theories are straightforwardly computational; they are based on static representations of options, utilities, probabilities, and the like, and processing is the algorithmically specifiable internal manipulation of these representations to obtain a final representation of the choice to be made. Consequently, utility theories are strictly sequential; they presuppose some initial temporal stage at which the relevant information about options, likelihoods, and so on, is acquired; a second stage in which expected utilities are calculated; and a third stage at which the choice is effected in actual behavior. And, like the computational governor, they are essentially atemporal; there are no inherent constraints on the timing of the various internal operations with respect to each other or changes in the environment.

What we have, in other words, is a model of human cognition which, on the one hand, instantiates the same deep structure as the computational governor, and on the other, seems structurally incapable of accounting for certain essentially temporal dimensions of decision making behavior. At this stage, we might ask: what general *kind* of model of decision making behavior we would get if, rather, we took the *centrifugal* governor as a prototype? It would be a model with a relatively small number of continuous variables influencing each other in real time. It's behavior would be defined by low-dimensional nonlinear differential equations. And it would be a model in which the agent and the choice environment, like the governor and the engine, are tightly coupled.

It would, in short, be rather like the "motivational oscillatory theory" (MOT) model described by mathematical psychologist James Townsend (Townsend 1992). MOT enables modeling of various

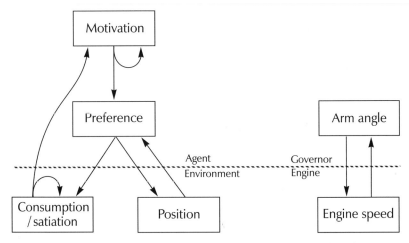

Figure 16.2: The MOT model of decision making compared to the centrifugal governor. Boxes represent variables and arrows represent influence. In each case, coupled variables evolve
continuously in time, and the system spans a kind of agent/
world divide. The MOT system is significantly more complex than the governor, but still very simple compared with
many dynamical models of cognition. Note that these diagrams should not be interpreted in a connectionist fashion;
the lines are not connections and do not have weights. (The
MOT diagram is adapted from Townsend 1992).

qualitative properties of the kind of periodic behavior that occurs
when circumstances offer the possibility of satiating desires arising
from more or less permanent motivations. An obvious example is regular eating in response to recurring natural hunger. It is built around the
idea that in such situations, your underlying motivation, transitory
desires with regard to the object, distance from the object, and consumption of it are continuously evolving and affecting each other in
real time; for example, if your desire for food is high and you are far
from it, you will move toward it, which influences your satiation and
so your desire. The framework thus includes variables for the current
state of motivation, satiation, preference, and action (movement), and
a set of differential equations that describe how these variables change
over time as a function of the current state of the system.[7]

MOT stands to utility theories as the centrifugal governor does to
the computational governor. In MOT, cognition is not symbol manipulation, but rather state-space evolution in a dynamical system that is
in certain key respects rather like the centrifugal governor. It is a

system that demands dynamical tools in its analysis. MOT produces behavior which, if one squints while looking at it, seems like decision making—after all, the agent will make the move that offers the most reward, which in this case means moving toward food if hungry enough. There is, however, a sense in which this is decision making without decisions, for there never are, in the model, any discrete internal occurrences that one could reasonably characterize as decisions. In this approach, decision making is better thought of as the behavior of an agent under the influence of the pushes and pulls that emanate from desirable outcomes, undesirable outcomes, and internal desires and motivations; in a quasi-gravitational way, these forces act on the agent with strengths varying as a function of distance.

The MOT model is a special case of a more general dynamical framework that Townsend and Jerome Busemeyer (1993) call "decision field theory". That framework, too complex to describe succinctly (an overview is provided in Busemeyer and Townsend 1995), faithfully models a wide range of behavior more easily recognizable as decision making, as studied within the traditional research paradigm. Indeed, their claim is that decision field theory "covers a broader range of phenomena in greater detail" than do classical utility theories, and even goes beyond them by explaining in a natural way several important paradoxes of decision making. The important point is that the general decision field theory works on the same fundamental dynamical principles as MOT. There is thus no question that at least certain aspects of human high-level cognitive functioning can be modeled effectively using dynamical systems of the kind that can be highlighted by reference to the centrifugal governor.

8 Is the dynamical conception viable?

In order soundly to refute a What-else-could-it-be? argument, a proposed alternative must be viable—that is, plausible enough that it is reasonably deemed an open empirical question whether the orthodox approach or the alternative is ultimately more promising.

One measure of the viability of an approach is whether valuable research can be carried out within its terms. On this measure, the dynamical approach is certainly in good health. Dynamical models have been or are being developed for a very wide range of aspects of cognitive functioning, from (so-called) "low level" or "peripheral" aspects such as perception and motor control, to (so-called) "central" or "higher" aspects such as language and decision-making, through to related areas such as psychiatry and social psychology. As already mentioned, a good deal of connectionist work falls under the dynamical banner, and this work alone would qualify the dynamical approach as worth taking seriously. However there are now also *non*connectionist dynamical models of numerous aspects of cognition, and their ranks are swelling. Further, in a number of fields under the broader umbrella of cognitive science, dynamics provides the dominant formal framework within which particular theories and models are developed; these include neural modeling, autonomous agent ("animat") research, ecological psychology and, increasingly, developmental psychology.[8]

Of course, it is quite possible for a research program to flourish, even though, for deep reasons, it will eventually prove inadequate— either in general or in particular respects. (Remember behaviorism.) So, in evaluating the plausibility of an alternative, we should also consider whether any known *general* considerations either support it or— perhaps more importantly—undermine it. Many general considerations have been raised in favor of the computational conception of cognition; and, given the stark contrasts, these might appear to argue *against* the dynamical alternative. It isn't possible to address all (or even any) such arguments adequately here; but I will briefly comment on one of the most powerful—not, however, to refute it, but rather to reveal something of the potential of the dynamical approach.

Cognition is often distinguished from other kinds of complex natural processes (such as thunderstorms or digestion) by pointing out that it depends on *knowledge*. One challenge for cognitive scientists is to understand how a physical system might exhibit such dependence in its behavior. The usual approach is to suppose that the system contains internal structures that *encode* or *represent* the knowledge. Further, it is often thought that the best way to encode or represent knowledge is to use *symbolic* representations, manipulated by some computational system. Thus, insofar as the dynamical approach abjures representation completely, or offers some less powerful representational substitute, it may seem doomed.

But, while the centrifugal governor is clearly nonrepresentational, and while (as argued above) representation figures in a natural cluster of deep features that are jointly characteristic of computational models, in fact there is nothing to prevent dynamical systems from incorporating some form of representation. Indeed, an exciting feature of the dynamical approach is that it offers opportunities for dramatically reconceiving the nature of representation in cognitive systems, even within a broadly noncomputational framework. A common strategy in dynamical modeling is to assign representational significance to some or all of the state variables or parameters (see, for example, the Townsend and Busemeyer decision-field-theory model mentioned above, or consider a connectionist network in which units stand for features of the domain).

Though representations of this kind may be exactly what is needed for *some* cognitive modeling purposes, they don't have the kind of combinatorial structure that is often thought necessary for *other* aspects of high-level cognition. However, within the conceptual repertoire of dynamics there is a vast range of entities and structures which might be harnessed into representational roles; individual state-variables and parameters are merely the very simplest of them. For example, it is known how to construct representational schemes in which complex contents (such as linguistic structures) are assigned in a recursive manner to points in the state-space of a dynamical system, such that the representations form a fractal structure of potentially infinite depth, and such that the behavior of the system can be seen as transforming representations in ways that respect the represented structure. Yet even these methods are doing little more than dipping a toe into the pool of possibilities. Representations can be trajectories or attractors of various kinds, trajectories obtained by the sequential chaining of attractors, even such exotica as transformations of attractor arrangements as a system's control parameters change (Petitot 1995).

Dynamicists are actively exploring how these and other representational possibilities might be incorporated into cognitive models, without buying the rest of the computational worldview. Consequently, while the dynamical approach is certainly a very long way from having actual solutions to most concrete problems of knowledge representation, it clearly holds sufficient promise to maintain its current viability as an alternative.

What positive reasons are there to think that the dynamical approach is actually on the right track? Again, space does not allow serious treatment of the arguments, but some are at least worth mentioning. In practice, an important part of the appeal of the dynamical approach is that it brings to the study of cognition tools that have proved extraordinarily successful in many other areas of science. But is there anything about *cognition*, in particular, that suggests that it might best be understood dynamically?

One central fact about natural cognitive processes is that they always happen *in real time,* which means not merely that, like any physical process (including ordinary digital computation), they occupy some extent of actual time, but that details of *timing*—durations, rates, rhythms, and so on—are critical to how they operate in real bodies and environments. As we saw above, dynamics is all about how processes happen in real time, whereas timing details are in a deep sense extrinsic to computational systems. Cognition also has other general features for which a dynamical approach appears well-suited. For example, it is a kind of complex behavioral organization which is emergent from the local interactions of very large numbers of (relatively) simple and homogenous elements. It is pervaded by both continuous and discrete forms of change. At every level, it involves multiple, simultaneous, interacting processes. Dynamics is a natural framework for developing theories that account for such features. Further, the systems within which cognition takes place (the brain, the body, the environment) demand dynamical tools for their description. A dynamical account of cognition promises to minimize difficulties in understanding how cognitive systems are real biological systems in constant, intimate, interactive dependence on their surroundings.[9]

A final way to underpin the viability of the dynamical conception is to place it and the computational conception in broad historical perspective. Computationalism, as cognitive science orthodoxy, amounts to a sophisticated instantiation of the basic outlines of a generically Cartesian picture of the nature of mind. The prior grip that this picture has on how most people think about mind and cognition makes the computational conception seem intuitively attractive. This would be unobjectionable if the Cartesian conception itself were basically sound. However, the upshot of philosophical evaluation of the Cartesian framework over the last three centuries, and especially in this century, is that it seriously misconceives mind and its place in nature.

Cognitive scientists tend to suppose that the primary respect in which Descartes was wrong about mind was in subscribing to an interactionist dualism: the doctrine that mind and body are two distinct substances that causally interact with one another. However, already by the eighteenth century the inadequacy of this particular aspect of Cartesianism had been exposed (Berkeley 1710/1977; Leibniz 1714/ 1977) and thoroughgoing brain-based materialism espoused (Hobbes 1651/1962; La Mettrie 1748/1912). Some of the greatest achievements of twentieth-century philosophy of mind have been to expose various other, more subtle, pervasive and pernicious epistemological and ontological misconceptions inherent in the Cartesian picture. These misconceptions are very often retained even when substance dualism is rejected in favor of some brain-based materialism, such as functionalism in its various guises.

Among the most important of these anti-Cartesian movements is one spearheaded by Ryle in Anglo-American philosophy (Ryle 1949/ 84) and Heidegger in continental philosophy (Heidegger 1927/62; Dreyfus 1991). Its target has been the generically Cartesian idea that mind is an inner realm of representations and processes, and that mind conceived this way is what causally explains intelligent behavior. This movement comprises three interrelated components. The first is a relocating of mind. The Cartesian tradition is mistaken in supposing that mind is an inner realm or entity of any sort, whether mental substance, brain states, or whatever. Ontologically, mind is much more a matter of what we *do* within environmental and social possibilities and bounds. Twentieth-century anti-Cartesianism thus draws mind *out*— in particular outside the skull. That aspect of mind that remains inside, and *is* the causal basis of our behavior, is *cognition*.

The second component is a reconceiving of our fundamental relationship to the world around us. In the Cartesian framework, the basic relation of mind to the world is one of representing it and thinking about it, with occasional "peripheral" interaction via perceiving and acting. It has been known since Berkeley that this framework has fundamental epistemological problems. But only more recently has it been shown that escaping these problems means reconceiving the human agent as essentially embedded in and skillfully coping with a changing world, and that representing and thinking about the world is secondary to and dependent upon such embeddedness (Guignon 1983).

The third component is an attack on the supposition that the kind of behavior we exhibit (such that we *are* embedded in our world and can be said to have minds) could ever be causally explained utilizing only the generically Cartesian resources of representations, rules, procedures, algorithms, and so on. A fundamental Cartesian mistake is to suppose, as Ryle variously put it, that practice is accounted for by theory, that knowledge *how* is explained in terms of knowledge *that,* or that skill is a matter of thought. In other words, not only is mind not to be found inside the skull, but also cognition, the inner causal basis of intelligent behavior, is not itself to be explained in terms of the basic entities of the general Cartesian conception.

My concern here is not to substantiate these claims or the post-Cartesian conception of the person to which they point (see, for example, Dreyfus 1972/92); it is simply to make the computational conception of cognition seem less than inevitable by casting doubt upon the philosophical framework within which it thrives. Orthodox computational cognitive science has absorbed some of the important lessons of seventeenth-century reactions to Cartesianism, but so far has remained largely oblivious to the more radical twentieth-century critiques. If, however, if we *begin* with a thoroughly post-Cartesian approach, the dynamical account of cognition will, in many ways, be immediately attractive. The post-Cartesian conception rejects the model of mind as an atemporal representer, and, like the dynamical approach to cognition, emphasizes instead ongoing, real-time interaction of situated agents with a changing world. The post-Cartesian agent is essentially temporal, since its most basic relationship to the world is real-time skillful coping; the dynamical framework is therefore a natural choice since it builds time in right from the start. The post-Cartesian agent manages to cope with the world without necessarily representing it. A dynamical approach suggests how this might be possible by showing how the internal operation of a system interacting with an external world can be so subtle and complex as to *defy* description in representational terms—how, in other words, cognition can *transcend* representation. In short, from the philosophical perspective that has managed to overcome the deep structures of the Cartesian world-view, the dynamical approach looks distinctly appealing; the Watt governor is preferable to the Turing machine as an archetype for models of cognition.

Notes

1. Here I am using the term 'computer' to refer specifically to digital computers rather than the wider class that includes so-called "analog computers". It is the narrower class which lies at the heart of the mainstream computational conception of cognition.

2. *Distance* is captured mathematically by a *metric*—a function that maps pairs of values of a variable onto real numbers in a way that satisfies certain familiar constraints. Any *quantity*, as such, will have a nontrivial metric associated with it. (An example of a trivial metric would be the same/different "metric", a function that returns 1 if two

values are different and 0 if they are the same. Applied to sequences, this kind of metric is known as "Hamming distance". It is a useful function for some purposes, but is not a metric in the relevant sense.)

3. Hence the ubiquitous "sigma" (Σ) term in connectionist equations.

4. The general field of dynamical systems theory studies many systems that are defined in terms of discrete maps. Some of these are just discretized versions of continuous systems that are *in* time in a full-blooded sense. Others, however, are not (including some that exhibit chaotic behavior). These systems are dynamical, but only in a wider sense than is used here. They bear interesting similarities both to dynamical systems and to computers.

5. The presence of a connection between two units is not enough for coupling in the full sense. Genuine coupling requires bidirectional connections and simultaneous update.

6. Relative to what? There are many ways to cash this out, but for non-linear systems, "large" is roughly *so many that we find it hard to understand the behavior of the system.*

7. The equations, with rough and partial translations into English, are:

$$\frac{dm}{dt} = M - m - c$$

(The change in motivation depends on how the current levels of motivation and consumption compare with some standard level of motivation, M.)

$$\frac{dz}{dt} = m \times \left[\frac{1}{z_1^2 + z_2^2 + a} + 1 \right]$$

(The change in *preference* for a goal depends on current motivation and distance from the object of preference.)

$$\frac{dc}{dt} = (x + C - c) \times \left[\frac{b}{z_1^2 + z_2^2 + r} + 1 \right]$$

(The change in consumption depends on the level of preference, the level of consumption, and the distance from the object of preference.

$$\frac{dz_1}{dt} = -(x \cdot z_1) \qquad\qquad \frac{dz_2}{dt} = -(x \cdot z_2)$$

(Movement toward or away from the object depends on the current level of preference for it.)

8. Rather than cite individual examples, I merely list here some overviews or collections which the interested reader can use as a bridge into the extensive realm of dynamical research on cognition. Kelso (1995) is both a manifesto for the dynamical approach and an accessible encapsulation of one powerful research program. A representative sampling of current research is contained in Port and van Gelder (1995), which also contains guides to a much larger literature. An excellent illustration of the power and scope of dynamical research, in a neural network guise, is Grossberg (1988). Serra and Zanarini (1990) present an overview of a variety of dynamical systems approaches in artificial intelligence research. For the role of dynamics in developmental psychology, see Smith and Thelen (1993) and Thelen and Smith (1993).

9. For more detailed treatment of these arguments, see van Gelder and Port (1995).

Acknowledgments

Four of the sixteen essays included here are retained from the first edition of *Mind Design* (Newell and Simon, Minsky, Dreyfus, and Searle). Seven of the remaining twelve (Turing, Dennett, Rumelhart, Smolensky, Rosenberg, Ramsey et al., and Clark) have appeared previously in essentially their present forms. The essays by Churchland and by Fodor and Pylyshyn have been abridged, slightly and substantially, respectively. The essay by Brooks has been assembled from two earlier works of his. And those by Haugeland and van Gelder are new.

All of the diagrams in this volume have been prepared afresh by the editor, and appear here for the first time.

1 HAUGELAND

"What is Mind Design?" appears for the first time in this volume.

2 TURING

"Computing Machinery and Intelligence" was first published in *Mind* 59: 433–460, 1950; it has been reprinted many times, and is included here by permission of *Mind*.

3 DENNETT

"True Believers: The Intentional Strategy and Why it Works" was originally presented as a Herbert Spencer Lecture at Oxford in November 1979, and was first published in *Scientific Explanation*, edited by A. F. Heath (Oxford: Oxford University Press, 1981); it is reprinted in Dennett 1987, and is included here by permission of the author and Oxford University Press.

4 NEWELL AND SIMON

"Computer Science as Empirical Inquiry: Symbols and Search" was the tenth Turing Award Lecture, delivered to the annual conference of the Association for Computing Machinery in 1975. It was published in the *Communications of the Association for Computing Machinery*, 19 (March 1976) 113–126. It is reprinted here by permission of the authors and the ACM.

5 MINSKY

"A Framework for Representing Knowledge" was originally published as Memo 306 of the Artificial Intellignece Laboratory at MIT. Excerpts were reprinted in *The Psychology of Computer Vision*, edited by Patrick H. Winston (New York: McGraw Hill, 1975). Different (but overlapping) excerpts are reprinted here, by permission of the author. (Note: these excerpts were so selected as to ensure that every part of the original Memo appears either here or in Winston.)

6 DREYFUS

"From Micro-Worlds to Knowledge Representation: AI at an Impasse" is excerpted (with minor revisions) from the introduction to the second edition of *What Computers Can't Do: A Critique of Artificial Reason* (New York: Harper and Row, 1979). It is reprinted here by permission of the author and Harper and Row.

The author is grateful to John Haugeland for editorial suggestions on transforming the original text into a self-standing article.

7 SEARLE

"Minds, Brains, and Programs" was first published in *Behavioral and Brain Sciences* 1: 417–424, 1980. Copyright © Cambridge University Press. It is reprinted here by permission of the author and publisher.

The author acknowledges his debts to a rather large number of people for discussion of these matters and for their patient attempts to overcome his ignorance of artificial intelligence—with special thanks to Ned Block, Hubert Dreyfus, John Haugeland, Roger Schank, Robert Wilensky, and Terry Winograd.

8 RUMELHART

"The Architecture of Mind: A Connectinist Approach" first appeared in *Foundations of Cognitive Science*, edited by Michael I. Posner (Cambridge, MA: Bradford/MIT Press, 1989). It is reprinted here by permission of the author and The MIT Press.

9 SMOLENSKY

"Connectionist Modeling: Neural Computation / Mental Connections" first appeared in this form in *Neural Connections, Mental Computation*, edited by Lynn Nadel, Lynn A. Cooper, Peter Culicover, and R. Michael Harnish (Cambridge, MA: Bradford/MIT Press, 1989). It is a slightly revised version of "Connectionist AI, Symbolic AI, and the Brain", *Artificial Intelligence Review* 1: 95–109 (1987). It is reprinted here by permission of the author and The MIT Press.

The author acknowledges research support from NSF grant IST-

8609599 and from the Department of Computer Science and the Institute of Cognitive Science at the University of Colorado, Boulder.

10 CHURCHLAND

"On the Nature of Theories: A Neurocomputational Perspective" first appeared in *Scientific Theories: Minnesota Studies in the Philosophy of Science,* volume 14, edited by C. Wade Savage (Minneapolis: University of Minnesota Press, 1990). It is reprinted in Churchland 1989, and is included here by permission of the author and The University of Minnesota Press. (The present version is slightly abridged, six paragraphs and two diagrams having been omitted from section 6.)

11 ROSENBERG

"Connectionism and Cognition" first apeared in *Acta Analytica* (Dubrovnik) 6: 33–46 (1990). It is reprinted here, slightly revised, by permission of the author.

The author gratefully acknowledges research support from The Center for Interdisciplinary Research (ZiF) in Bielefeld, Germany, and the Alexander von Humboldt-Stiftung.

12 FODOR AND PYLYSHYN

"Connectionism and Cognitive Architecture: A Critical Analysis" first appeared in *Cognition* 28: 3–71 (1988), and is reprinted in Pinker and Mehler, 1988. The present abridged version contains just over 60% of the original main text, but with less than 20% of the footnote text. It is included here by permission of the authors and Elsevier Science Publishers B. V., Amsterdam.

13 RAMSEY, STICH, AND GARON

"Connectionism, Eliminativism, and the Future of Folk Psychology" appeared previously in *Action Theory and Philosophy of Mind—Philosophical Perspectives* 4: 499–533, edited by James E. Tomberlin (Atascadero, CA: Ridgeview, 1990) and in *Philosophy and Connectionist Theory,* edited William Ramsey, Stephen P. Stich, and David E. Rumelhart (Hillsdale, NJ: Lawrence Erlbaum Associates, 1991). It is included here by permission of the authors.

The authors would like to thank Ned Block, Paul Churchland, Gary Cottrell, Adrian Cussins, Jerry Fodor, John Heil, Frank Jackson, David Kirsh, Patricia Kitcher and Philip Kitcher for useful feedback on earlier versions.

14 CLARK

"The Presence of a Symbol" first appeared in *Connection Science* 4: 193–205 (1992). It is reprinted here by permission of the author and Carfax Publishing Company.

15 BROOKS

"Intelligence without Representation", in its original form, was first presented at the *Workshop on Foundations of Artificial Intelligence* at Endicott House in June 1987, and subsequently appeared in *Artificial Intelligence* 47: 139–159 (1991). The version in this volume differs from that earlier one in two main ways: about thirty paragraphs have been added, and ten deleted. The added paragraphs now make up subsection 6.3 and section 8; they are extracted from "Intelligence without Reason", by Rodney A. Brooks, MIT AI Memo #1293 (1991), later published in the proceedings of the 1991 International Joint Conference on Artificial Intelligence. The deleted paragraphs were all taken from the final section (8.1–8.3 in the earlier version). There have also been a few other changes, including new photos. This version, compiled by John Haugeland, is published by permission of the author.

Phil Agre, David Chapman, Peter Cudhea, Anita Flynn, Ian Horswell, David Kirsh, Pattie Maes, Thomas Marill, Maja Mataric, and Lynn Parker were helpful in the preparation of one or both of the two essays that were combined to make this one.

The research described here was done at the AI Laboratory at MIT. Support has been provided by an IBM Faculty Development Award, by grants from the Systems Development Foundation, the Hughes AI Center, Siemens Corporation, and Mazda Corporation, by the University Research Initative under ONR contract N00014-86-K-0685, and by ARPA under ONR contract N00014-85-K-0124.

16 VAN GELDER

"Dynamics and Cognition" appears for the first time in this volume. It is loosely based on an earlier essay, "What Might Cognition Be, If not Computation?", which appeared in *The Journal of Philosophy* 92: 345–381 (1995). It appears here by permission of the author.

The author is grateful for assistance from many people, but especially from Robert Port, John Haugeland, and James Townsend.

Bibliography

If an entry has two dates, the year before the slash is that of its first publication, and the one after the slash identifies the edition to which page citations are given. If there are two page citations in an article, the one in brackets gives the page number in this volume. The numbers in brackets following the entries below indicate which chapters cite them.

Abelson, Robert P. 1973. "The Structure of Belief Systems", in Schank and Colby 1973. [5]

Agre, Philip E., and David Chapman. 1987. "Pengi: An Implementation of a Theory of Activity", in AAAI-87, Seattle, WA, 268–272. [15]

Altmann, Gerry, ed. 1992. *Computational and Psycholinguistic Approaches to Speech Processing.* New York: Academic Press. [14]

Anderson, John. 1976. *Language, Memory and Thought,* Hillsdale, NJ: Lawrence Erlbaum Associates. [13]

— 1980. *Cognitive Psychology and Its Implications,* San Francisco: W. H. Freeman and Co. [13]

— 1983. *The Architecture of Cognition.* Cambridge, MA: Harvard University Press. [13]

Anderson, John, and Gordon H. Bower. 1973. *Human Associative Memory.* Washington, DC: Winston. [13]

Artificial Intelligence. 1980. Special issue on non-monotonic logic, volume 13, numbers 1-2. [9]

Asquith, Peter D., and Thomas Nickles, eds. 1983. *Proceedings of the 1982 Biennial Meeting of the Philosophy of Science Association.* East Lansing, MI: Philosophy of Science Association. [13]

Ballard, Dana H. 1986. "Cortical Connections and Parallel Processing: Structure and Function", *The Behavioral and Brain Sciences* 9: 67–120. [12]

Bartlett, Frederic C. 1932/61. *Remembering: A Study in Experimental and Social Psychology.* Cambridge: The University Press. [5]

Barto, A. G. 1985. "Learning by Statistical Cooperation of Self-Interested Neuron-like Computing Elements", *Human Neurobiology* 4: 229–56. [10]

Bear, Mark F., Leon N. Cooper, and Ford F. Ebner. 1987. "A Physiological Basis for a Theory of Synapse Modification", *Science* 237: 42–48. [10]

Bechtel, William. 1988a. "Connectionism and Rule-and-Representation Systems: Are They Compatible?", *Philosophical Psychology* 1: 5–16. [11]

— 1988b. "Connectionism and the Philosophy of Mind: An Overview", *Southern Journal of Philosophy* 26 (supplement): 17–41. [11]

Beltrami, Edward. 1987. *Mathematics for Dynamical Modeling.* Boston: Academic Press. [16]

Bennett, Jonathan. 1964. *Rationality: An Essay Towards an Analysis.* London: Routledge and Kegan Paul. [11]

Berkeley, George. 1710/1977. *A Treatise Concerning the Principles of Human Knowledge*, in Cahn 1977. [16]

Berliner, Hans. 1975. *Chess as Problem Solving: The Development of a Tactics Analyzer.* Unpublished Ph.D. thesis, Carnegie Mellon University. [4]

Biro, John I., and Robert W. Shahan, eds. 1982. *Mind, Brain, and Function.* Norman: University of Oklahoma Press. [3]

Bobrow, Daniel G., and John Seely Brown. 1975. "Systematic Understanding: Synthesis, Analysis, and Contingent Knowledge in Specialized Understanding Systems", in Bobrow and Collins 1975. [15]

Bobrow, Daniel G., and Allan M. Collins. 1975. *Representation and Understanding.* New York: Academic Press. [15]

Bobrow, Daniel G., and Terry Winograd. 1977. "An Overview of KRL, a Knowledge Representation Language", *Cognitive Science* 1: 3–46. [6]

Boole, George. 1854/1961. *An Investigation of the Laws of Thought.* New York: Dover. [9]

Brady, Michael, and Richard Paul, eds. 1984. *Robotics Research: The First International Symposium.* Cambridge, MA: MIT Press. [15]

Brentano, Franz. 1874/1973. *Psychology from an Empirical Standpoint.* Leipzig: Duncker and Humblot. Translation, Antos C. Rancurello, D. B. Terrell, and Linda L. McAlister, 1973. London: Routledge. [1]

Broadbent, Donald E. 1985. "A Question of Levels: Comments on McClelland and Rumelhart", *Journal of Experimental Psychology: General* 114: 189–192. [12][13]

Brooks, Rodney A. 1986. "A Robust Layered Control System for a Mobile Robot." *IEEE Journal of Robotics and Automation* 2: 14–23. [15]

—— 1987. "A Hardware Retargetable Distributed Layered Architecture for Mobile Robot Control." *Proceedings IEEE Robotics and Automation,* Raleigh NC, 106–110. [15]

Brooks, Rodney A., and Jonathan H. Connell. 1986. "Asynchronous Distributed Control System for a Mobile Robot." *Proceedings SPIE,* Cambridge, MA, 77–84. [15]

Busemeyer, Jerome R., and James T. Townsend. 1993. "Decision Field Theory: A Dynamic-Cognitive Approach to Decision Making in an Uncertain Environment", *Psychological Review* 100: 432–459. [16]

—— 1995. "Dynamic Representation of Decision Making", in Port and van Gelder 1995. [16]

Butler, Samuel. 1872/1981. *Erewhon.* London: Trübner and Company; reprinted 1981, Hans-Peter Breuer and Daniel F. Howard, eds. Newark: University of Delaware Press. (See chapters 23–25, "The Book of Machines".) [2]

Cahn, Steven M., ed. 1977. *Classics of Western Philosophy.* Indianapolis: Hackett. [16]

Carroll, Lewis. 1956. "What the Tortoise Said to Achilles and Other Riddles", in Newman 1956, volume 4. [12]

Chalmers, David J. 1990. "Syntactic Transformations on Distributed Representations", *Connection Science* 2: 53–62. [14]

Charniak, Eugene. 1974. *Toward a Model of Children's Story Comprehension.* Unpublished Ph.D. thesis, MIT, and AI Lab Tech Report 266. [5]

Chase, William G., ed. 1973. *Visual Information Processing.* New York: Academic Press. [13]

Cherniak, Christopher. 1986. *Minimal Rationality.* Cambridge, MA: Bradford/MIT Press. [3][13]

Chomsky, Noam. 1957. *Syntactic Structures.* The Hague: Mouton. [5]

Church, Alonzo. 1936. "An Unsolvable Problem of Elementary Number Theory", *Americal Journal of Mathematics* 58, 345–363. [2]

Churchland, Patricia Smith. 1980. "A Perspective on Mind-Brain Research", *Journal of Philosophy* 77: 185–207. [10]

— 1986. *Neurophilosophy: Toward a Unified Understanding of the Mind-Brain.* Cambridge: Bradford/MIT Press. [10][12]

Churchland, Paul M. 1970. "The Logical Character of Action Explanations", *Philosophical Review* 79: 214–236. [13]

— 1975b. "Karl Popper's Philosophy of Science", *Canadian Journal of Philosophy* 5: 145–156. [10]

— 1979. *Scientific Realism and the Plasticity of Mind.* Cambridge: Cambridge University Press. [3][10][13]

— 1981. "Eliminative Materialism and the Propositional Attitudes", *Journal of Philosophy* 78: 67–90. [10][13]

— 1985. "The Ontological Status of Observables: In Praise of the Superempirical Virtues", in Churchland and Hooker 1985. [10]

— 1986. "Some Reductive Strategies in Cognitive Neurobiology", *Mind* 95: 279–309. [10][11][13]

— 1988. "Perceptual Plasticity and Theoretical Neutrality: A Reply to Jerry Fodor", *Philosophy of Science* 55: 167–187. [10]

— 1990/89. "On the Nature of Theories: A Neurocomputational Perspective", in Savage 1990; reprinted in Churchland 1989; and included (somewhat abridged) as chapter 10 of this volume. [11]

— 1989. *A Neurocomputational Perspective: The Nature of Mind and the Structure of Science.* Cambridge, MA: Bradford/MIT Press. [11]

Churchland, Paul M., and Clifford A. Hooker, eds. 1985. *Images of Science.* Chicago: University of Chicago Press. [10]

Clark, Andy, and Annette Karmiloff-Smith. 1993. "The Cognizer's Innards: A Psychological and Philosophical Perspective on the Development of Thought", *Mind and Language* 8: 487–519. [14]

CogSci-5. 1983. *Proceedings of the Fifth Annual Conference of the Cognitive Science Society.* Hillsdale, NJ: Lawrence Erlbaum Associates. [9]

CogSci-6. 1984. *Proceedings of the Sixth Annual Conference of the Cognitive Science Society.* Hillsdale, NJ: Lawrence Erlbaum Associates. [9][12]

CogSci-8. 1986. *Procedings of the Eighth Annual Conference of the Cognitive Science Society.* Hillsdale, N.J: Lawrence Erlbaum Associates. [8][12]

CogSci-9. 1987. *Proceedings of the Ninth Annual Meeting of the Cognitive Science Society.* Hillsdale, NJ: Lawrence Erlbaum Associates. [8]

CogSci-10. 1988. *Proceedings of the Tenth Annual Conference of the Cognitive Science Society*. Hillsdale, NJ: Lawrence Erlbaum Associates. [14]

Cohen, Robert S., and Marx W. Wartofsky, eds. 1965. *Boston Studies in the Philosophy of Science*, volume 2. Dordrecht: Reidel. [10]

Collins, Allan M., and M. Ross Quillian. 1972. "Experiments on Semantic Memory and Language Comprehension", in Gregg 1972. [13]

Cottrell, Gary W., Paul W. Munro, and David Zipser. 1987. "Learning Internal Representations from Grey-Scale Images: An Example of Extensional Programming", *CogSci-9*: 461–473. [8]

Cummins, Robert. 1983. *The Nature of Psychological Explanation*. Cambridge, MA: Bradford/MIT Press. [12]

Dell, G. S. 1985. "Positive Feedback in Hierarchical Connectionist Models: Applications to Language Production", *Cognitive Science* 9: 3–23 (= Feldman 1985). [9]

Denker, John, Daniel Schwartz, Ben Wittner, Sara Solla, Richard Howard, and Lawrence Jackel. 1987. "Automatic Learning, Rule Extraction, and Generalization", *Complex Systems* 1: 877–922. [8]

Dennett, Daniel C. 1969. *Content and Consciousness*. London: Routledge and Kegan Paul. [3]

— 1971/78. "Intentional Systems", *Journal of Philosophy* 68: 87–106; reprinted in Dennett 1978, and in Haugeland 1981. [1][3][11]

— 1976/78. "Conditions of Personhood", in Rorty 1976; reprinted in Dennett 1978. [3]

— 1977/78. Critical notice: *The Language of Thought* (Fodor 1975), *Mind* 86: 265–280; reprinted in Dennett 1978 as "A Cure for the Common Code?". [14]

— 1978. *Brainstorms: Philosophical Essays on Mind and Psychology*. Cambridge, MA: Bradford/MIT Press. [1][3][11][14]

— 1978a. "How to Change Your Mind", in Dennett 1978. [3]

— 1981/87. "True Believers: The Intentional Strategy and Why it Works", in Heath 1981; reprinted in Dennett 1987; and included as chapter 3 of this volume. [11]

— 1981/87b. "Making Sense of Ourselves", *Philosophical Topics* 12: 63–81; reprinted in Biro and Shahan 1982, and in Dennett 1987. [3]

— 1982/87. "Beyond Belief", in Woodfield 1982; reprinted in Dennett 1987. [3]

— 1987. *The Intentional Stance.* Cambridge, MA: Bradford/MIT Press. [3][11]

— 1987a. "Evolution, Error, and Intentionality", in Dennett 1987. [3]

Dretske, Fred. 1988. *Explaining Behavior. Reasons in a World of Causes.* Cambridge, MA: Bradford/MIT Press. [14]

Dreyfus, Hubert L. 1972/92. *What Computers Can't Do: A Critique of Artificial Reason.* New York: Harper and Row. (Third edition: *What Computers* Still *Can't Do.* 1992. Cambridge, MA: MIT Press. The second and third editions have the same pagination.) A modified version of the introduction to the second edition is included as chapter 5 of this volume. [6][16]

— 1991. *Being-in-the-World: A Commentary on Heidegger's Being and Time, Division 1.* Cambridge MA: MIT Press. [16]

Elman, Jeffrey L., 1988. *Finding Structure in Time.* Center for Research in Language Tech Report 88-01, University of California, San Diego. [8]

— 1992. "Structured Representations and Connectionist Models", in Altmann 1992. [14]

Elman, Jeffrey L., and David Zipser. 1987. *Learning the Hidden Structure of Speech.* Institute for Cognitive Science, Report #8701, University of California, San Diego. [8]

Fahlman, Scott E. and Geoffrey E. Hinton. 1987. "Connectionist Architectures for Artificial Intelligence", *Computer* 20: 100–109. [12]

Farey, J. 1827. *A Treatise on the Steam Engine: Historical, Practical and Descriptive.* London: Longman, Rees, Orme, Brown and Green. [16]

Feigenbaum, Edward A. 1977. "The Art of Artificial Intelligence: Themes and Case Studies of Knowledge Engineering", in *IJCAI-5*: 1014–1029. [6]

Feigenbaum, Edward A., and Julian Feldman, eds. 1963. *Computers and Thought.* San Francisco: McGraw-Hill. [15]

Feigl, Herbert, and Michael Scriven, eds. 1956. *The Foundations of Science and the Concepts of Psychology and Psychoanalysis: Minnesota Studies in the Philosophy of Science,* volume 1. Minneapolis: University of Minnesota Press. [11][13]

Feldman, Jerome A. 1981. "A Connectionist Model of Visual Memory", in Hinton and Anderson 1981. [9]

— ed. 1985. Special issue: "Connectionist Models and their Applications", *Cognitive Science* 9, number 1. [8][9]

— 1985a. "Connectionist Models and their Applications: Introduction", *Cognitive Science* 9: 1–2 (= Feldman 1985). [8]

— 1986. "Neural Representation of Conceptual Knowledge", Report TR189, Department of Computer Science, University of Rochester; reprinted in Nadel et al. 1989. [12]

Feldman, Jerome A., and Dana H. Ballard. 1982. "Connectionist Models and Their Properties", *Cognitive Science* 6: 205–254. [9][12]

Feldman, Jerome A., Dana H. Ballard, C. M. Brown, and G. S. Dell. 1985. *Rochester Connectionist Papers: 1979-1985*. Technical Report TR 172, Department of Computer Science, University of Rochester. [9]

Fetzer, James H., ed. 1988. *Aspects of Artificial Intelligence*. Dordrecht: Reidel. [10]

Feyerabend, Paul K. 1965/81. "Reply to Criticism: Comments on Smart, Sellars, and Putnam", in Cohen and Wartofsky 1965; reprinted in Feyerabend 1981. [10]

— 1970. "Consolations for the Specialist", in Lakatos and Musgrave 1970. [10]

— 1978. *Science in a Free Society*. London: New Left Bank. [3]

— 1981. *Realism, Rationalism and Scientific Method: Philosophical Papers*, volume 1. Cambridge: Cambridge University Press. [10][13]

Fodor, Janet D. 1977. *Semantics: Theories of Meaning in Generative Grammar*. New York: Crowell. [12]

Fodor, Jerry A. 1975. *The Language of Thought*. New York: Crowell. [9][12][14]

— 1983. *The Modularity of Mind*. Cambridge, MA: Bradford/MIT Press. [13]

— 1984. "Observation Reconsidered", *Philosophy of Science* 51: 23–43. [10]

— 1987. *Psychosemantics: The Problem of Meaning in the Philosophy of Mind*. Cambridge, MA: Bradford/MIT Press. [12][13][14]

— 1988. "A Reply to Churchland's 'Perceptual Plasticity and Theoretical Neutrality'", *Philosophy of Science* 55: 188–194. [10]

Fodor, Jerry A., and Brian P. McLaughlin. 1990. "Connectionism and the Problem of Systematicity: Why Smolensky's Solution Doesn't Work", *Cognition* 35: 183–204. [14]

Fodor, Jerry A., and Zenon W. Pylyshyn. 1988. "Connectionism and Cognitive Architecture: A Critical Analysis", *Cognition* 28: 3–71;

reprinted in Pinker and Mehler 1988, and included (abridged) as chapter 12 of this volume. [13][14]

Giere, Ronald. 1988. *Explaining Science: A Cognitive Approach*. Chicago: University of Chicago Press. [10]

Glymour, Clark. 1988. "Artificial Intelligence is Philosophy", in Fetzer 1988. [10]

Gödel, Kurt. 1931. "Über formal unentscheidbare Sätze der Principia Mathematica und verwandter Systeme, 1", *Monatshefte für Mathematik und Physik* 38: 173–189. [2]

Goldmeier, Erich. 1972. *Similarity in Visually Perceived Forms*. New York: International Universities Press. [6]

Goldstein, Ira. 1974. *Understanding Simple Picture Programs*. Unpublished Ph.D. thesis, MIT, and AI Lab Tech Report 294. [5]

Goldstein, Ira, and Seymour Papert. 1975; revised 1976. *Artificial Intelligence, Language, and the Study of Knowledge*. MIT AI Memo 237. [6]

Goodman, Nelson. 1965. *Fact, Fiction and Forecast*. Indianapolis, Bobbs-Merrill. [13]

Gorman, Robert P. and Terrence J. Sejnowski. 1988. "Learned Classification of Sonar Targets Using a Massively-Parallel Network", *IEEE Transactions: Acoustics, Speech, and Signal Processing* 36: 1135–1140. [10][11]

Gould, James L., and Peter Marler. 1986. "Learning by Instinct", *Scientific American* 255 (December): 74–85. [15]

Gregg, Lee W., ed. 1972. *Cognition in Learning and Memory*. New York, Wiley. [13]

Grossberg, Stephen. 1976. "Adaptive Pattern Classification and Universal Recoding: Part I. Parallel Development and Coding of Neural Feature Detectors", *Biological Cybernetics* 23: 121–134. [8]

— 1988. *Neural Networks and Natural Intelligence*. Cambridge MA: MIT Press. [16]

Guignon, Charles B. 1983. *Heidegger and the Problem of Knowledge*. Indianapolis: Hackett. [16]

Guzman, Adolfo. 1968. *Computer Recognition of Three-Dimensional Objects in a Visual Scene*. Unpublished Ph.D. thesis, MIT, and Project MAC Tech Report 59. [6]

Hanson, Philip P., ed. 1991. *Information, Language, and Cognition*. Vancouver: University of British Columbia Press. [14]

Hartree, Douglas R. 1949. *Calculating Instruments and Machines*. Urbana: University of Illinois Press. [2]

Haugeland, John, ed. 1981. *Mind Design* (first edition). Cambridge, MA: Bradford/MIT Press. [3][6][11]

— 1985. *Artificial Intelligence: The Very Idea*. Cambridge MA: Bradford/ MIT Press. [16]

— 1997. *Having Thought*. Cambridge, MA: Harvard University Press. [1]

Hayes, Patrick. 1979. "The Naive Physics Manifesto", in Michie 1979. [3]

Heath, A. F., ed. 1981. *Scientific Explanation*. Oxford: Oxford University Press. [11]

Hebb, Donald O. 1949. *The Organization of Behavior*. New York: Wiley. [8][9][10]

Heidegger, Martin. 1927/62. *Being and Time*. Tübingen: Max Niemeyer Verlag. Translation, John Macquarrie and Edward Robinson, 1962. New York: Harper and Row. [6][16]

Hempel, Carl G. 1945/65. "Studies in the Logic of Confirmation", *Mind* 54: 1–26 and 97–121; reprinted in Hempel 1965. [10]

— 1965. *Aspects of Scientific Explanation*. New York: The Free Press. [10]

Hewitt, Carl. 1977. "Viewing Control Structures as Patterns of Passing Messages", *The Artificial Intelligence Journal* 8: 232–364. [12]

Hillis, W. Daniel. 1985. *The Connection Machine*. Cambridge, MA: MIT Press. [12]

Hinton, Geoffrey E., and John A. Anderson, eds. 1981. *Parallel Models of Associative Memory*. Hillsdale, NJ: Lawrence Erlbaum Associates. [9] [12]

Hinton, Geoffrey E. and Terrence J. Sejnowski. 1983. "Analyzing Cooperative Computation", *CogSci-5*, session 7 (no page numbers). [9]

— 1986. "Learning and Relearning in Boltzmann Machines", in Rumelhart, McClelland, et al. 1986. [8][10]

Hobbes, Thomas. 1651/1962. *Leviathan*. New York: Collier Books. [16]

Hofstadter, Douglas R. 1985. "Waking Up from the Boolean Dream, or, Subcognition as Computation", in Hofstadter 1985a. [9]

— 1985a. *Metamagical Themas*. New York: Basic Books. [9]

Holland, John, Keith Holyoak, Richard Nisbett, and Paul Thagard. 1986. *Induction: Processes of Inference, Learning and Discovery*, Cambridge, MA: Bradford/MIT Press. [13]

Hooker, Clifford A. 1975. "The Philosophical Ramifications of the Information-Processing Approach to the Mind-Brain", *Philosophy and Phenomenological Research* 36: 1–15. [10]

— 1981. "Towards a General Theory of Reduction", Parts I, II and III, *Dialogue* 20: 38–59, 201–236, and 496–529. [13]

— 1987. *A Realistic Theory of Science.* Albany: SUNY Press. [10]

Hopfield, J. J. 1982. "Neural Networks and Physical Systems with Emergent Collective Computational Abilities", *Proceedings of the National Academy of Sciences, USA* 79: 2554–2558. [8]

Hopfield, J. J. and D. Tank. 1985. "'Neural' Computation of Decisions in Optimization Problems", *Biological Cybernetics* 52: 141–52. [10]

Hubel, David H., and Torsten N. Wiesel. 1962. "Receptive Fields, Binocular Interactions, and Functional Architecture in the Cat's Visual Cortex", *Journal of Physiology* 160: 106–154. [10]

Husserl, Edmund. 1929/60. *Cartesian Meditations.* Translation, Dorion Cairns, 1960. The Hague: Martinus Nijhoff. [6]

IJCAI-3. 1973. *Third International Joint Conference on Artificial Intelligence, Proceedings.* Palo Alto: SRI International. [8]

IJCAI-5. 1977. *Fifth International Joint Conference on Artificial Intelligence, Proceedings.* Pittsburgh: Computer Science Department, CMU. [6]

Jefferson, G. 1949. "The Mind of Mechanical Man", Lister Oration for 1949, *British Medical Journal* 1: 1105–1121. [2]

Jordan, Michael I. 1986. "Attractor Dynamics and Parallelism in a Connectionist Sequential Machine", *CogSci-8:* 531–546. [8]

— 1989. "Supervised Learning and Systems with Excess Degrees of Freedom", in Touretzky, Hinton, and Sejnowski 1989. [8]

Kant, Immanuel. 1787/1929. *Critique of Pure Reason,* 2nd edition. Riga: Johann Friedrich Hartknoch. Translation, Norman Kemp Smith, 1929. London: Macmillan. [9][11]

Karmiloff-Smith, Annette. 1986. "From Metaprocesses to Conscious Access: Evidence from Children's Metalinguistic and Repair Data", *Cognition* 23, 95–147. [14]

Kelso, J. A. Scott. 1995. *Dynamic Patterns: The Self-organization of Brain and Behavior.* Cambridge MA: Bradford/MIT Press. [16]

Keramidas, E. M., ed. 1991. *Interface 91—Twenty-Third Symposium on the Interface.* Interface Foundation of America. [8]

Kintsch, Walter. 1974. *The Representation of Meaning in Memory*. Hillsdale, NJ, Lawrence Erlbaum Associates. [13]

Kirsh, David. 1991. "When is Information Explicitly Represented?", in Hanson 1991. [14]

Kitcher, Philip. 1978. "Theories, Theorists and Theoretical Change", *Philosophical Review* 87: 519–547. [13]

— 1981. "Explanatory Unification", *Philosophy of Science* 48: 507–531. [10]

— 1982. "Genes", *British Journal for the Philosophy of Science* 82: 337–359. [13]

— 1983. "Implications of Incommensurability", in Asquith and Nickles 1983 (= *PSA* 1982), volume 2. [13]

— 1984. "1953 and All That: A Tale of Two Sciences", *Philosophical Review* 93: 335–373. [13]

— 1989. "Explanatory Unification and the Causal Structure of the World", in Kitcher 1989a. [10]

— ed. 1989a. *Scientific Explanation: Minnesota Studies in the Philosophy of Science*, volume 13. Minneapolis: University of Minnesota Press. [10]

Kleene, Stephen Cole. 1935. "General Recursive Functions of Natural Numbers", *American Journal of Mathematics* 57: 153–173, and 219–244. [2]

Kuhn, Thomas S. 1962/70. *The Structure of Scientific Revolutions*. (Second edition, 1970.) Chicago: University of Chicago Press. [5][6][10][12] [13]

— 1983. "Commensurability, Comparability, Communicability", in Asquith and Nickels 1983 (= *PSA* 1982). [13]

Lakatos, Imre. 1970. "Falsification and the Methodology of Scientific Research Programmes", in Lakatos and Musgrave 1970. [10]

Lakatos, Imre, and Alan Musgrave, eds. 1970. *Criticism and the Growth of Knowledge*. Cambridge: Cambridge University Press. [10]

La Mettrie, Julien Offray de. 1748/1912. *Man a Machine*. La Salle, IL: Open Court. [16]

Laudan, Larry. 1981. "A Confutation of Convergent Realism", *Philosophy of Science* 48: 19–49. [10]

Lavoisier, Antoine. 1789/1949. *Elements of Chemistry*. Chicago: Regnery. [5]

Lehky, S. and Terrence J. Sejnowski. 1990. "Computing Shape from Shading with a Neural Network Model", in Schwartz 1990. [10]

—— 1988b. "Network Model of Shape-from-Shading: Neural Function Arises from Both Receptive and Projective Fields", *Nature* 333: 452–454. [10]

Leibniz, Gottfried Wilhelm von. 1714/1977. *Monadology*. In Cahn 1977. [16]

Lewis, Alcinda C. 1986. "Memory Constraints and Flower Choice in *Pieris rapae*", *Science* 232: 863–865. [15]

Linsker, R. 1986. "From Basic Network Principles to Neural Architecture: Emergence of Orientation Columns", *Proceedings of the National Academy of Sciences, USA*, 83: 8779–8783. [10]

—— 1975. "The Cortex of the Cerebellum", *Scientific American* 232 (January): 56–71. [10]

Loewer, Barry, and Georges Rey, eds. 1991. *Meaning in Mind: Fodor and His Critics*. Oxford: Blackwell. [14]

Lovelace, Mary Caroline, Countess of (Ada Augusta). 1842. "Translator's Notes to an Article on Babbage's Analytical Engine", in *Scientific Memoirs*. R. Taylor, ed., volume 3, pp. 691–731. [2]

Lycan, William G. 1988. *Judgement and Justification*. Cambridge: Cambridge University Press. [13]

Mackworth, Alan K. 1987. "Constraint Propagation", in Shapiro 1987, volume 1. [12]

Madell, Geoffrey. 1986. "Neurophilosophy: A Principled Skeptic's Response", *Inquiry* 29: 153–168. [13]

Martin, W. 1974. Memos on the OWL System, Project MAC, MIT. [5]

Maxwell, James Clerk. 1868. "On Governors", *Proceedings of the Royal Society* 16: 270–283. [16]

McCarthy, John. 1960. "Recursive Functions of Symbolic Expressions and Their Computation by Machine", *Communications of the Association for Computing Machinery* 3: 184–195. [4]

—— 1968. "Programs with Common Sense", in Minsky 1968. [13]

—— 1979. "Ascribing Mental Qualities to Machines", Stanford AI Lab Memo 326; reprinted in Ringle 1979. [3][7]

—— 1980. "Circumscription: A Form of Non-Monotonic Reasoning", *Artificial Intelligence* 13: 27–41. [13]

— 1986. "Applications of Circumscription to Formalizing Common-Sense Knowledge", *Artificial Intelligence* 28: 89–116. [13]

McClelland, Jay L., Jerome A. Feldman, B. Adelson, Gordon H. Bower, and Drew McDermott. 1986. *Connectionist Models and Cognitive Science: Goals, Directions and Implications.* Report to the National Science Foundation, June 1986. [12]

McClelland, Jay L. and David E. Rumelhart. 1981. "An Interactive Activation Model of Context Effects in Letter Perception: Part 1. An Account of the Basic Findings", *Psychological Review*, 88: 375–407. [9]

McClelland, Jay L., David E. Rumelhart, and Geoffrey E. Hinton. 1986. "The Appeal of Parallel Distributed Processing", in Rumelhart, McClelland, et al. 1986. [12][14]

McClelland, Jay L., David E. Rumelhart, and the PDP Research Group. 1986. *Parallel Distributed Processing: Explorations in the Microstructure of Cognition. Volume 2: Psychological and Biological Models.* Cambridge, MA: Bradford/MIT Press. [8][9][13]

McCulloch, Warren S. 1961. "What is a Number, that a Man May Know It, and a Man, that He May Know a Number?", *General Semantics Bulletin*, Nos. 26 and 27: 7–18. [4]

McDermott, Drew. 1976. "Artificial Intelligence Meets Natural Stupidity", SIGART Newsletter, number 57: 4–9; reprinted in Haugeland 1981. [6]

Meltzer, Bernard, and Donald Michie, eds. 1970. *Machine Intelligence,* Volume 5. Edinburgh: Edinburgh University Press. [5]

Melville, Herman. 1851/1952. *Moby Dick.* New York: Modern Library College Editions. [6]

Michie, Donald, ed. 1979. *Expert Systems in the Microelectronic Age.* Edinburgh: Edinburgh University Press. [3]

Millikan, Ruth Garrett. 1984. *Language, Thought, and Other Biological Categories.* Cambridge, MA: Bradford/MIT Press. [11]

Minsky, Marvin, ed. 1968. *Semantic Information Processing.* Cambridge, MA: MIT Press. [6][13][15]

— 1970. "Form and Content in Computer Science", *Journal of the Association for Computing Machinery* 17: 197–215. [5]

— 1974. "A Framework for Representing Knowledge", MIT AI Lab Memo 306; exerpts reprinted in Winston 1975; other exerpts included as chapter 5 of this volume. [6]

— 1986. *Society of Mind.* New York: Simon and Schuster. [15]

Minsky, Marvin, and Seymour Papert. 1969. *Perceptrons*. Cambridge, MA: MIT Press. [8][10]

— 1970. Draft of a proposal to ARPA for research on artificial intelligence at MIT, 1970-71. [6]

— 1972. Progress Report on Artificial Intelligence. MIT AI Lab Memo 252. [5]

— 1973. *Artificial Intelligence*. Condon Lectures, Oregon State System of Higher Education, Eugene, Oregon. [6]

Miyata, Y. 1987. *The Learning and Planning of Actions*. Unpublished Ph.D. thesis, University of California, San Diego. [8]

Moravec, Hans P. 1984. "Locomotion, Vision and Intelligence", in Brady and Paul 1984. [15]

Mozer, Michael C. 1988. *A Focused Back-Propagation Algorithm for Temporal Pattern Recognition*. Report number 88-3, Departments of Psychology and Computer Science, University of Toronto. [8]

Munevar, Gonzalo. 1981. *Radical Knowledge: A Philosophical Inquiry into the Nature and Limits of Science*. Indianapolis: Hackett. [10]

Nadel, Lynn, Lynn A. Cooper, Peter Culicover, and R. Michael Harnish, eds. 1989. *Neural Connections, Mental Computation*. Cambridge, MA: Bradford/MIT Press. [8][12]

Nagel, Ernst. 1961. *The Structure of Science*. New York: Harcourt, Brace and World. [13]

Newell, Allen. 1973. "Production Systems: Models of Control Structures", in Chase 1973. [13]

— 1973a. "Artificial Intelligence and the Concept of Mind", in Schank and Colby 1973. [5]

— 1980. "Physical Symbol Systems", *Cognitive Science* 4: 135–183. [7][9][12]

— 1982. "The Knowledge Level", *Artificial Intelligence* 18: 87–127. [9][12]

— 1990. "Are There Alternatives?", in Sieg 1990. [16]

Newell, Allen, and Herbert A. Simon. 1972. *Human Problem Solving*. Englewood Cliffs, NJ: Prentice-Hall. [5][9][13]

Newman, James Roy, ed. 1956. *The World of Mathematics*. New York: Simon and Schuster. [12]

Nilsson, Nils J. 1971. *Problem Solving Methods in Artificial Intelligence*. New York: McGraw Hill. [4]

— 1984. "Shakey the Robot." SRI AI Center Technical Note 323, April. [15]

Norman, Donald A. 1973. "Memory, Knowledge and the Answering of Questions", in Solso 1973. [5]

Papert, Seymour. 1972. "Teaching Children to be Mathematicians vs. Teaching about Mathematics", *International Journal of Mathematical Education for Science and Technology* 3: 249–262. [5]

Papert, Seymour, and Marvin Minsky. 1973. "Proposal to ARPA For Research on Intelligent Automata and Micro-Automation", MIT AI Lab Memo 299. [6]

Petitot, Jean. 1995. "Morphodynamics and Attractor Syntax", in Port and van Gelder 1995. [16]

Pinker, Steven, and Jacques Mehler. 1988. *Connections and Symbols.* Cambridge, MA: Bradford/MIT Press. [13][14]

Pollack, J. 1988. "Recursive Auto-Associative Memory: Devising Compositional Distributed Representations", *CogSci-10:* 33–39. [14]

— 1990. "Recursive Distributed Representations", *Artificial Intelligence* 46: 77–105. [14]

Port, Robert F., and Timothy van Gelder eds. 1995. *Mind as Motion: Explorations in the Dynamics of Cognition.* Cambridge MA: Bradford/ MIT Press. [16]

Putnam, Hilary. 1981. *Reason, Truth, and History.* Cambridge: Cambridge University Press. [10]

Pylyshyn, Zenon W. 1980. "Cognition and Computation: Issues in the Foundations of Cognitive Science", *Behavioral and Brain Sciences* 3: 154–169. [12]

— 1984a. *Computation and Cognition: Toward a Foundation for Cognitive Science.* Cambridge, MA: Bradford/MIT Press. [12]

— 1984b. "Why Computation Requires Symbols", *CogSci-6:* 71–73. [12]

Quillian, M. Ross. 1966. *Semantic Memory.* CMU Ph.D. thesis, 1967. Published 1966, Cambridge, MA: Bolt, Beranak and Newman. [13]

Quine, Willard Van Orman. 1948/53. "On What There Is", *Review of Metaphysics,* 2: 21–38; reprinted in Quine 1953. [11]

— 1951/53. "Two Dogmas of Empiricism", *Philosophical Review* 60: 20–43; reprinted in Quine 1953. [1]

— 1953. *From a Logical Point of View.* Cambridge, MA: Harvard University Press. [1][11]

— 1960. *Word and Object.* Cambridge, MA: The MIT Press. [1]

Ramsey, William. 1989. "Parallelism and Functionalism", *Cognitive Science* 13: 139–144. [13]

Ramsey, William, Stephen Stich, and Joseph Garon. 1991. "Connectionism, Eliminativism, and the Future of Folk Psychology", in Ramsey, Stich, and Rumelhart 1991, and included as chapter 13 of this volume. [14]

Ramsey, William, Stephen Stich and David E. Rumelhart, eds. 1991. *Philosophy and Connectionist Theory.* Hillsdale, NJ: Lawrence Erlbaum Associates. [14]

Reddy, D. R., L. D. Erman, R. D. Fennell, and R. B. Neely. 1973. "The Hearsay Speech Understanding System: An Example of the Recognition Process", *IJCAI-3:* 185–194. [8]

Riley, Mary S. and Paul Smolensky. 1984. "A Parallel Model of (Sequential) Problem Solving", *CogSci-6:* 286–292. [9]

Ringle, Martin, ed. 1979. *Philosophical Perspectives on Artificial Intelligence.* Atlantic Highlands, NJ: Humanities Press. [3][7]

Rorty, Amelie O., ed. 1976. *The Identities of Persons.* Berkeley: University of California Press. [3]

Rosch, Eleanor. 1977. "Human Categorization", in Warren 1977. [6]

Rosenblatt, Frank. 1962. *Principles of Neurodynamics: Perceptrons and the Theory of Brain Mechanisms.* Washington, DC: Spartan. [8][10]

Rumelhart, David E. 1980. "Schemata: The Building Blocks of Cognition", in Spiro, Bruce, and Brewer 1980. [9]

— 1984. "The Emergence of Cognitive Phenomena from Sub-Symbolic Proesses", *CogSci-6:* 59–62. [12]

Rumelhart, David. E., Geoffrey E. Hinton, and Jay L. McClelland. 1986. "A General Framework for Parallel Distributed Processing", in Rumelhart, McClelland, et al. 1986. [12]

Rumelhart, David. E., Geoffrey E. Hinton, and R. J. Williams. 1986. "Learning Internal Representations by Error Propagation", in Rumelhart, McClelland, et al. 1986. [8][10]

— 1986a. "Learning Representations by Back-Propagating Errors", *Nature* 323: 533–538. [10]

Rumelhart, David E., Peter H. Lindsay, and Donald A. Norman. 1972. "A Process Model for Long Term Memory", in Tulving and Donaldson 1972. [13]

Rumelhart, David E. and Jay L. McClelland. 1982. "An Interactive Activation Model of Context Effects in Letter Perception: Part 2. The Contextual Enhancement Effect and Some Tests and Extensions of the Model", *Psychological Review* 89: 60–94. [9]

— 1985. "Level's Indeed! A Response to Broadbent", *Journal of Experimental Psychology: General* 114: 193–197. [12][13]

— 1986. "PDP Models and General Issues in Cognitive Science", in Rumelhart, McClelland, et al. 1986. [12]

Rumelhart, David E., Jay L. McClelland, and the PDP Research Group. 1986. *Parallel Distributed Processing: Explorations in the Microstructure of Cognition. Volume 1: Foundations.* Cambridge, MA: Bradford/MIT Press. [8][9][10][12][13][14]

Rumelhart, David E., Paul Smolensky, Jay L. McClelland, and Geoffrey E. Hinton. 1986. "Schemata and Sequential Thought Processes in Parallel Distributed Processing Models", in McClelland, Rumelhart, et al. 1986. [9]

Russell, Bertrand. 1945. *A History of Western Philosophy.* New York: Simon and Schuster. [2]

Ryle, Gilbert. 1949/1984. *The Concept of Mind.* Chicago: University of Chicago Press. [16]

Sandewall, Erik. 1970. "Representing Natural Language Information in Predicate Calculus", in Melzer and Michie 1970. [5]

Salmon, Wesley C. 1966. *The Foundations of Scientific Inference.* Pittsburgh: University of Pittsburgh Press. [10]

Savage, C. Wade, ed. 1990. *Scientific Theories: Minnesota Studies in the Philosophy of Science,* volume 14. Minneapolis: University of Minnesota Press. [11]

Schaffner, Kenneth. 1967. "Approaches to Reduction", *Philosophy of Science* 34: 137–147. [13]

Schank, Roger C. 1972. "Conceptual Dependency: A Theory of Natural Language Understanding", *Cognitive Psychology* 3: 552–631. [6]

— 1973. The Fourteen Primitive Actions and their Inferences, Stanford AI Lab Memo 183. [5]

— 1975a. "The Primitive Acts of Conceptual Dependency", in *TINLAP-75.* [6]

— 1975b. "Using Knowledge to Understand", in *TINLAP-75*. [6]

Schank, Roger C., et al. 1977. Panel on Natural Language Processing, in *IJCAI-5:* 1007–1013. [6]

Schank, Roger C., and Robert P. Ableson. 1977. *Scripts, Plans, Goals and Understanding.* Hillsdale, NJ: Lawrence Erlbaum Associates. [6][7]

Schank, Roger C., and Kenneth Colby, eds. 1973. *Computer Models of Thought and Language.* San Francisco: W. H. Freeman. [5][6]

Scheffler, Israel. 1963. *The Anatomy of Inquiry.* New York: Knopf. [10]

Schneider, Walter. 1987. "Connectionism: Is it a Paradigm Shift for Psychology?", *Behavior Research Methods, Instruments, and Computers* 19: 73–83. [12]

Schwartz, Erik L., ed. 1990. *Computational Neuroscience.* Cambridge, MA: Bradford/MIT Press. [10]

Searle, John R. 1979. "What Is an Intentional State?", *Mind* 88: 72–94. [7]

Sejnowski, Terrence J. 1981. "Skeleton Filters in the Brain", in Hinton and Anderson 1981. [12]

Sejnowski, Terrence J., Paul K. Kienker, and Geoffrey E. Hinton. 1986. "Learning Symmetry Groups with Hidden Units: Beyond the Perceptron", *Physica D* 22D: 260–275. [10]

Sejnowski, Terrence J., and Charles R. Rosenberg. 1987. "Parallel Networks that Learn to Pronounce English Text", *Complex Systems* 1: 145–168. [8][10][11]

Sellars, Wilfrid. 1956/63. "Empiricism and the Philosophy of Mind", in Feigl and Scriven 1956; reprinted in Sellars 1963. [11][13]

— 1963. *Science, Perception and Reality.* London: Routledge and Kegan Paul. [11][13]

— 1981. "Mental Events", *Philosophical Studies* 39: 325–45. [11]

Serra, Roberto, and Gianni Zanarini. 1990. *Complex Systems and Cognitive Processes.* Berlin: Springer-Verlag. [16]

Shapiro, Stuart C., ed. 1987. *The Encyclopedia of Artificial Intelligence.* New York: John Wiley and Sons. [12]

Sharkey, Noel E., ed., 1986. *Directions in the Science of Cognition.* Chichester: Ellis Horwood. [9]

Sharp, R. 1987. "The Very Idea of Folk Psychology", *Inquiry* 30: 381–393. [13]

Shepard, Roger N. 1989. "Internal Representation of Universal Regularities: A Challenge for Connectionism", in Nadel, et al. 1989. [8]

Shortliffe, Edward H. 1976. *MYCIN: Computer-based Medical Consultations*. New York: Elsevier. [6][15]

Simmons, R.F. 1973. "Semantic Networks: Their Computation and Use for Understanding English Sentences", in Schank and Colby 1973. [5]

Sieg, Wilfried, ed. 1990. *Acting and Reflecting: The Interdisciplinary Turn in Philosophy*. Dordrecht: Kluwer. [16]

Simon, Herbert A. 1969/81. *The Sciences of the Artificial*. Cambridge, MA: MIT Press. [15]

— 1977. "Artificial Intelligence Systems that Understand", in *IJCAI-5:* 1059–1073. [6]

Simon, Herbert A., and William G. Chase. 1973. "Skill in Chess", *American Scientist* 621: 394–403. [12]

Smith, Linda B., and Esther Thelen. 1993. *A Dynamic Systems Approach to Development: Applications*. Cambridge, MA: Bradford/MIT Press. [16]

Smolensky, Paul. 1983. "Schema Selection and Stochastic Inference in Modular Environments", *Proceedings of the National Conference on Artificial Intelligence*. Washington, DC. [9]

— 1984a. "Harmony Theory: Thermal Parallel Models in a Computational Context", in Smolensky and Riley 1984. [9]

— 1984b. "The Mathematical Role of Self-Consistency in Parallel Computation", *CogSci-6:* 319–324. [9]

— 1986a. "Information Processing in Dynamical Systems: Foundations of Harmony Theory", in Rumelhart, McClelland, et al. 1986. [8][9]

— 1986b. "Neural and Conceptual Interpretations of Parallel Distributed Processing Models", in McClelland, Rumelhart, et al. 1986. [9]

— 1986c. "Formal Modeling of Subsymbolic Processes: An Introduction to Harmony Theory", in Sharkey 1986. [9]

— 1988. "On the Proper Treatment of Connectionism", *The Behavioral and Brain Sciences* 11: 1–74. [12][13]

— 1991. "Connectionism, Constituency and the Language of Thought", in Loewer and Rey 1991. [14]

Smolensky, Paul, and Mary S. Riley. 1984 *Harmony Theory: Problem Solving, Parallel Cognitive Models, and Thermal Physics*. Technical Report 8404. Institute for Cognitive Science, UCSD. [9]

Solso, Robert L., ed. 1973. *Contemporary Issues in Cognitive Psychology: The Loyola Symposium.* Washington, DC: V. H. Winston and Sons. [5]

Spiro, Rand J., Bertram C. Bruce, and William F. Brewer, eds. 1980. *Theoretical Issues in Reading Comprehension.* Hillsdale, NJ: Lawrence Erlbaum Associates. [9]

Stabler, Edward P., Jr. 1985. "How are Grammars Represented?", *Behavioral and Brain Sciences* 6: 391–420. [12]

Stich, Stephen P. 1983. *From Folk Psychology to Cognitive Science.* Cambridge, MA: Bradford/MIT Press. [12][13]

— 1989. *The Fragmentation of Reason.* Cambridge, MA: Bradford/MIT Press. [10]

Suppe, Frederick. 1974. *The Structure of Scientific Theories.* Chicago: University of Illinois Press. [10]

Sussman, Gerald J. 1973/75. *A Computational Model of Skill Acquisition.* MIT Ph.D. thesis and AI Lab Tech Report 297; published 1975, New York: American Elsivier. [5]

Thelen, Esther, and Linda B. Smith. 1993. *A Dynamic Systems Approach to the Development of Cognition and Action.* Cambridge, MA: Bradford/ MIT Press. [16]

TINLAP-75. 1975. *Theoretical Issues in Natural Language Processing, Proceedings.* [6]

Todd, Peter. 1988. "A Sequential Network Design for Musical Applications", in Touretzky, Hinton, and Sejnowski 1989. [8]

Touretzky, David S. 1986. "BoltzCONS: Reconciling Connectionism with the Recursive Nature of Stacks and Trees", *CogSci-7:* 522–530. [12]

Touretzky, David, Geoffrey E. Hinton, and Terrence J. Sejnowski, eds. 1988. *Prceedings of the 1988 Connectionist Models Summer School.* San Mateo, CA: Morgan Kaufmann. [8]

Townsend, James T. 1992. "Don't be Fazed by PHASER: Beginning Exploration of a Cyclical Motivational System", *Behavior Research Methods, Instruments and Computers,* 24: 219–227. [16]

Tulving, Endel, and Wayne Donaldson, eds. 1972. *Organization of Memory.* New York: Academic Press. [13]

Turing, A. M. 1937. "On Computable Numbers, with an Application to the Entscheidungsproblem", *Proceedings of the London Mathematical Society* 42: 230–265. [1][2]

— 1950. "Computing Machinery and Intelligence", *Mind* 59: 433–460; included as chapter 2 of this volume. [1][4][7]

Van Fraassen, Bas C. 1980. *The Scientific Image.* Oxford: Oxford University Press. [10]

van Gelder, Timothy. 1990. "Compositionality: A Connectionist Variation on a Classical Theme", *Cognitive Science* 14: 355–384. [14]

van Gelder, Timothy, and Robert F. Port. 1995. "It's About Time: An Overview of the Dynamical Approach to Cognition", in Port and van Gelder 1995. [16]

von Neumann, John, and Oskar Morgenstern. 1944/80. *Theory of Games and Economic Behavior.* Princeton: Princeton University Press. [16]

von Uexküll, J. 1921. *Umwelt und Innenwelt der Tiere.* Berlin. [15]

Waltz, David. 1972/75. *Generating Semantic Descriptions from Drawings of Scenes with Shadows.* MIT Ph.D. thesis, published in Winston 1975. [6]

Warren, Neil C., ed. 1977. *Advances in Cross-Cultural Psychology*, volume 1. London: Academic Press. [6]

Watson, J. 1930. *Behaviorism.* Chicago: University of Chicago Press. [12]

Weizenbaum, Joseph. 1965. "Eliza—A Computer Program for the Study of Natural Language Communication between Man and Machine", *Communications of the Association for Computing Machinery* 9: 36–45. [7]

Wertheimer, Max. 1959. *Productive Thinking.* New York: Harper and Row. [5]

Widrow, G., and Hoff, M. E. 1960. "Adaptive Switching Circuits", in *Institute of Radio Engineers, Western Electric Show and Convention, Convention Record, Part 4.* pp. 96–104. [8]

Weigend, A. S., and David E. Rumelhart. 1991. "Generalization through Minimal Networks with Application to Forecasting", in Keramidas 1991. [8]

Wilkes, Kathleen V. 1978. *Physicalism.* London: Routledge and Kegan Paul. [13]

Wilks, Yorick. 1973. *Preference Semantics.* Stanford AI Lab Memo AIM-206. [6]

Winograd, Terry. 1972. "Understanding Natural Language", *Cognitive Psychology* 1: 1–191; also published separately, New York: Academic Press. [6][7]

— 1973. "A Procedural Model of Language Understanding", in Schank and Colby 1973. [6]

— 1974. Five Lectures on Artificial Intelligence. Stanford AI Lab Memo 246. [5][6]

— 1976a. "Artificial Intelligence and Language Comprehension", in *Artificial Intelligence and Language Comprehension.* Washington, DC: National Institute of Education. [6]

— 1976b. "Towards a Procedural Understanding of Semantics", *Revue Internationale de Philosophie* (Foundation Universitaire de Belgique), numbers 117-118: 260–303. [6]

Winston, Patrick H. 1970/75. *Learning Structural Descriptions from Examples.* MIT Ph.D. thesis, published in Winston 1975. [6]

— ed. 1975. *The Psychology of Computer Vision.* New York: McGraw Hill. [6]

Winston, Patrick H. and the staff of the MIT AI Laboratory. 1976. Proposal to ARPA, MIT AI Lab Memo 366. [6]

Wittgenstein, Ludwig. 1922/74. *Tractatus Logico-Philosophicus.* London: K. Paul, Trench, Trubner, and Company. German/English edition with translation by David F. Pears and Brian F. McGuinness, revised, 1974. London: Routledge and Kegan Paul. [11]

— 1953. *Philosophical Investigations.* German/English edition, with translation by G. E. M. Anscombe. Oxford: Basil Blackwell. [6]

Woodfield, Andrew, ed. 1982. *Thought and Object: Essays on Intentionality.* Oxford: Clarendon Press. [3]

Zipser, David, and Jeffrey L. Elman. 1988. "Learning the Hidden Structure of Speech", *Journal of the Acoustical Society of America* 83: 1615–1626. [10]